THE NATIONAL
CHURCH OF SWEDEN

THE HALE LECTURES, 1910

THE NATIONAL CHURCH OF SWEDEN

BY

JOHN WORDSWORTH, D.D.
BISHOP OF SALISBURY

President of the Anglican and Foreign Church Society,
The Henry Bradshaw Society,
and the Central Society for Sacred Study;
and Member of the British Academy

DELIVERED IN ST. JAMES' CHURCH, CHICAGO,
24-29TH OCTOBER, 1910

A. R. MOWBRAY & CO. LTD.
LONDON: 28 Margaret Street, Oxford Circus, W.
OXFORD: 9 High Street
MILWAUKEE, U.S.A.: The Young Churchman Co.

1911

Fs

A.252159

EXTRACTS

From the Will of the Rt. Rev. Charles Reuben Hale, D.D., LL.D., Bishop Coadjutor of Springfield, *born* 1837; *consecrated July* 26, 1892; *died December* 25, 1900.

 In the Name of the Father, and of the Son, and of the Holy Ghost. Amen.

I, Charles Reuben Hale, Bishop of Cairo, Bishop Coadjutor of Springfield, of the City of Cairo, Illinois, do make, publish, and declare this, as and for my Last Will and Testament, hereby revoking all former wills by me made.

First. First of all, I commit myself, soul and body, into the hands of Jesus Christ, my Lord and Saviour, in Whose Merits alone I trust, looking for the Resurrection of the Body and the Life of the World to come.

.   .   .   .

Fourteenth. All the rest and residue of my Estate, personal and real, not in this my Will otherwise specifically devised, wheresoever situate, and whether legal or equitable, I give, devise, and bequeath to "The Western Theological Seminary, Chicago, Illinois," above mentioned, but nevertheless *In Trust*, provided it shall accept the trust by an instrument in writing so stating, filed with this Will in the Court where probated, within six months after the probate of this Will—for the general purpose of promoting the Catholic Faith, in its purity and integrity, as taught in Holy Scripture, held by the Primitive Church, summed up in the Creeds and affirmed by the undisputed General Councils, and, in particular, to be used only and exclusively for the purposes following, to-wit:—

.   .   .   .

(2) The establishment, endowment, publication, and due circulation of Courses of Lecturers, to be delivered annually forever, to be called "The Hale Lectures."

The Lectures shall treat of one of the following subjects :
- (a) Liturgies and Liturgics.
- (b) Church Hymns and Church Music.
- (c) The History of the Eastern Churches.
- (d) The History of National Churches.
- (e) Contemporaneous Church History: *i.e.*, treating of events happening since the beginning of what is called "The Oxford Movement," in 1833.

It is the aim of the Seminary, through the Hale Lectures, to make from time to time some valuable contributions to certain of the Church's problems, without thereby committing itself to agreement with the utterances of its own selected Preachers.

ix

CONTENTS.

PAGE.

PREFACE.

ORIGIN OF THE BOOK. HELP FROM FRIENDS AND OTHER BOOKS.

I think that I may expect that most readers of this book will be aware, in a general way, of the circumstances which have led to its being written. But, as memories are short and historical accuracy is important, I will describe them as simply as possible.

One of the most remarkable features of the Lambeth Conference of 1908 was the presence at one of its meetings of Dr. Henry William Tottie, Bishop of Kalmar, who bore a Latin letter from the Archbishop of Upsala (Dr. J. A. Ekman), dated 20th June of that year, which contained the following sentences :—

" We rejoice that you Anglican bishops have for some time had in view the binding together of your Church and ours in some sort of alliance. I would ask that you should deliberate as to the points and the method of such an alliance with Henry William Tottie, Bishop of Kalmar, my beloved colleague, who, with your kind permission and under the orders of our most gracious King, is about to come to the council which you are soon to hold."

Bishop Tottie also addressed the conference, on which he made a remarkable impression by his fine presence, his dignified bearing and his sympathetic and intelligent attitude.

At the same time the conference received a report of the committee " on re-union and inter-communion " (of which I had the honour to be chairman), which contained a chapter on *the Scandinavian Churches*,[1] in which it dealt particularly with the Church in Sweden.

[1] See *Lambeth Conference of* 1908, pp. 179-182, S.P.C.K. Report No. XI., c. vi.

The conference subsequently passed the following resolution, No. 74 :—

"This conference heartily thanks the Archbishop of Upsala for his letter of friendly greeting, and for sending his honoured colleague, the Bishop of Kalmar, to confer with its members on the question of the establishment of an alliance of some sort between the Swedish and Anglican Churches. The conference respectfully desired the Archbishop of Canterbury to appoint a Commission to correspond further with the Swedish Church through the Archbishop of Upsala on the possibility and conditions of such an alliance."

This Commission was appointed in March, 1909, and consisted of the following persons :—The Bishop of Winchester (Dr. Herbert Ryle), chairman; the Bishop of London (Dr. Arthur Foley Winnington-Ingram), the Bishop of Salisbury, the Master of Pembroke College, Cambridge (Dr. Arthur James Mason), Vice-Chancellor of the University and Canon of Canterbury, and Canon Edward Russell Bernard, Chancellor of Salisbury Cathedral, from England, and the Bishop of Marquette (Dr. G. Mott Williams) from U.S.A.

Its members were invited by the Archbishop of Upsala to meet him in his cathedral city in the autumn. They were all able to attend with the exception of the Bishop of London, and had a most interesting three-days' conference on 21st, 22nd, and 23rd September. On the Swedish side were the Archbishop and the Bishop of Kalmar, the Provost or Dean, Dr. Herman Lundström, the well-known Church historian, editor of the *Kyrkohistorisk Årsskrift*; Dr. Nathan Söderblom, Professor of Comparative Religion; Dr. J. O. Quensel, the learned liturgiologist; Dr. Waldemar Rudin, a much-loved pastor and preacher; Dr. J. E. Berggren, formerly Provost, author, amongst other works, of *Olaus Petris Reformatoriska Grundtankar*; Dr. Erik Stave, an authority on the Swedish versions of the Bible; Dr. J. A. Kolmodin, Professor of Exegesis, one of the leaders of the "Evangeliska Fosterlands Stiftelse," an evangelical society for carrying on both Home and Foreign Missions; Dr. Carl Roland Martin, Assistant Professor of Practical Divinity, author of *Sveriges Första Svenska Mässa*; Dr. E. Billing, Professor of Dogmatic Theology, son of the Bishop of Lund; and Dr. Söderberg, Chancellor of the Cathedral. The only layman present was the well-known historian, Dr. Harald Hjärne, Professor of Modern History, a member of the Swedish Academy.

Some account of this conference was given in the London *Guardian*, 20th October, 1909, pp. 1668-9, in an article headed "The Conference at Upsala," which was written by Dr. Mason.

Since then a committee has been appointed in Sweden to correspond with ours, consisting at first of the Archbishop, Bishop H. W. Tottie of Kalmar, Bishop Otto Ahnfelt of Linköping, Provost H. Lundström and Dr. N. Söderblom. Bishop Ahnfelt, having unfortunately died in the spring of this year (1910), Dr. Gottfrid Billing, Bishop of Lund, one of the most important personages in the Church of Sweden, has been appointed to take his place. Neither committee, however, has yet reported, though many letters have passed, and important communications have been received.

My own published contribution to this subject hitherto is contained in a little volume of diocesan addresses delivered in 1909, called *Unity and Fellowship* (S.P.C.K., 1910). It was an address to a conference of the Dean, Archdeacons, and Rural Deans, of the diocese of Salisbury, delivered 2nd November, 1909, and consisted of a slight sketch of the visit of the Commission, and of the history and organization of the Church of Sweden.

My interest in the work in which we are engaged led, however, to my receiving an invitation from the trustees of the Western Theological Seminary, dated 10th December, 1909, to deliver the Hale Lectures on the foundation of my old friend, Bishop Hale of Cairo, on the Mississippi, Bishop Coadjutor of Springfield, the subject chosen being "The National Church of Sweden." This invitation, which fell in with my own inclination to go more deeply into the history of a Church which appeared to be so like our own, must be my excuse for my audacity in undertaking such a task with so little of previous study. But, in the execution of my design, the encouragement and help of friends have not been wanting. I may specially name the Bishop of Kalmar, Dr. Söderblom and Chancellor Bernard, who have most kindly read the proofs of these lectures, and given me constant and brotherly assistance. Next to them I must place Dr. Herman Lundström and Dr. Hjalmar Holmquist, who have freely placed their great historical learning at my disposal; Mr. K. B. Westman, to whom the third lecture is much indebted; Dr. Quensel, who, like Dean Lundström, and others, has aided me by the gift of valuable books, as well as by letters. I owe also a great debt of gratitude to Bishop G. Mott Williams for his valuable little book, *The Church of Sweden and the Anglican Communion* (A. R. Mowbray and Co., 1910), which worthily supplements the late Dr. A. Nicholson's *Apostolical Succession in the Church of Sweden* (Rivingtons, 1880) and its supplement *Vindiciæ Arosienses* (Griffith, Farran and Co., 1887), both of which are now scarce.

I have done my best in the nine months during which these lectures have been in preparation both to obtain the necessary books and to find time to study them—a study which included the attempt to learn a new language. Dr. Söderblom's counsel has been invaluable to me, especially in the matter of books, and many of these to which reference is made in the footnotes have been bought, borrowed or received at his suggestion.

I cannot give a complete list of these books without needlessly encumbering these prefatory pages, but I should like to mention a few of them. In the first place I wish to record my sense of the great value of the *Nordisk Familjebok*, of which, however, I only have the first edition (20 vols., 1876-1899). The *Biografhiskt Lexicon* (23 + 10 volumes, 1835—1907) is sometimes very useful, sometimes disappointing. The fine illustrated volumes of the *Sveriges Historia* (of which I have both editions), the *Sveriges Medeltid* of Hans Hildebrand (8 parts, 1885—

1903) and the *Illustrerad Svensk Litteratur Historia* of
Henrik Schück and Karl Warburg (3 vols., 1896—1897) are
works of which any country might be proud. All of them
would, however, be more useful to the student if they had
larger tables of contents, lists of the illustrations, and more
references to authorities. The first edition of the *Sveriges
Historia* has, it should be said, an admirable index; and
the covers of its fasciculi supply a list of illustrations
which last help the (unfinished) second edition sadly needs.

As far as I can judge, J. H. Turner's English translation
of Geijer's famous history (up to 1654) is a good one, but
that of Anjou's first volumes, by H. M. Mason, is sometimes unintelligible, and sometimes misleading. I have
seen it stated that Anjou's second work (1593—1693 A.D.)
has also been translated; but, if so, I have been unable to
find a copy. Anjou is an able writer, but his method in-
volves a good deal of unchronological arrangement, and is,
therefore, puzzling to the reader. Reuterdahl and Cornelius are both duller, but it is easier to find in them what
one needs.[2] I am glad to hear that my friend, Mr. G. C.
Richards, of Oriel College, has translated Cornelius'
Handbok i Svenska Kyrkans Historia, which has a good
chronological table, and a fair index. The reader will
find some useful detailed criticism of Cornelius in Dean
Lundström's article in the second volume of the *K. H.
Årsskrift* (for 1901), in which the learned author also
sketches his own idea of the division of the subject in
hand.[3]

[2] Reuterdahl's *Svenska Kyrkans Historia* is in four volumes
(six parts) and goes down to 1533 (Lund, 1838—1866). Cornelius' *Svenska Kyrkans Historia efter Reformationen* in two
volumes, covering the period 1520—1883, was published in
1886—1887. It has no index, but a good table of contents. His
Handbok i Sv. K. H. covers the whole ground in one volume,
3d. ed., 1892.

[3] *Anmärkingar och tillägg till C. A. Cornelius' Handbok i
Svenska Kyrkans Historia, m.m.*, pp. 173-216. I shall have
occasion to cite many articles from this review, and I have to
thank the editor for his very great kindness in giving me copies
of the whole ten volumes (1900—1909) at present issued.

Part of Anders Fryxell's lively and readable *Berättelser ur Svenska Historien* (up to 1577) has been pleasantly translated by Anne von Schoultz, and edited by Mary Howitt, two vols., Lond., 1844; and E. C. Otté's *Scandinavian History* (1874) is a very useful compendium.

Less known in England is Th. Norlin's *Svenska Kyrkans Historia efter Reformationen*, of which only the first volume was completed before the author's premature death (1864—1871). It describes the period from 1594 to 1649; that is a large part of the period covered by my sixth lecture. It is a book of more than usual originality and power, and I much regret that it is unfinished. The author's *Kort Ofversigt af Svenska Kyrkans Historia*, published in 1866, is also valuable, and with Dr. Hjalmar Holmquist's article, *Schweden* in *P. R. E.*[3], vol. 18, will give a reader who has little time to spare a good idea of the course and character of the history. Besides these, I may mention R. Keyser: *Den Norske Kirkes Historie under Katholicismen*, 2 vols., Christiana, 1856—1858, and Elis Bergroth *Den Finska Kyrkans Historia*, Helsingfors, 1892.

Of other books covering a considerable period Bishop John Baaz' *Inventarium Suiogothicum*, Lincopiæ, 1642, though wanting in accuracy and judgment, contains a convenient collection of documents, which must be used with care. I have found A. O. Rhyzelius' *Episcoposcopia Suiogothica* (2 parts, Linköping, 1752) exceedingly useful, and so is S. A. Hollander's smaller book, *Biskopar och Superintendenter*, Stockholm, 1874, which only deals with prelates in Sweden and Finland since the Reformation. Rhyzelius and Hollander are said to be often inaccurate, but they are indispensable. All the above are in my own library. References to the *Scriptores rerum Suecicarum* in three volumes, folio, printed at Upsala (I. ed., E. M. Fant, 1818; II. ed., E. G. Geijer and J. H. Schröder, 1828; and III. ed., Cl. Annerstedt, 1871—1876) are to a copy kindly lent me by the London Library through the friendly intervention of our dean, Dr. Wm. Page Roberts.

The names of more special books on constitutional and liturgical matters, single biographies and monographs of various kinds may be gathered from the notes, in which I have endeavoured to guide the reader to further studies, and to preserve some convenient record of my own. Of course, I make no claim to have mastered the contents of all the books I refer to, but merely to assert that I know them well enough to vouch for their value. I need, I hope, hardly say that I am profoundly conscious of the defects and imperfections of this little book. I am particularly sorry not to have found space for an account of Swedish hymnody and its influence. The book also needs information on some constitutional topics.

I hope that I may have leisure for further study of this subject. Whether that is granted or not, I hope that I may encourage others to it. Though laborious it has been to me a labour of love, and I rise from it, on the eve of my journey to the United States, with a heart full of thankfulness to God, who has given His Holy Spirit to men of different races and ages in such manifold richness and strength. Surely He wills that those whose aims in life have so much in common, whose natural piety is so similar, whose interests are so closely akin, and whose history has so many points of contact and often of striking resemblance, should draw closer again to one another on both sides of the Atlantic.

It remains for me to offer my most respectful thanks to H.R.H. the Crown Princess Margaret for allowing me to connect this volume with her honoured name. All the members of our Commission who were in Sweden last year will remember with peculiar pleasure the welcome which they received from the gracious lady who so happily links together the two nations in a living bond.

JOHN SARUM.

SALISBURY, 14th September, 1910,

POSTSCRIPT.—I add a few lines to this preface after my return from a two months' absence and a six weeks' tour in U.S.A. from 21st September to 2nd November—during which I have travelled some 4,500 miles by railroad, although I have not gone beyond the Mississippi. My halting places have been New York, Philadelphia, Washington, New York (again), Long Island, Boston, Albany, Cincinnati (Ohio), Sewanee and Nashville (Tennessee), Chicago, Rock Island (Illinois), Minneapolis, Chicago (for the lectures), Buffalo and New York. The lectures were delivered in St. James' Church, Chicago, on the six nights from Monday, 24th October, to Saturday, 29th. In delivery it was necessary to compress the first three into one and to omit considerable portions of the rest. Those who were good enough to attend will, therefore, find in the book much which they did not hear. The last section of the book has been written partly on shipboard and partly since my return home.

In the latter part of my journey, as well as at Cincinnati, I had the great advantage of the company of the Bishop of Marquette. I have also to thank Dr. J. P. Billings, head of the New York Public Library; Rev. G. Hammarsköld, of Yonkers; Dr. Tofteen, of Chicago, and Dr. J. N. Lenker of Minneapolis (a recognized authority on Luther and Lutheranism), for much help in regard to Swedish-American literature and statistics. On 19th October the Bishop of Marquette and I were most hospitably welcomed by Dr. Andreen and his colleagues at the Augustana College, Rock Island. On the 26th we were with equal kindness entertained by Dr. Hjerpe and his colleagues at the North Park College of the "Mission Covenant" at Chicago. At Minneapolis we had the pleasure of meeting ex-Governor Lind and several Swedish professors of the University. I must also express my particular thanks to Vice-Consul Henry S. Henschen, who gave me the opportunity of meeting a number of the leading Swedes of Chicago at luncheon, and of speaking to them after it on the 28th. I have embodied something of what I have thus learnt in the eighth section of the last lecture. To my kind travelling companion and chaplain, Rev. J. Spence Johnston, I owe the index and other help.

To my previous acknowledgments I must add hearty thanks to younger friends, to Rev. S. Gabrielsson, of Venjan, for help in correcting the proofs, and to him and Rev. M. Åmark for valuable letters on the present condition of the Church in Sweden. The Bishop of Lund has also honoured me with a similar letter. Docent Gustaf Aulén of Upsala has kindly sent me his valuable book on Reuterdahl's theology, and the secretaries of the "Evangeliska Fosterlands Stiftelse" and the "Missions Förbundet," the reports of their respective societies. I am indebted to Regements-pastor E. Schröderheim, for the eight numbers of the interesting *Sv. Kyrkoförbundets Skriftserie*, and to the editor of *Vår Lösen*, for that spirited fortnightly paper.

To God the giver of the great gifts of life and friendship be praise and glory!

SALISBURY, *Christmas*, 1910.

THE NATIONAL CHURCH OF SWEDEN.

I.

INTRODUCTORY.—THE COUNTRY AND ITS INHABITANTS IN
THE HEATHEN PERIOD UP TO 1000 A.D.

THE NATIONAL CHURCH OF SWEDEN.

LECTURE I.

INTRODUCTORY. THE COUNTRY AND ITS INHABITANTS IN THE HEATHEN PERIOD.

§ 1.—OBJECT OF THESE LECTURES: TO PROMOTE BROTHERLY INTERCOURSE.

The National Church of Sweden deserves, on many accounts, to be better known than it is by English-speaking races. It is the Church of a nation closely akin to the English, and, at many periods, largely influenced by men of English birth. Its history pursues a course in many ways comparable to that of the English Church. It has been ornamented by the lives of many distinguished men, and it has fostered a type of national character by the examples of which other Churches may well strive to profit. It has also lessons of warning to offer, and it suggests a number of problems to those who look for light upon the future of Christendom.

While the lessons of this history must be directly valuable to the Churches of the Anglican Communion, whether in Europe or America, or in the other parts of the globe where British and Swedish missions are in contact, it may be hoped that a considerate and sympathetic study of the subject will be acceptable also to dwellers in Sweden itself, and to the great body of Swedish settlers in the United States of America, who come into very close relation to members of our own Churches.

I have implied that the main object which I have set before me in these lectures is the promotion of mutual knowledge between the Churches and peoples of the Anglican Communion and the Swedish Church and people, and the

mutual affection and self-improvement which may grow
from such knowledge. This object suggests a treatment of
the subject which will differ somewhat from that which
would be proper in a course of University lectures.   A
basis of knowledge must be taken for granted, or, at any
rate, an interest which can readily be turned into knowledge; but, above all, a basis of common feeling. I shall
venture to count on my hearers' sympathy as fellow-workers
in the cause of unity and fellowship. The consciousness
of this sympathy will enable me sometimes to adopt a
lighter and more familiar tone in addressing them than a
purely scientific treatment might seem to demand, while
at the same time I shall not forget our deep agreement on
the tremendous truths of the Gospel and in the way of salvation opened to us by the Holy Spirit in the Church of
Christ. Church history is sacred ground, and those who
tread it must be ever looking onwards and upwards. We
are handling the eternal truths and watching the operation of the unseen laws of God's kingdom.   These two
thoughts then—our intimate brotherly relation as
Christians and our agreement on the most serious concerns of the soul—will be constantly present to us, I hope,
during the hours which we are allowed to spend together
in this great western city of the new world so far removed
both from England and Sweden, but equally near to our
divine Master.

§ 2.—THE COUNTRY AND ITS INHABITANTS.   NATURAL
FEATURES OF THE COUNTRY.

It will be convenient to preface our studies of the history
of the Church with a short sketch of the country and its
inhabitants, and a few words on the ancient religion which
was displaced by Christianity, and on the organization of
society in heathen times. The name of Sweden is now
given to the eastern and southern part of the great peninsula which runs from north to south between the North
Atlantic Ocean and the Baltic Sea. It has a very long

coast line, but very little of it is exposed to the full force of the Atlantic, as its western shores are protected partly by the southern projection of Norway, and partly by the northern part of the Danish peninsula of Jutland, the old Chersonesus Cimbrica.   It has, therefore, naturally had closer relations, whether for war or peace, with the nations bordering on the Baltic, the Finns, the Slavs or Russians, and the Wends or Vandals, and the nations beyond them, than the other Scandinavian peoples have had. Compared also with the Danes and Norwegians, the Sveas and Goths, who are the two great stems from which modern Sweden has grown, have been not only inclined to adventures by sea, but have frequently prosecuted adventures by land.   In historical times the journey to Constantinople was made in boats up the northern rivers, which were then dragged overland, and then down the Dnieper or the Volga.   (Cp. Constantine Porph.: *De Administrando Imp.*, c. 9).   But all three peoples have had close contact from time to time with their island neighbours in Great Britain.

Before entering upon any discussion of the relation of these tribes with other nations, and of their development in historical times, we may look at some of the natural features of the country which are very marked, and which have largely influenced its history.   Sweden is pre-eminently a land of woods and lakes; indeed, at the present day, about one half of the land is said to be forest, and about one-twelfth of the area is covered by water.   The depression which lies across the country from west to east, from the North Sea, or rather the Skager-rack, to the Baltic, is largely filled by two great lakes, Venern and Vettern, and by a multitude of smaller ones, including the Mälar Lake, on which Stockholm and Upsala, Vesterås and Strengnäs lie. This depression doubtless represents an arm of the sea, which, in not very distant geological time, separated the island of Scandia, as the ancients called it, from the north land.   The project for uniting the two seas by a canal, and so making it again an island, is an old

one. It was advocated by Hans Brask, Bishop of Linköping, in the time of Gustaf Vasa, and taken up by Charles
XII., but was not completely executed till 1832.   The
extent of lakes in this region may be estimated by the fact
that while the distance between the seas along the waterway
is 240 miles, only 56 of it is actual canal (Baedeker : *Norway
and Sweden*, p. 298, 1903).   The largest of these lakes,
Venern, flows into the sea by the Göta-Elf, the old boundary between Norway and Sweden, at the great port of
Göteborg.   Between it and the other lesser lake, Vettern,
lies the thick forest of Tived, the acknowledged though
somewhat indefinite boundary between the two leading
tribes.   To the east again of Vettern lies a chain of smaller
lakes which extends to the Baltic, and north of them the
other boundary forest of Kolmord with its marble quarries.

In early days the forests were probably much larger than
they are now, and the lakes considerably so, since the land
has been gradually rising, and many of the old lakes have
become moor and moss, or have been reclaimed for cultivation.   In this way, it may be remarked that many of the
spoils of war devoted by the victors, and thrown into sacred
lakes, as offerings to the gods, and supposed to have been
swallowed up for ever, have been recovered by antiquaries,
and are used to show the mode of life of the inhabitants of
Sweden at the close of the Bronze Age and the earlier part
of the Iron Age.   As to the forests, it is interesting to note
that Olaf Trätälja, or the tree-cutter, the last of the half-
mythical Yngling kings of Sweden, got his name from
clearing the forests on the borders between Norway and
Sweden.   Some think that the province of Vermland
(or Warmland) was so called because of the fires with
which he consumed the trees of these clearings (Otté :
Scand. Hist., p. 62).   Others say that Vermland is called
from a lake, Vermelen, which never freezes.   Others
derive it from the name of the first settlers.   As to the
forest trees, if I am rightly informed, the dwarf birch is the
hardiest species, which rises to the highest altitude, and
that in the farthest northern latitude.   Then come larger

birches, then pines, or, as we call them, Scotch firs, then firs, then oaks, then beeches, each following the other further north as the ice has receded. So that the forests give a sort of picture in nature of what has gone on in human nature, Cwens and Finns, or Lapps, receding before Swedes and Goths—as the birch has before the pine, and the oak before the beech.

The country is rocky, with much granite, and with much chalk in Skåne, but the hills in the more fertile and populous districts rise to no great height, and the lakes have flat or gently sloping sides like the tamer part of the English lakes, rather than crags or overshadowing mountains. Even the higher mountains in the northern provinces which, on the coast of Norway, rise abruptly from the sea, slope gently down on the Swedish side. On the other hand the coast of Norway has the advantage of the Gulf Stream, or some similar current, and is much warmer than the east coast of Sweden.[1] In fact, the Gulf of Bothnia is sometimes frozen over so completely as to enable people to walk and sledge from one side to the other. This is indeed always a dangerous procedure, and only possible when the winter is unusually cold. Yet it can be cold even on the west coast, and the Great Belt and the Little Belt were once so strongly frozen as to enable the whole Swedish Army to cross them in 1658—a famous occasion which led to the transference of the southern provinces from Denmark to Sweden.[2]

As regards inland travelling, the comparative flatness of the country and the absence of precipitous mountains make

[1] Baedeker's Guide : pp. 39-40.   The temperature of the Lofoden Islands is much the same as that of Copenhagen. Some eminent modern geographers deny that this current is the Gulf Stream, but the water is undoubtedly warmer than elsewhere.

[2] I have to thank private correspondents for this information. The ice on the Gulf of Bothnia is always dangerous from the large holes in it made by the storms. But it may easily have been the bridge for the migration to and fro of smaller or larger bodies of persons. In 1809 part of the Russian Army crossed the gulf where it is narrowest—the Qvarken, near Umeå.

the Swedish lakes better waterways than those of other
countries (though Lake Vetter is liable to sudden storms);
and when the forests were thick and the roads few they
afforded the easiest modes of travel. Even now in great
part of Sweden the winter travelling over ice and snow is
preferred to the summer travelling over ill-kept roads.

§ 3.—THE INHABITANTS.   THE STONE AGE UP TO 1500 B.C.
CULT OF THE SPIRITS OF THE DEAD.

The southern part of this country—which I will continue
to call Scandia, as distinguished from Svithiod, the country
of the Swedes—was undoubtedly the earliest inhabited.
This is evident from the many relics of the Stone Age
which are found particularly in its south-western and
southern provinces, and very frequently near the sea coast.
This age, which lasted in Sweden till about 1500 B.C., was
one in which stone and bone and wood were the chief
materials used for the service of man.   A glance at
Montelius' revised map in the new edition of the *Swedish
History*, p. 52, will show the distribution of the old graves,
which are the chief monuments of the Stone Age.   There
are none in the more northern provinces of Dalarne, Vermland, Vestmanland, and Upland, and very few north of
the great forests of Tived and Kolmord (Nerike and
Södermanland).   There are many in the western and
south-western provinces, near Norway and Denmark,
particularly in Dal, West Gothland, Bohuslän, Halland
and Skåne, and fewer in East Gothland, Småland and
Blekinge, and in the two islands of Öland and Gotland.

This evidence makes it probable that the mainland of
Sweden was originally settled from the west and south-
west, and not from the mouths of the Vistula and the Gulf
of Danzig; and it makes it probable that the northern part
of the country was very scantily inhabited.   We may suppose that the different tribes which immigrated as the
severity of the glacial period diminished pushed one
another upwards from south to north.   This agrees with

the fact that about five-sevenths of all the relics of the Stone Age in Sweden have been found in Skåne.

There are, however, a certain number of antiquities of a somewhat different character, which are called, for the sake of distinction, "arctic," as opposed to the South Scandinavian antiquities of the Stone Age.[3] These arctic antiquities are now attributed by good authorities to the primitive Lapps. Montelius writes:—"The comparatively large number of such stone implements which are found in the northern coast provinces not now inhabited by Lapps, from Vesterbotten to Gestrikland and in Dalarne, seem to give evidence that this people once dwelt more to the south than they do now. Sometimes, though very rarely, the peculiar spear points and knives of slate which characterize the 'arctic' Stone Age have been found even in Svealand, south of Dalarne, and in Gothland" (l.c., p. 56). In the island of Gotland implements of the two Stone Ages have been found together, and this is also the case at Åloppe in Upland and Jäderen in south-west Norway. The arctic Stone Age doubtless lasted much longer among the Lapps than among the South Scandinavians, just as it did among the North American Indians. When Tacitus wrote in the first century after Christ, the Fenni (by whom he may be supposed to mean the Lapps) were scarcely acquainted with bronze or iron. He speaks of their fleetness and of their skill in the use of bows and arrows, "which they point with bone in the absence of iron" (*Germ.*, ch. 46). Even now the Lapps are called Finns by the Norwegians.

The absence of graves among these "arctic" antiquities agrees also with what Tacitus tells us of the Fenni, viz., that they had no permanent dwellings, but only huts of boughs of trees. We may take it for granted that a race which uses stone cists, or dolmens, or tree-coffins, or even grave mounds, is civilized enough to have permanent cottages of stone or earth for the living. Conversely,

[3] See Montelius : *Sveriges Historia*[2], Vol. i., p. 55 foll., and Hans Hildebrand : *Sveriges Medeltid*, Book i., p. 299.

those who have no permanent dwellings do not have permanent sepulchres. The grave is a house for the dead, as we read in the book of Job; and in early ages at any rate it bore a considerable analogy to the house used by the living.

I conclude, therefore, that the original Lapps were a Stone Age people, who have left few traces except their slate implements, and were gradually pushed northwards by the South Scandinavian Stone Age people who were closely allied to the present inhabitants of Sweden. This agrees with the traces of the name of Finns, which we find in various parts of Sweden, particularly in Småland. It would be worth while to inquire whether "arctic" implements are found in the district of Finn-heden to substantiate the belief in an ancient Lappish settlement there. We must, of course, be careful not to draw into this discussion the various Finnmarker and Finn-skogar, which denote the settlements of modern Finns in the sixteenth and seventeenth centuries in Vermland, Dalarne, etc.

A trace of the religion of the South Scandinavian Stone Age is to be found in the cup-like depression on the upper roof-stones of the stone cists or passage-chambered graves in which the dead were laid unburnt. These were clearly intended to receive offerings; and, indeed, we are told that, even to present times offerings are secretly made in them (Montelius: *Civilization in Heathen Times*, E. T., p. 36; see fig. 37). The suggestion is that the offering was made to the spirit of the departed. It is, of course, also quite possible that the men of this age had another and a higher worship (as many primitive peoples have had) of which no trace now remains.

§ 4.—THE BRONZE AGE 1500 B.C.—500 B.C.   THE AGE OF FRÖ OR FREY: WORSHIP OF THE SIMPLE POWERS OF NATURE.

The Bronze Age, which is roughly dated in Scandinavia from 1500 B.C.—500 B.C., is the period in which metals first came to be known. They were in this case two, bronze (a mixture of copper and tin, with sometimes a little zinc— but brought into the country already in combination) and gold.   For, although gold is the oldest metal used by man, it is not found in the Stone Age in Sweden. There is no reason to think that the introduction of bronze was due to any large foreign immigration which destroyed the previous inhabitants.   It is rather due to intercourse by trade, and with the coast land of eastern Germany and Sarmatia and the countries of the hinterland descending to the sea by the course of the River Vistula and the Gulf of Danzig.   The chief evidence as to the continuance of the same population is afforded by the likeness of the graves and modes of burial during the later period of the Stone Age and the earlier Bronze Age.   Both buried their dead in large stone cists, either in a sitting or recumbent posture, and in an exactly similar manner, and used at first, and side by side, instruments of stone and bronze of closely similar shape.

We have, therefore, reason to think that the influence of trade coming from the south of Europe, particularly by what is sometimes called the " amber route "[4] from the head of the Adriatic to the Baltic, was the chief cause of the changes which at first took place in the Bronze Age (cp. *British Museum Guide to Art of Bronze Age*, p. 12, 1904). We cannot doubt that, with a greater knowledge of the world, the possession of more powerful weapons, and a greater taste for luxury and ornament, a fuller and more adventurous life began.   The most direct evidence of this life of the Bronze Age is to be found in the rock-gravings (häll-ristningar) which have been discovered especially in the old Norwegian province of Viken (Bohuslän, near Göteborg), East Gothland and South-Eastern Skåne. They are also found, though rarely, in Dal and Blekinge, and in the more northern provinces of Vermland and Upland.   They are not, however, found in Denmark or

[4] Amber was known in Sweden in the Stone Age and used for ornament (Montelius : *Civ.*, p. 25).

Norway. They bear witness to a civilization advancing by somewhat different roads from that of the Stone Age, probably from Vendland and the Vistula, as well as from the south, but not necessarily by only one or two routes— since there is no commoner feature of these rock-gravings than the presence of numerous ships.

These rock-gravings are cut on the surfaces of granite boulders and sloping scarps, and they are pictures, on rather a large scale, evidently recording historic events, and apparently such as afterwards became the subjects of the most ancient northern poems, especially sea-fights and the combats of single champions. They are nevertheless not so much pictures as picture-writings, although the key to them has not yet been found. They seem, however, to be contemporary with smaller gravings on the walls of burial chambers, of which the most important are at Kivik on the east coast of Skåne (S. H.[1], figs. 126-9). The most frequent objects on the rock-gravings are men and ships, but we find also a number of domestic animals, horned cattle, reindeer, horses and birds. There seem to be even representations of such south-country creatures as the turtle, the ostrich, the camel, and, possibly, the lion. Then we have footprints, shoes, cup-marks, weapons, shields, sledges, trees, and various nondescript signs.[5]

The human figure is always drawn naked, usually fighting or on shipboard, but in one or two cases ploughing (Du Chaillu: Figs. 902, cp. 912), rarely riding (fig. 899), or skating (fig. 909). The combatants carry shields (always round), sometimes with a central boss, sometimes with a cross. This wheel-shaped shield or hjul also appears as a sign by itself. The Thor-cross, hook-cross, or svastika, which seems to be a development of it, is not

[5] The fullest collection of illustrations of these gravings accessible to me is that in P. Du Chaillu's *Viking Age*, Vol. ii., ch. 8, Lond. 1889, figs. 890-913, to which reference is made in the text. See also Montelius: *Civ.*, figs 84-88, and *Sv. Hist.*[1], Vol. i., p 107. Special works by A. E. Holmberg: *Skandinaviens häll-ristningar* and L. Baltzer are referred to in these books.

found till the Iron Age. This agrees with what will presently be said as to the date of the worship of Thor.

No buildings of any sort are represented on these rock-gravings.

The only suggestion as to religion which these monuments afford is in their frequent representation of a gigantic elongated figure, of a very coarse description, usually with a tail, holding an upraised battle-axe or club, or more rarely two clubs. His weapon is sometimes stretched towards or over the heads of combatants, or at the stern of a ship over the mariners. But he is rarely himself engaged in fight. This can hardly be anything else than a figure of the battle-god of the Bronze Age protecting or inspiring his heroes, as in later days Odin was supposed to do, down to the great Battle of Bråvalla.[6]

Similar gigantic figures, standing, however, alone, and stout of body, were found cut on the chalk or other downs of Southern England, and two still exist. One of them, the " Cerne giant,"[7] 180 feet high, and covering about half an acre of ground, is cut on the side of a beautiful valley in one of the counties in my own diocese, that of Dorset. Near to it, well away from the village, a Maypole used to be erected.

Another, the " Long Man of Wilmington,"[8] in Sussex,

---

[6] In East Gothland, when he appeared for the last time in the fight between Sigurd Ring, of Sweden, and old Harald Hildetand, of Denmark, probably in the eighth century (see Geijer, *H. of the Swedes*, p. 11, E. T., and Otté, l.c., p. 26).

[7] See Hutchings' *Dorset*, Vol. iv., pp. 35-6, ed. 1870, where the figure is somewhat imperfectly represented, and a paper by Dr. H. Colley March in *Dorset N. H. and Antiq. Field Club*, Vol. xxii., pp. 101-18.

[8] It is figured in Rev. W. C. Plenderleath's *White Horses and other Turf Monuments*, p. 36, London, and Calne (1885), and in *Victoria County History (Sussex)*, Vol. i., p. 325, 1905. A hoard of Bronze Age antiquities was found at Wilmington in 1861 (*ibid.* 320). I am indebted to a clerical friend for an interesting and exact account of this figure. The names of Polhill Farm and Polegate close by suggest the connection with Phol, on whose personality see Grimm : *Deutsche Mythologie,*

is 240 feet high, and holds in each hand a stick or club,
on which he seems to rest, so placed, it is said, as to indicate
the vernal and autumnal equinoxes. This may be a figure
of Phol or Balder, a god of light, whose name some would
connect with that of Apollo. Some of you may remember
Rudyard Kipling's lines in his praise of Sussex (in the
Five Nations), which hint at the fact that the figure was
so placed as to catch the light :—

> " I will go out against the sun,
> Where the rolled scarp retires,
> And the Long Man of Wilmington
> Looks naked towards the shires."

Another such figure is said to have been cut on the turf
of Shotover Hill, near Oxford.

But if we are to find a name for the Cerne giant and the
tall figures of Swedish rock-gravings, I should conjecture
that they represented Frö or Frey rather than one of the
Aesir, like Balder.

Frö is merely an old Teutonic name for Lord, and
Fráuja is so used by Ulphilas to translate the Greek
κύριος. But, historically, he is a nature god, one of the
Vanir, who are allied with the Anses or Aesir, but on a
lower level than they. The Vanir are the gods of a less
civilized period, possibly of a less civilized race, who have
been accepted into their pantheon by conquerors, or retained
by a nation after they became acquainted with a higher
cult. The Aesir are somewhat more spiritual, and their
name may simply be a word meaning spirits.[9] The Vanir,
whatever may be the origin of the name, which has been
connected conjecturally with the Vendish people, or with

---

s.n., and Wolfgang Golther : *Germanische Mythologie*, p. 383
foll., Leipz., 1895. Dr. Söderblom suggests that Phol = Paul,
as in a newly-found text of the Merseburger-spell. But is not
" Paul " an attempt to give a Christian colour to the spell?
Local tradition asserts that the shining of the sun upon the whole
length of either club marks the equinox.

[9] See Golther : *G. M.*, p. 195, but the etymology is very
obscure.

a word meaning light and glittering[10]—possibly akin to the Latin Venus—were gods of the earth and water; whereas the Aesir were gods of the sky.

However Frö may have come into Swedish religion, his worship was particularly strongly established in the country. He formed a third with Thor and Odin in the great Upsala Temple even in the eleventh century—Thor being throned in the middle, Odin on his right, and Fricco, as Adam de Bremen calls him, on the left.[11] He embodies the elemental powers of nature—force, productiveness and riches. The Aesir are more human. To them belong the attributes of skill, wisdom, foresight, cunning, poetry, inspiration and the like—used no doubt pre-eminently in or with regard to war, the chief game, as Northmen always thought it, of human life, but quite separable from it. Frö, on the other hand, is the son of Niord, the earth or sea, at any rate of the lower world beneath the sky,[12] and the goddess of the waterfall. Frö is a purely nature god. His father is sent by the Vanir, who are subdued by the Aesir, to dwell among the latter. Frö takes a lower place than he had at first occupied, which the myth indicates by saying that he gave away his marvellous sword. His magic ship, " Skidbladnir," was large enough to take all the Aesir on board it, but could be taken to pieces and put away in the pocket. I suppose it was a gigantic skate or snow-shoe or pair of snow-shoes. Some may remember the poet Tegnér's use of this myth, as a

[10] See Geijer: *H. of S.*, p. 12, E. T., *Corpus Poeticum Boreale*, Vol. ii., pp. 465-6, Golther: *G. M.*, p. 220. The latter refers to the adjective " wanum," found in the Heliand in the sense of "bright." There is a lake and a parish called Vendel, with many remarkable heathen tombs, a few miles north of Upsala, which possibly may be connected with this matter. Wendel is a name for the devil in some parts of Germany (See Grimm: *D. M.*, p. 375, E. T., *s. n. Orentil*).

[11] *Gesta Pontif. Hammaburgensium* § 233 ; cp. *C. P. B.*, Vol. i., p. 97, Golther: l.c., 218 foll.

[12] Some connect the names with Nereus, some with νέρτεροι, (gods of the lower world), others with " Nertu " good-will (cp. Golther : p. 219, *C. P. B.*, Vol. ii., p. 465).

symbol for the power of imagination.[13] Historically, I
conceive it implies that the worship of the Aesir and Vanir
was already conjoined when the Suiones came to Lake
Mälar. At any rate, Frö remained a special patron of the
Sveas, and expresses, it seems to me, something of their
character—their love of ease and peace and wealth. He
was also specially venerated at Trondhjem, in Norway.

Another feature of the worship of the Bronze Age has
already been referred to in passing, the habit of throwing
the spoils of victory into a sacred lake. Swords and spears
and armour were bent and broken in pieces, conquered
enemies, captives and slaves, were killed and thrown into
such lakes in the later Bronze Age, and the earlier Iron
Age—no doubt as offerings to the god or gods.[14]

It is natural to compare with this the passage of Tacitus
(*Germ.*, ch. 40), which mentions certain tribes, amongst
whom he numbers the Anglii, as all worshipping "Nerthus,
that is to say, mother earth," a deity which is evidently the
female form of the northern Niord. He then describes a
sacred wood in an island, which is supposed to be Rügen,
in the midst of which is a lake where secret rites are performed at her annual festival, which ended with washing
of the image of the goddess in the lake, and the drowning
of the slaves who ministered in the rite. A lake now called
the Hertha-see, on the promontory of Jasmund, is often
visited by antiquarian pilgrims as the scene of this gloomy
festival, as many English readers have been reminded by
a recent story (*Elizabeth in Rügen*, p. 235). Other Latin
historians describe the devotion of captives and spoils in
sacred lakes or rivers, and we may believe that this form
of worship was widely spread. The cave of Grendel, at
the bottom of a deep lake, described in the poem of
Beowulf, fills up the picture. The god or demon of the

[13] See J. E. D. Bethune's *Specimens of Swedish and German
Poetry*, p. 74 foll., Lond. 1848.

[14] See *S. H.*[2], Vol. i., p. 118, for the Bronze Period ; *ibid.*,
167 for the Iron.

lake ate up the sacrifices, and the arms were treasured in his hall.

Beside these deities, who belong to the Germanic tribes in general, there is a less known god, who belongs more distinctly to the north, and who was certainly widely worshipped. This is Ull, or Ullr, the Ollerus of Saxo, who seems to have been a god of winter, or of winter sport. He is a consummate archer, snow-shoe runner and skater, and is also a very skilful magician. It is wise to invoke his aid in a single combat. We may suppose him to have been a god of the aboriginal population, whom, for convenience, we call Finns in the old sense, or Lapps. His name, indeed, like that of Frey, is Gothic, meaning glorious or noble (*ulthus*), an epithet which might be applied to any divinity. It is interesting to note that the sacred places, groves, altars and enclosures (ending in lund, or lunda, harg, vi, etc.), in which the names of Frey and Ull occur, are more numerous than those which are connected with Thor, and much more numerous than those named from Odin.[15] This shows the persistence of old traditions in the country and the greater antiquity of the worship of Frey and Ull in Sweden.

[15] See the evidence collected by M. F. Lundgren, and quoted by Hans Hildebrand (*Sv. Med.*, Book v., pp. 5 foll.). Names like Fröslunda, Frösvi occur twenty-five times ; Ullalund or lunda and Ullavi, twenty times; Torsharg, Torslund or -a, Torsvi, sixteen ; Odensharg, Odenslunda, Odensvi, only six. Thus we have Ulceby (2), in Lincolnshire ; Ulleswater, Westmorland ; Ullesthorp, Leicestershire ; Ulleskelf, Yorkshire ; Thoresby (2), Thoresthorp, Thoresway, Thorrock, all in Lincolnshire, and many others ; Frisby (2), Leicestershire, and Friston, Suffolk and Sussex. There are, of course, many places in England named from Woden, probably more than from Ull or Frey. A collection of all such place-names in this country is a desideratum.

§§ 5 TO 8.—THE IRON AGE (500 B.C.—1000 A.D.).

§ 5.—FIRST OR PRE-ROMAN PERIOD, 500 B.C. TO JUST
    BEFORE THE CHRISTIAN ERA. THE AGE OF
    THOR AND THE HAMMER.

The Iron Age of Sweden, which was till lately supposed
to have begun about the Christian era, is now found to
have extended for a period of about 500 years before it.
Of this first period comparatively few traces are found in
the country, though sufficient to prove the early introduction of the metal. It is to this period that I should assign
the introduction of the worship of Thor and the myths of
his victory over and association with the nature gods. I
should venture to call it the Age of Thor and the hammer.
The great difference between bronze and iron is this : That
bronze can be cast in moulds, and bronze weapons can be
imported ready made, or easily made from ingots, while
iron requires the smith's craft and the use of the hammer
and other powerful tools. A new god would naturally
come in with such a momentous gift or discovery. It is
interesting to notice that, though Montelius does not draw
this inference, he supposes independently that Thor was
the god of the early Iron Age in Sweden (*Civ.*, p. 121). As
Grimm says :—" The hammer, as a divine tool, was considered sacred. Brides and the bodies of the dead were
consecrated with it. Men blessed with the sign of the
hammer as Christians did with the sign of the cross, and
a stroke of lightning was long regarded in the Middle Ages
as a happy initiatory omen to any undertaking " (*D. M.*,
pp. 180-1, E. T.). The worship of Thor is an advance
upon that of the pure nature gods. He represents something spiritual, even though it be rough and turbulent, in
human nature. He is the Northmen's home god while
they still lived apart and before the introduction of any
kind of literature or writing, except a rough kind of native
poetry and jest.

§ 6.—Second Period of the Iron Age, 50 b.c.—400 a.d.
    The Suiones already in Sweden. The Age
    of Gothic Immigration and Migration, of
    the Runes and of Odin.

The opening of the second period of the Iron Age coincides with the Gallic wars of Julius Cæsar and the impulse given to the Germanic tribes by the pressure of Roman conquests up to and beyond the Rhine. The defeat of Varus in the Teutoberger Forest left the North German tribes free from the actual presence of Roman rulers, but one tribe naturally communicated the backward impulse to another, until, in time, it reached the Baltic and the Cimbric Chersonese and Scandia. It is to this pressure that I should assign three things, the migration of the Goths to Scandia, the introduction of writing and poetry, and the worship of Odin. This period extends from the Christian era to about the year 400 a.d.

Different opinions have been held as to the relative date of the settlement of the two great tribes of Sweden in that country; but the balance of evidence seems to me to tell strongly in favour of the priority of the Sveas. Not only do we find the latter always to the north of the Goths, but the few early historical notices which we have coincide with the natural presumption that they retired or concentrated northward under pressure of the Goths from the south. The Goths, or Gythons, indeed, are mentioned in classical literature earlier than the Sveas, but as inhabitants of the German mainland, not of the peninsula. When the Suiones are first mentioned by Tacitus it is as being *in ipso oceano*. If the Goths had been then beside them it was part of his plan to mention them. My conclusion then is that the Goths were still on the mainland. Let me give the evidence in some detail.

The first writer of antiquity who is quoted as naming these regions, Pytheas of Marseilles, a contemporary of Alexander the Great, speaks of the Guttones as a German

people inhabiting an estuary of the ocean, towards which
amber was brought by the waves from an island a
day's voyage distant (cp. Plin., *N. H.*, Book 37, ch. 11).
Tacitus, who wrote about the end of the first century after
Christ, speaks of the Guthones, who must be the same
people, as occupying a position between tribes who
inhabited the modern West Poland and Silesia, and those
who dwelt by the ocean in the modern Pomerania (*Germ.*,
ch. 43). This description suggests the lower course of the
Vistula, but somewhat south of the Gulf of Danzig, where
Pytheas seems to place them.[16]   They form a kingdom
which is ruled more strictly than the other German tribes.
Tacitus writes:—"That which distinguishes all these
peoples is the round shield, the short sword, and their
reverence to their kings." The German tribes usually had
oblong shields and long swords, and were very independent. His description of the Suiones which follows
(ch. 44) places them by contrast *in ipso oceano*—that
is, in an island or peninsula, and he tells us that they are
powerful by their fleets as well as in men and arms. He
describes their ships as equally fit for landing at the stern
and the bow—a remark which applies to many later
northern vessels.   They have no sails, nor even regular
banks of oars, but are rowed, as in some rivers, now on
one side, now on the other, of course by paddles.   The
Suiones honour wealth, and are governed by a monarch,
who has great power. Men are not allowed to bear arms
freely, partly because it is not necessary, since the ocean
prevents sudden hostile raids.

Next to them (proceeds Tacitus) are the Sitones, who
are like the Suiones in other respects, but fall even lower
than the condition of slaves, being governed by a woman.
This is the end of Suevia.   So far Tacitus.

[16] Pliny also makes the Guttones a German people, evidently
of the Mainland (*N. H.*, Book iv., ch. 28).   His account of
Scandinavia, which he makes an immense island of unknown
extent, is that it is inhabited by the Hilleviones in 500 villages,
who call it a second world.   The island of Eningia is thought to
be no smaller (*ibid.* 27.)

This notice is interesting, especially on two accounts; first, because it distinctly describes the Suiones as a Suevic tribe, together with the Semnones, Lombards, Angles (Anglii), Hermunduri, Marcomanni and Quadi, Gotini, Gothones, and many more. So that Sweden has a double claim to its name, as a Suevic country and as the special country of the Suiones. The mention of their neighbours, the Sitones, as governed by a woman, is also very interesting. We may suppose that in old Swedish their country was called " Queen-land," meaning land of the Quains or Finns, but it might also be translated " Women's land," and this ambiguity apparently gave rise both to the mistake which Tacitus made, and to the frequent description of their country about a thousand years later as a land of Amazons.[17] Yet I should not like to assert that women of martial character were not known in Finland. If the myths of the giants are rightly connected with the Finns[18] we must remember the great part that the giantesses play in these myths. Martial women certainly were known in Sweden. Three valiant shield-maidens fought at the Battle of Bråvalla; and what Olaus Magni writes about " the piracy of famous virgins," Alflida and the rest (Book v., ch. 24), does not wholly read like fable.

Ptolemy, who wrote his geography some fifty years later than Tacitus, also mentions the Gythones as an inland people, among the smaller nations of Sarmatia. He tells us that they dwell on the course of the Vistula below the Wends, who dwell all along the Venedic Gulf, that is, the Gulf of Danzig (3, 5, § 20). In another place he describes Scandia (that is, Southern Sweden) as a great island opposite the mouths of the Vistula, and gives

[17] See *Smith's Dict. Geography*, s. v. *Sitones*, and Bosworth and Toller : *A. S. Dict.*, s.v., *Cwénas* and *Cwén-land*, and Adam of Bremen, §§ 222 and 228, who speaks of the " terra feminarum " and the Amazons. See also Montelius : *S. H.*[1], Vol. i., p. 263 n.

[18] In the *Ynglinga Saga* the king of Jotunhem is called Finn. This is also the name of the giant who (according to popular legend) built Lund Cathedral.

the names of six tribes who inhabit it, amongst whom the southernmost are the Gutae (Γοῦται) and Dauciones. The mention of the Gutae as a southern tribe implies that they were newcomers; and they may well have immigrated between the age of Tacitus and that of Ptolemy. They may, or may not, have been close kindred of the Gythons to the south-east, or of the Gothini to the south-west, but their connection with the south-faring Goths of history does not seem to have been a practical one after their separation, as far as life in Scandia was concerned, at any rate for a long period after their southward migration.

I am aware that in thus insisting on the immigration of the Gothic tribes into Scandia I am opposing a popular belief, and that there is no direct tradition of such immigration. Dr. Söderblom would derive the name from " Gaut," in the sense of waterflow or waterfall, and connect it with the great Trollhättan Fall on the Göta River, where it descends about 110 feet shortly after leaving Lake Venern. He would make this the original home of the Goths of Sweden. I can only answer that etymological explanations of tribal names, though very tempting, are risky things, and that the historical notices of Tacitus and Ptolemy seem to me to be in favour of the suggestion which I have made.

We may, perhaps, reconstruct the course of the history of these migrations somewhat as follows, starting from the later part of the Bronze Age. First come the Suiones, in part possibly from the Gulf of Riga and the East, bringing with them a certain contingent of Wends and many Slavonic associations, and occupy Scandia, and probably also the neighbourhood of Lake Mälar, driving out, or subjugating, the primitive population, the majority of whom go further to the north. The myths of giants and dwarfs are, perhaps, relics of memories of conflicts with two aboriginal peoples, answering to, though possibly not identical with, modern Finns and Lapps, just as the myths of the Vanir are of more friendly contact with the Wends and Slavs (cp. Geijer, *H. of S.*, pp. 10, 12 and 30, E. T.).

Then, early in the second century, A.D., the northern Goths break away from the main body settled on the Vistula, and cross to Scandia by way of the islands of Öland and Gotland. In Gotland they must have had a wealthy settlement, the precursor of the greatness of Visby, since not less than 3,234 silver coins of the early Roman Emperors from Augustus to Alexander Severus (29 B.C. to 235 A.D.), were found in that island, the only others found in any quantity of that epoch being 88 in Öland and 584 in Skåne (Du Chaillu: *Viking Age*, Vol. ii., p. 556, Lond. 1889). The Goths, when established in the peninsula, and probably reinforced by kindred tribes from the south and southwest, especially arriving by the Göta River, still find Finns or Lapps, who here left their name (Finni) in Småland and West Gothland (Geijer, pp. 17 and 30). Of early serious conflicts between Goths and Sveas we have no striking record, except to some extent in Beowulf (canto 35), and we may presume that the latter withdrew of their own accord, or by agreement with the Goths, from Scandia, and concentrated themselves beyond the great lakes and forests at Sigtuna on Lake Mälar and elsewhere in Upland. We may also suppose, in view of the legends preserved by Jordanis in the sixth century,[19] that a swarm of Scandian Goths, under their king, Berig, rejoined and reinforced the Gythons of the Vistula in their southward movements.

These south-faring Goths, as is well known, had a marvellous history. Towards the end of the second century they came in contact with the Roman Empire in Dacia,

[19] Jordanis (a Bishop of Bruttium, c. 552 A.D.), *de rebus Geticis*, cc. 1 and 2. In the first chapter he speaks of the "Suethans" among the northern inhabitants of the Isle of Scanzia, and says that, like the Thuringians, they use excellent horses. Amongst the names of tribes there he mentions the Vagoth, Gautigoth ("acre hominum genus et ad bellum promptissimi") and Ostrogothæ, as well as the Finni. This looks as if West and East Gothland were already separate provinces. The "Gautigoth" may be the Goths of Göta-Elf.

where the names Daci and Getae stand curiously near to one another as synonyms for the same people, much as Gutae and Dauciones do in Ptolemy's account of southern Scandia. It may be a mere coincidence, but the southern Goths certainly liked to think of themselves as the same people as the Getae, just as the Swedes identified themselves with Scythians. However this may be, the Goths soon became Christians, and their bishop, Theophilus, sat at the Council of Nicæa in 325. Before the end of the fourth century their bishop, Ulfilas—himself a Cappadocian captive—provided them with an alphabet, a nearly complete Bible and the beginnings of a Christian literature. In a short time they overran Europe, established themselves as rulers in Italy, and founded a dynasty in Spain. But they never seem to have thought of evangelizing Scandia, or conferring upon it the blessings of civilization which they acquired so rapidly and so thoroughly.[20] One gift only, and that a fatal one, can we trace to the southern Goths. I have already pointed out that the introduction of Roman silver coin into the islands and Scandia was probably due to the first immigration of Goths from the Vistula. The influx of coins seems to have nearly ceased shortly after the time of Alexander Severus, and it does not begin again in any quantity till the time of Theodosius the Great. Then the character of these coins changes. Instead of silver they are almost all gold, and from the Eastern Empire. They are not, of course, so many in number as the silver,

[20] The attempts of Baaz to establish a connection between Romano-Gothic and Swedish Christianity are very ineffective (*Inventarium Ecclesiæ Sveogothorum*, pp. 85-6). They amount to this : That Rodolf, once a king somewhere in Scanzia (he misquotes Jordanis, chap. 1), took refuge with King Theodoric, and that among the subscriptions to the eighth Council of Toledo are several signed " Comes scantiarum et dux." On the meaning see Ducange s.v. *Comes* and *Scancio*. The title may mean " Master of the banquets " or " of the cupboards." See Diez : *Etymologisches Wörterbuch der Roman. Sprachen*[3], p. 163, s.v. *Escanciar*. Cp. Germ : *Schenken, Schanz*, etc. The title might be rendered " High Steward."

but they are in the aggregate of considerable value, and again appear in Öland and Gotland more than in the peninsula.[21] Many more must have been melted down to serve as material for ornaments. It is clear that the gold pieces which the Goths received from the Eastern Emperors, under the name of " subsidies," to buy off their attacks or to ensure their alliance, travelled northwards in large quantities. With them they carried the lesson that the barbarians had only to ask with sufficient vehemence and stoutness to grow rich without labour. Thus the Scandinavians learnt a lesson of avarice which they put in practice in England in their demands for danegeld, and, indeed, in all their piratical exploits. Thus the criminal weakness of the fifth century Emperors of the East bore bitter fruit for five centuries or more in the West. The hoards of gold coins of the fifth century Emperors, set side by side with the hoards of silver coins of our own Ethelred the Un-ready (or ill-advised), read a moral lesson, which nations may well take to heart, even in our own days—the duty of being prepared and able to fight for your country.

The introduction of runes for writing is dated by Montelius about 300 A.D. Our English antiquary, George Stephens, dates them somewhat earlier. In any case, they belong to the second period of this Iron Age. The first alphabet, or, as it is more correctly termed, Futhorc, from its opening letters, consisted of twenty-two characters. It is thought to have been founded on the Latin alphabet. " Probably " (says Montelius, *Civ.*, E. T., p. 118), " these signs were invented a little before the Christian era by a south Teutonic tribe, in imitation of the Roman writing which the Teutons received from one of the Keltic tribes living just to the north of the Alps." The great affinity for culture of all kinds shown by the south-faring Goths makes it natural by analogy to connect this gift to Sweden with the agency of a Gothic rather than a Swedish people.

[21] Du Chaillu's table *Viking Age*, Vol. ii., p. 586, gives 226 gold coins of this period, Mainland 37, Scania 19, Öland 106, Gotland 64.

But it is not probable that runes were introduced from the Vistula. It is more likely that they came by the Elbe. As far as I know no early runic stones are found in the islands, though there are gold bracteates with runes of a later date. The earliest rune-stone is from Bohuslän, and others are from neighbouring central provinces, and not from Skåne.

The third element of social progress which we assign to the same period is the worship of Odin, who is always connected in poetry with the runes, as Thor with the hammer. He is especially called the Goth (Gauti or Gautr). Probably, like the runes, his worship came from the South Germanic races (cp. Craigie: *Religion of A. S.*, 20 foll.). As Grimm says, the Swedes and Norwegians seem to have been less devoted to Odin than Gothlanders and Danes (*D. M.*, vol. 1, p. 160, E. T.). Names of places connected with Odin are more frequent in England, Germany and Denmark than in Sweden. Our own Wiltshire has some remarkable ones, such as Wansdyke and Wansborough, and Somerset has its Wanstrow—probably a place of sacrifice, and there is a Wansborough in Mells parish, and a number of others. As regards the characteristics of this divinity, he is god not only of craft and cunning and human strength, but of wisdom and poetry, and inspiration, and of a later and more courtly civilization. To quote a recent English writer, who contrasts Odin and Thor in an effective manner: " Odin was the god of the warrior, the poet, and the friend of kings, while Thor retained his former place in the hearts of those who still followed the old way of life in the secluded valleys of Norway and Iceland. Something of this distinctly appears in the figures of the two gods. Odin bears all the stamp of the new life and culture about him, while Thor is rather a sturdy yeoman of the old unpolished type. Odin is a ruler in whom knowledge and power are equally combined; Thor has little more to rely upon than his bodily strength. Even in small matters the contrast is marked. Odin lives by wine alone, while Thor eats the

flesh of his goats, and drinks the homely ale.   Odin's
weapon is the spear, Thor's is the more primitive hammer.
It is to Odin that all the warriors go after death ; Thor gets
only the thralls " (Craigie, l.c., p. 22).

Thor is specially the god of the Norwegians.

§ 7.—The Third Period of the Iron Age, 400 A.D.—700 A.D. Hugleik's Raid. The Romance of Beowulf and West Gothland.

The age of Byzantine gold dates from about 400 A.D.,
and extends to 700 A.D., the beginning of the Viking Age.
I have already noticed one striking phenomenon of this
period—the great influx of Byzantine gold.   Besides the
coins, gold rings of two pounds weight and more have
been found in Sweden, and as much as twenty-seven
pounds weight in one hoard.   These may be presumed to
have been made from gold coins melted down.   No native
coins were in use, but bracteate ornaments, stamped with
figures and runes, barbaric copies of Roman coins, are
rather frequent.   Spiral rings of gold seem to have been
used in the place of money.   The art of this period has
much beauty, and it shows traces of Celtic influence.   To
this period belong certain remarkable finds at Lake Vendel
and the three great barrows at Old Upsala (See Montelius:
Civ., pp. 139-141).   In this period we begin to touch
European history in another direction through Hugleik or
Hygelak, king of the Weder-Goths, and uncle of Beowulf,
who may plausibly be identified with the " Danish "
Chlochilaicus, whom Gregory of Tours describes as making a raid upon the kingdom of Theoderic I., one of the
sons of Clovis (Hist. Franc., Bk. iii., c. 3).   This places
him in the years 511 A.D.—533 A.D.   The romance of
Beowulf itself, which is preserved only in Anglo-Saxon,
and has a faint Christian tinge, is probably later, but it is,
I suppose, substantially the earliest monument of Scandinavian literature, and the civilization described in it is
really pre-Christian.   If the Weder-Goths lived in the

neighbourhood of Lake Vettern we may consider it a picture of early life in that province of West Gothland, which had so much to contribute to the early progress of Sweden, both in religion and in law, as well as in moral character. There is a noble tone of unselfishness and chivalry in the poem, and it is singularly free from any trace of sympathy with immorality, or vice, or trickery.

The raid described by Gregory of Tours is also interesting, as being the earliest Viking raid of which we have an account.   In this age not only the Gothic and Swedish provinces, but the coast of Northland (Norrland) beyond Gestrik and Helsingland, and up to Medelpad was inhabited.   It was a period of growing wealth and even of rude luxury.

§ 8.—FOURTH PERIOD OF THE IRON AGE, 700 A.D.—
1000 A.D.   THE YNGLING KINGS.   THE VIKING
AGE.   CHRISTIANITY AND THE UNION OF THE
KINGDOM.

Finally we come to the last period of the dark age of Swedish history, the stirring Viking Age, during which Christianity was at last introduced into Sweden, and at the end of which the first Swedish king received baptism—four hundred years later than our Ethelbert of Kent.   This period covers about 300 years from 700 A.D. to 1000 A.D. It is the period also in which Sweden for the first time became one kingdom, and for a time aspired to a wider northern empire.

The first Swedish royal family of Upsala kings, like the early kings of Wessex, claimed divine descent.   They were called Ynglingar from their first monarch, Yngwe Frey, who was said to be descended from Odin, Niord and Frey, and bore the name of the latter.   Twenty-two kings are named of this line ending with Ingiald, but some only reigned for a very short time, and some simultaneously. It was a period in which there were many petty kings, some with no lands, whose royalty was only acknowledged in war.   No doubt many of the Viking raids were simply undertaken to give an outlet to the ambition of such men, who were not wanted at home. As in Svealand so in Gothland there was probably a line of superior kings, and an even larger number of inferior ones.

The *Ynglinga Saga*, which gives the poetical history of the kings of Sweden, is a later document, and Norwegian not Swedish, but it has some interesting notices bearing on religion. The sixth of this line, Domald, is said to have been offered as a sacrifice to the gods by his subjects, as a last resort at the end of a long period of famine. Of the fifteenth, " Ane the Old," it is said that he purchased ten years of life by offering a son to Odin every ten years, and so lived to the age of 110, when the Sveas prevented him from sacrificing his last son, whereupon he died. Of the last, Ingiald, we are told that he was called " Illråda," or the Ill-counsellor (just as our Ethelred was called the Un-ready or Un-counselled, and Sigrid Stor-råda, or the High-minded)—his evil counsel being to put to death a number of petty kings by fraud and murder, and so to consolidate his kingdom. This, however, was frustrated; and his son, Olof Trätälja, of whom I have spoken, had to flee to Vermland.

A new line began under Ivar Vidfamne, of whom we read that he " brought all Sweden under his own sway. He made himself master also of the Danish kingdom, and a great portion of Saxon land, besides the Eastern lands, and the fifth part of England " (*Ynglinga Saga*, c. 45). According to the Saga, he died in our country, and was buried on the coast of England. His grave-mound was, it is said, opened by William the Norman, who found his body and burnt it, and then went up on land and got the victory (*Ragnar Lodbrok's Saga*, c. 19). It is the time of Sigurd Ring, the hero of the Battle of Bråvalla, in which Odin appeared for the last time, and of Ragnar Lodbrok and his sons. The latter was the most renowned hero of the Viking expeditions of the Northmen, and he died in England on a marauding expedition, perhaps a little before 800 A.D.

A few words are necessary as to these expeditions. I have already pointed out that the raid of Hugleik in the sixth century was the first on record. But what is generally called the Viking period dates from the last quarter of the eighth century. In the year 787 our Saxon chronicle notes for the first time the appearance of three ships of Northmen on the English coast. It is questioned whether they came from Norway or Jutland; but they seem to have come up the Thames as far as Kingston. This was the beginning of the Viking age of adventure and rapine, in which Danes, Norwegians and Swedes all took part, and renewed again, with more brutality and less readiness to acquire civilization, the wonderful achievements of their Gothic kinsmen in the third and following centuries. Doubtless many Swedes, like Ragnar Lodbrok and his sons, or descendants, were prominent in these Western exploits; but, as I said before, the Swedes had a greater aptitude than the other Northmen for adventures on the shores of the Baltic and its hinterland. It was a Swedish family that founded the Russian Empire under Rurik at Novgorod, or Holmgård, as they called it, in 862. Indeed the name Ros or Rus of the old writers was a name for the Swedes who had that lively intercourse with the Byzantines, to which reference has already been made. It was Swedes who furnished the famous Varangian guard at Miklagård, or Constantinople.[22] The runes on the Piræus lion, now at Venice, are, I believe, Swedish.

It is not my duty to enter upon the details of the half legendary, half historical exploits of the Viking Age, but to point out, as a historian of religion, how the neglect of the Scandinavian nations, particularly the Swedes, by their Christian neighbours, brought disaster upon those who neglected them. That sure punishment of neglect of duty and opportunity falls upon nations and churches as well as individuals is one of the laws of God's kingdom. The neglect of Arabia by Eastern Christians permitted the up-

[22] They were transferred from Vladimir the Great to Constantinople about 980 (*S. H.*[1], Vol. i., p. 280).

growth of the power of Islam, an Islam which pretended to improve the Gospel without really knowing the contents and nature of the Gospel. The neglect of Britain by the papacy, and by the Churches of the West under its influence, for the century and a half that followed the death of Pope Leo, had a great effect in alienating British from Western Christianity. We may still trace its effects in the sphere of religion in the movement for the creation of a separate province for Wales from which we are now suffering. The neglect of Scandinavia by the papacy and by the Christian Goths, Franks, Angles and Irish was rewarded by the ravage and rapine of the Viking Age; the horrible sufferings of many innocent men and women; the destruction, especially in the ninth century, of many churches, and of many treasures of literature and art which we should love to possess. The Viking Age continued until the North itself became Christian. It did not, however, entirely die out, but it had a revival in a milder form in the Crusades—understanding by the word expeditions to force Christianity upon the nations alien from the faith. This spirit of the Crusades appears indeed in the action of Charles the Great towards the Saxons just before the Viking Age, as well as in the missions of Olaf Tryggvason and Olaf Haraldson the Saint, in Norway, at the end of it, and in the crusade of the Swedish St. Eric against the Finns, and others of later kings, as much as in the Eastern expeditions of Godfrey, Tancred, Bohemond, and the rest.

As to the character of the Viking Age, the poet Esaias Tegnér has painted its heroic and brighter aspects in lively and sentimental colours in his *Frithiofs Saga*, while Geijer has portrayed it from another point of view. I will quote the passage of Holmberg, himself a warm admirer of the early age of his country, which Montelius has embodied in the *History of Sweden*[1] (Vol. i., p. 264):—

" It is true that there rests a rose-coloured light upon the northern Viking Age. But if we apply the spy-glass of history to our eyes we shall soon find that the rose-colour is nothing else but a blending of the hues of blood and tears. . . . The conception which we form of a subject often depends upon the name by which we are accustomed to designate it.   The term Viking-voyage suggests a chivalrous pursuit of dangers and warlike adventures, but the thing is better defined as a voyage for the purpose of killing and plundering.   We translate it, therefore, with perfect truth as piracy undertaken as a means of livelihood.''

It must, of course, be added that the pirates were often men who became valuable settlers in the countries which they raided, and that they infused new blood and vigour into Normandy and England, Apulia, Naples and Sicily and other countries.   They also had something to give to the Christianity of the older lands.   But the good was done at the expense of much needless sorrow, misery and confusion.

§ 9.—General Idea of the Character and Life of the People. Foreshadowings of later days.

The stories of early Sweden in the dark millennium which follows the birth of Christ are conspicuously full of a particular kind of interest—the interest attaching to revelations of national character.   For this purpose it makes little difference whether the legends are historically true or represent what the people loved to think, or naturally thought, of as true.   In them we have remarkable foreshadowings of later history, both in the lives of men and in the institutions which form the framework of their lives. In studying them we are struck by the persistence of certain types of character and social habit even to the present day.   This is what we should certainly expect in a people of simple temperament, and, to a great extent, unmixed blood, living under the conditions which have prevailed, and to a great extent still prevail, in Sweden.   People of homogeneous race in which both father and mother have the same kind of thoughts and prejudices, century after century, are naturally fuller than others of racial instincts and promptings in the blood. Their dreams, whether waking or sleeping, are not interrupted by cross-currents. And the isolation of Sweden, its sparse settlement, its climatic conditions, all contribute to make these dreams a real part of the life. The long winters and the bright summers bring out the contrast of darkness and light in a way with which dwellers in lower latitudes cannot be familiar. The beautiful silent starry nights of winter, the fantastic forms of ice and snow, the long-drawn summer days melting gently into a night which is scarcely night, all do their part in nourishing a poetic temper. Fairyland is revealed, in a way unknown to us, by the electric glow and coloured waves of shimmering, pulsing light, when the aurora borealis spreads over the heavens, or when the summer meadows, after sunset, are clothed with the white transparent veil of the " elf-dance."[23] Again, both lake and forest contribute their part to the production of the dreamy temperament. The lake is alternately, and almost at will, a mirror of the familiar shapes of cloud and landscape, subject to the beautiful changes wrought by sun and wind, and a transparent medium, through which the world beneath the earth is revealed to the gazer's fancy. The forest, with its deep glades and glancing half-seen forms of wild life, excites the imagination in another manner. A sense of these mysteries of lake and forest is emphasized by the isolation in which so many lives are passed. The whole experience seems to produce at once an intense love of the Fatherland, and, strangely enough, an intense desire to escape from its monotony into other lands. This double attraction to and from home is shared by the Swedes with the Irish. There is, indeed, much that is akin to the Celtic temperament in the Swedish, but the poetic turn takes a different line. Both love to dwell on the past, and to dream of the future. But, with the Swedes, the dreaming is of a much more practical character. While the Irish and the Highlanders, in their myths and in their aspira-

---

[23] See for good descriptions of both Du Chaillu's *Land of the Midnight Sun*, Vol. ii., pp. 46 and 420.

tions, dream of a life in contrast with their present
condition, the future life has generally appeared to the
Scandinavians as a glorification of their present state. The
Valhalla of Odin is only a glorified royal banqueting hall.
This characteristic also appears in Swedenborg's thoughts
of heaven. Again, both Celts and Norsemen are full of race
memories, inherited in the blood and fostered by tradition,
and both look to a sort of reincarnation of old heroes in
their descendants. But in the Swedes this takes a more
practical line, and from a dream becomes a kind of vision,
sending forth gallant processions of men to do the deeds of
their forefathers on the great stage of history. We cannot
wholly put this down to greater opportunity and greater
independence. There has been a conquering, adventurous
spirit in the Swedish people, as well as in their sovereigns
and leaders, a genius for war which is not inherited by the
Celtic peoples in anything like the same degree. With the
genius for war is joined a genius for law of a marked character, and for organisation in the arts of peace and all
that makes for prosperity and comfort, which also is not
Celtic, though the Land Banks and agricultural societies
show that there is considerable aptitude for it in Ireland.

   To come a little closer to the details of this ancient life.
The society which we find established in Sweden in
historical times, and that which previous legends describe,
is such as we should expect in a Suevic people settling
down peaceably, or with slight effort, in territory very little
occupied before. We have a historical account of such a
Scandinavian settlement in the Icelandic Landnama bok—
the " land-taking book "—in which we read how different
families occupied fresh ground, and divided it up amongst
themselves. Society, both in Iceland and Sweden, was
based on household ownership of land. It was a society in
which every freeman was equal in time of peace, and in
which all questions were decided in the popular assembly.
But the Sveas and the Goths had, as Tacitus witnesses, an
institution which the Icelanders tried to escape from,
namely, that of kingship. Tacitus naturally got his in-

formation from those who were familiar with Swedish customs from the outside, from those who, perhaps, fought against them, and, therefore, described the power of the kings as more absolute than it actually was in time of peace. But in war it was always absolute.

This observation as to the early settlement of Sweden by a party of colonists rather than of hostile invaders is very important as a key to many incidents and phenomena of its later history. A society composed of a large number of freemen holding land with equal rights was eminently favourable to domestic peace and to mutual respect. Each man was responsible for the religion of his family, and it concerned no one else what he thought and taught. Hence we may trace the national dislike of persecution. Hence, too, we explain the continuance of law and custom under the lagmen, or peasant judges, even when the country was most disturbed. Hence came the respect for the elective principle, both in Church and State.

This observation also explains the comparatively slight hold which the feudal system obtained over Sweden. It explains also the warlike instincts of so many Swedish sovereigns, and the readiness for adventure shown by many of the royal family and the nobility, who looked to find honour and distinction abroad for which their home life did not afford an opening.

There are many points of likeness between the history of England and that of Sweden, but there are also not a few contrasts. The principal point of contrast is to be found in this: England, not once only, but twice or thrice in historical times, under Saxon, Dane and Norman, was a conquered country, in which the leaders in war, especially the kings and their companions, obtained large estates, and held them as military fiefs. Sweden was a peaceably settled country, and, therefore, more equally divided, and had fewer serfs. The kings had comparatively small estates and small powers, and had to enlarge them by marriage, treaty, compact, gradual development of rights, as well as by warfare outside. The smallness of the revenues

of the crown accounts very much for the weakness of the
monarchy in the mediæval period, and explains the necessity which Gustaf Vasa felt for confiscating the revenues
of the Church. The bishops also in Sweden were, in the
Middle Ages, greater potentates in comparison to the
kings and nobles than they were in England.

How the kingly families, of which there were a great
many, arose we have no evidence. The Upsala kings, who
were the chief among the Sveas, claimed divine origin as
the descendants of Odin, Niord and Frey.[24] As head of
this family the Upsala king, who was elected from the
family, and by no means necessarily the eldest son, was
also priest of the temple in which his ancestors were worshipped. In the earliest times of which we know anything
there was a great assembly, both of Sveas and Goths,
every nine years at this temple, at which the king naturally
took the lead, and thus had a good opportunity of increasing his prerogative. How the alliance between the Sveas
and Goths arose, and when they first had the same king, is
not easy to say. According to legend it began with the
second dynasty in the eighth century. Probably it was at
first a matter of temporary arrangement, as the result of
some successful foreign campaign, and then (as experience
showed the usefulness of unity) it tended to become permanent. Certainly it was a fairly settled thing about the
middle of the ninth century, when Harald Fairhair was
encouraged by the example of Gorm the Old in Denmark
and Eric Emundson in Sweden, to attempt the unification
of Norway. After a king was elected by the Sveas he had
to make a circuit round the Gothic and other provinces in
order to obtain recognition. This was called his " Eriks-
gata," by which we are perhaps to understand his " journey through *all* the realm " from the old Norse " e "=
" all." At any rate, this is a just description of it. As he
came to the boundary of each province in turn he was

[24] For some of the paragraphs which follow cp. Geijer : *H. of
S.*, pp. 30 foll., E. T., and *Corpus Poeticum Boreale*, Vol. i.,
pp. 401-17, etc.

called upon to give hostages for his conduct as king, and to take an oath to observe the provincial laws. The right of the Sveas to have the prerogative voice in choosing the king was disliked by the Goths, but never denied by them.

The life which centred round the king and his family can best be described in one word as " Homeric "—an epithet which I find that Carlyle has anticipated. Religion was especially concerned with two things—sacrifice as a propitiation of the gods and a way of securing their favour at the beginning of an enterprise, and divination as a means to enquire their will.[25] It was also a shield and protection to human intercourse. To judge by parallel descriptions of other Scandinavian temples, the Upsala Temple had in its centre a table, on which lay an unjointed gold ring or bangle reddened with the blood of victims, on which oaths were sworn, and which was worn by the king or head of the assembly on his wrist at all gatherings of the people.[26] The oath ran as follows:—" I take so and so as witnesses herein that I take oath on the ring, a lawful oath—so help me Frey and Niord, and the Almighty Anse, as I shall pursue (*or* defend) this suit, *or* bear witness, *or* give verdict, *or* judgment, according to what I know to be most right and true in accordance with the law."

This oath was held to be very sacred and binding. The perjurer was treated as a vile and worthless person, a social outcast or *niding*, on a level with the adulterer. Besides the ring there was a bowl for the blood of victims, and in it twigs for divination by lot. Apparently, before the lots were drawn, the bystanders were sprinkled with the blood contained in the bowl. We shall find instances of this divination in the history of the mission of Anskar.

Idols were in use by the south-faring Goths, in the form of human busts on pillars draped with cloths, as early at

[25] Compare *C. P. B.*, Vol. i., p. 403, and Craigie, l.c., especially chapters 4 and 5.

[26] Compare *C. P. B.*, Vol. i., p. 422, and Craigie, l.c., p. 43. The " Anse " may probably be Thor.

least as the fourth century. They were figured on the storied column of Theodosius as part of the spoils of war brought to the city of Constantinople in the fourth century (*The Goths*, by Hy. Bradley, pp. 9 and 14, Lond., 1888). In Iceland they seem not to have been in early use, for we rather read of nails driven into the pillars of the high-seat. But there were certainly three images in the Upsala temple; and Odin, on his eight-legged horse, " Slepne," is several times represented on rune-stones (Montelius: *Sv. H.*¹, fig. 335, 403, from Tjängvide and Hablingbo in Gotland).

As to the victims offered to Odin, they were too often men (for women are never mentioned), as well as dogs, horses, cocks, etc. The king himself might be chosen in times of emergency, as Domald was, or he might have to sacrifice his sons (as Agamemnon sacrificed Iphigenia), or he might devote himself as King Eric the Victorious did at the Battle of Fyrisfield in 983, to gain victory from Odin. It is no doubt from such compacts with the old gods that the mediæval idea of compacts with Satan has grown up. Eric, it is said, died just ten years after the battle.[27]

If there was much that was terribly cruel in the human sacrifices in Sweden, there was often a heroic spirit mingled with it. In a later day we find Christians in Iceland offering to devote themselves to Christ for a purer life (not, I suppose, to actual death, but to a life of renunciation) if the heathen would do the same (*C. P. B.*, Vol. i., p. 410, from the *Kristni Saga*). The reverence for and impulse towards the monastic ideal thus had its natural root in the country.

These sacrifices, of whatever kind, were great occasions of popular concourse. The word " Ting," the old name for such a gathering, meant at once sacrifice, banquet, diet or parliament, assize for justice, and fair or market. The

[27] Compare the idea in *Gösta Berlings Saga*, by the novelist, Selma Lagerlöf, of the supposed compact made by the Majorska with the Devil, under which one of the cavaliers was to die every ten years. The scene of the novel is laid in the eighteenth century.

acknowledged central character of the Upsala Ting, and the custom of all the provinces to attend it every nine years, helped to establish the pre-eminence of the Sveas from very ancient times. The image of a State Church was thus presented at a very early stage of the nation's history, with the Upland king as its pontiff, and this thought had an influence in Sweden, just as the fact that Constantine the Great was Pontifex Maximus had an influence upon the Council of Nicæa and the Church of the fourth century and on later Byzantine religion.

The king was, therefore, a national priest, and every father of a family was priest in his own household. Just as in the temple there was a high-seat on which the priest sat, adorned with emblems or images of the gods, so it was in the household of which the father was priest, judge and leader. Marriage was held in honour, and adultery and rape were considered great crimes, but much laxity was allowed to the man. This was a blot upon Swedish character, of which Adam de Bremen speaks, and on account of which he contrasts the Swedes unfavourably with the Norwegians, while he has much to praise in the Swedish character in other respects. Polygamy was practically permitted, and no reproach attached to the man who had children born to him from handmaids or slaves in his house—a point which we must remember when we come to speak of the mediæval clergy and even of much later days. I feel bound, however, to say that equal laxity seems to have prevailed in such Norwegian households as that of St. Olaf and his son Magnus the Good, and in a number of other cases. The father (as in ancient Greece or Rome) was free to take up or expose an infant born in his house. If he took it up and had it sprinkled with water (the heathen form of baptism) and named in the presence of his chief kinsmen it became his child.[28]

[28] This ceremony of heathen baptism is well attested. So we read in *Halfdan the Black's Saga*, ch. 7 : " Queen Ragnhild gave birth to a son, and water was poured over him, and the name Harald given him." This was Harald Harfager. His

Even in Christian times the clergy on the spot do not seem to have censured this laxity, although, of course, it appeared wrong to Adam. But even he does not mention the vice of drunkenness as prevalent in Scandinavia, probably because it was so common all round him in Germany as to excite no remark. The Sagas make many references to it, although it was not so much of daily occurrence as an incident of festivity. In King Sigurd's well-ordered household at Ringarike, when Olaf the Saint visited him and his mother, the food was milk and fish one day, alternating with meat and ale on another. Games of chance were also played very largely, and we find evidence from the first centuries after Christ that dice were used for gambling (Montelius: fig. 371). Draughts were also played, and the game of chess was introduced as early as the eighth or ninth century, and was evidently much in favour.

Among such a people the sentiment of family life was naturally very strong. The graves of the dead were near the houses, and were places for religious worship and meditation. On these family-howes (ätt-högar), as they were called, the head of the family was wont to sit, according to old custom, for hours together, no doubt to hold converse with the spirits of the departed and to look forward to the uncertain future.[29] These howes were also places for games and athletic sports, as in the Iliad and Aeneid. The use of the churchyard for festivals is clearly a relic of this custom, which prevailed also in England.

The most distinctive virtue of the Swedes, which yet characterizes them, was their hospitality. "It is the greatest disgrace among them (says Adam, § 230) to deny hospitality to wayfarers; they in fact vie with one another as to which of them is worthy to receive a guest. After

son, Hakon the Good, by a slave-girl, Thora Mosterstang, was baptized by Earl Sigurd (H. Harfager's Saga, ch. 40). So Sigurd (Sigfrid) was baptized in the house of King Hjalfrek, not indeed as his son (see Völsunga Saga, chap. 13, trans. by Morris, published in the Scott Library).

[29] See the quotation from Hallfred's Saga about Thorlaf in C. P. B., Vol. i., p. 416.

showing him all the rights of humanity for as many days as he desires to spend in a place his host sends him on to his friends from one halting place to another."

As to the highest ideal of independent manly character all over Scandinavia we cannot, I suppose, have a better picture of it than as it appears in the persons of Beowulf, the Weder-Goth, and of Sigurd in the *Völsunga Saga*. The poem of Beowulf does not, I think, contain any summaries of good advice to heroes, but we have in the later poem the remarkable "wise words" of Brynhild, addressed to Sigurd, which read like an extract from a Scandinavian book of Sirach :—

"Be kindly to friend and kin, and reward not their trespasses against thee : bear and forbear, and win for thee thereby long enduring praise of men." . . . "Let not thy mind be over-much crossed by unwise men at thronged meetings of folk; for these speak worse than they wot of; lest thou be called a dastard, and art minded to think that thou art even as is said; slay such an one on another day, and so reward his ugly talk. . . . Let not fair women beguile thee such as thou mayst meet at the feast, so that the thought thereof stand thee in stead of sleep and a quiet mind; yea draw them not to thee with kisses or other sweet things of love."

"If thou hearest the fool's word of a drunken man, strive not with him being drunk with drink and witless; many a grief, yea, and the very death groweth from out such things."

"Fight thy foes in the field, nor be burnt in thine house.

"Never swear thou wrongsome oath; great and grim is the reward for the breaking of plighted troth."

"Give kind heed to dead men—sick-dead, sea-dead, or sword-dead; deal heedfully with their dead corpses" (*Völsunga Saga*: ch. 21, translated by W. Morris).

This was advice to a hero who went about the world with his sword ready to maintain his honour and that of his kinsmen and friends, and being a law to himself.   But there was another side to Swedish life, the law-making, law-abiding peasant life, which is the real heart of the country.   As I have said, Sweden was peaceably settled by a large body of freeholders, and never took to the feudal system.   There was, therefore, always a strong democratic basis to society in it.   The monarchy was always held to be elective, and a bad king might be deposed and stoned, as their history often witnesses.   To quote Adam again (ch. 231): "The king's power depends upon the vote of the people.   What all have decided in common he must confirm, unless his decree prevails, which they sometimes follow against their will.   And so they rejoice in thinking that at home all are equal.   When they go to battle all yield obedience to the king, or to him who for his skill in war is made captain by the king."   The fighting was done by the kings and their kindred and attendants, but chiefly in foreign expeditions, starting generally in the spring and returning before winter.   Thus the country people in the most laborious time of the year were often left to rule themselves.   This led to the peculiar institution of the "Lagman" (or lawman), who was a peasant judge chosen by the people, and had the law (probably originally in verse) in his memory, and was its expounder to the people and their spokesman in the great assemblies of the nation.   The Roman tribunate (as Geijer has observed) offers a certain analogy to this office, though under very different conditions.   This office was known also in Norway, but not in Denmark.   The earliest traces of it seem to be in West Gothland, which was often a connecting link between Norway and Sweden, where the name of "Lumb" is mentioned in heathen times (ninth or tenth century), as having composed a large number of laws.   Viger Spå (the wise), who may have been his contemporary, is mentioned in similar terms in the preface to *The Law of Upland*.[30]

The name of Torgny is well known as that of the Lagmen of Upland, one of whom was prominent, as we shall

[30] See *Sv. Medeltid*, Book iii. p. 42 foll., and L. Beauchet : *Loi de Vestrogothie*, pp. 2 foll. and 10 foll., Paris, 1894.

see, in the time of Olof Skötkonung.   In these independent social and political institutions we have features of
Swedish life which have been in one form or another very
persistent throughout its history, and which account for
much which would be otherwise inexplicable, especially for
the recuperative power of the nation after its exhaustion by
foreign wars.

This concise sketch of a great subject, the Heathen
Period of Swedish history, may, I hope, be sufficient to
interest you in what is to follow.   We cannot fail to see the
unity and continuity of this history.   We comprehend
already that certain great principles underlie it and penetrate it.   We perceive that we have to do with a noble and
a strong people, and we can trace the hand of God already
beginning their education for their destiny among the
nations.

This little poem describes how a noble young Norwegian, Gaute, on a pilgrimage to the holy land, wanders in the woods and finds himself exhausted by a river he cannot cross. After a dream a boat appears and carries him over, and near a hermitage he sees an old man praying in monkish dress, who rises, looking like an ancient warrior. The old man asks him about Norway, and whether people remember Olof, and what they think of him. Gaute replies that most people think he was drowned. The old man angrily retorts that to so athletic a swimmer this was impossible. Others, says Gaute, think God took him alive to heaven. This, says the old man, is improbable : Olof had many sins.

"Last (said Gaute) some believe thus,
That he cleft the foaming billows,
And found safety on a vessel
That appeared outside the battle.
For his valiant fellow-warriors
Who were bound in Danish fetters—
But few lived indeed—were loosened,
       Loosened by an unknown hand.
Many thought that must be Olof's."
    "Lives then Einar Tambar skälver?"
    "Lives he? Yea (thus answered Gaute)
Wealthiest man in Tronde county."

Now the cloister bell resoundeth,
Goes the old man to the temple,
Says his mass, and then returning
Calls to him his guest, and bids him
"Greet him.   No man fought more bravely
Of the Long Serpent's crew than Einar."
From the astounded guest he turneth,
Slowly goes, is found no longer.

Years go by ; Gaute wanders homeward,
Greets the well-known shores of Norway,
Tells the folk what fortune met him.
Then with tears thus answered Einar :
    "In good troth, my brother Gaute,
Olof Tryggvason thou sawest."
    So the story runs in Norway.
Dear at heart to all its people :
By Christ's holy grave far distant
Sits the hero : there King Olof,
Intercedes for Norway's realm."

II.

THE CONVERSION OF SWEDEN (830 A.D.—1130 A.D.).

LECTURE II.

THE CONVERSION OF SWEDEN (830 A.D.—1130 A.D.).

§ 1.—INTRODUCTION. DIVISION OF THE SUBJECT.

It is the function of the historical lecturer, as distinguished from the professed historian, to create a personal interest in his subject in the minds first of his hearers and then of his readers. The historian must record everything that a student may reasonably expect to find in his book, whether the latter consults it on a particular point, or reads it straight on for full information. The lecturer may be satisfied if he leaves a clear mental picture traced in broad outline which the student can fill up for himself. There should be enough detail and local colour to heighten the effect, but not enough to weary the memory. The great object is to make a strong impression on the mental retina.

In discharging this function I shall ask you to consider the first great period of Swedish Church history—the mission period of three hundred years—under three successive aspects. First, it is a mission from Northern Germany, finding a centre in Hamburg, or rather Bremen, in which the work is done by emissaries from Corbey, Frisia, Germany and Denmark. In this period far the most striking figure is Anskar, the founder of the Church in Sweden. For, after his death, little by comparison is done for about a hundred years. This period, which is the longest of the three, extends to a hundred and fifty years, from 830 A.D.—980 A.D. We have a good life of Anskar by his successor, Rimbert; but, besides this, almost our only authority is Adam of Bremen, the North-German Tacitus, who give us both accurate annals of the archbishops of Hamburg and a valuable Scandinavian geography. Adam had as his friend and informant one of the most remarkable men of his time, Sven Estridsson, King of Denmark, son of a Jarl Ulf and

Estrid, sister of King Knut. This man (1018 A.D.—1076 A.D.) was friend and son-in-law of the Swedish King, Anund Jakob, and resided much in Sweden. He made several attempts to conquer England, and five of his fifteen sons sat successively on the throne of Denmark. Two of them, St. Canute and Eric Eiegod, are well known in northern history.

The second period occupies a space of some ninety years (980 A.D.—1066 A.D.). It extends from the time of Eric Segersäll (the Victorious), with whom history proper in Sweden begins, up to the Norman Conquest of England and the failure of the lofty enterprise of Archbishop Adalbert, who desired to establish a great North German patriarchate, including Scandinavia. It is a time when the failing energies of the Bremen mission are reinforced by the missionary spirit which bursts forth in Norway under the two Olafs, and is welcomed by the Swedish Olof—the first Christian king—and his successors. It is a time when English missionaries, brought from Norway, or directly sent over by Knut, co-operate, more or less independently, with the old line of missionaries from Germany and Denmark. It brings us into close contact with many men of strong character. Adam is still our chief guide to the end of it, but his mainly ecclesiastical and German point of view is enlarged by the brilliant personal records of the Icelandic Sagas.

The third period is the shortest of the three, and covers less than seventy years (1066 A.D.—1130 A.D.). It describes a time of transition, during which Sweden first comes into direct contact with the papacy in the person of Gregory VII. The most important ecclesiastical event in it is the establishment of the Archbishopric of Lund in 1103 A.D. It corresponds with the reign of Stenkil and his family in Sweden, and is brightened by the names of several sainted bishops of English origin or consecration. At the close of it nearly all Sweden was nominally Christian.

I shall add a few words in conclusion on the reasons for

4

the slowness of the conversion of the country and the expectation which it enables us to form.

§§ 2 AND 3.—THE HAMBURG-BREMEN MISSION FROM ANSKAR TO ODINKAR (830 A.D.—980 A.D.).

§ 2.—EBO AND ANSKAR. GAUTBERT.

Efforts for the conversion of the two southern Scandinavian nations began almost simultaneously in the earlier part of the ninth century, but they succeeded much more rapidly in Denmark than in Sweden.   Charles the Great had been satisfied with the conversion of his own subjects in great measure by force, and considered that the only policy to be pursued as regards the Danes was to defend his empire from their incursions.   His son, the Emperor Louis the Pious (814 A.D.—840 A.D.), preferred to try the gentler way, and sent Ebo, Archbishop of Reims, with the approval and authority of Pope John X., probably in the year 823 A.D., as the first Christian missionary beyond the Eider.   A few years later a Danish prince, Harald Klak, desiring alliance with the Franks, determined to become a Christian, and was baptized, with his wife, at Mainz in 826 A.D.   On his return to Denmark he took with him Anskar,[1] a monk of Corbie, near Amiens, who had recently

---

[1] The authorities for the life and mission of Anskar are fortunately excellent.   They are his life by Rimbert, his deacon and intimate friend and successor in the Archbishopric, and the chronicle of the archbishops of Hamburg (*Gesta Pontificum Hammaburgensis Ecclesiæ*), written by Adam, a canon of Bremen, and master of the schools there about the year 1075 A.D.   Rimbert's life has often been printed.   A rather convenient, but not very correct, text of it is to be found in Fabricius *Scriptores Septentrionales*, and another in the second volume of the *Scriptores Rerum Suecicarum*, published in 1828, with a Swedish version.   The best text is probably that in Pertz' *Monumenta Germaniæ*, Vol. ii.   I have had access to all of these, but I have found the one most convenient for reference to be the reprint of Mabillon's text from the *Annales Benedictini*, Vol. vi., in Migne's *Patrologia*, Vol. 118, and I have referred to the chapter numerals and pages of that edition.   I have used Pertz's, or rather Lappenberg's edition of Adam of Bremen's

been transferred to the northern colony of that house called Corbey, or Corvey, in Westphalia.   Anskar set up a school, which he supplied with pupils, as some Roman missionaries still do nowadays, by the purchase of children, but he was not very successful.   Harald was again driven out, and Anskar's companion died, and he himself returned, in company with Harald, who became a Frankish vassal over Walcheren and Dorstad in Holland.   The latter place, which is on the Lek, a branch of the Rhine, about thirty-five miles east of Rotterdam, and a little south-east of Utrecht (Wyk by Duurstede) was a port which did a large trade with Scandinavia, and was a place where many Northmen settled, and many also were baptized long before their own homes were Christian.[2]   In the autumn, probably of 829 A.D., Swedish ambassadors came to the Frankish court, reporting that their people had learnt something of Christianity from merchants and captives, and would be glad to receive missionaries.   Anskar was again asked to go north.   He consented, and, after a perilous sea journey, in which he and his companions were robbed by Vikings, and suffered other hardships by the way, he at length reached Sweden.   His companions would have turned back, but his courage led them on. They made a dangerous over-land journey, partly by lake, partly through the forests, and at length arrived at Birka,

Gesta Pontificum as reprinted in Vol. 146 of the *Patrologia Latina*. I have referred to the continuous series of chapter numerals in round brackets in that edition which are also to be found in the text in the *Scriptores Septentrionales*, and are more convenient than the references to the different books, each with a different series of chapters.   There is a good survey of all this literature in an essay, *Om Källorna till Nordiska missionens historia*, by H. Holmquist, *Kyrko-historisk Årsskrift*, Vol. ix., pp. 241-283, 1908.   See also Hans von Schubert : *Kirchengeschichte Schleswig-Holsteins*, Vol. i., 1907.   A good popular account of the period is contained in Professor N. Söderblom's lecture to the Students' Missionary Association at Upsala (*Om Sveriges förste Kristne lärare*), published in their *Meddelanden* of June, 1889.

[2] See Rimbert : *Vita Anscharii*, 33, 42 and 48.

a much frequented port on an island in Lake Mälar, still called Björkö, about eighteen English miles west of Stockholm and twenty-two south of the old city of Sigtuna.[3]

It is possible that there were already the beginnings of a Christian congregation, in the persons of Frisians who had settled at Birka for the purpose of trade. The further objective of the mission was evidently Upsala and the region round it. Upsala was the chief seat of heathenism, of which the centre was a gilded temple surrounded by a sacred wood, on which the bodies of sacrificed men and animals were constantly hanging. Here every nine years a great national festival was held, in which the whole of Sweden was represented, so that the country had a kind of religious unity before its political unity was established. This place is only some twenty or twenty-five English miles to the north of old Sigtuna (Signildsberg), and is accessible from it by water. It is about three English miles from the present cathedral and university city which now bears the name of Upsala. Anskar was kindly received by King Bern or Biörn, who consulted his people, and, with their consent, gave him leave to preach and baptize. The chief of the district, Herigar (Härgar), a trusted counsellor of the king, was converted, and built a chapel for the mission on his own ground, and continued a stanch Christian for the rest of his life.

Anskar remained two winters at Birka, and returned to Germany in 831 A.D. in order to report his progress to the Emperor. The party brought back with them an assurance from experience that the mission was likely to be successful, and some kind of a written evidence of the

---

[3] The situation of Birka is described by Adam of Bremen with some detail, chapters 47 and 237. The inhabitants defended themselves against the pirates by filling up the channels with stones, which made navigation difficult for themselves as well as for their enemies. The remains still found on the island of Björkö are the most remarkable in point of quantity and interest of all in Sweden. Some 2,500 grave-mounds are visible besides a multitude of Christian interments. See, *e.g.*, Dr. Söderblom's paper referred to in note 1.

king's good will. The phrase used is rather obscure, "cum literis regia manu more ipsorum deformatis." It was probably not a letter in runic characters, as some have thought, but the king's monogram perhaps on a wooden tablet or tally (*Vita Anscharii* 18, alias 11; cp. Reuterdahl: i. 205). In the meantime an important and statesman-like plan, partly conceived by Charles the Great, was being matured for the establishment and government of the Church in Northern Germany, and was enlarged so as to embrace the newly-opened regions. Without following in detail the changes which it was found necessary to intro-duce into this plan, owing to untoward circumstances and conflicting ecclesiastical interests, it is sufficient to state that Anskar was consecrated first Archbishop of Hamburg in 831 A.D., by Drogo of Metz (one of the sons of Charles the Great), Ebo of Reims and others, with a view to the oversight of the northern missions. This arrangement received the approval of Pope Gregory IV., who gave Anskar the pallium, and entrusted the mission to him with-out withdrawing the authority already given to Ebo. The two archbishops, however, seem to have worked together, not only without friction, but with genuine affection. After considerable difficulties caused by the loss of the estate of Turholt, given by the Emperor Lewis as an endowment of the see, and the burning of Hamburg by the Danes, it was at length decided that the see of Ham-burg and the older foundation of Bremen should be united. This took place with the consent of Pope Nicolas I. in 864 A.D., and Bremen became the archbishop's residence. During the interval between his consecration and his re-moval to Bremen Anskar again prosecuted the Danish mission, and joined with Ebo in consecrating Ebo's nephew, Gautbert, under the name of Simon, as bishop for Sweden (*V. A.*, ch. 21; Adam, ch. 14).

Gautbert must therefore rank as the first Swedish bishop. He was a friend of the famous Rabanus Maurus, Arch-bishop of Mainz, who addressed a letter to him, *Ad Simonem magnum sacerdotem* and "Bishop of the

Sueones," of which a portion has been preserved to us.
Rabanus counts up a great number of presents, which he
sends to Simon, including a missal "cum lectionibus et
evangeliis," a psalter, a copy of the Acts of the Apostles,
three altar cloths, three sets of vestments, two chasubles
and two tunics (camisæ) or albs, a corporal and a pallium.[4] These presents must have been of great
value to the infant Church, but we know nothing
further of their history.   Gautbert's mission seems to
have been, on the whole, ineffective, and he was driven out
by a local conspiracy, in which his nephew, Nithard, was
murdered or martyred.   For seven years the few converts were left without a shepherd.   Gautbert became
Bishop of Osnabrück, and was unwilling to return.
Anskar then sent a hermit, Ardgar, who was able to support those who had remained firm, including, besides
Herigar, a noble lady, Frideburg, and her daughter.   A
rather interesting incident is reported concerning Frideburg, that, after the departure of Bishop Simon or Gautbert, she reserved a little wine [5] in her house in order that
she might have a death-bed communion in case no priest
was at hand (*V. A.*, ch. 32).   She had so kept it three
years when Ardgar arrived.   Clearly communion of the
dying was at this time in both kinds as Anskar's own was.

Anskar, whose personal interest in the mission still continued, came again to Sweden, in 848 A.D., in the time of a
king called Olof, and remained for about the same time
as before. He arrived at a critical moment, when much
discussion on matters of religion was going on amongst
the people; and had he been able to remain or been better
supported, the conversion of the province of Upland might
more speedily have followed. Two tendencies have been
observed in Scandinavian heathenism about this period, a
tendency to monotheism of a somewhat sceptical character

[4] See H. Holmquist : *Källorna*, etc., p. 271.
[5] "Aliquantulum vini," which I believe to be the right reading, as it is in Mabillon's text and the Swedish version.
Fabricius and the *S. R. S.* read " aliquid emptum vini."

and a tendency to increase the number of deities. Both seem to be discernible in the account of Anskar's second mission. Complaint was made that the gods were angry because their sacrifices were neglected; and an enthusiast came forward to announce a vision which he had received from the gods bidding the people deify their late king, Eric. Tales of the power of Christ were also circulated by those who had been in Germany and Holland, especially at Dorstad. On Anskar's arrival the king and his nobles determined to ask counsel of the gods as to whether the mission should be encouraged or not. They were consulted by means of lots taken in the open air, the ritual being probably somewhat more elaborate than that described by Tacitus, but generally similar (*Germ.* 10, *Vita Ans.* 24).

It would seem that the bowl of blood, with twigs in it, was taken from the temple table, and the people sprinkled with the blood. Then the twigs were thrown at random on a white cloth in the open air. The priest said a prayer over them, and then, looking up to heaven, took up three of them in succession. If each indicated the same answer, " yes " or " no," that was, we must suppose, the answer given by the oracle.[6] Or the answer might, apparently, be a less simple one. On this occasion it was favourable to Anskar. After this the question was put before two public assemblies, probably one at Birka and one at Upsala. At length the full consent of the people was obtained, and it was determined that the mission should be allowed to continue its work and to make converts without opposition; and the king gave a hall for a church. Anskar then left Eribert, another nephew of Bishop Gautbert, as priest-in-charge, and returned to Germany. He died himself at Bremen on the 3rd of February, 865 A.D., and was shortly afterwards canonized by Pope Nicolas I.

There can be no question of Anskar's saintliness, accord-

[6] Golther, *G.M.*, 631, discusses divination by lot at considerable length, but without making the process very clear, on account of the lack of evidence.

ing to the standard of any age of Christendom.   His missionary zeal and courage, his uncomplaining patience, his generosity, his spirit of foundation, whether at home or abroad, his austere self-discipline and his diligence in the work of his calling were all striking features of his character.   He struggled hard and successfully against two faults, a temptation to vainglory and to discontent, the latter caused by his failure to achieve actual martyrdom, a death which he thought had been promised him in a vision in early youth.   His relations with Ebo, who might so readily have been regarded as his rival, seem to have been more than friendly.   He clearly regarded Ebo as his counsellor and inspirer.   He evidently felt the great importance and future possibilities of their joint mission, and he seems to have done his best to leave it as a legacy to be fostered by the whole Church of Germany.

Before his death he drew up a short account of the work of the mission, and sent a copy of it to each of the bishops in that part of the empire which was ruled by Lewis, King of Germany (840 A.D.—876 A.D.), who was the third son of the Emperor, Lewis the Pious, with the following touching letter.   It will be observed that he makes no mention of himself in it, but only of Ebo and others who had helped the work :—

"In the name of the holy and undivided Trinity, Ansgar, Archbishop by the grace of God, to all the prelates of the Holy Church of God, that is to say, to those dwelling within the realm of King Lewis.

"I desire that you should know that in this little book is contained how that Ebo, Archbishop of Reims, inspired by the divine Spirit, in the days of our Lord Emperor Lewis, with his consent and that of a synod gathered from almost the whole Empire, went to Rome and there obtained from the venerable Pope Paschal public licence to preach the Gospel in the parts of the North; and how afterwards the Emperor Lewis promoted this work and showed himself bounteous and kind towards it in all ways; and the other circumstances which have attended this mission (legatio).   Wherefore I make earnest prayers to you that you will intercede with God, so that this mission may be permitted to increase and bear fruit in the Lord. For already, both among the Danes and the Swedes, the Church of Christ has been founded, and our priests, without hindrance, discharge their proper office.   I pray also that you will cause this letter to be preserved in your library for a perpetual memory ; and that, as occasion shall serve you and your successors, when you shall have found it convenient, you will make it known to all men.   May Almighty God make you partners in this work by your kind good will and joint heirs with Christ in heavenly glory " (*P. L.*, 118, 1031).

§ 3.—RIMBERT.   GROWTH OF POLITICAL UNITY IN THE NORTH.

Notwithstanding this solemn appeal, little or nothing was done for Sweden by the German mission for seventy years after Anskar's death.   His successor and sympathetic biographer, Rimbert, did not indeed forget his old master's work during the twenty-three years of his episcopate (865 A.D.—888 A.D., Adam : ch. 33).   But he lived in troubled times, and had to spend his resources largely in redeeming captives.

In the last half of the ninth century we find all three of the Scandinavian Powers making progress towards internal unity.   Denmark was first united under Gorm the Old, who used his central position of high priest of Odin at Lejre in Seland, very much as the Upsala kings did in Svithiod.   He not only ruled over the Danish islands, but over Slesvig and part of Holstein, and over Blekinge and Skåne in Sweden.   At the same time Eric Edmundson (who died about 885 A.D.) was undisputed sovereign both of the Swedes and Goths.   Their example encouraged Harald Fairhair (850 A.D.—933 A.D.) to attempt the even more difficult task of uniting the thirty-one little kingdoms of Norway, in which he succeeded under the inspiration of love,[7] and reigned for fifty years.

About this time it would seem that Christianity was introduced into the island of Gotland, although we do not know the means.   Apparently it was from some other direction than the Bremen mission.   The antiquary, Dr. Ekhoff, has found the remains of three stone churches in the foundations of the twelfth century church of St. Clement at Visby, the earliest of which may go back to about 900 A.D.

A later archbishop, Unni, was more personally interested in the mission than Rimbert had been, and actually died of sickness at Birka in 936 A.D.   But he stood rather alone; and, if we may judge Adam of Bremen's apostrophe to bishops of his own day, Unni's example did not much appeal to his countrymen.   Adam turns to those who sit at home and place first amongst the advantages of the episcopate the brief delights of glory, gain, gluttony and sleep, and bids them look at the example of this poor and modest but really great and glorious priest of Christ, who, braving all the perils of land and sea, and making his way among the fierce tribes of the North, laid down his life for Christ in the most distant regions of the world (ch. 49). Yet we know no details of Unni's work.   His successor at Bremen was Adaldag, a young man of high birth, who sat for the long period of fifty-three years (935 A.D.—988 A.D.), and had himself been a missionary to the Slavs. He ordained many bishops for Denmark, and a Dane of good birth, Odinkar, for Sweden (ch. 69).   But we only hear of the latter that he was a good and able man, and we hear of no congregation of the mission in Sweden except at Birka.

The Bremen mission had not become extinct, but it had made little progress.   Sweden needed other help, and it came to it, in a somewhat unexpected way, from England.

[7] He was anxious to win a girl called Gyda, daughter of King Eirik of Hordaland, who returned answer that she would never come to him unless he subjected to himself the whole of Norway as fully as Kings Gorm of Denmark and Eirik of Sweden had done (*Harald Harfager's Saga*, ch. 3).

§ 4.—English Missionaries from Norway chosen by the Kings reinforce the German and Danish Missionaries. The first Christian King and his contemporaries and sons.

The history of Sweden, as distinguished from learned conjecture or doubtful legend, begins, as I have said, with Eric the Victorious, father of Olof Skötkonung, the first Christian king. In order to understand the course of the forward movement for the conversion of Sweden, which now undoubtedly commenced, we must make acquaintance with two remarkable men, Olaf Tryggvason and Olaf Haraldson, Kings of Norway, from whom the main impulse to the conversion came. We must also understand their relation to the Danish kings, the conquerors of England, Sven Forkbeard and his son Knut, as well as to the royal family of Sweden. We must further collect the few particulars which we can glean about the English missionaries who worked with and under them. For they are strangely shadowy personalities beside the striking figures of the princes of that wild and heroic age. It will be convenient first to sketch the political relations, and then to add to our sketch what we know of the growth of the Church in the country.

Eric the Victorious was a great warrior of the Ivar race, grandson of that Eric Edmundson who had united the Swedes and the Goths. He is said himself to have added Finland, Livonia and Esthonia to the Swedish crown. He and his brother Olof at first reigned together. After his brother's death he not unnaturally refused to share the kingdom with his nephew, Styrbiörn, then quite a boy. But this boy, when only fourteen years of age, mastered the great pirates' stronghold of Jomsburg on the mainland and made himself head of their remarkable celibate brotherhood. He attacked his uncle in Mälar Lake, but was defeated at the important Battle of Fyrisvall in 983 A.D. Eric, as you have heard, devoted himself on this occasion to Odin, while Styrbiörn gave himself to Thor, and was killed. After the victory Eric naturally wished to secure

the succession to his own infant son, and induced the
nobles and people to do him immediate homage—an incident from which, according to the common story, he is
said to have received the surname of Skötkonung or Lap-
King.[8]

Eric's wife, Sigrid Stor-råda (the high-minded), who we
may suppose held the child in her arms, was herself a
powerful instrument in working out the tragic history of
the three kingdoms at this time, being closely connected,
in one way or another, with all the chief actors in it. Her
haughty temper caused her husband to separate from her,
and he married another wife. He then invaded Denmark,
and drove the king, Sven Forkbeard, into exile. While
in Denmark the Swedish king for a time became a
Christian, though he afterwards relapsed into paganism
(Adam, ch. 79). It may have been while he was ruling
for a time in Denmark, or, as Saxo (lib. x., p. 338, ed.
Holder, Strassburg, 1886) puts it, rather later, that Poppo,
a bishop of Slesvig, came as legate of the German Emperor
and Archbishop Adaldag, to persuade the Scandinavian
peoples to live at peace with their neighbours, and performed some remarkable miracles in the presence of the
multitude—holding a hot iron in his hand, and allowing a
waxed shirt to be burnt upon his body (Adam : ch. 77 ; cp.
Saxo : l.c.). Other Danish bishops, such as Odinkar
junior, ordained by Adaldag's successor, Libentius, or
Liavinzo (988 A.D.—1013 A.D.), also worked occasionally
in Sweden (Adam : l.c.). Eric the Victorious is said to
have died ten years after the Battle of Fyrisvall, according
to his compact with Odin, in the year 993 A.D. (cp. *Harald
Greyskin's Saga*, ch. 11, in *Heimskringla*, ed. Laing, ch.
2, p. 63).

His widow, Sigrid, who was very rich, had many

[8] This is the common story; but others suggest a different
origin to the name. Hans Hildebrand : *S. H.*[2], pt. 2, p. 80,
derives it from a land tax or skatt (English " scot ") laid by him
on the royal estates and domains, and connects it with his
coinage.

suitors, as she was now regent for her son. Among them were Harald Grenske, father of St. Olaf, and a king from Russia, whom she caused to be burnt in the house in which they were resting after a drinking bout, in order, as she said, to make these petty kings tired of coming to court her (*ib.* p. 135; *Olaf Tryggvason's Saga*, ch. 48). She was more ready to listen to the famous Olaf Tryggvason, who had now fairly settled himself on the throne of Norway. But, when the latter asked her to be baptized, she refused, and he struck her on the face with his glove, calling her an old heathen jade.[9] Sigrid replied, "This may some day be thy death" (*O. T. S.*, ch. 68; *ib.* p. 150). Many here will remember how Longfellow gave poetical expression to this and many other scenes from Olaf's life in his *Tales of a Wayside Inn.*

Soon after this she accepted the addresses of Sven Fork-beard, who was at this time an ally of her son Olof, and bore him the famous Knut, our English Canute, about the year 995 A.D. Others, however, make her marriage with Sven later, and some suppose Knut to have had another mother.[10]

§ 5.—OLAF TRYGGVASON FIRST TO REIGN AS A CHRISTIAN KING IN NORWAY (995 A.D.—1000 A.D.).

The exact chronology of this period is not easy to make out in detail, but we receive much light on it from our own Saxon chronicles, which write at some length both of Sven and Anlaf, by whom they mean Olaf Tryggvason. Both are, in their different ways, links between Scandinavian and English Christianity. Olaf Tryggvason was the first Christian king who actually reigned with full acceptance as a Christian king in Norway, but two of his predecessors

[9] Saxo x., p. 340, says that Olaf invited her to come on board his ship. As she was climbing the ladder she was let down into the water and nearly drowned, and the Norwegians only neighed at her in derision. In any case, Olaf behaved with great discourtesy.

[10] See the *Dictionary of National Biography*, s.n. *Sweyn*.

had been Christians at heart as well as in profession, and
had done something to make the teaching of Christ known.
The first was Hakon the Good, the youngest son of Harald
Fairhair, whom Harald sent to be fostered by King
Athelstan in England, and who long reigned in Norway
(934 A.D.—961 A.D.). Hakon tried to introduce Christianity
quietly into his country, but public opinion was too strong
for him and he was obliged to take part in heathen sacrifices. Much the same thing may be said of Harald Greyskin. Olaf Tryggvason's reign in Norway was a much
shorter one, only five years (995 A.D.—1000 A.D.), but it was
fruitful of lasting consequences for the whole north. He
was a man of much more impetuous and daring character,
and probably of greater nobility, notwithstanding his discourtesy to Sigrid and his occasional acts of ferocity.   I
should like, though I find it somewhat difficult to do so, to
accept the portraiture of him which has been drawn in a
very effective manner by my friend, Mr. Vigfusson, in the
Corpus Poeticum Boreale (Vol. ii., pp. 83-90).   It is based
on Ari's report, preserved in the *Heimskringla* and other
Sagas, from which Mr. Vigfusson rejects what he supposes
to be later monkish legends, such as the scarcely credible
one of the torture of Raud the Sorcerer (ch. 87).   He writes
of Olaf :—" The greatest of all the northern kings, his life is
an epic of exceeding interest.   Coming out of the darkness
he reigns for five short years, during which he accomplishes
his great design, the Christianizing of Norway and all her
colonies; and then, in the height of his glory, with the
halo of holiness and heroism undimmed on his head, he
vanishes again.   But his works do not perish with him.
He had done his work, and though, maybe, his ideal of a
great Christian empire of the Baltic was unfulfilled, he had,
single-handed, wrought the deepest change that has ever
affected Norway.   His noble presence brightens the Sagas
wherever it appears, like a ray of sunshine gleaming across
the dark shadowy depths of a Norway firth.   All bear
witness to the wonderful charm which his personality
exercised over all that were near him; so that, like the holy

king, Lewis (who, however, falls short of Olaf), he was felt
to be an unearthly superhuman being by those who knew
him. His singular beauty, his lofty stature, golden hair
and peerless skill in bodily feats, make him the typical
Norseman of the old heroic times, a model king.''

He was baptized, according to his Saga, in the Scilly
Isles by a hermit who had won his confidence by foretelling
him what was to happen to him.[11] In any case he was a
nominal Christian when he took a leading part in the
famous raids on England in 993 A.D.—994 A.D., which are
described with more than usual detail by the Saxon
Chronicles.

After defeating the brave Alderman Brithnoth at Maldon
in Essex—a battle famous in English song—he attacked
London in company with Sven of Denmark, but they were
driven off by the citizens. Then came a visit to the south
coast and parleys and negotiations, which ended in Olaf
receiving a lengthy hospitality for his army from King
Ethelred, and a very large subsidy or '' Danegeld,'' the
first, or one of the first, on record, while he himself received
confirmation, the English king acting as his sponsor, in
994 A.D. He was confirmed by Aelfheah the Bald, Bishop
of Winchester, afterwards known as St. Alphege of Canterbury, at Andover, near the eastern border of my own
diocese. It is quite possible that the bishop's influence
with Olaf and others stirred up the hatred of the heathen
Northmen, who barbarously murdered him in 1012 A.D.

[11] Adam suggests in one place, ch. 77, that he was baptized
by one of the Bremen missionaries settled in Denmark, Poppo
or Odinkar junior. In two other places he supposes that he
was baptized with his people by the English bishop, John,
'' qui regem conversum cum populo baptizavit '' (ch. 242, cf.
ch. 78), but this is probably due to a confusion between him and
Haraldson. His own Saga (ch. 32) gives a description of his
baptism by a hermit, who was also a fortune-teller, together
with his followers, in the year 988 A.D. This may be true, as
it fits in with the fact that he was not confirmed when he came
again to England. We learn from other sources that he was
anxious to pry into the future, and especially regardful of omens
and presages of the future.

After his confirmation Tryggvason promised that he would never attack England again, which promise (says the chronicle) he kept. Notwithstanding the remnants of ferocity and superstition which remained in this remarkable man, we cannot doubt that his confirmation was a real turning point, a moment of conversion, in his life (cp. *C. P. B.*, Vol. ii., p. 84). It is one of the most remarkable instances in history of the effect of that holy rite, as an opening to new life when baptism has been received somewhat hastily, though in adult years. It is interesting to compare this change with that which came upon Knut when he realized his responsibilities as King of England.

Tryggvason, when he left England, went over to Dublin, where a Danish settlement had long been formed. He was there found out by a spy from Norway, who, however, seems to have been drawn to him—as most men were —and to have given him correct information. It was an opportune moment for return to that country. Jarl Hakon, who had long governed, and at first governed well, had now alienated the people by his licentious conduct. Olaf made a sudden descent on the country, and was well received. He brought missionaries with him, and wherever he went, as far as possible by persuasion, but if necessary by threats and violence, he brought people to baptism. He seems to have preached himself in the churches where there were any.[12]   After his election as King of Norway at Trondhjem, he preached first at Viken on the estuary of the Göta River, where Christianity already had a footing. It was at Ringarike in this district that he stood godfather to the youthful Olaf, son of Sigrid's old suitor, Harald Grenske, who was living as a child with his mother, Asta, and her second husband, the farmer-king, Sigurd, whose idyllic life is so pleasantly pictured in the Sagas. Tryggvason visited in turn the other Norwegian districts and colonies, including Iceland and Greenland. The greater part of his five years was spent in this half-crusading, half-missionary tour,

[12] *Laxdale Saga*, ch. 40, p. 138, Dent, London, 1899.

which was something like a Swedish king's " Ericsgata "
—a tour to acquire recognition of his election, but at the
same time to establish the new religion. Unfortunately,
Wineland, in Massachusetts, was not discovered till a few
years later by one of his followers. Otherwise this great
continent of America might have looked to Olaf Tryggvason and one of his English bishops, John, or Sigfrid, or
Grimkil, as the first missionaries of the Christian faith.[18]

I am afraid that antiquaries will not allow us to think
that the old circular building at Newport in Rhode Island [14]
is an old Norse church or baptistery, but the discovery of
Wineland is quite independent of this identification.

We cannot doubt that it was with Tryggvason's good
will, and very probably at his instigation, that one of his
bishops from England, Sigfrid, whom the Norwegians
called Sigurd, extended his labours to West Gothland,
where Olaf's sister, Ingeborg, had married the Jarl or
regent on condition of his becoming a Christian (*O. T.
Saga*, chs. 106-7). We shall hear more of Sigfrid later.

But all this zeal for conversion, which was clearly very
genuine, was to come to an untimely end. Sigrid never
forgave the rebuff to which she had been so rudely exposed,
and used all her influence, whether on her second husband,
Sven, or on her son, the Swedish Olof, to make her threat
effective. Sven himself had several grudges against
Tryggvason, who had not helped him when he was in
need, and had recently married his sister, Thyra, against
his will. Thyra, for her part, had run away from a disagreeable marriage with the Vendish king, Burislaf, into

[18] On the discovery of Vinland, see S. Laing's *Heimskringla*,
Vol. i., pp. 192-230, ed. 2, 1889.

[14] There is a picture of this circular building in *S. H.*[1], Vol. i.,
p. 291, fig. 348. It is now generally said to have been built by
Governor Arnold in the seventeenth century as a windmill
(Baedeker : *U.S.A.*, p. 250, ed. 4, 1909), and to have been
copied from one at Chesterton in England, designed by Inigo
Jones (Richman : *Rhode Island, its Making and its Meaning*,
Vol. ii., p. 151, quoted in a letter by Rev. Walter Lowrie, of
St. Paul's, Rome, sent me by the kindness of Commendatore
Rivoira).

which Sven had forced her in 999 A.D., and thrown herself on the protection of Tryggvason (*O. T. S.*, chs. 99, 100). Thyra, who was as proud as Sigrid herself, was eager for war against her brother.

Under these circumstances a conflict was unavoidable. The Swedish and Danish kings, now forming one family, combined with malcontents from Norway. They lay hid in a " vik " or fiord and allowed the main body of Tryggvason's fleet to go onward, and then came out and attacked his ship, the "Long Serpent," almost alone, at a place called Svoldr.[15]   After a magnificent fight against tremendous odds, Tryggvason leapt into the sea and was drowned; though the affection of his friends and countrymen deemed him to have escaped and to be still alive, and long expected his return.

Thyra, however, did not share these hopes.   She refused to survive her husband, and starved herself to death.

The abiding sorrow that followed his disappearance, and the mysterious whisper of the sea, which is still supposed to sing a sort of dirge for the lost hero, has been well described in a pathetic ballad by Björnson.   After telling of the impatience of the Norwegian fleet of six and fifty Dragons waiting for him to come up, and the murmured questions of the men, he goes on :—

> But when the sun, after night was past,
> Showed up the sky-line without a mast,
>   Burst their words like a storm-wind :
> " Oh ! the ' Long Serpent ' where is she?
> Cometh not Olaf Tryggve's son?"

[15] Adam puts the battle in the Sound.   He does not agree with the high estimate of Tryggvason which appears in the Sagas, but affirms that he put much trust in auguries and divination by lots, and in prognostications from birds, and hints that he had given up Christianity (ch. 81).   But, with all his merits, Adam writes in the Danish and German interest, his chief authority being King Sven Estridsson, grandson of Sven Forkbeard and nephew of Knut.   Saxo also speaks of Olaf's trust in auguries (ch. x., p. 339).   Geijer puts the battle in the bay between Rügen and Greifswald.   He has a charming ballad on Olaf's supposed survival, *Skaldestycken*, pp. 143-9, Stkh., 1869.   See above p. 44.

Then in a moment 'twas stillness all,
For from the deep there uprose a call,
    Round the fleet rippled a sighing,
" Oh ! the ' Long Serpent ' is taken :
Fallen is Olaf Tryggve's son."

Henceforth for many a hundred year,
Northern shipmen behind them hear,
    Mostly when night-time is moon-lit,
" Oh ! the ' Long Serpent ' is taken :
Fallen is Olaf Tryggve's son."

§ 6.—CHARACTER OF SVEN.   KNUT IN ENGLAND.   OLAF
    HARALDSON, 1015 A.D.—1030 A.D.).

Sven and Olof Skötkonung then divided the three kingdoms between them (giving part of Norway to the sons of
Hakon Jarl), and made a binding agreement that they
should maintain the Christianity planted in their kingdoms
and should propagate it among foreign nations (Adam : ch.
80). Skötkonung was, therefore, at least, already a
catechumen. Sven, for his part, put down idolatry and
proclaimed that Christianity was to be everywhere received
in Norway, and appointed Gotebald, a bishop who had
come from England, to be a teacher in Skåne. Of this man
we learn that he preached sometimes in Sweden and often
in Norway (ch. 82). Sven, like many men of this age, was
double-minded and unstable, with good impulses but with
sudden bursts and periods of ferocity and wickedness. In
early life he had been baptized. Then he relapsed into
paganism, and became a bitter persecutor. Then,
apparently before the Battle of Svoldr, he repented and was
reconverted, and some say was rebaptized. He died at
Gainsborough, after the Conquest of England in 1014 A.D.,
leaving a great northern empire to his son, Knut. His
body was first buried in England, but afterwards embalmed
and sent to the Minster of Roskilde in Seland, which he
had built.
    As long as Sven lived Olof Skötkonung was undisputed
ruler of great part of Norway, and naturally clung to his

new possessions. It was, therefore, a matter of great displeasure to him when the young son of his mother's old suitor, Harald Grenske, namesake and godson of Olaf Tryggvason, appeared to claim the crown of Norway, to which he had no particular title. Skötkonung's half-brother, Knut, was for ten years occupied in England with consolidating his power there, and the Swedish king could not make war on Norway alone, especially as such a war, for the purpose of conquest, was against the traditions of his country, and unacceptable to the feelings of the Swedes. He had, therefore, for the time, to make the best of a disagreeable position.   The new claimant of the throne of Norway was a remarkable man.   " He was no Olaf Tryggvason come back, as the people hoped " (writes Mr. Vigfusson), " this short, thick-set, ruddy young man, that carried his head slightly stooping, like the hard thinker he was.   Here was a lover of order, who drove the courts, enforced the laws with the strong hand, and who, as other kings in like case, ruled through poor men he could trust rather than the nobles whom he suspected; who was the organizer of the public and the Church law, and the severe scourge of those that broke it; in short, as a man of Henry II.'s type rather than that of Tryggvason, essentially a secular business-like hard-working man—such was Norway's saint that was to be " (*C. P. B.*, Vol. ii., p. 116).

This young man had become a Viking at the age of twelve, and in that capacity was an ally of King Ethelred in England, though a very troublesome and expensive one. After his victories in Norway he reigned for ten years as acknowledged sovereign till 1025 A.D.   He not only annoyed Skötkonung by depriving him of his Norwegian possessions, but gave him just offence by attacking him in his own country in Lake Mälar, and perhaps disgusted him even more by the cleverness with which he escaped from the trap in which he seemed to be caught, by cutting a canal for his ships in an unexpected place.

Skötkonung could never bear to hear him spoken of, and always called him " Digre " (that thick fellow), or some

other opprobrious name. Yet Haraldson was wise
enough to see that an alliance with the proud and noble
royal family of Sweden would be an advantage to him, and
made clever approaches towards Ingegerd, the king's elder
daughter, to which she was quite ready to respond. When
this hope was frustrated by Ingegerd's marriage to the
Prince of Novgorod, he was glad to marry her half-sister
Astrid, daughter of a captive Vendish lady, who was
brought up in the house, as such children usually were, and
only in a slightly lower position than the legitimate children
of the family. This marriage was arranged by the Jarl,
Ragnvald Ulfsson, and his wife, Ingeborg, with whom we
are already acquainted, without Skötkonung's knowledge.
The king was naturally very angry, and the Jarl was glad
to escape from Sweden in the train of the Princess
Ingegerd.

Skötkonung's antipathy to Olaf of Norway was, as I
have said, unpopular in Sweden, and it nearly cost him his
crown. We see a reflection of the people's feeling in
Ingegerd's petulant jest at her father's pride, after he had
killed five blackcock in one morning, when she reminded
him that the King of Norway had taken five petty kings
and subdued their kingdoms in the same space of time
(*St. Olaf's Saga*, ch. 90). We see it in the very remarkable speech of the lagman, Thorgny, at the Upsala Ting,
reminding the king of the eastern expeditions of his father
and predecessors, and rebuking his haughtiness and his
desire to have Norway under him " which no Swedish king
before him ever desired " (*St. Olaf's Saga*, ch. 81). Very
remarkable, too, both as exhibiting the democratic character of the Swedish constitution and the popular love of
domestic tranquillity, was the peaceful revolution operated
by the parables of the lagman, Emund, of Skara—no doubt
a friend of Ragnvald's—and the wise counsels of the three
brothers, Arnvid the Blind, Thorvid the Stammerer, and
Freyvid the Deaf (*ib.* ch. 96). Under the arrangement
made in consequence Skötkonung had to make peace with
Haraldson, and to allow his son, Anund Jakob, who was

ten or twelve years old, a share in the government, with right of succession to the throne (*ibid*), while he himself retired to another province.   This was about 1019 A.D.

This arrangement, as described by the Saga, fits in very well with the account given by Adam from the religious side, and is creditable to the accuracy of both our sources. I shall speak of it presently when I come to the Christian history.   Skötkonung, who had hitherto lived at Upsala, now retired to West Gothland, very probably to the estates left vacant by the Jarl and his own daughter, Ingegerd. He died shortly after, while Haraldson was still king of Norway.   The latter, after ten years of quiet, was called upon by Knut in 1025 A.D. to show him allegiance, which he refused.   Haraldson, in alliance with his brother-in-law, Anund Jakob, was defeated somewhere in the south of Sweden, and took refuge in Russia.   In 1030 A.D. he made an effort to regain his throne.   He was again defeated, and was slain at the Battle of Sticklestead (29th July), which stands next to Svoldr in the prominence given to it in northern history.   He had made many enemies in Norway, but, after his death, a revulsion of feeling in his favour very quickly took place, which was skilfully promoted by his English court-bishop, Grimkil.   Miracles were wrought at his tomb at Trondhjem; the missionary labours of Tryggvason came to be attributed to him, and the stern politician was transformed into the martyr missionary, the St. Olaf who became the patron saint of Norway, and who was scarcely less venerated in Sweden. The process was accelerated by the death of Knut in 1035 A.D., when the Danish Empire began to fall to pieces, and Norway recovered its independence.

I make no apology for the space given to this survey of the political history.   It is not only necessary to enable us to understand the religious history, but it gives us a sense of the reality of the characters and persons with whom we are dealing—a reality which can easily be made more perceptible by the detailed study of the wonderful portraits drawn by the Icelandic story-tellers in their dark low cham-

bers sitting round their winter fires, or writing busily on
their vellums, six or seven hundred years ago.   If only the
Swedes had had the Icelandic faculty of story telling and of
humorous insight into character, how much richer would
have been the record of their own history!

§ 7.—RELIGIOUS HISTORY. SKÖTKONUNG (993 A.D.—1021 A.D.) BAPTIZED BY SIGFRID, NEAR SKARA, 1008 A.D.

We turn now to the religious history, as far as it is re-
corded. Skötkonung, by his compact with Sven after the
Battle of Svoldr in the year 1000 A.D., was bound to maintain and propagate Christianity in his dominions, both in
Norway and Sweden.   This brought him into contact with
Tryggvason's bishops who still remained.   He found the
most ready welcome in the provinces on each side of the
Göta River, particularly Viken and West Gothland.
The latter was now a Christian province under his first
cousin, Jarl Ragnvald Ulfsson, whose father was brother
of Sigrid Stor-råda.   It was probably in this family that the
young king became acquainted with Bishop Sigfrid, from
whom he received baptism at the well of Husaby near Skara
in 1008 A.D., according to the old Swedish tradition.[16]
Why had he not been baptized before? and who was the
Sigfrid who baptized him?   As regards the first question,
I am inclined to presume that his mother, Sigrid, had remained a heathen, and that it was her influence which
retarded his baptism.   Skötkonung had now married a
Christian wife, Astrid, member of a noble Irish family.
As regards Sigfrid, I think we may accept the tradition
that he was an Englishman, and the same as the
Sigurd who appears in *Olaf Tryggvason's Saga* as attending him on his journey to the dangerous Salten Fiord in
the north of Norway—a place which is still visited by
travellers on account of the rushing tide of which the Saga
speaks (*O. T. Saga*, chs. 86, 88).   The bishop's prayers

---

[16] The well is still shown and the churchyard contains a remarkable monument, said to be the king's (see *S. H.*[1], Vol. i.,
figs. 326-9).

and holy water are then supposed to have given the ships a calm and peaceful entrance in the midst of high waves on each side.   The name Sigfrid is English or German, not Norse, but the substitution of the name Sigurd in the north for that of Sigfrid or Sifrid in the south is well known in the case of the hero of the *Volsunga Saga* and the " Nibelungen Lied."

Some recent historians have doubted the identity of St. Sigfrid with the Sigurd of Olaf Tryggvason, but, as I think, on insufficient grounds.   It has been said that Sigfrid is not an English name, but this is a pure mistake. Bede has much to tell us of an Abbot of Wearmouth, who bore it in the seventh century (†688), and it was borne by Bishops of Selsey and Lindsey.   It is, indeed, very common in our annals, and as many as thirty-six-persons of the name (Sigefrith, etc.), are enumerated in Searle's *Onomasticon Anglo-Saxonicum*.   There is, therefore, no reason to look to Germany for traces of such a missionary, or to quote the letter of Archbishop Bruno, of Querfurt, the apostle of Prussia (997 A.D.—1009 A.D.) to the Emperor Henry II., which describes the conversion of the chief (senior) of the *Suigii* by a bishop whom he does not name, whom he had sent, together with a monk, Rodbert, " beyond the sea."   Dean Lundström supposes that these Suigii or Svigii are to be sought in Circassia, near the Black Sea.[17]

---

[17] This letter, which exists in a Donatus MS. from Fulda, of the eleventh century, now in the Landesbibliothek at Cassel, may be found in Fr. Miklosich and Fiedler : *Slavische Bibliothek*, Vol. ii., p. 307 foll., Wien, 1858.   The passage in question is as follows (p. 311) : " Inter hec non lateat regem quod episcopus noster cum egregio monacho, quem nostis, Rodberto ultra mare in evangelium Suigis *transmiserat*.   Quomodo venientes nuncii verissime dixerunt ipsum seniorem Suigiorum, cuius dudum uxor christiana erat, gracias deo, baptizavit.   Cum quo mille homines et septem plebes eandem graciam mox ut receperunt. Quos [quod *ed.*] ceteri indignati interficere querebant," etc. See H. G. Voight : *Bruno von Querfurt*, pp. 289 and 436 *n*, Stuttgart, 1907, who supposes this to refer to the conversion of the King of Sweden.   Emil Hildebrand, *S. H.*[2], Vol. ii., p. 75, 1905, also adopted this opinion.

Dean Lundström identifies the " Suigii " or " Svigii " with

It may be mentioned that William of Malmesbury (*P. L.*, Vol. 179, p. 1722) gives the obit of " Sigefrid, Bishop of Norway, monk of Glastonbury," as the 5th of April, whereas the legend of St. Sigfrid makes it 15th of February. But this legend was only written in 1205 A.D. (see *S. R. S.*, Vol. ii., pt. 1., p. 345) This introduces another element of uncertainty, though it confirms the name Sigfrid as that of an English missionary to the north.

It is unfortunate that we know so little of this bishop. His legendary life appears to be of little value. It represents him as an Archbishop of York and as a volunteer sent out by an English king, Mildred. Now, we do not know of any king called Mildred, though the name occurs in the Durham *Liber Vitæ*, as that of a Northumbrian king or duke. There was certainly no Sigfrid Archbishop of York, though there was a Bishop of Lindsey of that name, *circa* 1000 A.D. The description of him as wearing a mitre is also a mistake, as mitres were not worn so early. The story of his three martyred nephews, Unaman, Sunaman and Winaman, and their speaking heads is a puerile extravagance. The fact, however, that Adam of Bremen clearly knew only of one Sigfrid, and that a famous man, makes it probable that there was one man bearing

the Ζιγχοί of Ptolemy v. 9, 18 (who places them in Sarmatia Asiatica), and Pliny's " Zingi," and " Zigæ," *N. H.*, vi. 7, and Strabo's Ζύγοι, Ζυγοί or Ζύγιοι (books ii. and xi.). These people are described by ancient geographers as dwelling near the north-east shore of the Black Sea, south of the River Hypanis, and about half way between the Cimmerian Bosporus and the mouth of the River Phasis. In later Christian times their country was called Zecchia or Zichia. Their bishop attended a council at Constantinople in 536 A.D. (Labb. : *Conc.*, v. 259). They are mentioned also several times by Procopius. Their existence as a people in the same district in the tenth century is proved by a number of references in Constantine Porphyro-genitus (imp. 911 A.D.—959 A.D.), *de administrando imperio*, cc. 6, 42, 53. In the last passage he speaks of their country as producing mineral oil. The names seem sufficiently near for the Dean's purpose, but I do not know how far " ultra mare " can be naturally interpreted in Bruno's case of the Black Sea. Dr. Söderblom inclines to think that it may.

the name of Sigurd in Norway and Sigfrid in England
and Sweden, who was at once a monk of Glastonbury, and
Tryggvason's court-bishop and companion at Salten Fiord,
and who meets us in the central part of *Olaf Haraldson's
Saga* (chs. 55, 257, 258). This man, according to Adam
(speaking of him under the name of Sigfrid), " preached
alike to the Swedes and Northmen " (ch. 242), and has the
first place among the English bishops and presbyters, " by
whose advice and teaching St. Olaf prepared his own heart
for God, and to whom he committed the rule of the people
subject to him " (ch. 94). He was clearly a missionary,
not a territorial bishop, and, therefore, we may well believe
that he also preached in the district of Verend in Småland,
where he is venerated as the founder of the Church in
Vexiö. That see, however, did not have a regular suces-
sion till much later.

The last definite notice of Sigfrid in the Bremen history
is as attending a funeral of one bishop and the consecration
of another (Adam : ch. 98) after 1029 A.D.   But if he was, as
I believe, the consecrator of St. Eskil, he lived till after the
Norman Conquest. He was evidently dead when Adam
wrote in 1072 A.D. He was buried under the altar in Vexiö
Cathedral, where his tombstone was visible about the year
1600.[18]

As regards the Church in West Gothland, we have a
passage in Adam's Chronicle which throws much light
both upon the religious and the political history. He is
comparing Skötkonung with St. Olaf (ch. 94).   " The
other Olaf in Sweden" (he writes) "is said to have been
eminent for a like love of religion. He, in his desire to
convert his subjects to Christianity, was actively zealous
that the idol temple, which is in the middle of Sweden, at
Ubsola, should be destroyed.[19]   The heathen, fearing this

---

[18] J. Baaz : *Inventarium Eccl. Sveogothorum*, p. 105, Lincopiæ, 1642, who says it was found forty years before, when the
altar was removed by Bishop Petrus Jonae.

[19] It was perhaps in connection with these efforts that an English missionary, Wolfred, attacked an image of Thor and cut
it to pieces, for which he suffered martyrdom (Adam : ch. 97).

intention, are said to have passed a statute (placitum), together with their king, that if he wished to be a Christian he should hold as his own the best district of Sweden, wherever he desired to live, and might there establish a Church and Christianity, but should not use force to make any of the people give up the worship of the gods, and only admit such as wished of his own free will to be converted to Christ. The king, gladly accepting this statute, founded a Church to God and a Bishopric in West Gothland, which is close to the Danes or Norwegians. This is the great City of Skara, for which, on the petition of the most Christian king, Thurgot was first ordained by Archbishop Unwan (1013 A.D.—1029 A.D.).[20] He vigorously discharged his mission to the Gentiles, and, by his labour, gained to Christ the two noble peoples of the Goths.''

Although this gives a different reason for Skötkonung's unpopularity from that which is recorded in the Saga, the facts all fit well together, and agree with the well-known dislike of the Swedes to religious persecution and their adherence to the old precedents from the time of Biörn, which allowed each to maintain or advance their faith by persuasion. We shall have other evidence of this feeling later on.

The foundation of the see of Skara is, therefore, fixed to about the year 1020 A.D., a year or two before Skötkonung's death.

No doubt Skötkonung's request to Archbishop Unwan to consecrate a bishop for Skara was a very acceptable one. There was a natural, and sometimes a very strong, jealousy on the part of the Archbishops of Hamburg against the English missionaries, who were brought in first by Tryggvason, and then by St. Olaf, and also by Knut.

In any case, it was during the pontificate of Unwan, but, perhaps, about its close, as it is recorded in connection with the death of Haraldson, 1030 A.D.

[20] Thurgot's name is not, however, mentioned in the early lists of the Bishops of Skara in *Scr. Rer. Suec.*, t. III., cp. Rhyzelius : *Episcoposcopia*, pp. 163-4. (See the names in note 23).

There was a struggle, sometimes successful, to get these men, who were chosen by the civil power, and ordained in England at the request of these kings, to regularize their position by entering into engagements of fidelity to the see of Hamburg. Unwan caught one of Knut's bishops, Gerbrand of Seland, who had been ordained by Ethelnoth, Archbishop of Canterbury (1020 A.D.—1038 A.D.), and forced him to promise obedience to Hamburg. He then censured Knut, who promised to work with him in future (ch. 92). St. Olaf similarly made excuses for two of his bishops, Rudolf, who returned to England in 1050 A.D. and became Abbot of Abingdon, and Bernard (chs. 94 and 242). Unwan also had to maintain his rights against two other bishops ordained in Rome—Asgoth and Bernard (ch. 242)—the first instance we have of direct ecclesiastical intercourse between Rome and Scandinavia. Clearly the general tendency of the northern kings was to have bishops as much as possible dependent on themselves and to use the English hierarchy for their purposes. While, therefore, we rejoice at the zeal of such men as Sigfrid and others of our countrymen who followed him, we need not suppose that the court-bishops generally were men of very great earnestness. Unwan seems to have taken the opportunity of the opposition to St. Olaf to send a certain Sigward, a Dane, to be bishop to his malcontent subjects (Adam: ch. 242, cp. *O. T. S.*, chs. 229, 230, 251, 257, which speak of him as taking the part of the bönder against the king). But, on the whole, his policy seems to have been a reasonable one, and in the interests of Church order and civil peace. The Church of Sweden has always needed some counterpoise to the influence of the civil power. It found it first in Bremen, then in Rome. Both our Churches, that of England and that of Sweden, now need greater ecclesiastical freedom within and closer alliance with other Churches outside.

The reign of the first Christian king of Sweden was, on the whole, peaceful and progressive, as well as comparatively long. When he died, perhaps in the winter of

1021 A.D.—1022 A.D., he had been king for nearly thirty years since his father died, but he was, if the story is correct, only forty-two years old. He was thus probably older in years than the other prominent kings of this period— the two Norwegian Olafs and Knut—who may all be supposed to have been about forty at the dates of their deaths. The short reigns of some, and the early deaths of most, of these kings contrast with the long lives of the lagmen and of the bishops, so that we can readily see how it was that a quiet order in Church and State might continue and make progress, while the nominal rulers, after a brilliant display of force, passed away and left less definite results behind them. Two things Sweden seems to have acquired in the reign of Olof, the use of money coined in the country instead of in England or elsewhere (*S. H.*[1], Vol. i., p. 261), and the use of letters for correspondence. The first instance recorded in the Sagas of written private letters, instead of verbal messages and tokens, is in the correspondence of Olof's daughter, Ingegerd, with Jarl Ragnvald, and his wife, Ingeborg, about her projected marriage with Haraldson (*St. O. S.*, ch. 71). Of course, the clergy had long been accustomed to write letters, and, on this account, were constantly used as ambassadors. The later futhorc of sixteen runes had probably been in use on monuments from the latter part of the ninth century, and was, I presume, the one used by Ingegerd.[21]

§ 8.—Accession of Anund Jakob (1021 A.D.—1050 A.D.).

Olof of Sweden was succeeded about the year 1021 A.D. (*St. O. S.* ch. 120) by his son, Anund Jakob, who, according to Adam, "was superior to all his predecessors in wisdom and piety: no king being more loved by the Swedish people than Anund" (Adam: ch. 94). He had a long and fairly quiet reign of some thirty years, in the

---

[21] The letters on Olof's coins are, however, like those on Ethelred's, of Anglo-Saxon type, not runes (*S. H.*[1], figs. 330, 349). The new edition of *S. H.* has considerably more on this subject of coinage.

first part of which he took the side of St. Olaf against Knut, but not very vigorously. During his reign Christianity was widely diffused throughout the country (l.c. ch. 107). He continued his father's friendly relations with the see of Hamburg, and received from Libentius II. (1029 A.D.—1032 A.D.) Gotescalk,[22] as second Bishop of Skara, in succession to Thurgot, about the year 1030 A.D. Sigfrid was apparently present on the occasion of Gotescalk's consecration, and is now described as coming from Sweden, probably from Småland (l.c. ch. 98). Anund Jakob was only about forty-five years old at the time of his death. His coins are more developed than his father's, but, after his time, no money was coined in Sweden for 100 years— an evidence of the disturbed state of the country.

He was succeeded about 1050 A.D. by his elder half-brother, Emund, called "the old"—son of the Vendish lady who had been a captive in Olof Skötkonung's household, who was also mother of Astrid, the Queen of Olaf the Saint. Such children, as we have seen, were brought up in the family, and recognized as belonging to it, though without quite so high a position as those of legitimate origin. Many of the mothers were ladies of good birth taken prisoners in war. Magnus, son of Alfhild and Olaf the Saint, of whose birth and baptism there is a quaint tale in the Saga (*St. O. S.*, ch. 131), was afterwards king of both Norway and Denmark, which he ruled from 1042 A.D. to 1047 A.D.

The most remarkable events, from our special point of view, in Emund's reign are the efforts which he made to be independent of the see of Hamburg, and the attempt made by Archbishop Adalbert to hold a general council of the northern nations nominally subject to his rule. Adalbert, who sat for a long period of twenty-seven years (1045 A.D.—1072 A.D.), was an able, ambitious and magnificent person, of high rank, and possessed of great wealth and wide influence in Church and State. He endeavoured to establish a patriarchate in the north, to embrace North

[22] He also is not named in the early lists.

Germany as well as Scandinavia, and possibly to be a rival to Rome itself. He received from Pope Leo IX. (1049 A.D.—1054 A.D.) the position which St. Boniface had previously held as legate of the Apostolic see. He became the guardian and Chief Minister of State of the young Emperor, Henry IV. of Germany (1058 A.D. onwards). It is to be feared that his missionary zeal was largely tempered with a desire to consolidate his own power and prerogative. On the other hand, the King of Sweden was naturally anxious to maintain his independence of the German Empire. He thought no doubt that as St. Olaf had his own court-bishop, Grimkil, and others chosen by himself, and brought from England, and Jarl Hakon had Sigurd chosen by Knut, and previous kings of his own race had favoured Sigfrid, both in West Gothland and Småland—Skara and Vexiö—so he might be entitled to have his own court-bishop, Osmund. This man was a nephew of Bishop Sigfrid, though apparently not himself an Englishman. He had been sent by his uncle to study in the schools of Bremen (Adam: ch. 132; cp. 242). According to the accounts of his enemies, he tried to get ordination at Rome—as two others called Bernard and Asgoth had done—but was repulsed. He then was consecrated bishop by a Polish archbishop, and posed in Sweden as a representative of the pope. There may have been something in this last pretension. Adalbert, however, was determined not only to maintain, but to enlarge the jurisdiction of his see. He consecrated Adalward, Dean of Bremen, as Bishop of Sigtuna (ch. 205), which had now taken the place of Birka, and sent him with a retinue of priests to obtain recognition from the king in Svithiod. They found Osmund having an archiepiscopal cross carried before him, and acting as head of the Church in Sweden, and professing to treat Adalward and his party as intruders, because they could not produce a commission from the Apostolic see (ch. 132).

The representatives of the Archbishop of Hamburg were for the time driven away with contempt, and Adalward

himself seems to have tried to set up for himself at Skara
(*ib.* ch. 132; cp. ch. 205). Osmund (Asmund), like his
uncle, Sigfrid, appears as bishop both of Skara and Vexiö
on the old lists.[23]

This attempt of Adalbert's to get a footing in the court
of Sweden was certainly connected with another of his
ambitious projects, that of holding a general council of the
North at Slesvig. The reasons of discipline given for this
effort were possibly only too true in that age " that bishops
sell their benediction—*i.e.*, give orders for money—and
that the peoples are unwilling to pay tithes, and that they
all are enormously gluttonous and unchaste."

But the bishops from the other side of the sea—*i.e.*,
Norway and Sweden—refused to come, and hence the
council fell through. Adalbert seems to have tried for
several years to get his suffragans to meet him, but to no
purpose (Adam : chs. 203-5).

In time, however, Emund was moved by the misfortunes
of his own family and his country to recall Adalward, and
it seems that Adalbert was also reconciled to Osmund (*ib.*
ch. 206). The Archbishop also ordained five others for
Sweden, including a second Adalward, Stenfi, whom he
called Simon or Symeon, for Helsingland, and John the
Monk, Bishop of Birka (ch. 206). The latter is the first
monk whom we know to have worked in Sweden after the
time of Anskar.

The elder Adalward laboured successfully in Vermland
(ch. 134). The younger Adalward was active in mission
work in the time of King Stenkil, and converted the people
in the city of Sigtuna and its neighbourhood, and tried to
destroy idolatry at Upsala (ch. 237). Simon, or Stenfi,
became the apostle of the Scritefinni, or Skating Finns, or
Lapps—to the far north—who, on their snow shoes, or
runners, could beat the wild beasts (ch. 232). His memory
still lives in Helsingland and Norrland under the name of
St. Staffan.

[23] The list of Skara begins 1, Sigfrid ; 2, Unno ; 3, Asmund ;
4, Stenfrid ; 5, Adalward I.; 6, Adalward II. That of Vexiö
begins 1, Sigfrid ; 2, Asmund ; 3, Siward ; 4, John.

§ 9.—THE HOUSE OF STENKIL (1066 A.D.—1130 A.D.).

After Emund Gammal's death the old divinely descended line of Swedish kings came to an end, and the West Goths seem to have been able to carry an election in favour of Stenkil, son of Ragnvald. His father has been identified, perhaps without sufficient reason, with the old Jarl Ragnvald Ulfsson, who has been already mentioned more than once. Stenkil had previously shown kindness to the Bremen bishop, Adalward I., and the latter hoped by this means to carry out the destruction of the idols of Svithiod, and to introduce a reform after the Norwegian model. In this he was abetted by Bishop Egino of Skåne. But Stenkil knew the temper of the Sveas too well. He told the bishops that if they persisted they would lose their lives, he would lose his kingdom, and the people would relapse into paganism (Adam : ch. 238).

This prudent king did not, however, live long, and a period of confusion and civil war followed, in which force was used on both sides to promote the interests of Christendom and heathendom. Inge, son of Stenkil, abolished the sacrifices in Svithiod, and enjoined that all folk should be christened, and, in consequence, was pelted with stones, and obliged to abdicate, for a time, as his father had predicted (*Appendix to Hervarar Saga*; cp. Geijer: p. 41). This use of force in matters of religion was alien from the Swedish character, and stands very much alone in Swedish history, although crusades to convert other peoples were undertaken by Swedish kings later on. But the forcible conversion of Småland a little later was the work of a Norwegian, not a Swedish, king, Sigurd, the Jerusalemfarer (1121 A.D.—1130 A.D.). In Sweden, at this time, the heathen Sven, Inge's brother-in-law, reigned for three years, and received the name of Blot-Sven, or Sven the Sacrificer. Inge then recovered his kingdom, but did not destroy the Upsala Temple. It was left for one of the later kings, Sverker I., in 1138 A.D. (as we are told) to lay the foundation of old Upsala Cathedral and to work into it the materials of the pagan temple of the three gods (E.

6

Benzelius filius: *Monumenta Hist. Vet.*, p. 20, Upsaliæ, 1709).

The independence of Hamburg, which Emund had desired, came from another quarter. The other prince-bishops of Germany combined against Adalbert, and the Vends attacked him and his people, and obliged him, in 1066 A.D., to flee for his life, and restored paganism for a time in Bremen. He had to take refuge at Goslar, where he died 16th March, 1072 A.D. This heathen reaction naturally co-operated with that in Sweden, and Christians were persecuted in both countries. Among the Swedish martyrs of this period, the most celebrated is St. Eskil, 12th June, who preached in Södermanland, and ranks as the first bishop of Strengnäs. His see was, however, at Fors, some miles away, now a part of the modern Eskilstuna (the Sheffield of Sweden), which takes its name from the saint. He was an Englishman, and was not only invited by St. Sigfrid, but, it is said, ordained by him. This might well be the case in the confusion that filled the German archbishopric after 1066 A.D. The zeal of Eskil led him to encounter Blot-Sven when he came to sacrifice at Strengnäs. He prayed to God for a sign from heaven, and a great storm of thunder, hail, snow and rain over-whelmed the assembly, and overturned the altar. This enraged the heathen, who murdered him. His martyrdom is celebrated on the 12th June, but the year is uncertain.

The old see of Skara also had as its bishops at the close of the eleventh century, three Englishmen in succession—Rodulward, Ricolf and Edward. Of the latter we are told that, having a wife and family in England, he managed to collect enough money from the revenues of his see, and to return home again with a competency.

The neighbouring see of Vesterås, in Vestmanland, also claims another English saint, the monk and abbot, David, as its founder. He was martyred, it is supposed, in the year 1082 A.D. Last of this company comes St. Botvid, the first native Swedish missionary, who was baptized in England, and from whom Botkyrka takes its name.

§ 10.—Commencement of Roman Influence and of Intercourse with the Papacy.

The collapse of the power of the see of Hamburg opened the way for another power to appear on the scene, besides that of the English Church. This was that of the papacy, which, in the person of the wonderfully energetic pope, Gregory VII., addressed its first known letters to Sweden in the years 1080 and 1081 A.D. The first is to I(nge), king of the Swedes, and congratulates him on the advent of missionaries from the Gallican Church, which, however, has only instructed him from the treasures of its mother, the holy Roman Church. It requests him to send to the Apostolic see a bishop or other sufficient clerk to give information as to the habits and character of the nation, and to receive the Apostolic (*i.e.*, Roman) mandates to bring back with him (4th October, 1080 A.D., *Reg.* viii., *ep.* 11; *P. L.*, 148, 585). The second, dated 24th October, 1081 A.D., is addressed to the kings of the West Goths, I(nge) and A(lstan), after a visit from their bishop. It is thought that this may have been Rodulward, Bishop of Skara. The letter rejoices over the news of the conversion of their people. It exhorts to concord and to reverence of churches, compassion towards the poor and afflicted, reverence and obedience to bishops and clergy, and urges them to give tithes for the use of the clergy, the churches, and the poor —thus setting forth the tripartite division of tithes which afterwards prevailed in Sweden—and to proclaim the duty of doing so to the whole realm. It refers to their predecessor's good fame—by whom, I suppose, Stenkil is meant—and urges them frequently to send their clerks to Rome for further instruction in the manners of the Roman Church (*Reg.* ix., *ep.* 14; *P. L.*, 148, 617-8). The address "to the kings of the Visigoths," or West Goths, instead of " to the king of the Swedes," as the first was directed, is interesting as showing an increase of local knowledge. At this time there were two joint kings of the West Goths, reigning also over Svithiod; but the title " king of the Swedes and Goths " was not yet

admitted. The reference to the " Gallican Church " is not
quite clear. Possibly it is an allusion to Anskar as a monk
of Corbey; possibly Norman monks, perhaps from Bec, had
now begun to come (as was natural) to the North. Rodulward, Ricolf and Edward, bishops of Skara, in the end of
the eleventh century, are all, however, called Englishmen.

The next step towards incorporation of Scandinavia into
the system of the Western Church was the establishment of
the Archbishopric of Lund. This was the result of a visit
to Rome in 1093 A.D. of Eric Eiegod, so called from his
constant kindness and gentleness, the pious king of Denmark, in the time of Pope Urban II., of which the court
poet, Mark Skeggison, has preserved an interesting record.

I will quote some verses of it from Mr. Vigfusson's
translation (*C. P. B.*, Vol. ii., p. 236) :—

" It shall be told how the king went the long-path to
Rome to win a share in its glory; there he saw the fenced
land of refuge. . . . Harold's brother visited the great
halidoms in Rome; he adorned the rich shrines with rings
and red gold; he went, with weary feet, round the realm
of the monks for his soul's good; he passed on from the
East and came to Rome withal. Eric carried from abroad
an archbishop's see over the Saxon March, hither in the
North. Our *spiritual* state is the better by his act. It is
impossible that another king could do as much for our
souls' needs. The pope, Christ's friend, in the South,
granted all that he asked of him."

Eric's prayer was granted by the pope, who also
canonized for him his brother Canute, but there was some
delay in the establishment of the Archbishopric of Lund,
which was obviously unpleasing to the see of Hamburg.
From a letter of our own Anselm to the first archbishop,
Asser or Atser, it seems that Anselm had intervened to
overcome the difficulty by putting some pressure upon
Cardinal Alberic (*Epp. lib.* iv., *ep.* 90, also repeated as
127; *P.L.*, 159, 247). The dignity was not actually conferred until after Eric's death, which occurred on his second
pilgrimage, in Cyprus, and was given, not by Urban, but

by the new pope, Paschal II., in 1103 or 1104 A.D. The rights of Hamburg were not entirely abrogated, and Asser seems to have had no jurisdiction at first in Sweden. Indeed, Popes Calixtus II., in 1123 A.D., and Innocent II. in 1133 A.D, reaffirmed the rights of Hamburg. It was not till the time of Eskil, Asser's nephew and successor, that the primate of Lund became also primate of Sweden (1152 A.D.).

In the meantime Pope Gregory's correspondent, Inge I., had died (1111 A.D.), and was succeeded by his nephews, Philip and Inge the younger. The period was one of uncertain government, and, with their deaths, ended the line of Stenkil and a period of even greater confusion followed. In the meantime the conversion of the outlying provinces was going on; Eastern Småland was still heathen, and St. Botvid, the first Swedish missionary, found work to do in Södermanland. The temple at Upsala was still standing and heathenism had many powerful adherents in Upland. But, generally speaking, we may say that Sweden had become a Christian country about 1130 A.D., just three hundred years after Anskar's mission began.

§ 11.—CONCLUSION.

We can hardly be surprised that it took three hundred years for a country, in which individual or at least family life was so independent as in Sweden, to become Christian. It was a country to which forcible conversion was abhorrent, and where the example of the kings, if contrary to public sentiment, did not go for very much. Conversion demanded an extremely difficult change in life and habits, even when it did not penetrate very deeply into the character, especially among the men. A man had to give up the Viking life. He was forbidden to follow the old law of private vengeance, and to have more than one wife. He had no longer unlimited power over his wife and children, nor the right to acknowledge or expose his children at his own will. The Church's rules as to marriage with near relations and others, as to penance, fasting

and observance of holy days and Sundays, and, in particular, the prohibition to eat horse-flesh, were all burdensome.   Hitherto the laws of Sweden had been of the
people's own making.   Now they had, in part at least, to
be accepted from outside.

That in time all these difficulties were overcome tells
much for the zeal and earnestness of the first preachers of
the faith.   Anskar's memory was a precious possession.
None of those who followed were, perhaps, equal to him,
but, whenever they were true to their profession, they made
definite progress.   The experience of appeals to Christ in
times of danger evidently had a great effect, and miracles
were certainly believed to have been wrought.   The old
faith had little that was beautiful, and much that was re-
pulsive about it.   It was easy to see that the old gods were
powerless, when a man like the English missionary,
Wolfred, hewed down the idol of Thor (Adam: ch. 97).
But, above all, perhaps, the successes of the two Norwegian
Olafs weighed with the people.   They were heroes after
the Scandinavian heart, one with his athletic vigour and
personal charm, the other with his energy and craft.
All their home work had been done as Christians, and their
early deaths did not seem in that age a misfortune,
especially in the case of Haraldson, whose acceptance by
the people as a saint only gave his name fresh power.

Thus God, in one way or another, was working out His
will, and Sweden, having slowly become Christian, may
be supposed, I trust, to have accepted the faith more deeply
and unchangeably than other nations to whom it came more
speedily.   On the other hand the fact that Sweden had no
such long connection with the earlier type of Western
Christianity as England, for instance, had, and received
the system of the Church after the development of about
a thousand years had moved it some way from primitive
Christianity, was not to its advantage.   It has not had the
same depth or breadth of Christian experience as the older
Western Churches.   I venture to think that Swedes on both
sides of the Atlantic are already beginning to feel the wis-

dom of cultivating a greater variety of types of religious character and of using the religious freedom, which Lutherans prize so much, in a positive more than in a negative direction. Two lines of effort seem particularly to suggest themselves in connection with the subject of this lecture, a broader study of Church history, and indeed of all history, as exhibiting the providence of God, and a practical participation in the work of foreign missions to the non-Christian races and peoples of mankind. The former enlarges our intelligence, the latter our experience, of the manner in which the manifold wisdom of God is intended by Him to be manifested by means of the Church. We may thank God that in both these lines of effort the Church and people of Sweden are exerting themselves and making large and substantial progress.

Adam de Bremen's Statements as to Scandinavian Bishops.

It will be convenient to the reader to have Adam's statements in his own form. The principal passage is ch. 242 : " The first (missionary) to come to Norway (*Nortmannia*) from England was a certain Bishop John, who baptized the king (Tryggvason) on his conversion with the people. To him succeeds Bishop Grimkil, who afterwards (*tunc*) was ambassador to Archbishop Unwan (1013 A.D.—1029 A.D.) from King Olaph (Haraldson). In the third place came the well-known Sigafrid [uncle of Esmund (*or* Osmund, ch. 132)], who alike preached to Swedes and Norwegians. And he continued up to our own time with other prelates (*sacerdotibus*) equally eminent (*non obscuris*). After whose departure our metropolitan (the Archbishop of Hamburg) ordained Thoolf bishop in the city of Trondhjem, and Sigward to the same regions. As for Asgoth and Bernard, though he was offended that they were consecrated by the pope, yet when they apologized he sent them away with gifts." They seem to have lived up to Adam's own time. Then he proceeds to say that in Norway and Sweden, on account of the recent planting of Christianity, no fixed boundaries were set to dioceses, but each bishop chosen by a king or people did his best all round in building up the Church.

In ch. 92 Adam gives a list of Knut's bishops, of whom " he brought many from England to Denmark. He placed Bernard in Skone, Gerbrand in Seland, Reginbert in Fune. Our Archbishop Unwan was jealous of this." It is said that he caught

Gerbrand returning from England, knowing that he had been ordained "Bishop by Elnoth (Ethelnoth of Canterbury, 1020 A.D.—1038 A.D.) archbishop of the English." Gerbrand was forced to promise fidelity to Hamburg, and became a great friend of Unwan's. Unwan complained to Knut, who apologized, and promised to act with him in future.

In ch. 94 Adam gives a list of Haraldson's bishops : " He had with him many bishops and presbyters from England, by whose advice and teaching he prepared his own heart to God, and to whose rule he committed the people subject to him. Amongst whom, renowned for their learning and virtues, were Sigafrid, Grimkil, Rudolf and Bernard. These also, at the king's command, went to Svithiod and Gothland, and all the islands which are beyond Norway, preaching the Word of God and the kingdom of Jesus Christ to the barbarians. He sent also ambassadors to our archbishop with presents, asking that he would give a kind welcome to these bishops, and send his own men to himself who might strengthen the rude people of Norway in their Christianity." Then follows the passage about Olaf Skötkonung already quoted (See above, pp. 74-5).

In ch. 78 he had already mentioned John as one of Tryggvason's bishops, " et alii postea dicendi." He, therefore, clearly distinguishes John from Sigfrid, mentioning them together, as we have seen in ch. 242. Sigfrid is also mentioned in ch. 98 as being present at the funeral of Thurgot, about 1030 A.D. I do not know on what authority Swedish writers often identify John and Sigfrid. No doubt it was quite possible for a man to take a new name at his consecration, as Gautbert and Stenfi took the name of Simon or Symon. But I see no evidence that this was the case here.

III.

THE ROMANIZED CHURCH UNDER THE SVERKERS, ERICS AND FOLKUNGAR (1130 A.D.—1389 A.D.).

LECTURE III.

The Romanized Church under the Sverkers, Erics and Folkungar (1130—1389).

§ 1.—Introduction. Division of the Mediæval Period into Three Sections.

The history of Scandinavia is at all times complicated on account of the close relations which existed between Swedes, Danes and Norwegians, whether for peace or war. It is impossible to understand the development of any one of the three without frequent reference to the annals of the others. The history is often further complicated by the intestine troubles which have from time to time separated different parts of the same land into hostile camps. I have, therefore, thought it best to omit much of the details of secular history, which could only be made intelligible by lengthy explanations, and to take for granted that those who listen to or read these lectures are generally acquainted with the three periods covered by the title of this and the following lecture. I have called it *The Romanized Church*, in order to suggest the main truth that up to the commencement of this period Roman influence had been very slight in Sweden, and that it only extended to a period of about 390 years. In England Roman influence began much earlier, and penetrated much deeper into the national life. It had been felt in Britain from the earliest times up to the pontificate of Leo the Great, in the fifth century. After his time there was a break in our relations with other Western Churches for about 150 years. Then normal relations were resumed,

and went on from Augustine's time till the breach with
Rome under Henry VIII., which occurred a little later
than it did in Sweden. No doubt the relations between
England and Rome became more binding after the Norman
Conquest, which coincided with the great development of
papal power under Hildebrand, but these relations were
only an extension of much that had long existed.

I shall divide the history of the Romanized Church into
three periods, according to the families which successively
ruled in Sweden.

First came the rival lines of the Sverkers and Erics for
about 120 years (1130—1250)—a period during which the
foundations of the mediæval Church were laid. Then
came the kings of the Folkunga dynasty, the descendants
of the all-powerful Birger Jarl, for about 140 years, in
which the chief names besides his own are those of his son,
Magnus Ladulås and St. Birgitta. The third period,
which I shall treat in a separate lecture, is that of the Union
of Kalmar, when Sweden was under foreign rulers, beginning with the able Queen Margaret and ending
with Christian the Tyrant (1389—1520)—a period of
about 120 years (1130—1250)—a period during which the
amongst ecclesiastics is that of Archbishop Nicolaus Ragvaldi, who attended the Council of Basel as Bishop of
Vexiö, amongst patriots that of Engelbrekt, and amongst
statesmen, of course, that of the Stures.

As a whole, this period of 390 years was a time of great
distraction, during which the central government was
often very weak, and the power of the nobles was hardly
held in check. The power of the Church, or at any rate
of the hierarchy, grew very much in these troubled days,
not so much from the greatness of any of its leaders in
Sweden, but because it was part of a centralized system,
having its direction outside Sweden. While other parties
were confused and vacillating in their aims, the Church
had a definite policy, and had the command of that kind
of religious influence which is particularly powerful in
times of ignorance and violence.

§ 2.—SKETCH OF THE PAPAL SYSTEM NOW INTRODUCED
        INTO SWEDEN.   POSTULATES OF THE INTERNA-
        TIONAL CHURCH-STATE.

Let me remind you of the chief aims and claims of the
papacy which were set before the Swedes for their acceptance under the Sverker kings in the first half of the twelfth
century and onwards.   They were not formed into a system all at once, but they were the growth of many centuries
of policy and experience, during which the minds of the
great statesmen, who at intervals filled the papal throne,
advanced step by step in the development of a very remarkable conception.   The mediæval papacy had its roots far
back in the past.   It owed much to Victor and Stephen, to
Damasus and Siricius, to Innocent I. and Leo. I., to Gregory the Great and to Nicolas I., as well as to Gregory
VII. and Innocent III.   These men, taking up St. Paul's
conception of a glorious and united Church, extending not
only to the limits of the earth, but conterminous with the
universe—a conception formed, we must remember, at
Rome—attached it not unnaturally to the imperial city,
the only apostolic see-city in the West.   The development
was the creation of the greater minds, of whom I have
mentioned the names of some; the establishment of the
tradition was the work of the lesser men who pursued the
same lines of policy with a unity and continuity of purpose which is exceedingly wonderful.   The idea which
they set before themselves, whenever they looked at the
matter as one of religious principle, was to establish an
international Church-state which was to rule the world, for
its good, in the name of God.   This state was to have
as its centre the city of Rome, or at any rate, the bishop
of the Roman see.   It was to be a spiritual state, but one
intimately allied with the powers of this world, and yet
independent of them and superior to them.   The conception of such an ecclesiastical society rested on two principal
foundations or postulates, one theological and one historical
—but both unsound.   The theological postulate was that
the visible Church of Christ was identical with the king-

dom of God, proclaimed by our Lord in the Gospel. The practical postulate was that it was right for this society to claim the prerogatives of the city of Rome, and to adopt, "mutatis mutandis," the methods of government of the Roman Empire of the West. This adoption of secular claims and methods was no doubt very effective up to a certain point. It led, however insensibly, to a claim to exercise secular authority, which inevitably came into collision with the growing power of nationalities.

It followed from this general conception that the Church-state was held to be a sacred and divine thing, even though its ministers or its monarchs might from time to time be very deficient in holiness. Whatever tended to exalt its power was held to be for the honour and glory of God, even though much mischief and misery might incidentally accompany the measures which promoted it. The great plan was to be pursued without faltering. The weakness of human nature was regarded as exceptional and unusual, but the triumph of divine grace in the body was assured.

§ 3.—THE POPE AS VICAR OF CHRIST. THE SYSTEM OF DELEGATION.

The pope, who was the centre of the whole, claimed first to be the vicar and successor of St. Peter, and then to be practically the sole vicar of Christ on earth. His supremacy was considered to be a divinely revealed truth expressed in certain texts of holy Scripture, and especially in certain sayings of our Lord to St. Peter, to which a very strained interpretation was given.[1]

He was already, in the Middle Age, supreme law-giver of the Church, as well as the supreme judge of appeal. Just as the Roman Emperor issued his rescripts to provincial governors, which became laws of the empire, so the pope's letters to his representatives became laws of the Church. He drew all business into his hands, and declared himself

---

[1] I have tried to elucidate the true meaning of these texts in a visitation address on *The Roman Church*, published in a recent volume, entitled *Unity and Fellowship*, S.P.C.K., 1909.

ready to decide all questions on which men disputed. He
also claimed to be the fountain and source of all power, the
dispenser of all privileges, and the director of all troubled
consciences. The claim to be the source of power grew
step by step with the custom, which first appears in the
sixth century, of sending an honorary scarf, called pallium,
from Rome to metropolitans of various provinces, whom
the pope desired to attach to himself or to recognize as his
agents. The fact that this woollen scarf had rested for a
night on the tomb of St. Peter gave it a special sanctity,
and carried with it an idea of the delegation of some of the
Petrine power to the recipient. At first this was given as
a personal honour. Then in time it came to be the official
duty of every metropolitan to ask for it after his consecration, and it was held that without it he was in some ways
in an irregular condition. From a gift to a metropolitan
after consecration it became a condition of his confirmation
before consecration, and thus the idea was gradually established that metropolitan power was held by delegation
from the pope. For a long time, certainly up to the thirteenth century, and the fourth Lateran Council under
Innocent III., it was generally held that ordinary episcopal
appointments within a province were to be confirmed by
the metropolitan, with the assistance of the comprovincial
bishops. But whenever there was a disputed or disputable
election an appeal to Rome was open, and many bishops,
in order to gain favour with the pope or a stronger position at home, voluntarily asked for confirmation where
there was no dispute. In process of time all bishops
were expected to get confirmation from Rome, and
to pay heavy fees for it. The financial necessities of
the papacy, as well as the desire for power, co-operated
in the extension of this system, which greatly restrained
episcopal and local liberty. Further, as time went on,
every bishop was expected to travel to Rome, every three
years, or to be subject to a heavy fine. In this way every
bishop was brought into subordination to the central
power.

The rights of metropolitans were further infringed upon by the system of delegating superior power to legates sent from Rome with a longer or shorter commission in wider or narrower terms. And if a metropolitan's power seemed to be growing too great his province could be sub-divided by the creation of a new metropolis.

The pope's agents for quickening and renewing spiritual life were, however, not merely occasional visitors, but much reliance was placed upon those religious orders which were composed of men for whom the ties of family and secular life had been broken, and who were, by the strongest life-long vows, devoted wholly to the service of the Church. They were to be the chief assistants to the bishops on the spiritual side, the supplements to the shortcomings of the secular clergy.

Besides having the help of these specially holy persons, the bishops were to rule with the aid of a body of religious men versed in practical affairs, their cathedral chapters. They were intended to preserve the continuity of diocesan administration, and to prevent a bishop—who might have much business on hand of all kinds—from letting the work of the diocese drop. They were also gradually substituted as elective and legislative bodies for the popular assemblies of clergy and people, which were hard to manage, and often tumultuous and erratic, and which tended to be superseded or swayed by the authority of the king or some great noble. For as long as the king and people had the upper hand in such elections the independence of the bishops was threatened. It was also felt necessary to check the rights of lay patrons and parochial congregations, and to give the bishops at least a veto upon the appointment of the secular clergy and the right and duty of admitting them to benefice as well as office.

The subjects of this state were to be the whole people of the land and any whom the secular power could win by conquest. Conversion by crusade, which thus became part of the system, was certainly not an invention of the papacy. It was an instinct of human nature, appearing

7

in such different characters as Mahomet, Charles the Great, the two Norwegian Olafs, and the Swedish St. Eric. But it received a considerable amount, not only of sanction, but of direct encouragement from the Church. Tithes for the proposed furtherance of such crusades became a valuable source of papal revenue. Similarly the different forms of persecution for heresy, on a larger or a smaller scale, were taken up rather than invented by Rome.[2] But the foundation principle, both of crusades and persecutions, that the general good of right belief was much more important than the wrongs or sufferings of individuals, became a specially Roman tenet. It was part of the general conviction that control of human life by the Church should be as extensive as possible. All crimes and offences which could be ranked as offences against religion were drawn as much as might be into the Church courts, and judged by Church laws. All breaches of morality and piety—adultery, incest, perjury, blasphemy, and the like—were to be judged and punished by Churchmen. All subjects in which the soul was concerned, marriage, wills, education, hospitals, charities, and the like, were to be subjected as far as possible to Church rule. The law of God, the law of the soul, was to be made and administered by those who understood His will and were devoted to His service. And, lastly, acceptance of the papal system, as a chief part of the law of God, came, by the end of the period, to be recognized, as the most practical duty of religion, and rejection of it as the gravest impiety and heresy of which a man could be guilty—and heresy was punishable with death.

For the purposes of this spiritual state it was necessary to have both clergy and the religious orders as free as possible from external control, as untrammelled by earthly ties and interests, as entirely devoted to the work of their callings, as subservient to their spiritual rulers, as well assured of the means of livelihood, as was possible under the conditions of human life. For these reasons it was

[2] Cp. Bishop Mandell Creighton : *Persecution and Tolerance.*

the object of the Church to free the clergy from the jurisdiction of secular courts, and to put them as decisively as
possible under spiritual discipline; to prevent them from
entering into obligations of service to secular lords, to
prohibit the inheritance of benefices, and particularly to
attach to their calling the obligation of celibacy. On the
other hand it was the business of the community, based
upon the teaching of Scripture, to give them an assured
income in the way of tithes and offerings, and certain possessions of houses and land free of taxes, otherwise payable to the crown and the community.

§ 4.—ENDOWMENTS. REVENUES. PETER'S-PENCE. CRUS-
ADING TITHES. ANNATES, ETC.

Further, since wealth was a means of acquiring power,
and power is needed for the Church's spiritual ends, men
and women were to be encouraged as much as possible to
make the Church their heir, and to build and endow
churches and monasteries. Such gifts they were taught
were well-pleasing to God, and made atonement for an ill-
spent life, or were the crown of a good one. Many a nobleman or high-born lady genuinely looked forward to the
quiet retirement of a convent at the close of life, or desired
to perpetuate their names by charity to such an institution
and to have the benefit of the prayers of its inmates after
death. Hence it became a great point of papal policy to
secure freedom to testators to make the Church their heir,
while it was a natural counter-policy of statesmen to dis-
courage and check such benefactions, which tended to en-
croach upon the disposable property of a nation, and to
force the burden of taxes upon a smaller area of the
country.

Such endowments might suffice for local needs; but besides them the central government naturally required the
support of the faithful. In addition to casual fees for legal
documents, dispensations, indulgences, promotions, and
the like, it was necessary to have a regular income. This

was already secured from England from Saxon times, in the form of Peter's-pence, a silver coin annually from every household.   The example of England had been followed in the eleventh century in Denmark and Poland, and the same example was in time to be set before Sweden. The payment of annates, or half-a-year's first fruits of benefices, was an exaction of the latter part of the Middle Age, whether such taxes were paid to the bishops or to the popes.   English clergy still pay such annates to the governors of Queen Anne's Bounty, who use them (since the reign of that sovereign) for the improvement of small benefices.   Tithes payable during the time of crusades, imposed on all Church incomes, were already known, but were nominally only levied in emergencies.   They became in time a very oppressive and almost constant tax on the clergy

§ 5.—STRENGTH AND WEAKNESS OF THIS SYSTEM.   IT GIVES UNITY AND DIGNITY TO EUROPE, BUT IGNORES THE RIGHTS OF THE INDIVIDUAL AND THE NATION, AND SETS CLERGY AND LAITY APART. CAUSE OF ITS FALL.

I need hardly comment on the strength and weakness of this magnificent system.   It was a strange mixture of iron and clay, of stable and unstable elements, of principle and expediency.   It started from the great principles of the divine fatherhood and of the brotherhood of man, and of the duty of uniting with men all over the world in the fellowship of an universal Church.   It lifted men's minds above matters of national, provincial, and local interest, into a higher sphere, both intellectual and spiritual.   It gave a union in particular to Europe, which it otherwise lacked.   It tempered the tyranny of feudalism (though that was not developed in Sweden, as elsewhere), and provided discipline even for kings and princes.   It made life to many persons bearable and even happy, in the midst of violence and barbarism, by offering the consolations and ideals of religion as a counterpoise to the pettiness and misery of present life. Through the doctrine of the Communion of Saints, it brought the great examples both of the present and the past into close relation to the lives of Christians dispersed throughout the world, and made life nobler by this sense of fellowship.

On the other hand, it had grave inherent defects. Its postulates were unsound and its interpretations of Scripture often crude and erroneous. It neglected the interests and stinted the growth of the individual soul, and it ignored the rights and duties of the Christian people. It separated the clergy into something like a caste, and made ambition on their part almost a duty. It treated laymen chiefly as useful instruments or passive recipients of instruction. It overlooked the design of God that every member of the Church should be a fully developed fellow-worker in the body. Further, it was largely a paper system, which broke down when applied to mankind on a large scale, and it needed men of herculean proportions and abilities to administer it even tolerably well. In the hands of ambitious, avaricious and sensual men, such as often filled the high places of the Church in the fourteenth and fifteenth centuries, the system rather spread corruption than promoted discipline.

Nevertheless, with all these defects on the spiritual side, the papacy might have continued to dominate Europe if it had merely maintained and developed its spiritual claims. Its fall was caused by its secular ambition. To put it quite simply, the possession of temporal sovereignty ruined its character. Yet the development of this temporal power was not an unnatural result of the spiritual system, and no doubt seemed all but inevitable to those who had been brought to think of the visible Church as the kingdom of God, and of Rome as the centre of the world. Let me point out how the secularity of the papacy arose.

§ 6.—CLAIM TO TEMPORAL SOVEREIGNTY. THE AVIGNON
    POPES AND THEIR AVARICE AND SIMONY.   THE
    GREAT   SCHISM.   FAILURE   OF   REFORMING
    COUNCILS.

Inasmuch as kings and princes were, for the good of
their souls, subjects of the pope, like other men, and could
be punished for their sins and crimes by him, or receive
pardon and abolition from him, and since they depended
on him for dispensations and were glad to have his assistance in their quarrels with their rivals and subjects, the
papacy gradually acquired a large and indefinite power
of interference in secular matters and concerns of State.
A rebellious or immoral king, who might be called a persecutor of the Church, could perhaps only be punished by
putting his kingdom under an interdict (since personal
excommunication was little felt), or by favouring some
rival to the throne.   From this habit of interference,
which, of course, was welcomed by those in whose interest
it was applied, grew up a monstrous claim to exercise universal temporal sovereignty, which culminated in the
bull *Unam Sanctam* of Boniface VIII. in 1302. Up to
this point the papal claims had been tolerated with an extraordinary amount of patience, because they seemed to
be the expression, however one-sided and defective, of
religious principle; but the fourteenth and fifteenth century popes destroyed the fabric which had been built up
with so much skill and zeal. The fourteenth century saw
the papacy reduced to a kind of vassalage under the kings
of France, and yet claiming more than ever the right to
interfere in other lands. It saw the Limousin popes re-
sorting to all sorts of oppressive expedients to maintain
their revenues and to supply their luxuries; simony,
rapacity and political intrigues, characterize this period.
After the seventy years at Avignon (1309—1379), the
papacy only returned to Rome to suffer from the effects of
the great schism between Urban VI. and Clement VII.
The question which was the rightful pope divided Europe
into two camps. If Urban was not pope he was merely

an old archbishop of Bari, not even a cardinal, who had been forced by popular tumult into the papal chair.   If Clement was not pope, he was merely young Robert of Geneva, who had been elected by cardinals in rebellion against their rightful master.   In this uncertainty it was impossible for thinking men or even for the people to look upon either of them with the old reverence which was given to a pope with an undisputed title.   It was seen also, very quickly, that neither would be able to reform the Church as a whole, and that a general council was needed, which, from the nature of the case, must be superior to both; and, therefore, to the papacy.   Even before this the very success of John XXII. in his conflict with the Emperor Louis of Bavaria had shattered one of the great mediæval ideals, the majesty of the Roman Empire.   The misconduct and mismanagement of the later popes deprived half Europe of its other ideal—the spiritual dignity of the papacy.   Thus, people on all sides began to think for themselves, and to be less under the dominion of traditions.   The Councils of Pisa, Constance and Basel, met and dissolved without effecting the serious reforms which all men agreed were needed.   The chief result was the abolition of papal " reservations " at Basel, and the partial restoration of the freedom of canonical election.   The papacy had its opportunity for self-reform in the seventy years that followed, but it had become an ambitious, intriguing, warring state among the other states of Europe, and had lost all desire for serious reform.   Even when one who had been in favour of reform became pope, as Pius II., he condemned himself for what he had done as Aeneas Sylvius in defence of the Council of Basel. Thus, the Protestant Reformation became necessary for Europe, and it was embraced by all those nations, including Sweden, in which there was a sufficient interest in theology, a sufficient knowledge of Holy Scripture, and a sufficient sense of personal dignity and love of liberty to enable them to venture upon a decided break with the past.   These   nations   were,   generally   speaking,   those

which had never been, or had only partially been, subjects
of the ancient empire of the West; and on the whole, the
thoroughness of their acceptance of the Reformation varied
inversely with the thoroughness of their previous incorporation into the empire.   The reason of this distinction is
to be found in the fact that conversion inside the Roman
Empire had been very largely formal and superficial—conversion outside it was more the result of persuasion or
conviction.

Even to the present day the instinctive attitude of different European nations towards the papacy is very
remarkable.   It is noticeable even in many who are personally alienated from the practice of religion.   Men of
Latin and Celtic race, especially in France and Ireland,
appear often unable to conceive of any other system of
Church government than an autocracy.   They have little
personal interest in theology, little sense of personal responsibility for the faith and life of the Church, but the
papacy seems to them a natural and logical outcome of
the only Christianity which they know.   Their sense of
the value of unity and orderliness outweighs all other considerations.   It is not, of course, so with Teutonic nations,
and we shall see that in the end the rejection of this system
in Sweden was more complete than in Germany and
England.

§ 7.—INTRODUCTION OF THE PAPAL SYSTEM INTO SWEDEN.

This survey has carried us rapidly to the eve of the
Reformation.   We must now retrace our steps to mark in
detail the manner in which the Romanized Church
developed in Sweden.

To the Northern nations at first the distant power of
Rome came with an immense and imposing prestige.
Let me quote to you two of the Norse poets who represent
the idea which was formed of the relation of Christ to
Rome, and of Rome to the world.   One of them, Eilif,

who lived, I suppose, about 1000 A.D., and wrote of Thor
as well as of Christ, thus speaks of the latter :—

> " They say Christ sits upon a mountain throne
> Far to the south beside the well of Fate :
> So closely has the Lord whom angels own
> With Rome and Roman lands entwined His state."

Another, a little later, writes :—

> " The Lord of monks has greater might than all.
> Who can put any limits to God's powers?
> Christ has not only formed this world of ours,
> But for Himself has reared Rome's glorious hall."[3]

No doubt the pilgrimage of the Danish king, Erik Eiegod, tended to keep up this feeling of sanctity and majesty
of the city, where Christ, in the person of His vicar, was
throned on the seven hills and sent out his emissaries bearing the decrees of Fate from the banks of the Tiber.

At first, however, this great southern power approached
Sweden cautiously and tentatively. Hildebrand did little
more than ask for information. After his death, Urban
II. and Clement III. divided the allegiance of Christendom as pope and anti-pope, and strong action was not
to be looked for. The establishment of the Archbishopric
of Lund, which was a move against the pretensions of
Clement, who was supported in Germany, was not backed
up by strong action as regards Sweden. All that we can
say is that after the time of its establishment by Urban II.
greater regularity of succession to bishoprics seems to
prevail in Sweden. They ceased to be missionary and
gradually became territorial. But as yet there was no
acceptance in Sweden of the papal system, which was

[3] See *Corpus Poeticum Boreale*, Vol. ii., pp. 22 and 115.
A more literal translation is : " They say that He sits on a
mountain throne in the south at the well of the Fates, so has
the mighty Lord of the Powers bound Himself to the lands of
Rome " ; and : " The might of the Lord of monks is the
greatest. God is able to do most things. Christ created the
world and reared the hall of Rome."

naturally introduced into Denmark by the Archbishop Asser in gratitude for the dignity conferred upon him, and in union with the pious feelings of the Danish kings. The decrees of the Synod of Reims in 1119, and of the first Lateran Council of 1122, both under Calixtus III., were received in Denmark shortly after they were passed in the South, under the guidance of the legate, Cardinal Alberic. They were directed against simony, lay investiture, the inheritance of benefices, and the marriage of the clergy. Thus, they were a mixture of right and wrong principles. Simony was disgraceful and sinful (though the way in which it grew up is explicable), and the inheritance of benefices highly inexpedient.   Lay investiture was a matter for compromise—such as was reached in England. The marriage of the clergy, on the other hand, was a right possessed by them as by all other men, and to deny it was so to run counter to human nature, as to promote immorality and a low standard of clerical life.

§§ 8 TO 11.—PERIOD I.

§ 8.—THE SVERKER AND ERIC KINGS (1130—1250). ESKIL OF LUND (1157—1178). ESTABLISHMENT OF FIXED SEES AND MONASTERIES.   COUNCIL OF LINKÖPING (1152) GRANTS PETER'S-PENCE.

We must now touch on the special history of Sweden after the extinction of the line of Stenkil.   For more than forty years, from 1137 to 1178, the see of Lund was filled by a strong, high-born and ambitious, but also pious man —Eskil—nephew of the first Archbishop, a contemporary and friend of St. Bernard of Clairvaux,, a man in whom the two prevailing impulses of the age, to fight for power and to take refuge in monastic seclusion, seem to have been equally balanced.   He was at home both in the battle-field and in the cloister.   He was the first to hold a council of northern bishops, in 1139 or 1140, at which representatives of Sweden, Norway and the Färö Islands met with men from Denmark—thus carrying out to some extent the project for which Adalbert of Hamburg had longed in vain. The papal legate, Theodignus, was present at this council, and preached the celibacy of the clergy, mostly, no doubt, to unwilling ears. In 1145, Eskil had the joy of consecrating the present stately cathedral of Lund, of which Asser had consecrated the crypt. On both these occasions the bishops of West and East Gothland, or, as we may now call them by their see-cities, Odgrim of Skara and Gislo of Linköping, were both present. In 1152, Eskil became Primate of Sweden, and began to intervene in its internal affairs, Lund still being in Danish territory.

Under Eskil fixed sees were established at five centres in Sweden—Skara, Linköping, Old Upsala (which took the place of Sigtuna), Strengnäs and Vesterås. Småland had been for some time in the diocese of Linköping, and its see-city, Vexiö, is not named as having a bishop of its own until 1183. Even then the diocese was very small and only included Värend. The last mediæval see, that of Åbo in Finland, was founded about the year 1200. It became important, and was, perhaps, next in importance to Upsala and Linköping at the time of the Reformation. With the assistance of Eskil the first monasteries were also established in Sweden, all of them being settlements of Cistercians from his beloved Clairvaux. Several had been established before that time in Skåne.

The first monastery in what was then Sweden was Alvastra, on Lake Vettern, at the foot of the Omberg, in East Gothland, founded in 1143, where the tombs of the Sverker kings may still be seen among the ruins. The next (1144) was Nydala, in Småland. Then came Varnhem in West Gothland, where a fine church, with an eastern apse, still remains, containing tombs of Biger Jarl, Jesper Svedberg and the De la Gardie family. The first convent of nuns was at Vreta, near Linköping in East Gothland, and another was founded at Gudhem in West Gothland. Södermanland, the province south of Lake

Mälar, had its monastery at Viby, afterwards moved to Julita.   Upland had Byarum, removed to Skokloster or Skogkloster (the forest monastery), long the chateau of the Wrangel family, but now that of the Brahes.   It contains the famous collection of spoils from the Thirty Years' War.

Lastly, the island of Gotland had Gutvalla or Roma, which has been state property since the Reformation. Thus, nearly every large province of Sweden proper came to have a seat of retired religious life, after the ascetic model, between the years 1143—1164, besides the cathedrals, with their clergy, more or less forming a society, though not yet a chapter, which were in the principal towns.   All this shows an intelligent plan, which many reasonably suppose to have been largely framed by Eskil, whose long episcopate gave time for the perfecting of carefully-planned measures of Church policy.

The pope was, however, quite ready to give Sweden further relative independence, coupled, of course, with closer dependence on the centre, on the principle " Do ut des." In 1152, the first Swedish Council was held at Linköping by the Englishman, Nicolas Brakespear, Cardinal of Alba, afterwards Pope Hadrian IV.   He had come as nuncio from Pope Eugenius III. (the pupil of St. Bernard), and had established an archbishop at Trondhjem for Norway, and was prepared to do the same in Sweden.   He made a greater impression on the North than any foreigner who had hitherto visited the country.   It was, however, impossible to get the rival kings and the prelates of the different parts of Sweden to agree upon the place and person.   For the pre-eminence of Upsala over Linköping was not yet quite settled, and the pallium which had been brought to invest the new archbishop was left with Eskil of Lund for future use.   At this Synod of Linköping, the East-Gothic king, Sverker, was present, and assented to the payment of Peter's-pence, thus following the example just set in Norway.   The custom of all men bearing weapons was also forbidden.   I imagine that the silence of this council in respect to the question of clerical marriage must have been a matter of arrangement between the legate and the bishops. It was, I presume, the price paid for the grant of Peter's-pence. It is almost necessary to suppose something of the sort, when we recollect what had been done in Denmark, and note the latter assertion of the Swedes (in 1213), that they had a papal privilege for their immunity from the law of celibacy (Innocent III., Reg. XVI., 118).

§ 9.—St. Eric, King in Upland, law-giver and church builder. His crusade. Death (1160). Becomes a popular saint.

About this time the rival king of the Sveas, afterwards known and widely honoured as St. Eric, was establishing laws and religion in Upland, and doing his best to Christianize Finland after the manner which the two Olafs, Tryggvason and Haraldson, had found successful in Norway. St. Eric was the son of a large peasant proprietor or bonde, not of royal race, but his mother, Cecilia, was daughter of the heathen Blot-Sven, who had rivalled King Inge, and she, too, like the rest of that family, was now a zealous Christian. It is probable that Sverker was also descended from Blot-Sven; and, if so, the kings of Gothland and Svealand were cousins, perhaps first cousins. Eric was a real benefactor to his country, and his reign is a landmark in its history. He was at once a law-giver and a Churchman. To him the married women of Sweden owe important rights.

The following quaint form was long used by the father in betrothing his daughter to her suitor. " I give thee this my daughter for honour and housewife, for half the bed, for doors and keys, and every third penny in thy goods movable and immovable, and for all the rights which Upper Sweden hath from St. Eric, and St. Eric gave. In the name of the Father, and of the Son and of the Holy Ghost. Amen." (Olaus Magni *De gent. Septent.*, XIV., c. 5; cp. *S. H.*, Vol. i., p. 381). This form seems to have been used without alteration up to the middle of the sixteenth century.   It was prescribed in the civil laws of Gustavus Adolphus in 1618, but with the omission of the references to Upper Sweden and St. Eric (*Sueciæ leges civiles*, lit. 2, c. 5, *de jure conjugii*, ed. Loccenius, Lund, 1675).   We possess a church that St. Eric built or finished at Old Upsala, on the site and with the materials of the famous heathen temple.   It is possible also that the Church of the Holy Trinity at the present Upsala in his work.

His missionary crusade in Finland was carried on in company with his bishop, St. Henry, an Englishman, who had come with Nicolas to the North.   It is called a crusade, but it was conducted, it may be, with more humanity and piety than many such expeditions.   It was necessary to cause the Finns to live at peace with their neighbours, and peace and baptism were offered to them before war was declared.   The king was evidently really in earnest in his prayers and efforts for the eternal salvation of his enemies, and he wept for those who fell in battle without having received baptism.   Henry was left behind as bishop in Finland, and some years later fell as a martyr.   It is re-corded that his thumb, which was cut off in the struggle, fell on the snow, and was found some time afterwards.   It long appeared as a charge on the seal of the chapter of Åbo.

Eric returned to New Upsala, then called Östra-aros, and was murdered by a Danish prince, who made a sudden and for a time successful raid in order to claim the crown.   Eric, who would not interrupt the mass which he was attending in Holy Trinity Church, Upsala, was killed outside it, about the year 1160, and on 18th May.   This historic church, I am glad to remember, was put at the disposal of my colleague, the Bishop of Winchester, for a celebration of Holy Communion, at the time of our recent visit to Upsala, in September, 1909.   Eric was elevated by the love of the Swedish people to the glory of saintship, and became the patron saint of the nation, though he was denied the dignity of official canonization.   The rival

Sverker kings opposed this honour, and their influence with the papacy was strong enough to prevent it: but his saintship was afterwards *de facto* recognized by various papal indulgences.

§ 10.—CHARLES SVERKERSSON, FIRST "KING OF THE SWEDES AND GOTHS." UPSALA MADE AN ARCHBISHOPRIC (1164). LETTERS OF POPE ALEXANDER III. PRIVILEGES AND IMMUNITIES OF THE CLERGY. INNOCENT III. LETTERS TO ABSALON AND ANDREAS OF LUND.

The Danes being driven out, Charles Sverker was elected king of the Swedes and Goths, and was the first in historical times to bear that designation. He did a real service to Swedish nationality by taking up again the project, which had been dropped for a time, of forming Sweden into a more or less independent province. No doubt, it was to conciliate his Upland subjects that he gave up any claims that Skara or Linköping might possess, and agreed to fix the Archbishop's throne at Old Upsala. This act fell in with the policy of many of the popes, who wished to prevent any of the great sees, such as Arles, Hamburg, Canterbury, or Lund, from acquiring anything like patriarchal rights which might make them rivals to Rome. Ever since the fifth century this policy had checked the development of the French Church, and the same policy checks it still. The German empire had for a time fostered and protected the great German sees, but Hamburg was first weakened by the establishment of Lund, and then Lund by that of Upsala. In England, the obedience of York to Canterbury had recently been abrogated, after a long struggle, at the instance of Archbishop Thurstan (1114—1140). Whatever may be thought of the other cases, Swedish nationality was certainly the gainer by the foundation of its Archbishopric. In August 1164, Pope Alexander II. (1159—1181) gave a constitution to the new foundation by issuing two bulls, one addressed to Stephen, the new archbishop, a monk of Alvastra, and, therefore, from East Gothland, who had just been consecrated at Sens by Eskil of Lund, in the pope's presence. This first bull made Upsala the metropolis of the new province, and put the bishoprics of Skara, Linköping, Strengnäs and Vesterås (naming them in that order) under the jurisdiction of the new archbishop (*P. L.*, 200, 301 foll.). It reserved, however, the due right and reverence of the Bishop (sic) of Lund. What the position of Åbo in Finland was intended to be, is not clear. The second was addressed to all the Bishops of Sweden, and directed them to show obedience to their new metropolitan, and gave them good advice as to carefulness and purity in ordinations (*ibid.* 303). But again nothing was heard of clerical celibacy.

About eight years later (1172), the same pope, who was a great jurist, wrote two important letters to the new archbishop and his suffragans, as well as two of a less detailed character to the Bishops of Linköping and Strengnäs. The two longer ones deal with many of the usual matters of discipline, but even here make no mention of celibacy. The first, dated 9th September, 1172 (*ep.* 975, l.c. 850), speaks of certain great crimes, and reprobates also the custom of certain clergy celebrating the Eucharist " with dried lees of wine or crumbs of bread steeped in wine " (thus touching a difficulty which we shall notice later), and censures the custom of clandestine marriages among the laity. The second, dated the next day (*ep.* 979, l.c. 854 foll.), mainly deals with promotion to benefices, which laymen are asserted to be in the habit of conferring without reference to the bishops. It expresses a wish that the clergy should be free from accusation before the civil courts. It discourages ordeal by fire or duel, and enjoins the payment of tithes. These letters show considerable local knowledge, and were no doubt on the whole very useful in consolidating the body of Church law in Sweden. By the year 1200 the clergy had obtained, as far as the king was concerned, the desired exemption from the jurisdiction of the civil courts. It was not, however, as yet

agreed to by the people.   In 1219 the goods of the Church
were declared free from the king's power to impose fines.
The same period saw the foundation of colleges of clergy
round the cathedrals of Upsala and Skara (about 1200 and
1222.   See Holmquist: *Schweden*, p. 21), which were furnished at first with regular canons.

At the end of the century, a very powerful and religious
pope, Innocent III., occupied the Roman see.   In his first
year (1198) he busied himself with the affairs of the North,
and tried to re-establish the authority of Absalon, Archbishop of Lund (1178—1201) over the Church of Sweden.
The case in which he particularly interfered illustrates the
manners of the time and the difficulties of Church government.   Three bishoprics had lately become vacant in
Sweden, and three men, who are described as not born in
lawful wedlock, had been elected to fill them.   These men
were almost certainly sons of clergy.   Absalon, Archbishop of Lund, forbade the Archbishop of Upsala, whose
name was Peter, to consecrate them; but Peter disregarded
the inhibition, and consecrated two of them.   Whereupon
Absalon suspended them all.   Innocent now wrote to
the next Archbishop of Upsala, Olaus I., directing him to
follow the commands of Absalon (*Reg.* I., *ep.* 444, *P. L.*
214, 421; cp. the letter to Absalon on his rights over
Sweden; *ibid. ep.* 419, p. 395).[4]   Olaus died soon after, and
the people, with the consent of the king, elected Valerius,
the son of a priest, to succeed him.   Andreas of Lund, who

---

[4] I may notice that we possess the will of Absalon, former
Archbishop of Lund, dictated on his death-bed.   Amongst other
pious bequests and friendly gifts he ordered the manumission
of several female slaves with their children, one of whom he had
received as a present from Biargaherred in Skåne.   There was
nothing remarkable in an archbishop having slaves at this
time.   But the manumission of their children would not have
been necessary in Sweden if the fathers were freemen.   In
Sweden, as distinguished from Denmark, Germany and France,
the children of slaves by a freeman followed the better half
(Geijer : p. 86).   Another noticeable gift is the remission of a
debt of several marks to his clerk, Saxo, who seems to be Saxo
Grammaticus, the Danish historian (*P. L.*, vol. 209, p. 760).

succeeded Absalon, naturally consulted the pope on this point. But the pope, perhaps having learnt more of the difficulties of the subject, while seeing the inconsistency of the position, left Andreas to settle it, and gave way by enclosing a dispensation and sending the pallium for Valerius (*Reg*. X., *ep*. 147, 1207, A.D., *P. L.* 215, 1244). Similar difficulties occurred later, and were met in much the same way by strongly-worded declarations in the way of canons and statutes, followed by weak action in the way of dispensations or relaxations.

As regards the general condition of the clergy, we have evidence from the later correspondence of the same pope, Innocent, with Andreas that the clergy of Sweden were publicly married and claimed to have a privilege from the pope for this indulgence (*Reg*. XVI., *ep*. 118, 3rd October, 1213). The pope desired to see this privilege, but we have no record of its production. It may have been, as I have suggested, merely a verbal bargain as the price of concessions to papal claims on the part of king and people.

§ 11.—INTRODUCTION OF THE FRIARS.   POWER OF DOMI-
NICANS.   GROWTH OF POWER OF BISHOPS.
CREATION OF CATHEDRAL CHAPTERS.   COUNCIL
OF SKENINGE UNDER WILLIAM OF SABINA (1248)
PROHIBITS CLERICAL MARRIAGE.

The weak reign of Eric III. (1222-1250) witnessed a further consolidation of the Romanized Church.   As the twelfth century brought in the Cistercians, so the thirteenth naturally introduced the friars—of whom the Dominican Friars Preachers were the most powerful in Sweden, and did most for education.   They had two great houses, one at Sigtuna, and one at Skeninge in the diocese of Linköping —besides minor ones.[5]

The bishops now began to be secular potentates, and to take their places in the more private Councils of State,

[5] A picture of the nave of Skeninge Church is given in *S. H.*[1], Vol. i., fig. 461. See also Vol. ii., fig 390, for the interior.

which were gradually superseding the large popular assemblies. They were often men of high birth. Thus Olaus II., for fifty years Archbishop of Upsala (1223—1273), was nephew of St. Eric; Charles I., Bishop of Linköping, was brother of the all-powerful Birger Jarl (†1220); just as a son of the Jarl's was later bishop of the same see. Several of the bishops of Skara were of noble or knightly rank. It was the interest of this powerful hierarchy to keep the succession in the hands of men like themselves, and they thus gladly promoted the rules of the fourth Lateran Council of Pope Innocent III. as to the election of bishops by their chapters (canons 23 and 24). Since the canons were for the most part nominated by the bishops there was great likelihood of the tradition represented by the bishops being maintained. The first secular chapter founded in Sweden was that of Bishop Benedict of Skara in 1222. Ten years later we find similar institutions at Linköping and Åbo. Archbishop Jarler organized a secular chapter at Upsala in the place of the old "capitulum monachorum," with the help of Cardinal William of Sabina. The other three followed suit before the end of the century.[6]

The mention of William of Sabina leads to a reference to the momentous step which was at last taken by the Council of Skeninge in 1248 to introduce the most practical and most difficult piece of the papal programme—the celibacy of the clergy, which was coupled with a requirement that bishops should procure and study the most recent collection of the Roman canon law. As Cardinal Nicolas had presided at Linköping, so another legate, William of Sabina, presided at this second council. Its statutes were sufficiently severe, dealing out excommunications and anathemas on the married clergy and their wives, with a

[6] I owe this information to a letter from Professor Hjalmar Holmquist. Dissertations on the subject have also been written by K. V. Lundquist, *Bidrag till kännedomen om de Svenska domkapiteln*, etc., Stockholm, 1897, and H. Lundström in *Skisser och Kritiker*, 1903 (See below, 171, n. 19).

view to the prevention of the inheritance of benefices, or even of any possessions by their children.   At the same time bishops were forbidden to exact anything but food and drink at their visitations, and only allowed to take a certain retinue with them.

The legate ordered these rules to be read and put in execution at the yearly synods.   He further enlarged them, with papal authority, a year or two later doing his best to get the elections of bishops entirely free from outside interference, and to prevent the clergy from taking any oath to the king or other secular person.   These rules were confirmed by Innocent IV., who was then pope, in 1250. They naturally produced opposition, and the law of celibacy was never really thoroughly enforced, though it was often talked about.

§§ 12 TO 16.—PERIOD II.   THE FOLKUNGAR (1250—1389).

§ 12.—JARL BIRGER AND HIS FAMILY.   GOOD LAWS. MAGNUS LADULÅS AND VALDEMAR.   GROWTH OF POWER OF THE POPE.   COUNCIL OF TELJE (1279). PRIESTS' MARRIAGES.   DISTINCTION OF "FREE" AND "UNFREE."   KNIGHT-SERVICE INTRODUCED.

With the death of Eric Erricsson, the third of the Eric line of Swedish kings, the rivalry between that dynasty and the Gothic line of the Sverkers came to an end.   During the latter part of Ericsson's nominal reign the Jarl Birger had been all powerful, and he continued to be so after the election of his son Valdemar until his own death in 1266. The election took place during the Jarl's absence on a crusade in Tavasteland against the Finns, where our countryman, Bishop Thomas, was at once zealous and imprudent.   The crusade was promoted by Pope Gregory IX., who gave the same indulgence to those who took part in it which was granted to crusaders going to the Holy Land (Celsii: *Bullarium*, p. 67, 9th December, 1237).

The Folkunga dynasty lasted in one form or another for nearly 140 years.   It was something like the line of Pepin in France taking the place of the Merovingian kings; something like that of the House of Lancaster in England in the fifteenth century. Only it was a rule of Swedish law up to the sixteenth century that the monarchy was elective, not hereditary, and hereditary right has never had so many votaries as in France and England. The Folkunga period was favourable to the growth of the immunities and privileges of the Church, and at the same time to the establishment of better laws. Jarl Birger is remembered as the founder of Stockholm, which, from its splendid position, was as important a move for Sweden as the foundation of Constantinople by Constantine, or of Petersburg by Peter the Great, to their dominions. It was also in his time (1258) that Pope Alexander IV. gave leave for the removal of the archiepiscopal see from Old Upsala, to the more convenient site near Östra-aros, or East-mouth, about three English miles distant, while it retained the name belonging to the old city. This was as important for the Swedish Church as (to compare small things with great) the movement from old Sarum on the hill to new Sarum in the valley, thirty years before, was to the diocese of Salisbury. The transfer at Upsala was not, however, complete till about 1273.[7]

The Jarl is also remembered for his legal reforms, and as substituting as far as possible process in the courts for private revenge. He proclaimed four laws for peace—the first protecting the church and churchyard; the second forbidding the forcible abduction of women; the third establishing a man's rights to personal security in his own house and on his land; and, lastly, when travelling to the Ting, or assize. He also did his best to stop trial by ordeal or wager of battle, and, in other ways, improved the position of women, slaves and shipwrecked mariners. In all this he naturally had the help and encouragement of the clergy.

His son, Magnus Ladulås, or Barn-lock, whom the Jarl

[7] See E. Benzelius fil. : *Monumenta*, pp. 20-1, and Celsii : *Bullarium*, s. annis., 1258, 1259.

had made a duke in order to balance his brother Valdemar,
is equally remembered for his improvement of the laws.
His surname was given to him because of the check which
he imposed on travellers, especially on nobles, who were
accustomed to help themselves to the peasants' stores without payment—thus abusing the old Swedish custom of
universal hospitality.   In the place of it innkeepers were
established everywhere to superintend the lodging of
travellers in different houses.   Magnus was an enlightened
and magnificent king, but he had, like our Henry IV., to
make terms with the clergy in order to cover the usurpation
by which he deposed his brother Valdemar.

Let me explain how the pope had cause to interfere.

In the year 1274 Pope Gregory IX. had obtained power
over King Valdemar by reason of a great sin which he had
committed, and for which he had gone to Lyons to obtain
pardon.   During this pilgrimage the pope inhibited the
realm of Sweden from electing a new king, and mentioned
that the king of Sweden had acknowledged the Roman
pontiff as his superior, and his kingdom as tributary to
Rome (9th January, 1274, Celsius, p. 85-6).   Seven
months later he wrote to Duke Magnus demanding that
testators should be free to leave their property to the
Church, and the clergy freed from the jurisdiction of the
civil courts.   He also condemned the practice of civil
magistrates excommunicating lay offenders (9th August,
1274, *ibid.* 86).   Magnus, who was at war with his brother,
purchased the support of the Church by giving way to
these demands (see Holmquist: 22-3).   After his coronation a council was held at Telje in October, 1279, which
reflects the alliance between himself and the hierarchy
(Reuterdahl: *Stat. Synod*, p. 37).   The sacredness of the
king's person was established and protected by threat of
excommunication.   At the same time prohibitions of
clerical incontinence were renewed, and it was laid down
that a fine for this fault was to extend to a quarter of the
clerical income, and was only to be taken once.   After that
punishment was to be more severe.

Yet the decree states that " few or none are exempt from this plague " (*ibid.*, p. 30). There could be little hope of stamping out a custom so inveterate. For, if all were involved in it, it was the interest of all that the law should be evaded. And inasmuch as the council went on to revoke the law against clerical inheritances and to allow the lawful heirs to succeed to all goods acquired by whatever means, the position of the children of the clergy was better than it had been before (*ibid.*, p. 32).[8]

It is difficult to form a judgment of the moral condition of any large body of persons, especially in a bygone age very different from our own. But the clergy in Sweden were probably a more independent and, if we may use the word, respectable class of men than in those countries where the feudal system, with its lay patronage in the hands of great landlords, prevailed. Sweden, as I have said, was not a conquered but a settled country, divided amongst a large number of small landowner or " bönder." A group of these men, acting as a parish, founded and endowed the churches and chose the clergy, men usually of their own class.[9] On the other hand, where the feudal system prevailed, the clergy often were dependents on the lord of the manor, often his slaves or villeins.

It is probable that the priests' families were much on a par with those of the " bönder " around them. How far they were able to continue to intermarry with these families after the council of 1248 it is not easy to ascertain. It is to be feared that as time went on they were forced to choose their partners from a less reputable class; and that the men themselves paid less regard to the tie, which was no longer respected by the law. Probably the rights of the children were better protected by the civil law than those of the mothers, who were denounced by Church law. We find

[8] See further on this subject J. A. and Aug. Theiner : *Einführung der erzwungenen Ehelosigkeit*, Vol. ii., pp. 331-7, Bremen [1892].

[9] The different rules of this period are described by Reuterdahl : *S. K. H.*, Vol. ii., pt. 2, p. 633.

the Council of Upsala in 1368 referring to and reinforcing
the decrees of Telje (1279), but heading this part of its
statutes with the significant words: "These rules that
follow are not to be published to the laity " (*Stat. Syn.*, 52).

The reign of Magnus Ladulås is not only an epoch in the
history of the growth of Church privileges, but it is also
marked by an extension of the power of the nobility. He
was the first sovereign who gave the nobility a charter of
exemption from taxation, with the intention of attaching
them to the personal service of the crown (Geijer, p. 52).
He also exempted from payments to the king "all persons serving on horse-back, in the service of whomsoever
they might be " (Ordinance of Alsnö, 1285, *ibid.*). Thus
arose the momentous distinction of " free " and " unfree "
(frälse and ofrälse), which in origin had nothing to do with
personal freedom or freehold of property, but only freedom
from taxation on account of services supposed to be rendered to the State. Thus also arose the order of knighthood, which was personal, not hereditary, just as it was,
and, indeed, still is in England.

These changes, though not directly intended to depress
the peasantry, certainly did so, especially in days when
foreign officials came in and treated liability to taxation as
if it were a condition almost of serfdom.

§ 13.—FRATRICIDAL WARS OF THE PERIOD.   GROWTH OF
    LITERATURE.   RHYME-CHRONICLE.   PETRUS DE
    DACIA.   CRUSADE AGAINST CARELIANS.   LATER
    SAINTS : BRYNIULF, HEMMING, NICOLAUS HER-
    MANNI

The Folkunga period was disturbed by frequent civil
wars and murders, especially amongst brothers of the royal
household.   " Not a king of this race " (writes Fryxell : i.,
265) " is to be found who did not commit violence on, and
act treacherously by, his nearest relations, father, brother
and children.   They were the cause of their own ruin by
their persecutions of each other, to the degree that no noble

branch remained of a family once so numerous." It is remarkable that these fratricidal wars first called out the spirit of Swedish poetry, which is manifested in the earliest anonymous rhyme-chronicle. This is the so-called Eric's-chronicle which describes the period 1229—1319, and was probably written down about the date of the final years recorded in it in the reign of Magnus Ericsson.[10]

The Folkunga period was, however, a time of intellectual progress, the leaders of which in Sweden were the Dominicans, and afterwards the Birgittines. The Franciscans had most influence in Stockholm, which was, however, very largely a German town. The Dominicans, by their establishments in foreign cities, such as Cologne and Paris (1285), introduced Swedes to the growing knowledge of the day. But scholasticism never took much root in the country. The first Swedish writer of importance was Petrus de Dacia, who had studied under Thomas Aquinas, but whose bent of mind was much more to allegory and mysticism than logical system. He conceived a deep platonic affection for Kristina of Stumbelen, a nervous and fantastic peasant girl, living in the neighbourhood of Cologne, whose acquaintance he made as a student there (1266-9), and to whom he afterwards wrote mystic love letters, which may be found in the *Acta Sanctorum* for the month of June, embodied in the life which he wrote of her (tome v., pp. 231-387). The following extract from one of his letters will give an idea of the strength of his affection :—

" O my most loving one! O inmost marrow of my heart! I beseech thee let us raise our eyes and lift our hearts to God, in whom all things are one; and from Him and in Him we find ourselves, as far as we are one, we who in ourselves are very much separated. O dearest! would I

[10] This first part of the *Chronicon Rhythmicum maius* may be found in *Scr. rer. Suecicarum*, Vol. i., pt. 2, pp. 1-52. The connecting part that follows is of little historical value. The better work begins again with the *Karlskrönika*, 1389-1452, and the *Sture-chronicles*, 1452-1520.

could talk to thee face to face, and abide with thee also in bodily presence! and this certainly I should prefer to all the comfort given to me by the relations and friends amongst whom I dwell, and I daily beseech God to do it before my death by whatever opportunity for it may be given. I, thy father, am well, dearest daughter; and I am deeply grieved because I have heard nothing lately about thy state." This was perhaps his last letter to her before his death.

The end of the thirteenth century was marked by a crusade conducted against the heathen Carelians, in Finland, who were assisted by the Russians who had long been adherents of the Greek Church. This war was waged during the minority of Birger, son of Ladulås. From this unfortunate war began the long-drawn contest with Russia. A few years later, in 1295, a check was put upon the primacy of Lund, and Archbishop Nicolaus Allonis of Upsala received the pallium direct from Rome (see Celsii: *Bullarium*, p. 97. Boniface VIII. writes: " Pallium illi per manus Cardinalium delegatorum Romæ tradi curavimus, salvo Lundensis jure ").

The latter part of the Folkunga period is memorable for the career of the great female saint, Birgitta. It was also brightened by the lives of the only later sainted bishops which Sweden has to show, Bryniulf, or Brynolphus I. of Skara (1278—6th February, 1317), Hemming of Åbo (1339 —22nd May, 1366), and Nicolaus Hermanni of Linköping (1374—13th September, 1391). Bryniulf was a man of high birth, son of the West Gothic lagman, Algot, who had studied for many years in Paris, a Latin poet and good administrator, who governed the see of Skara for nearly forty years, though often in conflict with Magnus Ladulås,

Hemming was a zealous missionary in Finland and its neighbourhood, and a great founder. Amongst his other foundations must be reckoned the establishment of the first the first Church Order of the province. He also procured library in Finland. His statutes published in 1352 were the representation of Finland in the election of the king of

Sweden at the Mora Stones. He is, therefore, rightly regarded as a sort of national hero in that province. He was
a friend of St. Birgitta, of whom I am about to speak, and
the first who brought her revelations to the notice of the
pope (*Nordisk F. B.*, s.v. Hemming).

Nicolaus Hermanni, the last Swedish saint before the Reformation, was even more closely connected with Birgitta,
who chose him as tutor for her children. After her death
he worked hard to get her canonized, and was the author of
a well-known hymn in her praise :—

> Rosa rorans bonitatem
> Stella stillans claritatem
> Birgitta vas gratiæ

in a metre which became popular for Swedish verse.

Nicolaus was the first Churchman of high rank to support Queen Margaret, and he is, therefore, an important
link between the Folkunga and Union periods. His contemporary, Archbishop Birgerus Gregorii (1366—1383),
another zealous friend of Birgitta's, may also be mentioned
as the principal Latin poet of the Middle Age, in company
with Bryniulf (*I. S. L. H.*, i., p. 110). His offices for St.
Botvid and St. Birgitta have some real poetical beauty
(See G. M. Dreves' *Lateinische Hymnen-dichtung*, I.,
pp. 437-41, Leipzig, 1909).

§ 14.—ST. BIRGITTA (1303—1373). HER FAMILY AND CHAR-
ACTER. EARLY IMPRESSIONS. MARRIAGE WITH
ULF. DEATH OF HER HUSBAND. REVELATIONS :
THEIR METHOD. POLITICAL INTERESTS.[11]

We must now turn our attention to Birgitta herself,
whose life (1303—1373) deserves a fuller treatment. She is
confessedly one of three representatives of religion in
Sweden, whose names are everywhere known—the other
two being Gustavus Adolphus and Swedenborg.

She was also the first who has left sufficient personal

---

[11] See the detached note at the end of this lecture.

memoirs (so to call them) to enable us to form a full estimate of her character and inner life.[12]   She was a lady of
noble—though not, as was sometimes said, of royal—birth,
and had a full consciousness of her dignity, and of her
duty to the Church, a consciousness which doubtless saved
her from many a false step, and supported her in many
trials.   Her father, Birger Persson (†1328) was lagman of
Tiundaland, the chief province of Upland.   He was nephew of the Archbishop of Upsala, Jacobus Israelis, and
other members of the family had been bishops.[13]

Her mother was descended from a brother of the great
Birger Jarl.   Her father was president of the royal commission which codified the laws of Upland in 1296.   He
was an adherent and friend of the dukes Eric and Valdemar in their struggle with their brother Birger, and
particularly of the chivalrous Eric, who, it is said, saved his
wife Ingeborg's life in a shipwreck off the island of Öland
shortly before Birgitta's birth.   Both of them were
Folkungar, that is to say, reckless in their family quarrels,
but the cruel revenge taken on them by their brother Birger
awakened the utmost horror and compassion among the
people throughout the North.

Birgitta's father, of whose name hers is, of course, a dimi-
nutive, was a man of great piety, and was a large benefactor to churches and convents, and made a pilgrimage as
far as to St. James of Compostella.   From him she clearly
inherited much besides her name.   Such striking features
in her character as her love of law and law-making, which
appears in the rule of her order, and in her general desire for
orderliness ; her tendency to utter decisive judgments, often
in tones of great severity and without respect of persons ;

---

[12] Cp. Lydia Wahlström: *Den heliga Birgitta*, Stockholm,
1905, p. 4 : " Den heliga Birgitta är den enda historiska personlighet under Sveriges medeltid, med hvilken vi kunna känna
oss stå öga mot öga, hvars själslif vi kunna studera i minsta
detalj och hvars lefnadsvanor vi kunna sluta oss till."

[13] See the table in *S. R. S.*, Vol. III.[2], p. 189.   The name
" Israel " seems to have been much in fashion in this family.

the tendency also to oppose the crown in politics, and to take the side of the nobility, and, lastly, the love of pilgrimage and of pious foundations—all these seem traceable to him.   From her mother she inherited both the hardness and the chivalry of the Folkunga character—the hardness shown often towards herself, the chivalry in many of her conceptions of religious life, in which she likens Christ to a noble warrior, and holds up the crusading knight to greater honour than the monk.   It may be traced also in her favouritism towards her son Karl, and her joy when her son Birger was knighted at Jerusalem.   The images of the whole family, including Birgitta, are still to be seen in the brass which is the oldest monument in Upsala Cathedral.[14]

Birgitta was naturally proud and ambitious, with a very strong will, and a powerful imagination, and (as I have said) a certain hardness, which she learnt to use towards herself quite as much as to others.   Probably her character was fixed in the years of childhood, passed first in her father's dark and rather dull country house of Finstad, in Eastern Upland, and, after her mother's death (1314), under her maternal aunt at Aspnäs in East Gothland, some thirty miles from Vadstena.   She became used to the society and conversation of religious men, and, happily, she seems to have fallen in with remarkably good ones, who, in succession, were devoted to her.   She was accustomed to hear legends and religious books read, and to discuss religious questions.   Quite as a child she began to have visions.   The two which impressed her most were the gift of a crown pressed upon her head, which she felt exactly fitted it, and some words spoken to her by the Saviour from His cross.   When she was thirteen years old both she and her younger sister Katharine were married to sons of Gudmar, lagman of Nerike, who belonged to the same party as her father.   Birgitta's husband, Ulf, was only eighteen, and her strong will largely moulded and controlled his.   He joined her in her religious exercises

[14] It is figured in *S. H.*[2], fig. 179.

and mortifications, and learnt to say the " hours " of the
Virgin with her, while she took care not to press him too
hard, and encouraged him to study books of law and justice, so that he might better discharge the duties of his
office. He succeeded his father as lagman of Nerike, but
they generally lived at Ulfåsa in East Gothland.

In one instance he took his own way in giving their
daughter Märta in marriage to Seved Ribbing—a rough
hard man whom Birgitta generally calls " the robber."
But, on the whole, Ulf was a man of excellent and honest
character, a good knight and a good man of business.

Amongst her particular occupations, probably begun at
Finstad, a high place was given to the reading of the Bible,
which she caused to be translated at least in part into
Swedish for her use.

It is interesting to know that she was not alone in her use
of the Bible, for King Magnus Ericsson, who succeeded
his uncle, Birger, " possessed a great book of the Bible in
Swedish."[15]

Some time in her married life Birgitta seems to have resided at the court as " court-mistress " to Blanche of
Namur, Queen of Magnus.   Her judgment on both the
gay young king and queen was very severe, and was perhaps dictated by her partisanship in politics—although
Magnus was son of Duke Eric, whom her father had followed.[16]   What is astonishing is that a woman should have
been bold enough, in this age, to take so decided a line in
politics in such a country as Sweden.

[15] Wetzer and Welte: *Realenc*, s.v. *Bibelübersetzungen*, p.
768.   This was probably the Pentateuch.   It is mentioned in
his will, dated 1340.   This and other pre-Reformation versions
were printed by Klemming in *Svenska medeltidens Bibel-
arbeten*, 2 vols.   Stkh., 1848—1855.

[16] For an interpretation of the passages in her revelations
touching the king and queen, which are contained in the
appendix *Extravagantes* 80, and in lib. iv., ch. 3, etc., we may
refer to *Commentarii historici super nonnullis Rev. S. Birgittæ*
in *Scr. rer. Suec.* III.[2], 16-20.   In *Extrav.* 59 Birgitta tells
a story about a box of relics given to her when she was " magi-
stra Reginæ Blancæ quondam Reginæ Sueciæ."

After the birth of their eight children (five of whom lived to grow up) Ulf and his wife visited the tomb of St. James at Compostella. On their way back Ulf fell ill at Arras, and Birgitta had a revelation of his recovery in a vision of St. Denis, patron of France—a vision which also spoke of a new life and work for herself. Ulf came home, but only to die (†1344) in the Cistercian monastery of Alvastra. On his death-bed he placed a ring on her finger as a reminder that she was to pray continually for his soul. Their friends were astonished to notice that in a few days she had given up wearing it. She declared that she felt the ring to be a clog binding her to the remembrance of earthly joys, and, though she had loved Ulf with her whole soul, she now intended to give her love wholly to God, and so she ended: "I will forget both the ring and my spouse" (*S. R. S.*, III., 2, 227). The first years after Ulf's death were spent in quiet retirement at Alvastra and in intimate friendship with the clergy there.

Shortly after it came her first distinct revelation. Our Lord appeared to her and said:—"Thou art my bride and the channel between myself and mankind. Thou shalt hear and behold spiritual things, and my spirit shall rest on thee till thy last day" (*ibid.* 193-4). Other revelations followed in succession, and the words which Christ or St. Mary or other of the saints spoke to her were written down by her or taken down from her lips and translated into Latin, and considered to be the very words of the speakers. She was a seer and a prophetess rather than a mystic enthusiast. She was throughout filled with a moral purpose like that of the Old Testament prophets, whose language she often recalls to us. Of her seven hundred revelations only three or four were corporal, or hallucinations of the senses (*I.S.L.H.*, i. 70).

Her first amanuensis was an excellent man and a good Latin scholar, Master Mathias, Canon of Linköping, the best theologian in Sweden, whose most famous work was *Concordancie super totam Bibliam*, a commentary in three folio volumes. He naturally did some editing, and cut out from the revelations anything that had a heretical or dangerous tendency, but without depriving them of their strong personal flavour.   About half of the books of the revelations passed through his hands.

The trances in which Birgitta's revelations were given came upon her suddenly, and generally in prayer.   Once when she was riding to what was then the king's house at Vadstena, she turned her thoughts to God, and in a moment she passed into an ecstasy, and lost consciousness.   She saw before her a great staircase, above which sat our Lord as judge, surrounded by saints and angels.   Half way up the stairs was a learned monk, whom she knew quite well. His face had a diabolic expression, and he put a succession of puzzling questions to Christ, who answered him calmly and without anger.

Meanwhile a servant rushed forward and grasped her horse's reins, and, after an hour, she returned to consciousness.   She remembered every word she had heard, and dictated it in Swedish to her confessor, who turned it into Latin.   This vision occupies the fifth book of the revelations, which contains sixteen chapters—an immense effort of memory.   Besides this, the first and second books and part of the rule of her order belong to the Swedish period of her life, as well as some scattered revelations in books six and eight and in the appendix (*Revel. extravagantes*), and probably the prayers.   Sometimes she herself wrote her revelations in Swedish, and the MS. of one or two of them remains written in a firm strong hand (see *I. S. L. H.*, i., p. 96, for a facsimile).

Birgitta was not a Protestant like Wycliffe or Hus, though she denounced the immoral life of priests and monks, and gave advice alike to kings and popes in the form of sharp reproof.   Her attitude to the papacy was thus expressed by herself :—" It is a true Christian belief that the pope, who is without heresy, however much he may be tainted with other sins, nevertheless is not so degraded by these or other bad actions, that he cannot exercise the power to bind and loose souls, which power he has received of God " (*Rev.* lvii., c. 7). On another occasion she heard the Blessed Virgin say that she had two sons, one our Saviour, the other he " who sits in the papal seat, that is the seat of God in the world, if he has obeyed His precepts and loved Him with a perfect charity " (*Rev.* iv. c. 138). This refers to Pope Urban V. Quite at the close of her life, in her last pilgrimage, she declared that it was the duty of the Greek Church to submit to Rome, and threatened it with perpetual slavery if it did not do so (vii. 19).

Dr. Schück, whose account of Birgitta's life is one of the best known to me, compares her to Fra Angelico. She is a poetess, with a keen eye for nature, and yet with a mediæval, not a modern, love of nature. She sees nature " with a background of gold and sky blue." " When one reads her writings," he says, " it is as if one stood on a height with clouds beneath one's feet, the vault of heaven arching over one's head, but without discerning a bit of earth " (*I.S.L.H.* i. 97).

But (as he goes on to say) Birgitta is far from being cold. " In her writings seethes a mystic passion. Childhood's dreams and youth's suppressed enthusiasms return in her revelations coloured by an already ageing woman's powerful imagination. ' My body (she says) is like an untamed colt, and my feelings like the wild birds of the forest ' " (*Rev. extr.* 52). She hears her bridegroom Christ whisper to her :—" If thou desire nothing beside me, if thou despise everything for my sake, not only children and parents, but honour and riches, so shall thy heart be in my heart, and inflamed with love for me, just as dry bushwood is burnt in the fire; and I shall be in thee, so that all worldly things shall become to thee bitter and the pleasures of the flesh as poison " (*Rev.* i. 50).

The following extracts, which I have chosen from those selected and translated (rather too freely) by Hammerich, will give a fair idea of Birgitta's style, and particularly of her eye for nature and her faculty of apt illustration :—

" Christ speaks : The world is like a broad desert, overgrown

9

with woods, so dense and dark, that nobody was able to penetrate through it.   There was only one made road, which ended
in an abyss.   And those who fell into it cried out : O Lord
God, come and help; show us the way, and give light to us who
are waiting for Thee.   In Thee alone is there salvation !   And
this cry has come up to heaven to my ears and touched my heart;
and I came into the desert as a pilgrim, in order to work here
and make a road.   Before me there sounded a voice : Now is the
axe laid to the root of the trees !   This was the voice of the
Baptist who was to prepare the way before me.   And I worked
from sunrise till the hour of rest ; I allowed myself to be
tempted ; I endured hatred and scorn ; I have cut the way to
heaven and cleared the trees and bushes which barred it.   The
sharpest thorns pierced my side, and iron nails wounded my
hands and feet ; my teeth and cheeks were cruelly smitten ;
but I turned not back ; I became the more ardent and went
onward like the animal which, driven by hunger, throws itself on
the hunter, and in its passions, runs the lance into itself, held
towards it by the hunter.   The more zealous man was to
murder me the more zealous I became to suffer for him " (*Rev.*
ii. 15).

"When coal is consumed and the brass is melting in the
fire, the air remains in the bellows nevertheless ; thus also
desire remains in the heart when the time of grace is passed "
(iii. 7).

"Whatever may come in the life hereafter must be indifferent
to me if only I can have my will in this life, so says the man
of the world with a hoarse voice.   Of a truth the humble bee
keeps humming and bumming and stays near the soil " (i. 44).

"The friendship of the world is light as snow, and at the
same time cold as the hoar-frost."

"The world is a poor-house ; there it is dark and dreary, full
of smoke—but what darkens the soul is love of the world—and
full of soot, that is to say, the lust of the flesh.   But thou art
introduced into a society of great people, into the House where
beauty is without blemish, warmth without smoke, sweetness
without disgust " (v. 9).

"With many people the will is like a mill-wheel which remains still and cannot grind, because it has no water.   Therefore break through the milldam of pride, and the water of the
Holy Spirit will be poured out, and will set thy will in motion "
(iv. 97).

"Man longs often for vain honour, which, like the froth of
the sea-wave, rises high like a mountain, but quickly vanishes.

As an owl desires the night so does man ; he hunts after vain things and hates those belonging to eternity " (i. 2; vi. 45).

" There are tears which are like the pouring rain, when man laments his temporal need ; others are like the snow or hail when man weeps after his God, but not out of love and longing, but with an icy cold heart full of fear of hell ; and would be content, be it in heaven or on earth, to find a little place, where he could get rid of the torment and satisfy for ever his desires. On the contrary, those tears which draw the soul to heaven, and heaven to the soul, are like the dew which falls on a rose-leaf.   When man bethinks himself of the love of the Lord and of His cruel and bitter passion ; then the eye is filled with tears which surround the soul as the dew drops lie round the flower ; which refresh the soul and make it fruitful and bring God the Lord into it " (i. 81).

" If the kernel of a date is planted in a fertile soil, it takes root, the palm branches unfold themselves, the tree throws off a beautiful perfume, and its fruit ripens.   So is the thought of the divine Judgment, when it penetrates a heart which has acknowledged its sin ; then the sacrifice of its own will, together with holy exercises, form the stem ; the branches grow by love ; the fruit which ripens under the word of preaching is the joy to proclaim the honour of God " (i. 43).

" The rock gave water when the staff of Moses touched it. Thus flow the tears of repentance when the hard heart is touched by the fear and love of God " (i. 2).

" The rose has a sweet scent, is lovely to look upon, and soft to the touch ; and yet it grows among thorns.   So the good among the bad ; the one cannot be without the other.   Bear thou also with the enemies of Christ, so long as He himself bears with them into that which."

" Love changes the beloved one into that which he loves " (cp. i. 54; vi. 17).

Hammerich thus concludes his selection of passages :—

" The ground thought on which everything rests, her principle of knowledge is the same as in Bernard and Hugo, namely, love. . . . We are changed into that which we love ; by love God is enclosed in the soul ; being loved, He is comprehended as the externally present One, and thus is He, and in Him His creation, enjoyed by us.

" Where the fulness of love is there is also knowledge ; he who loves sees God in everything.   But all true love rests on a thorough discernment of that which is loved by the loving one himself. The consciousness of this never leaves our Birgitta, and keeps her soul from that inclination of German mysticism, to lose itself in the divine formless nothing.''

And not only does Birgitta, in distinction from other mystics, preserve this sense of the persistence of her own personality, but she has a particular perception of beauty, as an attribute of God. This, says Hammerich, is peculiar to her among such writers (p. 209). It appears emphatically in her descriptions of our Saviour, and of the Blessed Virgin Mary. She assigned to the latter a very high place in the dispensation of God's grace and believed (with the Franciscans, not the Dominicans) in her immaculate conception. One of the most strikingly beautiful of her revelations is the vision of her son Karl's judgment in which the Virgin Mother appeared to reinforce his own mother's prayers in the struggle for his soul between good and evil powers (*Rev.* vii. 13, Partridge's *Life of St. B.*, pp. 231-7). This, in one form or another, was her special consolation on the pilgrimage to Jerusalem. To any mother who reads these revelations it will probably appear the most wonderful of all.

But the personal and spiritual elements are by no means the only ones. Her revelations often extended to practical matters and those of political importance. It was in a considerable measure due to her that the king, Magnus Ericsson, prosecuted his design of a war against the Russians in 1348. In the strife which followed between king and nobles she naturally took the part of the latter, and she even uttered revelations which advised the king's deposition. One of these, which gives us a darker picture of the king's character than any other historical document known to us, declares that God would drive the king and his whole house from the throne, and set on it a native Swede, who should guide the land in accordance with the will of God (*Rev. extrav.*, 80). By this she is supposed to have meant her own son, Karl Ulfsson, a man of pleasant and attractive manners, but apparently quite unfit for any great position.

§ 15.—Her ambition to bring back the Pope to Rome
  and to found an Order.   Characteristics of
  the Order.   Vadstena.   Journey to Rome.
  Life there.   Urban V. returns (1367) and sanc-
  tions her statutes (1370).   Journey to East,
  and death.   Canonized three times, but
  Revelations treated with caution.   Criticism
  at Basel.

She extended her messages to other European princes,
and she felt herself commissioned to declare in the name of
Christ that those two ferocious beasts, the kings of England and France, were to make peace on the basis of a
marriage, that so the kingdom might descend to the lawful
heir (*Rev.* iv. 104 and 105.   Cp. *Rev.* vi. 34 and 63, to
Pope Clement VII.).

But her chief concern was to bring the popes from Avignon, of the wickedness of which place she may have heard
from her father.   The exile of the papacy from Italy for
seventy years was very distasteful to all good churchfolk,
at least outside France.   In England it was made a reason
for the non-payment of the customary tribute and of Peter's-
pence.   Even in Sweden it provoked resentment.   Two
years after her husband's death Birgitta received a revelation, in which Christ thus spake to her :—" Go to Rome:
for there the streets are paved with everlasting gold; that
is, the blood of the martyrs and saints.   There, by the
merits of the saints and the absolution of the pope, lies the
shortest way to heaven.   In Rome thou shalt remain until
thou hast seen the pope and the emperor " (*S.R.S.* III. 2
202).

She wrote to the then pope, Clement VI. (1342—1352),
the implacable enemy of the Emperor Lewis, urging him
to break the fetters of his Babylonish captivity, and to return to the capital of Christendom.   The failure of her
entreaties, combined with other impulses, such as the wish
to attend the jubilee of 1350 and the desire to promote the
interests of her proposed order, led her to take her journey

to Rome—a journey from which she never returned. She
set out in the autumn of 1349.[17]

Her confessor, Mathias, was absent with the king as his
adviser on the Russian crusade, to which Birgitta had in-
cited him.   This was a foolish and fatal expedition, in
which Magnus treated the Russians as if they were heathen,
and pressed Latin baptism and allegiance to the pope upon
them at the sword's point, only to suffer loss, to return to
his country loaded with debt, and to meet the great plague
of 1350.   Mathias died shortly after his return.

Birgitta had, however, two other excellent friends and
companions, Petrus Olai, prior of the monastery of
Alvastra, and another priest of the same name, Magister
Petrus Olai, head of the Holy Ghost's Hospital at
Skeninge.   The latter was her confessor in place of Master
Mathias, though he was much inferior to Mathias as a
theologian and a scholar.

I have already indicated the objects of her journey and
ambition, especially her personal desire to found a new religious order, from which should grow the regeneration of
mankind.   She desired to be the equal of the great men
whose foundations had given them such renown and reputation for saintliness as to dim the glories of conquerors
and statesmen.   Magnus Ericsson had already fallen in
with her plan, and gave great gifts and grants to it, including the estate of Vadstena, which was well situated for the
central position she wished her order to occupy.   It was
placed half way down the eastern side of Lake Vettern,
behind the Omberg, and was naturally visited by all
travellers passing from one province of Gothland to the
other.   But, before this plan could be executed, it was
necessary to obtain the sanction of the pope.

[17] See *Rev.* book v., ch. 12, near the end of the book, which
shows the difficulties she had to contend with in Sweden.   Mrs.
Partridge's *Life of St. Bridget* makes her arrive in Rome in the
spring of 1347 (p. 88), and be a witness of Rienzi's election to
the tribunate in May (April?) of that year (pp. 96-7); but this
does not seem to agree with the other evidence of the date of her
journey.

The peculiar feature of the plan was one which naturally arose from Birgitta's own experience of the value of co-operation between men and women. Her " Order of the Holy Saviour " was to be lodged in a double-cloister. It was to be " first and principally " for women, but a certain body of men, mostly priests, was to be settled beside it The two bodies were hardly to meet except in church, and even then were not to see one another, but each sex was to supply its proper gifts for the advantage of the whole. The idea was not a new one, having been carried out in England in Saxon times, and more recently in the twelfth century by St. Gilbert of Sempringham and elsewhere. There were to be thirteen priests to represent the twelve apostles and St. Paul; four deacons to represent the four Latin doctors; eight lay-brothers, and sixty nuns—the deacons, lay-brothers and nuns forming a body of seventy-two to represent the Lord's evangelists. No nun was to be admitted younger than eighteen years; no man under twenty-five. Entrance was to be after repeated requests during a year's probation. The nuns were admitted with a marriage ring and crown, but carried out of church upon a bier. An open grave in the cloister and a coffin in the church were perpetual reminders of death. The rules as to fasting and poverty were, however, not too strict. Vadstena itself was in the diocese of Linköping, and subject to the bishop of that see —as the other houses were to the diocesan bishops. All this and much else was supposed to be matter of divine revelation. The object of the order was naturally not merely the edification of the members, but the promotion of learning and education, and the instruction of the people by popular preaching in the mother tongue. Attention was also paid to improved methods of cultivation, and to various kinds of husbandry and home industry, such as lace-making, which is still carried on at Vadstena.

With these two plans in mind Birgitta journeyed southwards, and reached Rome after a difficult journey. Here she was joined, after a time, by her son Birger and her daughter Katharine, and by other travellers from Sweden. Her revelations took the form of prophetic warnings addressed to Rome and to the popes, and to various leaders of the Church; but usually her life was a quiet well-ordered and serious round of study, devotion, careful meal-times and ministry to the poor. She was much too independent to enter a monastery, for, while she desired to live by rule, she did not wish to live under rule. She never even wore the habit of her own order. The city was distracted by the factions of the Orsini and the Colonna families, and was sometimes hardly safe to move in. She was protected by one of the Orsini family, and in time got a house lent her, which, after a while, became a priory of her order, and the agency of Vadstena, and almost of Sweden in Rome. It is near the Campo di Fiore and is still shown. She had a long and tedious time of waiting before her vision was fulfilled. Clement VI., and his successor, Innocent VI., lived and died at Avignon. At last, in 1367, she had the joy of seeing Urban V. enter Rome, and the Emperor Charles IV. came for a time in the next year. Urban showed her great favour, and in 1370 sanctioned the statutes of her order, though only " per modum constitutionum," as a branch of the Augustinians, and gave her many privileges. But he left Italy in September of that year, and Birgitta prophesied his death, which took place in Avignon after a few months. This event immensely increased her reputation as a prophetess. She now wished to fulfil her long-cherished design to visit Palestine. In 1372 she started on this pilgrimage, passing Naples, where her son Karl, a married man, boldly made love to the queen—Joanna—a lady of no good record—much to Birgitta's distress. But he died there, much to her relief, and, as she supposed, in answer to her prayers. I have already spoken of the consolation which she received in visions of the rescue of his soul in the other world. She went on with Birger, who was made a knight of the Holy Sepulchre at Jerusalem. Her strong

will struggled with sickness on the journey, and her revelations continued, and were extended to Cyprus and to the
prelates of the Greek Church. She lived to return to Rome,
and there breathed her last with great piety and trust the
23rd July, 1373. She did not foresee that a younger saint
than herself, Catharine of Siena, a friend of her own
daughter Katharine, would be more successful, and actually
would procure the return of Pope Gregory XI. only a few
years later. Birgitta herself was canonized in 1391 by Boniface IX. But, inasmuch as this took place during the great
schism, the interests of the order, which was subject to a
good deal of jealousy and suspicion, both theological and
practical, required a further confirmation of her sanctity,
and of the value of her revelations. The question of the
authority to be attached to the latter was raised at the Council of Constance in 1415 by the greatest theologian of the
day, John Gerson, Chancellor of the University of Paris,
in a tract written for the purpose, which he entitled *De
probatione spirituum* (*Opera*, t. i. 37-43, Antverpiæ,
1706). He notices the difficulty involved in either approv-
ing or rejecting her revelations, and complains that they
were not properly before the council for the purpose of
examination.

The eleventh *consideration* of this tract seems to be
especially directly against Birgitta. It warns the council
of the danger of a woman having long conversations with
her confessor under pretext of frequent confession, and
prolix narration of her visions, or any other excuse for excessive talking. "There is scarcely any other plague
which is more effective to do mischief or more hard to
heal," he exclaims, and then goes on to quote Virgil's
description of Dido's dangerous conversations with
Aeneas. The University of Oxford was also concerned
to oppose the multiplicity of canonizations. Birgitta's
second canonization was, however, solemnly performed by
Pope John XXIII., who had already issued an immense
bull, generally called, from its size, *Mare magnum*, the

1st May, 1413, in favour of the order, and this act was confirmed by the council in 1415.[18]

This, however, was not considered sufficient, and a fresh confirmation, both of the canonization and the privileges of the order was demanded and supplied by Pope Martin V. at Florence in 1419.[19]

All opposition was not, however, even then overcome, and the defenders of the order had to meet even more strenuous criticism at the Council of Basel in 1433, when 123 passages from the revelations were attacked.   The Roman Church then and later prudently refused to commit itself to the defence and sanction of all the revelations, though expressions were used asserting that Birgitta possessed a prophetic spirit, and was moved by divine grace.   Pope Benedict XIV., in his book *On the Canonization of Saints* (ii. 32), sums up the judgment of the Latin Church that they may be read for edification, but are in no sense matters of faith.[20]   The " ad instar " indulgences—which it was hoped would make a pilgrimage to Vadstena equal to one to " St. Peter ad vincula " in Rome, or to the Portiuncula at Assisi—were also withdrawn and not restored.

§ 16.—VALUE OF VADSTENA TO SWEDEN.   UNHAPPY
      CAREER OF MAGNUS ERICSSON.   HIS UNPOPU-
      LARITY.   REIGN OF ALBREKT OF MECKLENBURG.
      BO JÖNSSON GRIP, DROTSET OR STEWARD.

Although the Order of the Holy Saviour did not regenerate the world, and did not even acquire the same privi-

[18] Celsii *Bullarium*, p. 165, cp. L'Enfant *Concile de Constance*, I., p. 103.   The bull may be found in *Svenskt diplomatarium* (1401 onwards), II., 1714.   Cp. T. Höjer: *Vadstena Klosters . . . . Historia*, pp. 165-6, Upsala, 1905.

[19] See fuller details on most of these points in T. Höjer: l.c., p. 180 foll.   He speaks of the house given by Francisca de Papazuris and afterwards used as a hospitium for Swedish pilgrims (pp. 120-2).

[20] See Hefele: *Councils*, § 794.

leges as the Franciscan, it did great service to Sweden, and even to England, where the nuns of Syon did honour to the memory of their founder, King Henry V., and even now keep up a small house in Devonshire. The mother house of Vadstena was the centre of the religious life of Sweden and of its higher education. To it we may ascribe a great influence in forming the noble character of most of the Swedish ladies of the fifteenth and sixteenth centuries; for those who were not educated there were almost all interested in the convent of Vadstena, and on friendly terms with its inmates.

Its library was a remarkable one, and still forms an important portion of the university collection at Upsala. Its preachers went everywhere through the country, preaching in the mother tongue. From it issued (though doubtless in few copies) the first Swedish versions of the Scriptures and translations of famous mystical books and sermons. Its chronicle, the *Diarium Vazstenense*,[21] which covers the period from 1344 to 1545—just two centuries—is not only an indispensable document for Swedish history, but gives a picture of a quiet religious life, which it is very comforting to contemplate. The Church historian, Reuterdahl, writes of it with more than usual display of feeling in speaking of the moral and religious character of the Union period. After confessing that we have many evidences of mischief, both among the clergy and in the convents, he adds that we have also many which witness to inward piety, and deep reverence for Christ and His work on earth. " If anyone doubts this let him simply read without prejudice the old meagre inventories of gifts, and the registers of benefactions, and the monastic chronicles. Let him especially read through the Diary of Vadstena. Simple but warm faith and inward and humble love may be read there in almost every line. It would be unjust not to read it."[22]

[21] Printed in the first volume of the *Scriptores rerum Suecicarum*, Upsala, 1818.
[22] *Svenska Kyrkans Historia*, Vol. iii., pt. 2, p. 395, Lund.

So deeply rooted was Vadstena in the affections of the people that it lasted throughout the period of the Reformation, and was not closed till 1595, by order of Duke Charles, when it was a home of disaffection and conspiracy.   The other houses of the order had mostly disappeared, but four still remain, Altomünster in Bavaria, two in Holland, and one, as I have said, in England.   The houses at Valladolid and elsewhere in Spain are revivals, not survivals.

During Birgitta's absence in Rome the reign of King Magnus closed in Sweden with a period of great misery and unpopularity.   He returned from his Russian crusade, as I have said, loaded with debt, only to meet the calamity of the great plague of 1350—a plague which pressed with special severity upon the clergy.   A similar scourge appeared in 1360, which fell particularly upon the children. Magnus was especially unpopular on account of his unworthy favourite, Bengt Algotsson, and because of his retrocession to Denmark of the provinces of Halland, Skåne and Blekinge, which had revolted to Sweden early in his reign.   His object, of course, was to purchase the support of Denmark in his struggle with his son Eric and his subjects.   He was deposed in 1363 by the party with whom Birgitta was acting, and, after an imprisonment of some years, he retired with his son Haco to Norway, where he enjoyed a higher reputation than in Sweden.   His sister's son, Albrekt of Mecklenburg, was elected in his place, and had a precarious tenure of the crown—making himself very unpopular by the number and character of his German followers.   During Albrekt's reign Sweden was practically governed by a nobleman, Bo Jönsson Grip—so called because his arms were a Griffin's head—who was lord over two-thirds of the mainland and the whole of Finland, who oppressed the country in the king's name.   He bore the title of Drotset, or Drots, which may be rendered steward, or seneschal of the realm.[23]   After his death Albrekt tried

[23] See Ducange : s.v. *Drossatus*, which is rendered in Latin " Dapifer " and " Dapifer," again " Seneschal." But " Steward " is the word used in the English translation of

to govern more for himself, but he was conquered and treated with ignominy by the Danish princess, Margaret, widow of Haco, in 1389, and thus the once brilliant Folkunga dynasty came to an inglorious end.

DETACHED NOTE.—ON THE AUTHORITIES FOR THE LIFE AND CHARACTER OF ST. BIRGITTA AND HER LITERARY RELATIONS.

The earliest Life is that by her two later companions, Magister Peter and Peter the Prior, written in 1373 : this is the most important source next to the revelations themselves. It may be found in *Scr. rer. Suec.*, III., 2, pp. 185-206. The revelations were first printed at Lübeck in 1492. MSS. exist in various libraries even in England, as at Balliol, Merton and Magdalen Colleges in Oxford, and Lincoln Cathedral, but none of these are complete. The best English MS. is, I believe, in the British Museum, Harleianus 612, which belonged to Syon. This also contains the partly unpublished *Processus Canonizationis*, which is also found in MSS. of the Royal Library at Stockholm, and of the Vatican. Part of it is published in *S. R. S.*, III., 2, 218-40. There is an interesting copy of Koberger's edition, Nuremberg, September, 1521, in Lambeth Palace Library. It belonged to the monastery of Syon, and was given at the petition of David Curson, "a brother professed . . . by the consent of the reverent father and all hys brethern," to Mr. John Doo, of the College of Fotheringham, on condition that he should pray for the company of the said monastery, and leave it to the common use of the college aforesaid. I have myself used Durantus' full and convenient edition, printed with the revelations of SS. Hildegard and Elizabeth, Cologne, 1628.

Of modern books I have used Schück *Ill. Sv. lit. hist.*, H. Lundström *Birgitta* in *P.R.E.*[3], Vol. 3 ; Dr. F. Hammerich (of Copenhagen) *St. Birgitta*, German translation by A. Michelsen, Gotha, 1872 ; G. Binder *Die heilige Birgitta von Schweden*, München, 1891 ; Lydia Wahlström *Den heliga Birgitta*, Stockholm, 1905; Höjer : *Vadstena Klosters . . . . Historia*, Upsala, 1905, and MS. notes generously supplied by Mr. Knut B. Westman, of Upsala, who is writing a monograph on the subject. I believe that the latest and fullest biography is one by Hans Hildebrand, published about six years ago in *Svenska Akademiens Handlingar*, but I have not had access to it.

Geijer's History, and is familiar to us from the history of Scotland, where the Stewards or Stuarts became kings.

There is an English Life (*The Life of St. Bridget of Sweden*, by the late Mrs. F. J. M. A. Partridge, Burns and Oates, London, 1888), which only professes to be a condensation of the book of a German nun published at Mayence.   This latter is *Leben der Heiligen Birgitta von Schweden von einer Klosterfrau der ewigen Anbetung zu Mainz* [der Abtissin Maria Bernardina], 1st ed. Mainz, 1875, 2nd ed., 1888.   It is intended for edification, and must be read with this qualification in mind. But it is brightly written, and well conveys the feeling and spirit of the old authorities.   It also gives references to the books and chapters of the revelations which more pretentious books sometimes lack.   Mr. Westman has also most kindly helped me to identify a number of them.

As regards the literary relations of St. Birgitta the following letter from Mr. Westman will be read with interest :—

SYSSLOMANSGATAN 16, UPSALA, SWEDEN,

27th *March*, 1910.

RIGHT REVEREND SIR,

Professor Söderblom has asked me to tell you what is known about the books Birgitta owned or studied, especially with reference to a possible literary influence on her from some of the earlier mystics.   Unfortunately the notices in this respect are very few and not very significant.   She has surely known the following books :—

> The Bible ; Historiæ Scholasticæ (which I suppose to be the Historia Scholastica by Petrus Comestor); Dialogus Gregorii ; Vitæ patrum ; Pseudo-Bernhard, Liber de modo bene vivendi ; and Speculum Virginum (an ascetic book, later on translated into Swedish, now edited by Geete, Stockholm, 1897-8).

There is scarcely anything more to mention, if not some Italian heretical and apocalyptic books—no doubt emanating from the Fraticelli—which she disapproves (III., 33; VI., 68, 67).

So there is no explicit trace of any literary influence from any of the earlier female mystics.   To the question whether any such influence on the text of the revelations—for instance, from Gertrude, or either of the two Mechtilds—is, on inner reasons, to be supposed, I would personally answer in the negative.   At least, no such influence is needed to explain those rather un-literary writings of Birgitta.   If there can be found any detail, a thought or parable or something like that, that could be best explained by supposing such an influence (a possibility which I do not deny, though I have not found any), it must always be remembered that Birgitta and the above-named mystics are religious types of a very different kind. They are ecstatic, with their visions centred around a bridal mysticism on the lines of Bernhard's Sermones in Canticum, partly (Mechtild of Magdeburg) also devoted to the metaphysical trend of Dionysius Areopagita and the Victorines. She, even in her visions, is prophetical and practical, intent on finding and interpreting the intensely active and world-reforming will of God. To this type belongs, for instance, Savonarola, and, in some degree also, Hildegard of Bingen.—Believe me, yours very respectfully,

KNUT B. WESTMAN.

IV.

The Romanized Church under the Union Sovereigns
(1389 a.d.—1520 a.d.)

*Margaret, Eric of Pomerania, Christopher of Bavaria,
Karl Knutsson, Christian I., John and Christian
II.*

LECTURE IV.

THE ROMANIZED CHURCH UNDER THE UNION SOVEREIGNS (1389—1520).

§ 1.—MARGARET AND ERIC OF POMERANIA.

The history of the Union period is particularly important for our subject, as exhibiting the bishops, especially the Archbishop of Upsala, in the enjoyment of the fullest secular power, and so preparing the way for that reaction against the excessive wealth and independence of the Church, which was a very marked feature of the Swedish Reformation.

Queen Margaret was a Danish princess of great ability, goodness and beauty—her face may still be seen in the abbey of Roskilde—and she was acceptable in Sweden as a pupil of St. Birgitta's daughter, Märta. She was acknowledged as sovereign by the whole of Scandinavia at the Union of Kalmar 20th July, 1397. Experience of the misery caused by the constant warfare between the three kingdoms and the knowledge of their kinship and common interests naturally suggested the union, which was favoured by the accident of her unique position and by the admiration of her fine personal character. By the terms of the union each country was to be governed by its own laws, and fugitives from one were not to be protected in another, while each was to be allied with the others for mutual defence. Doubtless both enmity of Germany and jealousy and fear of Russia favoured the union, although the terms on which it was concluded were not at the time publicly known. It was at first accepted passively.

It was further agreed that Margaret should be succeeded in wearing the triple crown by her grand-nephew, Eric of Pomerania, who was at the time of the union in his sixteenth year. He was crowned at Stockholm in the next year (1398). This king is interesting to us from his marriage (in 1406) with Philippa, an English princess, daughter of our Henry IV., who was distinguished at once for her gentleness, her intelligence, and her courage. Unfortunately her marriage was childless; and it was rendered unhappy by her husband's misconduct. Nevertheless, she was of great service to Sweden as regent during his absence. Like the other royal ladies of Sweden, she attached herself to Vadstena, and it was clearly through her and one of her English companions that the Birgittines were introduced into England. The Diary of Vadstena mentions the name of " Henry Rawinzwatt " as coming in the year of the marriage, to ask for brethren to be sent to England. This, to us, rather strange designation, covers the name of a well-known person, Henry Fitzhugh, third Lord Fitzhugh, a great traveller, who was advanced to the office of constable of England on the coronation of Henry V., and was father of a Bishop of London.[1]

As long as Margaret lived Eric's faults were to a great extent controlled and concealed. Her chief fault, in the eyes of the Swedes, was that she considered herself as a Dane, and Denmark as the head of the union kingdom, and that she governed Sweden through Danish noblemen. Eric, however, regarded himself as a German, which was worse; and he had neither the ability for government nor the character of Margaret. He was a man of very inconsistent nature, learned and accomplished according to the standard of the times, and not without religious impulses and interests, but headstrong, obstinate and vain, lax in morals, and determined to use the power of the Church for secular ends. Much of his long reign was spent in vain

[1] See detached note at the end of this lecture. " Rawinzwatt," in Swedish books, is also called " Ravenswather " (*Sv. H.*[1], 2 p. 163). It perhaps means " Ravensworth," though I have not identified the name in connection with Fitzhugh. He married Elizabeth, heiress of Sir Robert Grey, of Rotherfield-Grays, Co. Oxon. See for some notices of them Collins' *Peerage*, ix., 467. Henry Fitzhugh, " noster Camerarius," was one of the witnesses to Henry V.'s deed of foundation of Syon on his manor of Isleworth, in the parish of Twickenham, Middlesex.

attempts to get hold of the German provinces of Pomerania and Slesvig, to which he had some claim, and he governed, or tried to govern, Sweden with German bailiffs, who treated the free Swedish peasantry with the contempt and roughness which German barons used towards their own folk.

We are, of course, specially concerned with Eric's interference in the Church, for which opportunity was given by the uncertainty as to who was the true pope. Already, in 1409, before Margaret's death, he offended the clergy by forcing his Danish chancellor, Johannes Jerechini,[2] into the Archbishopric of Upsala, and obliging the Chapter of Strengnäs to accept Andreas, the archbishop-elect, who was thus displaced, instead of their own dean, Georgius, whom they had elected. One rival pope, Gregory XII., confirmed Andreas; the other, Alexander V., confirmed Georgius. The latter, being opposed by the king, had to give way, and thus both the bishopric and the papacy were turned into the tools of a secular intrigue.

The chancellor-archbishop was so hated that he had at length to leave the kingdom. He became Bishop of Skalholt, in Iceland, where he also became unpopular, and was, in consequence, drowned by the people. After his removal King Eric was on better terms with the Chapter of Upsala, who submitted to him three names, from which he chose one, that of his own confessor, Brother Johannes Haquini of Vadstena. But, on the death of Haquini in 1432, a bitter conflict again arose. The king asserted that the archbishop could not be chosen without his consent, since he was the first councillor of the sovereign and of the realm, and the chief man in the kingdom when he himself was absent.[3] He, therefore, refused to accept Olaus Laurentii,

---

[2] It appears to be the Swedish custom to distinguish clerical persons by Latin names, even to a much later date, while laymen are described in Swedish. Although the custom is not universal, it is convenient, and so I have written Birger Persson for the layman, and Birgerus Gregorii for the archbishop, etc., etc. I have, however, not always been consistent.

[3] See Reuterdahl: III., 2, p. 16; cp. Celsii: *Bullarium*, 180-1.

who was chosen by the chapter, and tried to force on them his own man, Arend, or Arnoldus, Bishop of Bergen, a person of bad character.   On Arnoldus' death the king pressed another man of his own choice, Thorlak, a Norwegian; but the quarrel was suspended on account of the peasant rising under Engelbrekt, which, in the end, caused the king's downfall.

§ 2.—ENGELBREKT'S RISING (1433—1436). ITS PERMANENT RESULTS. KARL KNUTSSON AND THOMAS OF STRENGNÄS.

Engelbrekt Engelbrektsson,[4] the leader of this rising (1433), is the William Tell of Sweden.   He was a true patriot, and a worthy national hero.   He was just the sort of leader whom the people needed, a wealthy mine owner, and a member of one of the lesser noble families or gentry of the province of Nerike, in the chief town of which, Örebro, he was born.   His heart was stirred by the treatment of the free Swedish peasants, as if they were dogs or cattle, rather than human beings, on the part of the foreign bailiffs, and in particular the treatment of the Dalesmen of the neighbouring province by a Danish nobleman, Jösse Ericsson.   Jösse lived at Vesterås, but had authority over great parts of Vestmanland, Bergslagen and Dalarne.   He was accused, apparently truly, of forcing the peasants into obedience by hanging them up in the smoke of a fire and yoking their wives to their own hay-carts (för hölass). The rising, though it began in Dalarne, soon extended over the whole country, and it was remarkable for the rapidity of its success and the good conduct of the insurgents.   It was said that not a housewife lost a fowl.   It seemed a movement inspired by God, so that Bishop Thomas of

[4] There is a good popular account of Engelbrekt by Professor S. J. Boëthius in Heimdal's *Folkskrifter*, 1893.   The poem, *Engelbrekt och Karl Knutsson*, attributed to Bishop Thomas of Strengnäs, may be found in full in *Medeltids Dikter och Rim*, published by the Sv. Fornskrift Sällskapet, pp. 385-390, Stkh., 1881—1882.

Strengnäs does not scruple to write about it in his poem, entitled " Engelbrekt and Karl Knutsson " :—

> God roused up that little man Engelbrekt,
> Who had slight skill the work to direct ;
> He gave him might and wit.
> Castles and cities, folk, counties and lands
> Fell all right quickly into his hands ;
> As God willed He ordered it.

For three years this hero became the most powerful man in Sweden, and its true ruler. His great achievement was the winning of the Council of State, which he found sitting at Vadstena in East Gothland on its return from Copenhagen. He marched into the room, leaving his followers outside, and dealt straightly with its members, and in particular with the bishops. He first seized (we are told) Bishop Knut of Linköping by the throat, and threatened to drag him out to the people. He made as if he would treat Bishop Sigge of Skara in like manner. Bishop Thomas of Strengnäs, afterwards his great friend and elegist, was also in trouble. He persuaded the council, then and there, to write a letter, dated 16th August, 1434, to King Eric, renouncing his authority. The rebellion succeeded so well that in the next year, 1435, Engelbrekt was elected administrator of the kingdom at the Diet of Arboga. Unfortunately, however, the patriotism of the nobles was of short duration. They made terms of some sort with Eric, by which he was to rule through Swedish noblemen ; and the titles of steward and marshal were revived—the first being given to an old man, Christer Nilsson Vasa, and the second to a young and popular knight, Karl Knutsson Bondé, who was the rival of Engelbrekt in the affections of the people.

Christer Nilsson is interesting to us as the direct ancestor of King Gustaf Ericsson Vasa. The family acquired the name Vasa from the charge on their shield, a faggot or fascine used to fill up a ditch in storming a fortress. Christer's son-in-law, Bengt Jönsson Oxenstierna, was himself administrator in 1448, and father of the famous archbishop, Johannes Benedicti, who was administrator in 1457 and 1465. Christer was also grandfather in the male line of Ketillus Caroli Vasa, Bishop of Linköping, who was administrator in 1464. The Vasa family was at first Danish in sympathies, but it was reconciled to the nationalist party by the marriage of John Christersson with Brita, a daughter of Gustaf Sture, and a niece of Karl Knutsson's.[5] Engelbrekt was not elected administrator a second time, but the office was given to Karl Knutsson, much to the disappointment of many of Engelbrekt's followers. Engelbrekt, none the less, went on labouring for the public good, though with weakened health and spirits. He was, however, foully murdered in April 1436, by a nobleman whom he had, as administrator, checked in a course of piracy, but who now approached him seemingly as a friend.[6]

This murder ranks with the other public tragedies which have profoundly affected the national imagination, and few victims of revenge have more deserved popular sympathy than this good man. He was buried in his native town, where his memory and example, without doubt, appealed to the two foremost leaders of the Swedish Reformation of the sixteenth century, which was so closely connected with the reaction against foreign tyranny. The brothers, Olaus and Laurentius Petri, were, like Engelbrekt, born at Örebro. Though Engelbrekt's career was short, it was permanently fruitful. It revived in the peasants a sense of their old position and their power, which they were well-nigh losing, as for a time they quite lost it in Norway, where they had no such leaders to encourage them. It broke down the provincialism of Sweden, and created a fuller sentiment of nationality and of the value of duty to the country, as well as of affection for it. Two great institutions may be said to have grown out of it, the national parliament or Riksdag, and the national Kingship. The

---

[5] See the table of the Vasa family in *Sv. H.*², 2, p. 499. It is more exact than Geijer's account of the family, p. 97.

[6] This was Måns Bengtsson, son of Bengt Stensson, of the family of Natt och Dag. The murder took place on an island on Lake Hjälmar, near the Castle of Göksholm.

meeting at Arboga in 1435, at which Engelbrekt was
elected Rikets höfvidsman, or administrator, was the first
to which not only spiritual and temporal nobles, but one or
more burghers from every town, and some peasants from
every province, were summoned as representatives.   The
parochial clergy were not yet summoned, but in other
respects it was a true Parliament.   The office to which
Engelbrekt was elected was also a new departure.   For
though he was only administrator for one year, he prepared
the way for the Stures, and then for Gustaf Ericsson Vasa,
and finally for the strong-handed measures by which
Charles IX. and Charles XI. broke down the dangerous
privileges of the nobility.[7]   The peasant rising of the
Dalesmen was even more obviously a precedent for that
which assisted Gustaf Vasa in the liberation of the country
some eighty years later.

It is further to be noticed about this rising that only one
instance of revenge on the tyrants who had misgoverned the
people is recorded.   Jösse Ericsson took refuge from the
peasants in the monastery of Vadstena, where he resided
some three years, but in 1436 he was drawn from his retreat
by the East Gothland peasants, taken to Motala, and condemned to death and executed.   He had been a benefactor
to the Church, especially at Vadstena, and his punishment
was considered by zealous Churchmen as an act of
sacrilege.

After Engelbrekt's death, his rival in the affections of
the people, Karl Knutsson, the marshal, remained the
chief man in the kingdom; but the Union party soon took
courage again.   The nobility and the bishops for the most
part were in favour of a foreign ruler, under whose distant
oversight they might develop their own relative independence.   The important representative of Sweden at the
Council of Basel, Nicolaus Ragvaldi, Bishop of Vexiö,
had, indeed, defended Engelbrekt at the council, and he
had won the affection and admiration of Bishop Thomas of
Strengnäs, whose verses in his praise I have already cited.

[7] S. J. Boëthius, l.c., pp. 26-7.

The following rough but spirited lines at the end of his poem deserve to be remembered :—

> Scapes a bird from the fowler's snare
> It will again of such craft beware ;
>   Sweden, now hast thou scapen.[8]
> Wilt thou fall into the snare again,
> Which did so closely thy limbs constrain,
>   And now, maybe, still lies open?
>
> Stand thou firm then, O noble Swede,
> Better that which thy land did need,
>   And turn thee backward never.
> Venture thy neck and venture thy hand
> To ransom thy home, thy fatherland ;
>   God cheer thee in thine endeavour !
>
> Every bird will fight for its nest,
> So too will every savage beast ;
>   Mark then what now doth behove thee.
> God hath given thee sense and soul ;
> Keep freedom ; be not another's thrall—
>   So long as thy limbs can move thee.

Thomas was the first poet in the modern Swedish tongue whose name has come down to us, and he is a man who did honour to the Church both by his character and his talents. His other two poems on Freedom and Faithfulness (Troheten) are also well known.

§ 3.—Retirement of King Eric. Nicolaus Ragvaldi. King Christopher and his land's-law.

The bishops, however, as a body, were not in favour of attempting to set up a national kingship, and it was mainly through the influence of Nicolaus, who became archbishop in 1438, that they secured the election of the King of Denmark, Christopher of Bavaria, on the retirement of Eric,

[8] See for this form Shakespeare's *Pericles*, Act 2 (Gower). The original of these lines may be found in *Medeltids Dikter och Rim*, p. 390, and in Boëthius, l.c., p. 28 ; cp. *S. H.²*, II., pp. 392-3 and 409.   *Friheten* and *Troheten* are in *Medeltids D. o. R.*, pp. 391 foll., and 393 foll.

who was rejected everywhere, except in Gotland. It is characteristic of the times and of the man that for a number of years Eric lived there on the proceeds of piracy, exercised at the expense of his former subjects. He was, however, at last rejected even there, and died in Pomerania in 1459. King Christopher's coronation took place in 1440. Though his administration was weak, he was not unpopular, and his reign was memorable for improvements at least in the form of legislation both in Church and State.

The bishops now gave their consent (in 1442) to the promulgation of the land's-law for the whole of Sweden, which their predecessors had successfully resisted in 1337 in the days of Magnus Ericsson. The law of Christopher was very much the same as that of Magnus, and, in fact, so like it as to mislead many copyists. But, strange to say, it did not even now include the Kyrko-balk or Church code, although the bishops seem to have intended that it should do so; and such a section is generally found in the earlier provincial laws on which the land's-law was founded.[9] The land's-law, I may remark, was sufficiently complete to remain in use with more or less revision up to 1734, although for more than half that period it remained unprinted. The first edition of it was published by the authority of Charles IX. in 1608, who introduced a few modifications into it, besides the obvious one in the interest of his family declaring that the crown devolved " iure successionis," and not " iure electionis."[10]

[9] There is an interesting introduction to the early history of Swedish law by a French professor, Ludovic Beauchet : *Loi de Vestrogothie*, Paris, 1894. See pp. 97 foll. for various opinions as to what took place in 1347. For information as to the Kyrko-balk see p. 102, and for Christopher's land's-law see pp. 108 foll.

[10] I quote from the convenient, if not wholly accurate, version of Loccenius : *Leges provinciales regni Sueciæ*, Lund, 1675. The student who wishes to go deeper must consult the great collection of Schlyter : *Corpus iuris Sveo-gothorum antiqui* (Lund, 1838-1877). Instead of the old *tit.* I., *de Rege*, ch. 3 : "Ad Regnum Sueciæ Rex eligendus est, et non jure successionis assumendus." Charles wrote : "Ad regnum Sveciæ

The land's-law of Christopher states that the king has decided, in consequence of the variety and uncertainty of the laws, at the request of the Archbishop of Upsala and his suffragans, and of that the Royal Council and the nobles, to collect the laws of Sweden into one volume with certain additions.   These additions, as far as they differ from the earlier land's-law, are in favour of the king's prerogative.   The law also reserved all the privileges of churches and ecclesiastical persons.   It contained the provision that no new law was to be introduced into Sweden except with the consent and goodwill of the people (*De rege*, iv., §7).   It was not, however, apparently passed by any public assembly or series of assemblies (except the Royal Council).   This is remarkable since Eric's land's-law had at least been ratified in various provincial assemblies (Beauchet: p. 109).

A few words about the relation of the civil law of Sweden to the Church may be in place here.   There was never that rivalry in Sweden which existed in those other parts of Europe, which had been subject to the Roman Empire, between the canon law and the civil law.   The influence of the canon law dates naturally from the Council of Skeninge, under William of Sabina, in 1248, to which reference has already been made.   It is specially visible in the sections that refer to civil rights, and particularly to personal liberty.   It favoured the enfranchisement of slaves, and exhorted Christians to give it.   Instead of the Roman civil maxim " partus ventrem sequitur," it substituted the rule " a child follows the better half," *i.e.*, if

Rex jure successionis assumendus, non eligendus est." He also refused to confirm the Kyrko-balk as containing papal errors.   He prescribed the application of the divine law (Gudzlagh) to certain capital crimes.   He ordered that if no rule is to be found applicable to a particular case in the law of Christopher or later ordinances, as regards difficult matters (outside those in the Kyrko-balk) recourse may be had to the laws of Upland and East Gothland, which he had published. See Beauchet, l.c., p. 113, and Loccenius, l.c., " Confirmatio regia," 20th December, 1608.

one party is free, whether father or mother, the child is free. When Magnus Ericsson abolished slavery in West Gothland and Vermland in 1335 he declared that he did it " for the glory of God and of the Virgin Mary " (*Dipl. S.*, No. 3,106).

The same influence appeared in the sections touching marriage, the rights of the wife, and the dissolution of the tie.

Archbishop Nicolaus, owing to his influence with the king, obtained for his see in perpetuity the important castle of Almare-Stäket, on the road between Stockholm and Upsala, which he had built and fortified; and he thus prepared the way for the excessive power and political intrigues of his successors, which had so great influence afterwards upon their fortunes and the fortunes of the Church.

Although Nicolaus seems to have been in himself a good and able man, it can hardly be doubted that his policy was, on the whole, injurious to the Church.

§ 4.—Karl Knutsson elected king in 1448. His enemy, Johannes Benedicti (Oxenstierna), archbishop (1448—1468). Karl's feebleness. The archbishop's ambition and presumption. Drives Karl from the country. Struggle between Karl and Christian I. of Denmark.

Karl Knutsson, in the meanwhile, received Finland as a fief, and held Öland in pledge. Some months after Christopher's death he was elected king, notwithstanding the opposition of the powerful family of the Oxenstierna. They had, however, succeeded in getting the archbishopric for a member of their house, Johannes Benedicti (grandson of Karl's rival, Christer Nilsson), who was the enemy and rival of Karl for the next twenty years. Like Nicolaus, he was confirmed by the Council of Basel, but he seems also to have received confirmation from Pope Nicolas V., after his consecration, and probably on easy terms as to

fees.[11]   These instances are important as precedents which
were, no doubt, remembered in the dispute with Rome as
to the confirmation of bishops-elect at the time of the
Reformation.

The new archbishop was very ambitious, and took upon
him something of kingly state.   He had himself crowned
by four bishops.[12]   In 1455 he obtained from the pope the
right to be called Primate of Sweden.   In 1457 he was
elected administrator of the kingdom, and took an almost
royal title.   It has sometimes been asserted that he put
his own figure on his seal, wearing a crown, and holding a
sceptre in its right hand, and an orb in its left.[13]   Such a
figure, not unlike that on the great seals of Sweden,
certainly appears on his seal.[14]

[11] See Celsius : *Bullarium*, 1st October, 1438, p. 186, and
Reuterdahl, III., 2, p. 22, for Nicolaus, and *Bull.*, 27th April,
1448, p. 190, and Reuterdahl, l.c., p. 29, for John.   The latter
page of Celsius gives information as to a reduction of fees in
another case.

[12] Rhyzelius : *Episcopo-Scopia*, p. 48.

[13] Rhyzelius : p. 48.   This very interesting seal is figured in
S. H.[1], 2, p. 300, fig. 229 (but not in *S. H.*[2]).   The figure is
seated, and it is dressed in a cope or robe fastened under the
chin, with a cross where the morse would be.   Two angels
hold shields, one on each side : the dexter bears a cross for
Upsala, the sinister shield has the bearing of Oxenstierna, the
ox-yoke.   The legend is : Secretum · Johannis · Dei · gra
archiepiscopi · Upsalensis."

[14] The great seal of Magnus Ericsson (a king seated with
crown, sceptre and orb) is given in *S. H.*[1], I., fig. 507.   That
of the kingdom of Sweden in 1436 has a standing figure of St.
Eric in armour, with the legend " Sigillum regni Suecie.
Sanctus Ericus Suevonum Gothorum[q]ue [rex]," *S. H.*[1], II.,
fig. 176 = *S. H.*[2], 2, fig. 337.   That of King John of Denmark is
like that of Magnus Ericsson (*S. H.*[1], I., fig. 335), but more
elaborate.

The archbishops' seals figured in *S. H.*[1] are :—(1) Stephen,
1164, I., fig. 447, an archbishop standing with two-horned
mitre, a pastoral staff in right hand and book in left ; (2) Hemming, 1341, II., fig. 8, an archbishop seated, pastoral staff in
left hand, blessing with right hand ; (3) Birgerus Gregorii,
1366, fig. 161—using his predecessor, Peter's, die, but substituting his own name—very like No. 2 ; (4) Jerechini, 1408,

But, to judge by the similar design on the seal of Jacobus Ulphonis, later in the century, the figure is intended to represent our Lord, possibly with some suggestion that the archbishop was, like the pope, the vicar of Christ.

Karl himself was not strong enough for the position. He had been a brilliant party leader, but became (as Geijer says, p. 68) a feeble king. He was without heart for his office, and looked too narrowly at his own immediate advantage. His governors were as rapacious as the Danish and German bailiffs had been, and it mattered little that they robbed in the name of a Swedish king and plundered under the cloak of law. Amongst other things, his attack upon the freedom of testamentary bequests to the Church provoked bitter resentment. The archbishop, in fact, went to war with him, and drove him out of the kingdom. The result was that Christian of Oldenburg, who had been king of Denmark since 1448, and had ousted Karl from Norway in 1450, was now chosen king of Sweden also, and crowned in 1457. The peasants in Norway, who had no Engelbrekt to lead them, were utterly broken down in spirit, and were more or less content (notwithstanding their ancient traditions of independence) to be ruled from Denmark.

This union of Norway with Denmark lasted until the Treaty of Kiel on 14th January, 1814, which was followed by the union of Norway with Sweden in the next year. But Danish rule in Sweden was never long established without resistance. The struggles that followed are of little in-

fig. 149, three niches, in centre Blessed Virgin Mary and child, figures right and left; (5) Johannes Benedicti (1455?), already described, fig. 229; (6) Jacobus Ulphonis, 1470, fig. 278, much like No. 5, but with a cross on the crown and no morse. It has a three-quarter face looking to right of spectator—a rare attitude, found occasionally in Scotland, but only found, I think, in England on the seal of Richard de Bury of Durham, 1333; (7) Gustavus Trolle, 1514, fig. 353, an angel with a cross on his cap, holding a shield, Upsala and Trolle, quarterly, the latter being a headless Troll. No archiepiscopal cross staff is found on any of these seals.

terest to the Church historian, except as showing the decay of spiritual ideals and motives in the hierarchy.

The next ten years saw various changes of fortune on the part of the rival kings, with both of whom the archbishop was at bitter enmity. His first cousin, Ketillus Caroli Vasa, Bishop of Linköping, also took a prominent part in the warfare and intrigues of the times, sometimes acting as administrator of the whole or part of the kingdom.

After Archbishop Johannes Benedicti's death in 1467, in Öland, Karl summoned a council of nobles at Örebro, who recommended Thord, Dean of Linköping. He was accepted by the Chapter of Upsala, who sent his name to Pope Paul II. for confirmation. The latter refused to give it, and declared that the provision of an archbishop fell to himself. He, therefore, confirmed and consecrated Jacobus Ulphonis Archdeacon of Vexiö and Canon of Upsala, a young man of about thirty years of age, who was then residing at Rome, and was chosen by the cardinals. This arbitrary interference with the rights of the chapter took place in 1470, the year in which Karl died, or the claims of Thord might have been more seriously defended.[15]

Jacobus Ulphonis held office for forty-four years. He was the foremost man of the union party, but was for some time on good terms with the leader of the national party, Sten Sture, the elder, as well as with his successors, though sometimes at war with them. It had been supposed that Sture had supported Jacobus' promotion at Rome, having had some close relation to him in early life, perhaps as pupil to tutor, or the like.

§ 5.—THE STURES. CHRISTIAN II. AND GUSTAVUS TROLLE.

Karl left the government of the kingdom to his nephew, Sten Sture, whom he advised never to take the name or

[15] Reuterdahl: III., 2, p. 38. Anjou, p. 6, speaks of Thord as dead. There is a sketch by Archbishop A. N. Sundberg of *Jacobus Ulphonis: Svea Rikes Ärkebiskop*, 1470—1515, Upsala, 1877.

insignia of royalty.   Sten was chosen next year as administrator of the kingdom at the diet of Arboga (1471), and shortly afterwards defeated King Christian at the famous national battle of Brunkeberg, which took place in that part of Stockholm now called Norrmalm.   In the thirty years that followed this victory Sweden had greater rest and prosperity than in any other period of the fifteenth century.   Sten Sture's administration was fitly marked by the foundation and opening of the University of Upsala in 1477, which owed most to Archbishop Jacobus.   Such an institution had long been in contemplation, and certainly from the time of the Councils of Constance and Basel. Among the first professors was the historian, Ericus Olai. It did not, however, flourish long and continuously at first, but was suspended after about 1515.

Sture's nationalist policy was generally opposed, both by the higher clergy and the nobles, although he was able from time to time to co-operate with Archbishop Ulfsson. He had, however, one strong supporter in Hemming Gad, the humanist, a warm-hearted, impulsive man, and all his early life a great hater of the Danes, who was chosen Bishop of Linköping in 1501, but was never consecrated. Sture was specially obnoxious to the nobles, because of the encouragement and support which he gave to the peasants, in accordance with the old traditions of Swedish freedom. Through the combined influence of the clergy and the nobles, King John of Denmark was accepted as king of Sweden in 1483.   He was a man of popular character, though occasionally violent.

In the same year the act of union was again ratified by the Treaty of Kalmar, but upon conditions which embodied the demands of the nobility, and much restricted the power of the crown.   The tendency of this treaty may be gathered from its last article, which enacted that "Every good man, whether of the clergy or laity, should be king over his own peasants, excepting in such cases as concerned the rights of the sovereign."   This treaty in fact established the oligarchy which the nobles and higher clergy desired.

But King John was not crowned until the 25th November, 1497.   After a short period, during which the king attempted to reign in person and Sten Sture was driven from power by Jacobus Ulphonis, the archbishop and the administrator were again reconciled.   The latter died suddenly 13th December, 1503.   Early in the next year his friend and kinsman, Svante Sture, managed to get himself elected administrator.

Svante's father, Nils Bosson, was, by his father's side, a member of the family of Natt och Dag, so called from its shield, half black and half white—the family to which the murderer of Engelbrekt belonged.   But Nils took the name of Sture from his mother, and Svante continued to use it, as did his son, Sten Sture the younger—the noblest and most chivalrous of those who bore this name.

Svante died in 1512, and his young son, Sten, was chosen to fill his place, instead of Eric Trolle, head of the strongest rival family.   In the next year Christian II. succeeded his father John in Denmark—a man of secret, resolute, crafty, unforgiving, unscrupulous and violent temper, but not without good qualities and a desire to improve the conditions of life among his poorer subjects, especially the townsmen of Copenhagen, amongst whom he had been familiarly brought up.   Two years later Jacobus Ulphonis, now an old man, retired from his office, and was succeeded by Eric's son, Gustavus Trolle, another Johannes Benedicti.   Thus the stage was cleared for a new company of actors, and those young and sanguine ones, new to life and inclined to violent expedients; and thus the forces which had been gradually developing their strength in Sweden and Denmark came into vehement and more than usually tragic conflict.   The destruction of the union and the breach with Rome were occasioned by the conduct of the new archbishop and his allies and the hatred which they inspired.

Gustavus Trolle was sprung from a family which was closely linked with the interests of the union by its large possessions in Denmark.   Its chief members had for two generations been unsuccessful rivals and determined enemies of the Stures. Gustavus himself was of a stubborn and obstinate temper. It is said that as a wilful child he refused to follow his step-mother and the other children in a boat journey from Strengnäs, and in consequence escaped accidental death by drowning, which the other three suffered. He was persevering also in his studies at Cologne, and was one of the first of his countrymen to learn Greek. Like many others of them, he spent several years at Rome, from whence he only returned in 1512 to become Provost of Linköping. In less than two years he was elected archbishop (December, 1514), on the retirement of Johannes Ulphonis. His confirmation and consecration at Rome were procured from Leo X. by a letter from the young administrator and considerable sums of money forwarded by Eric Trolle, to which King Christian II. added four hundred marks of silver. But the new archbishop was not persuaded by the support of Sture to give up the family quarrel and the Danish alliance. He was of an ambitious character, and never forgot or forgave an injury real or fancied. His object doubtless was to displace Sture by the help of the Danes, and to get himself or his father elected administrator. When Sten came to Upsala and held out the hand of friendship and reconciliation to him in the cathedral he refused his overtures with scorn. Hostilities broke out between them, and it was decided at the Riksdag of Arboga, 1516, that Christian should not be received as king in Sweden. Again Sten offered Trolle peace, on the condition of his giving up his castle, which he refused. Then a Danish fleet appeared to support the archbishop, which was beaten off. A second Riksdag was held at Stockholm in 1517, at which the archbishop appeared and defied the assembled estates. This was too much for the nobles and people, who resolved unanimously that Stäket should be levelled to the ground, and the archbishop degraded from his office as a traitor to his country. He was kept in confinement therefore, and thus a formal breach was made with Rome by the civil power of Sweden, a year before Luther burnt the papal bulls of indulgence at Wittenberg.

A second invasion by Christian in the next year was repelled at the Battle of Brännkyrka, in which the administrator's banner was carried by the young Gustaf Ericsson Vasa, the future liberator of Sweden. Christian, however, still negotiated, and, on pretence of coming himself to Stockholm, required six hostages for his safety. Among them were sent Gustaf Ericsson, and the old Hemming Gad. But, when the king had received these hostages, he declared them his prisoners, and sailed away to Denmark. This was the political condition of things before the final and tragic end which took place in 1520.

We must now explain the ecclesiastical situation.

The case of Gustavus Trolle had, of course, been reported at Rome, and Leo X. at once prepared measures to vindicate his ecclesiastical rights. A spiritual court was appointed to sit in Denmark, and, in the spring of 1517, Birgerus, Archbishop of Lund, threatened to excommunicate Sten and his adherents, and to place Sweden under an interdict, unless Trolle was restored to his office.

These threats were lightly regarded, and the appearance of a papal legate in person was dexterously turned by the national party to its own advantage. This man was Giovanni Angelò Arcimboldi, son of a Milanese senator, who had been employed since 1514 by the cultivated but unspiritual Pope Leo X. as his agent for the sale of indulgences in Germany and Northern Europe. This sale had been begun by Pope Julius II. on the pretext of obtaining money for the building of St. Peter's Church, and was continued by Leo on the same ground. It was permitted by secular princes because of the large sums which they received from the pope's agents for allowing it in their dominions. Needless to say, it corrupted those agents as well as their dupes, who purchased the worthless pieces of paper, which assured them all that the Church could give in the way of pardon for almost all imaginable sins. It is not necessary to inquire what exact limits Roman theologians put upon the value of these indulgences.   Those who sold them magnified their value, and many of those who bought no doubt believed that they were receiving some great advantage.

Arcimboldi received a fresh appointment in 1516, after the dispute had broken out between Sten and the archbishop, and he was empowered as legate, *a latere*, to heal the breach and do other business in the pope's name, being furnished with a letter to the administrator, dated 6th September, 1516.   In January, 1517, he sent as his emissary Didrik Slagheck, a Dutchman, of whom we shall hear more later on, to negotiate for peace in the interests of King Christian.   In March, 1518, the legate himself came into Sweden, where he was allowed to set up his cross, and to sell his wares, and to dispense titles and judgments in the pope's name, without hindrance—thus showing that the events of 1517 were not intended to be a final breach with Rome.

By the end of the year Arcimboldi was completely won by the costly presents and personal attentions of the regent and his friends, and by the hopes of succeeding Trolle. He attended another Riksdag at Arboga in December, 1518, at which he confirmed the sentence upon the archbishop, and advised him to submit, whereupon Trolle solemnly resigned his office.   The estates of Sweden might now well think that they had received pardon for the informality of their earlier proceedings, but the legate's act had still to be ratified by the pope.   Arcimboldi's own plan seems to have been to get his appointment to Upsala confirmed at Rome, to continue himself to reside in Italy, and to receive the revenues of the see, while he appointed old Jacobus Ulphonis to act as his deputy in Sweden.

But this plan met with strenuous opposition from both the parties interested.   Christian and Trolle were furious at Arcimboldi's treachery to their cause, and the king used the opportunity of the legate's return to the south to deprive him of most of his ill-gotten gains, including a great deal of two specially Swedish products, iron and butter, in which he hoped to do a large trade. The legate, however, escaped in person to Rome, where he made his peace with the pope, though his plan was not confirmed. In 1525 he became Bishop of Novara, and in 1550 arch-bishop of his own city, Milan, where he died in 1555. Such were some of the men who disgraced the high places of the Church in the first half of the sixteenth century.

Christian then prepared a new campaign, using the gold of Sweden, as Gustaf Vasa afterwards wrote, for its own conquest.[16] He also got himself made the pope's agent for the re-instatement of Trolle, and thus, armed at all points, awaited a favourable moment for revenge.

§ 6.—Religious life of the Church. Elementary
        teaching. Character of the bishops. The
        chapters and their officers. Dioceses,
        Monasteries and religious orders. Wealth
        of the Church.

After this review of the external history we naturally turn to consider the inner life of the Church.   In the absence of any authoritative description of it in detail, and, in view of the tumult and confusion of secular life, and, considering the reformation that followed, it would be per-haps natural to paint a very dark picture, to which the history of the sixteenth century might stand out as in bright relief.   I doubt, however, whether we have a right to do so.   That learning, as represented by book know-ledge, was at a low ebb is indeed clear.   The first book printed in Sweden is generally considered to be the *Vita sive legenda cum miraculis Katherine*, the daughter of St. Birgitta, in or about 1483.   The first book in the Swedish language was issued in 1495 (Gerson's *Aff dyäfwlsens frästilse*), and the next in 1514.   There were only ten printed books in the language when Olaus Petri began his publications about 1526.   It may, indeed, be said of him that he taught the Swedes to read (H. Schück :

[16] See *P. R. E.*[2], s.v. *Arcimboldi*, Vol. 1, p. 618.

Olavus Petri, p. 49, 1906). The University of Upsala, though contemplated at the Council of Basel, was not founded until 1477—a year before that of Copenhagen— but its efficiency was small, and at first it did not long endure. After 1515 it was for a considerable time in abeyance.

Popular teaching was of the most elementary character. It is mentioned as rather a great step of progress that the sainted Bishop Nicolaus Hermanni of Linköping, of whom I have spoken (1374—1391), ordered the clergy to teach the people about the Lord's Prayer, the Apostles' Creed, the Ave Maria, the Ten Commandments and the seven works of mercy.[17] At the provincial synod in Söderköping (1441) it was ordered that the Lord's Prayer, Ave Maria, and the Apostles' Creed should be translated into Swedish, and read before the people every Sunday and festival. This latter council was held in the time of the able Bishop Nicolaus Ragvaldi (c. 13, Reuterdahl: *Stat. Syn.,* p. 127). The object, of course, was that they might be learnt by heart. The "Ave Maria" was, no doubt, still in the Biblical form, without the later accretion, in which the Blessed Virgin is invoked as "Mother of God." This same archbishop compiled a code of the statutes of his diocese, from which we may learn much as to the administration of the sacraments customary in Sweden. The three forms just named were to be taught to children by their parents and god-parents. Children of seven years old and upwards were to be confirmed by the bishop fasting—the implication being that if they were confirmed at an earlier age they need not fast. No one was to be confirmed more than once, and parents were frequently to remind their children by whom and where they were confirmed. Bishops might change names in confirmation, and no one is to be admitted to minor orders without confirmation. There are reasonable and prudent directions as to hearing confession, etc. In the communion the wine is to be red

[17] Reuterdahl : *Statuta Synodalia,* pp. 57-8, in a document of uncertain date.

rather than white, and more wine than water is to be in the chalice (*Stat. Syn.*, pp. 145-399).   I learn from Dr. Holm-quist that in distant and scantily populated districts it is probable that a bishop sometimes administered confirmation by deputy.

The learning of the priesthood also was small, and it would be easy to quote evidence of canons warning them against crimes and vices, and to relate instances of their misdoings.   But we have not that wealth of information for Sweden which Chaucer, Langland, Wycliffe, Pecock, etc., give us for England.   The case of the Dane, Johannes Jerechini, whom Eric of Pomerania foisted into the Archbishopric of Upsala in 1409, with the consent apparently of Gregory XII.[18], stands almost alone in Swedish annals.

The bishops of the mediæval Church, even in its last and most secular period, were generally men of good Swedish families, and of good education, according to the standard of the day, having mostly studied abroad and taken some degree in arts, or theology and canon law.   Even when they were immersed in political intrigues and engaged sometimes in actual warfare, they were patrons of art and literature, and anxious to promote good men.   We have already seen such inconsistent characters in the persons of Adalbert of Bremen and Eskil of Lund, while the fifteenth century popes exhibited even more striking instances of the same combination.   As to the clerical antecedents of the Swedish bishops, we find them, as was natural, taken mostly from the dignitaries of the cathedral chapters, particularly that of Upsala.   Comparatively few were members of religious orders.

The first archbishop (Stephen, 1164) was a Cistercian, but no other member of that order—so widely spread in Sweden—is known to have attained episcopal rank.   Of the twenty-eight archbishops who followed him up to and including Johannes Magni, three were Dominicans—

[18] See Celsii : *Bullarium*, p. 162, and Johannes Magni : *Hist. Metropol. E. U.*, s.n.

Jarler (1232), in whose time the Council of Skeninge was held, John III., Bishop of Åbo, a Pole (1289), and Petrus Philippi (1332). One was a Franciscan, Laurentius, who succeeded Jarler in 1285. One was a Birgittine of Vadstena, Johannes Haquini, in the time of Eric of Pomerania (1412). Two other Dominicans were bishops of Vesterås (1329, 1332), and two Birgittines bishops of the same see in 1441 and 1454.

In most cases the choice of the chapter fell upon dignitaries or canons of their own body, or at least secular clergy of their own diocese. Even when the popes " provided " clergy to high office, they mostly chose Swedes, who, of course, were obliged to pay heavily for their promotion. It seems to have been usual for the popes to choose Swedes even in the case of dignities less than episcopal. Hans Hildebrand, to whom I am indebted for much of my information on the subject, only names one Italian " provided " in 1353 to the Provostship of Upsala, being a man not in priest's orders, one German and one Dane (*Sv. M.*, book v., 148-9). Thus the Swedish Church was very national, even when it was most fully under Roman influence.

As regards birth, the bishops were mostly from families who had a right to bear arms. Few were townsmen or burghers, though some of the most important men in the last period were of this class. Such seem to have been the notorious Johannes Jerechini, and the two brothers, Johannes and Olaus Magni, Conrad Rogge, Bishop of Strengnäs, Hemming Gad, elect of Linköping, and Hans Brask, bishop of the same see.

These facts do much to explain the political attitude of the bishops and dignified clergy who sided on the whole rather with the nobility and the union party than with the peasants.

On the other hand, the failure of the papal curia to press the Roman international system to its full development, and the comparative absence of the scandals of indulgence-mongering (except in the last years of the period) account for that absence of bitterness in the Reformation movement which seems, to a foreigner, very remarkable.

As regards the personnel of the cathedral chapters [19] in the later middle age, they were, as I have said, bodies of secular canons, as in the English cathedrals of the old foundation. The Benedictines never got hold of the Swedish cathedrals as they did amongst ourselves of the chapters of the great sees of Canterbury, Durham, Winchester, Ely, Norwich and others. But the Swedish secular chapters had a shorter history than ours, and were not as fully developed as those of York, London, Lincoln, Salisbury, Wells, Exeter, Hereford, Lichfield, and Chichester, etc. Lund, then in Danish territory, shows by its beautifully furnished retro-choir what might have been. The development of the dignities in the cathedrals also differs considerably from our own. In the first period of the secular foundations the only officers were a provost and a certain number of canons. The provost continued to be the chief man in the chapter. Next to him, both in order of time and dignity, came the archdeacon, of whom there seems to have been only one in each diocese, instead of several, as among ourselves. Then came the dean, and while the provost was largely an officer with outside business, the dean was occupied with the interior concerns of

[19] I have not seen K..V. Lundquist : *Bidrag till kännedom om de Svenska Domkapitlet under medeltiden*, Stockholm, 1897, nor the German work of Ph. Schneider : *Die bischöflichen Domkapitel*, 2 ausg., 1892. There is a summary of the capitular system (without any particular reference to England or Sweden) in *P. R. E.*[3], by P. Hinschius (Hauck). I have found most information in H. Hildebrand's *Sv. Medeltid*, Book v., pp. 136-159, which seems to be chiefly based on Lundquist. The reader who is interested in the subject of English cathedrals will find much information in E. A. Freeman : *History of the Cathedral Church of Wells, illustrating the history of the cathedral churches of the old foundation*, Lond., 1870, and E. W. Benson (Bishop of Truro, afterwards archbishop) : *The Cathedral, its necessary place in the life and work of the Church*, Lond., 1878). There are some notices of a " Provost " at Wells in Freeman : pp. 33, 39, 150, 166.

the cathedral and the cathedral body.   Further, the office of cantor or precentor, which comes second among the English dignities in the old foundations, was not a high one in Sweden, and it is comparatively rarely mentioned. We are, perhaps, entitled to conjecture that the musical side of public worship was not nearly so widely developed as among ourselves.   We hear, indeed, of two fourteenth century organs in Gothland churches which have been preserved to our own day (*Sv. M.*, book v., 693), but there seems to be little reference to instrumental music in churches in Swedish literature.   The other officers who are more often mentioned are the scholasticus, or theological lecturer, who may answer in some measure to the chancellor in our cathedrals and the sacristan or treasurer.   There was also very frequently in later days a man of business, an œconomus, syssloman, or steward, answering, I suppose, to the seneschal at Canterbury, and to the chapter clerk or registrar of our other cathedrals.   But these officers were not at all necessary to every chapter, or at all times.

The canons who formed the general body of the chapter were naturally most numerous in Upsala.   About the year 1400 there were thus a provost, an archdeacon and eighteen canons.   Linköping had rather fewer than Upsala.[20] Vesterås seems to have been a much smaller body, with about four canons.   Strengnäs and Skara appear to have had about the same number, viz., twelve or thirteen canons. Vexiö had a provost and seven canons in 1382, and other officers are mentioned at different times.   Åbo, in Finland, had ten canons and an archipresbyter, besides the other usual officers (*Sv. M.*, book v., 141-3).

The appointment to the cathedral offices lay generally with the bishop, who was, however, to consult the chapter as regards his choice.   This system of co-optation was

---

[20] In 1470 we find a provost, archdeacon, dean, scholasticus, cantor and fifteen canons mentioned in the letter of Paul II. threatening all who opposed Jacobus Ulphonis with excommunication (Celsii; *Bull.*, p. 202)—that is exactly the same number as in 1400, since Jacobus himself was a canon.

sometimes interfered with by papal reservation or provision
(*Sv. M.*, v. 148-9).   At times also the kings petitioned the
popes to delegate to them rights of nomination.   These
rights were specially granted to King Magnus Ericsson in
1347 and 1352.   King Christian I. also made an agreement
with Pope Sixtus IV. that he should present suitable persons to the provostship, archidiaconate and decanate in
some of the principal cathedrals (*ibid.* 150).   But these
were exceptional cases, and the general independence of
the chapters were recognized as the rule.

The bishop presided in the chapter, and the provost was
vice-president.   The provost accompanied the bishop on
his visitations, and also visited, under the bishop's direction, in his own person.   He was also generally pastor of
the city church.   His relation to the archdeacon and dean
do not seem to have been very clearly defined.   Cathedral
statutes, such as those that are common in England, do not
seem to have been preserved, or, at any rate, are
not accessible in print.   But the general principle of the
chapter's work was here as elsewhere " to assist the bishop
when the see was full, to supply his place when it was
vacant."[21]   In Sweden the chapters seem to have been able
to maintain their independence in elections more than in
England, though when a bishop was a strong man we do
not find evidence of independent capitular action.

As regards the districts assigned to each bishop, the
great difference between mediæval and modern Sweden is
that the former contained the whole of Finland from
Viborg in the East to Torneå in the North, and did not
contain the Danish provinces which were in the diocese of
Lund, nor Bohuslän, which was Norwegian.   Gotland   ·
also was for a long time independent, then Swedish, then
Danish.   The Archbishop of Upsala had an enormous
diocese, extending up to Torneå in the North, and including Jemtland and Herjedalen, which were under the Norwegian crown.   Some attempt was made in the union

[21] " Auxiliari episcopo, sede plena : supplere, sede vacante,"
Benson : l.c., p. 52.

period towards the conversion of the Lapps.   Linköping diocese included East Gothland, and the two islands of Gotland and Öland, as well as considerable parts of Småland. Skara, the West Gothland see, also included Vermland and Dal. Vexiö was much the smallest in extent.

The dioceses were divided into "contrakter," or rural deaneries of ten to twelve parishes, each with its provost. The provosts and certain representative clergy were summoned to the prest-möte, or diocesan synod, which it was a bishop's duty to hold every year. Ruridecanal meetings also sometimes took place.

The parish priests (socken-presterna) were chosen in many cases by the peasants whose fathers had joined to found the parish.   In case of dispute various methods were provided by different provincial laws for securing an election.   Where the parish did not elect, the king or some other founder had the right of patronage, as with us. Institution was given by the bishops.

The chief income of the parish priests was derived from tithes which were laid on the produce of the chase and fishing, as well as on domestic animals and the fields. Only one-third of the tithes of corn came to the parish priest, the other part was divided among the bishop, the Church and the poor.   The "poor" tithe was administered by the bishop, and given to hospitals, education, building of cathedrals and support of canonries, etc.

The parish priests were not, however, rich, while the bishops and monasteries were.   Of the latter there were a large number in the peninsula, especially in the diocese of Lund, where there were thirty-eight.   In Sweden proper there were forty-five, with six in Finland, and four in Bohuslän, which then belonged to Norway, making a total of eighty-three.

It would be of little interest to give a list of these eighty-three religious houses.   The numbers belonging to the principal orders in what is now Sweden and Finland may, however, be mentioned.   The Franciscans were the most popular, having twenty-five houses, the Dominicans eighteen, and the Cistercians sixteen. The rest had between them twenty-four, which includes the old-fashioned Benedictines (7), Præmonstratensians (5), Carmelites (3), Birgittines (2), Johannites (2), Antony Brothers (2), Cluniacs (1), Carthusians (1), Augustinians (1). The latest foundation was one promoted by Jacobus Ulphonis and Conrad Rogge of Strengnäs, the Carthusian monastery of Mariefred, to which Sten Sture gave the castle and estate of Gripsholm in 1493. It was the first to be confiscated after the Reformation.[22] The Carmelite monastery at Örebro is memorable as having been the place of the early education of Olaus and Laurentius Petri.

It is not easy to estimate what the wealth of these various sees and chapters and religious houses was in the aggregate. It was certainly very large. Thus we are told that every nobleman was required to provide six able-bodied men for every four hundred marks rent. A report made to the diet at Stockholm in 1526 returns the quota of the archbishop at fifty men, of the Bishop of Linköping at thirty-six, and others less. The highest quota of a lay-lord was twenty-four, and of the 441 men, which had to be raised on that occasion, 156 were to be supplied by the bishops.[23]

It was not, perhaps, much of an exaggeration on the part of Gustaf Vasa in 1527 to say "that the crown and the nobility together hardly had here in the kingdom a third part of what the priests, monks, churches and monasteries had" (Anjou: p. 29).

§ 7.—CONCLUSION. DISSATISFACTION WITH ROME AND DISCONTENT WITH THE BISHOPS. CHRISTIAN'S TRIUMPH. EFFECT OF THE BLOOD-BATH AT STOCKHOLM ON CHURCH AND STATE.

Thus, from the little congregation founded at Birka in the time of Anskar, had grown up a great semi-independent society—an "imperium in imperio"—which con-

[22] See Cornelius : *Handbok*, pp. 149-50, and Lecture V., § 4.
[23] L. A. Anjou : *Reformation*, p. 28, E. T., 1859.

fronted, and, at times, overshadowed the State, and threatened the solidity and efficiency of the kingdom. When once it was perceived that the first duty of a State was to have a settled government, guaranteeing liberty and law to all men, it was impossible for those who guided the State to be content to let this " imperium in imperio " continue unregulated. There was dissatisfaction with the papacy, but much more discontent with the home administration of the Church. The papacy aroused dissatisfaction and a certain amount of contempt by the uncertain character of its interference, and the atmosphere of intrigue and corruption in which all business done with it was involved. It was felt that very many matters were decided by it from motives other than those of religion, and often on grounds of policy which made it the instrument of foreign and hostile powers. But, on the whole, the papacy had not done nearly as much harm to Sweden as to other nations, and it had done much good, especially by widening the outlook of the men who came in contact with it. The main causes of discontent were the excessive wealth, power and secularity of the higher clergy, and their disintegrating influence on the national life. The Archbishop of Upsala was a great secular potentate, able to make successful war upon kings and administrators. But he was not the ruler of the Church in Sweden, even when he was administrator of the kingdom. The Church in one sense was too strong, but in another it was too weak, because it failed in cohesion. Each bishop had his castle and his retainers, and was a sort of petty king in his diocese and upon his own estates, and a menace to the unity of the State. Such simple facts as these, brought home to the minds of everyone, were much more powerful than dissatisfaction with Rome. Members of the national party could not fail to see their relevance to the two problems, which the rising under Engelbrekt had first brought into prominence, and which had ever since been before their minds: First, how to free Sweden from a foreign dynasty, which burdened it with heavy taxes for the benefit of strangers, and involved it in affairs and wars not its own; secondly, how to give unity to the nation within.   The state of constant insecurity and of frequent civil war had become intolerable by the end of the fifteenth century.   What was needed was a strong native king, who would drive out the foreigner and consolidate the government.   Then came the deposition of Gustavus Trolle by the Riksdag at Stockholm in November, 1517, and the destruction of the Castle of Stäket.   This, as we have seen, was not intended to be an absolute breach with Rome.   The hope was that the pope would, in the end, confirm it and appoint a new archbishop of a more peaceable and patriotic temper, or at least assent to his legate Arcimboldi's plan.

But when Christian, in 1520—smarting from his own previous defeats, and mindful of his grandfather's defeat at Brunkeberg—was successful in his second invasion, in which Sten Sture fell, and left Sweden without a leader, he determined to have his revenge and to make future rebellion impossible.   He had succeeded in such a policy in Norway, why should he not succeed in Sweden?   He had with him, not only military, but spiritual power.   He brought papers from the pope pronouncing an excommunication on the administrator and his adherents, on account of their treatment of Trolle, and including an interdict of divine services and sacraments covering the whole of Sweden to be used if it were necessary.   He was brother-in-law of the Emperor Charles V., and had all the prestige of the Roman Empire, as far as it remained, to back him.   Why should he not then succeed?

By his own fair speeches and lavish promises, and by the help of those whom he had persuaded to serve him, he won entrance into Stockholm, and that mainly by the good offices of Hemming Gad.   He was there crowned with great pomp by Gustavus Trolle and the other bishops on Sunday, the 4th November.   For three days he entertained his guests, Swedish, German and Danish, with equal courtesy and pleasantness.   Everything was to be forgiven and forgotten, especially all the proceedings against the archbishop, who was now restored to office; the king had taken oath upon the sacrament that it should be so. But he was, under this mask, maturing a plan of revenge, to which he was instigated by Didrik Slagheck, once a barber, but now a bishop, and the bearer of Leo X.'s letters of excommunication against the Swedes. This plan is not attributed to Archbishop Gustavus by those who lived nearest the time, although he was used as an instrument by the king to work it out.

On Wednesday, the 7th, Christian held a council of the realm, to which the bishops, the chief lords and ladies, clerks and citizens were summoned. Gustavus Trolle came forward to demand satisfaction for the injuries he had received at the hands of the late administrator. He was supported by Otto, Bishop of Vesterås. The administrator's widow, Christina, stood up in her husband's defence, and declared that all the estates were equally responsible for the archbishop's deposition and the destruction of his castle in 1517. The king asked who of those present had signed the act of deposition. Hans Brask allowed that he had done so, but appealed to a secret writing under his seal, in which he asserted that he did it under compulsion. The others, including the two bishops, Mathias of Strengnäs and Vincentius of Skara, were imprisoned. Gustavus, it seems, wished the cause to be referred to Rome for judgment, but the king decided that it should be settled out of hand. Next day, the 8th, the prisoners were brought before a spiritual tribunal, of which the president was the Danish bishop, Jens Andersson Beldenacke. They were asked whether it was not heresy to confederate and conspire against the holy see of Rome, and they were constrained to answer " Yes. ' This was regarded by the court as a condemnation of themselves, by their own mouth, on a capital charge, and their immediate execution was decreed—even the consolation of the sacrament being denied them. All things had been prepared beforehand in the market place, scaffold, guards, cannon and executioners. First the two bishops

lost their heads, then twelve temporal lords, including Eric
Abrahamsson, Eric Johansson Vasa and Joakim Brahe;
then the burgomasters of Stockholm and the principal
citizens.   A Danish knight who was present informed the
people that the archbishop had thrice adjured the king
upon his knees so to punish the guilty, but Vincentius
declared that this was untrue, and that it was the king who
was the traitor.   As this is asserted by Olaus Petri, the
reformer, who was present as one of the company of his
bishop, it must be assumed to be true; and so far it clears
Trolle of the worst suspicion.   Olaus also notes the in-
gratitude of the king towards Bishop Mathias, who, since
the treaty was drawn up, had done more than any man in
Sweden to promote his cause, and without whom the king
would not have succeeded in his enterprise.   The
next day other victims were executed.   "The dead
bodies" (says Olaus Petri) "were left to lie in the market
place from Thursday till Saturday.   It was a pitiful and
terrible sight to see how, in that rainy season, blood, mixed
with water and filth, ran down in the gutters off the market
place."   Many of the citizens were taken from their business without a moment for thought, or for making their
peace with God.   Others were drawn from the crowd if
they showed any sympathy as spectators.   Men at arms,
who had come in the retinue of the lords who were executed,
were torn off their horses in their boots and spurs, and borne
straight to the gallows, which were often full and rarely
empty.   Another spectator, Olaus Magni, the historian,
afterwards titular archbishop of Upsala, saw ninety-four
persons beheaded; and others were hanged or butchered in
other ways.   Before the massacre terminated the king sent
letters to all the provinces, saying that he had caused Sten
Sture's chief abettors to be punished as notorious heretics,
according to the sentence of the bishops, prelates and the
wisest men in Sweden, and that he would henceforth govern
the kingdom in peace by the laws of St. Eric.   On the
Saturday the king ordered a great fire to be kindled in the
suburb of Södermalm, where the Church of St. Catharine

now stands, on which the bodies of the dead were consumed. To make his revenge complete, he caused the dead body of the administrator, which had been buried for half a year, to be dug up, and thrown upon the pile. The massacre was also extended to Finland, and Hemming Gad, who had escaped thither, was not saved by his recent services, and lost his head at the age of 80. The king's whole progress on his return from Stockholm was marked by similar cruelties, in which harmless monks and innocent children were slaughtered. More than six hundred heads had fallen before he quitted Swedish territory at the beginning of the next year.

This tragedy bears the name in history of the " Bloodbath of Stockholm," and by it Christian earned the name of " the Tyrant." He left the kingdom in the hands of Didrik Slagheck, Gustavus Trolle, Jens Andersson and others. Slagheck was made Bishop of Skara in the place of one victim, and Jens Andersson was nominated to Strengnäs in the place of the other. Slagheck retired to Denmark when Gustaf Vasa began to succeed in his revolt, and was made Archbishop of Lund; but was shortly afterwards burnt to death at Copenhagen by King Christian (1522). Trolle also retired to Denmark, where, on Christian's deposition and imprisonment, he crowned King Frederick in 1524. He was wounded in battle in 1535, and died in prison. Jens was neither elected, nor confirmed nor consecrated to Strengnäs, and he, too, shortly retired. But what became of him does not seem to be recorded. The miserable captivity and wretched fate of Christian is well known.

As regards its effect on Sweden, this tragedy had great influence on the history of the Church, as well as of the State. It settled any question of accepting a Danish ruler perhaps for all time. It was also a signal step in the interruption of relations with the Roman see in the interest of which Slagheck had planned it. However much it might have been dictated by policy and personal hatred on the part of Christian, it was carried out and defended by him as

a punishment of heresy, that heresy being opposition to
Rome.   It made the Swedes determined never to have
again such a powerful archbishop as Trolle, and, as two of
the bishops had been his supporters, the whole order were
objects of suspicion.   The breach was now made, and it
was seen that the power of the bishops must be checked,
and their wealth and independence diminished.

It made it easily possible for Gustaf Vasa to attack this
point in the Swedish constitution under the financial
necessities, which, from the first, pressed upon him.

When also the pope stiffly refused to confirm canonically
elected bishops because their fees were not forthcoming the
breach became still wider.   It was then that the new doctrines began to take hold of men's hearts, and the national
sentiment was strengthened and ennobled by the teaching
as to the value of individual faith in God which the
Lutheran preachers gave.   The new spirit of personal
piety which was engendered, the new force of character
which was created, were precious alike to the religion and
to the policy of Sweden.   The Church had brought Sweden
into the comity of nations, but had failed to make the best
of the national character.   The State was now to take the
moulding of this character in hand, in alliance with the
Church, but in an alliance which (as we shall see) did not
give the Church sufficient freedom of development.   On
the whole, however, the tangled web of destiny can be
seen by those who look back upon its progress to be surely
woven by the fingers of God, and not to be the working of
a blind and meaningless fate.   Good lives were woven into
it, and their influence is not yet exhausted.

DETACHED NOTE.—ON THE MONASTERY OF SYON IN ENGLAND.

The following is an extract from the introduction to the *Catalogue of the [Men's] Library of Syon Monastery, Isleworth*, by Mary Bateson, Cambridge, 1898, pp. xi. and xii. :—

The English interest in the Brigettine order dates from 1406, when Henry IV.'s daughter, Philippa, went to Sweden to become the wife of Eric, king of Norway, Sweden and Denmark. Immediately after the marriage the bridal party visited Wadstena, the parent house of the Brigettine order, already the richest monastery in Sweden ; and the result of the visit was that an Englishman, Henry Lord Fitzhugh, who was in Queen Philippa's suite, promised to endow the order in England with his manor of Hinton, near Cambridge. In 1408 John Peters, priest, and one deacon were sent to England. Peters stayed eight years [24] [he died in 1418, leaving many books to Wadstena], but it was not directly from his exertions that Syon sprang. Philippa visited Wadstena again January, 1415, and enrolled her name among the nuns, promising to live there if she should become a widow, and it is probable that at that time she began to use her influence to promote the interests of the order in England. In May of that year four Swedish nuns, three novices and two priests were sent to England. It appears that Henry V. had agreed to found a House for them, which was to be endowed from the spoils of the alien monasteries dissolved in 1414.

On the 22nd February, 1416, he laid the foundation of the Church of Syon, and of the monastery of St. Saviour and St. Briget of Syon, of the order of St. Augustine.

The Carthusian House at Sheen, called Jesus of Bethlehem, was founded about the same time, and the two Houses frequently acted together. The original Syon was near Twickenham, but after the manor of Isleworth was given to the nuns, 1422, and rich property fell into their hands, a new house was begun in Isleworth, 1426, on the present site of Syon House. In 1431 the convent moved and soon became enormously wealthy. At the dissolution of greater monasteries it ranked eighth in riches. It is possible that a search for Syon accounts might give some information on the purchase of books. [25]

[24] Fant's *Scriptores rerum Suecicarum* I., 125.
[25] The agricultural accounts of the Abbey's Home-farm yielded many of the statistics for Prof. Thorold Rogers' *History of Prices*.

V.

THE SWEDISH REFORMATION UNDER GUSTAF VASA AND
HIS SONS, ERIC AND JOHN (1520 A.D.—1592 A.D.).

LECTURE V.

The Swedish Reformation.

§ 1.—Gustaf Vasa (1496—1560). His early history
and adventures. Elected king at Strengnäs,
1523.

In order to understand the course of the Church history
of the Reformation period we must first remind ourselves
of the chief events in the romantic history of Gustaf
Ericsson Vasa, the liberator of Sweden, and the founder of
the most important dynasty of Swedish kings. We have
all of us at some time or another in our lives delighted to
read of his adventures, and, therefore, a detailed account
of them would be out of place here.

The family to which he belonged was an honourable one
in Upland. It first appears in history at Frötuna, in the
province of Upsala, in the middle of the fourteenth century. The most prominent member of it was the old
drots, or steward, Christian Nilsson, the rival of Karl
Knutsson, and great grandfather of Gustaf. His father's
first cousin, Kettil, was Bishop of Linköping (†1465).
He was born himself on the 12th May, probably in 1496,
and was brought up at the University of Upsala, and
in the court of Sten Sture the younger, where he attracted
the notice of King John of Denmark. He was only
twenty-two years old when he was treacherously carried off
as a hostage by Christian II., and kept in prison for about
two years. He escaped first to Lübeck and then to
Kalmar, and, on his return to Sweden, remained in retirement at his father's house of Räfsnäs, not far from the
bishop's see of Strengnäs, and close to the newly-founded
monastery of Mariefred on Lake Mälar. Here he heard of
the massacre of Stockholm on 8th November, 1520, in
which his father was one of the victims. Here, too, he

formed the plan of escaping to Dalarne, and rousing the Dalemen to revolt, as they had done under Engelbrekt some ninety years before. Towards the end of the month, in the darkness of winter, began that course of changeful adventures, in which, first on the Dalelf and in the Kopparberg, and then in the neighbourhood of Lake Siljan, he moved from place to place disguised as a peasant, hospitably received, and sheltered by some, betrayed by others, and always pursued by Danish spies and soldiers. These adventures are full of picturesque episodes, which are even more interesting to the Swedes than the wanderings of King Alfred are to ourselves. When, in despair of rousing the people he was flying into Norway, and had almost passed the boundary, he was recalled by swift snow-shoe runners, who brought him back to Mora. Here the assembled peasants (who were at last thoroughly shaken from their torpor by reports of the cruelties and further designs of Christian) chose him to be their leader, and made him, as far as they could make him, the administrator of the kingdom (January, 1521).

The revolution which followed was in an extraordinary degree the work of this single young man, not yet twenty-five years old. It is marvellous with what perseverance, cheerfulness and courage, with what skill, prudence and self-restraint, he kept the war going, with the aid of foreign mercenaries and undisciplined peasant levies, and with an empty treasury. At the end of April he was master of the central Swedish provinces of Dalarne, Gestrikland, Vestmanland and Nerike, except the castles. At midsummer he was able to besiege, though not to take, Stockholm. In the second half of August he was accepted as administrator of the kingdom (Rikets höfvitsman) at a council of nobles held at Vadstena in East Gothland. Two years more were required to take the castles and the towns. On the 6th June, 1523, he was elected king at the Riksdag in Strengnäs, which was, as you will remember, near his own home. Here also was the focus at that time of the reforming movement, which was quite in its infancy.

Here the new king came into close contact with two of the three men whose spiritual force was to turn the mind of Sweden into a new direction, Olaus Petri, who was a little older than the king, and his friend, the Archdeacon Laurentius Andreæ, who was some ten years older than Olaus. It needs but little imagination to picture with what eagerness the young preacher and the older thinker and organizer, who were already bound together, met and welcomed the representative of practical energy and triumphant hopefulness. Here (they must have felt) is one who will give us the political leadership which we need. Gustaf, for his part, must have recognized at once in them a moral power which he himself did not possess, and one which would give dignity to his cause. What dreams were dreamed in those early days, what ideals of new life for the Church and the community took shape from the contact of these remarkable men who met at Strengnäs in 1523!

§ 2.—Introduction of Protestant teaching. The brothers Olaus and Laurentius Petri and Archdeacon Laurentius Andreæ.

The introduction of Protestant teaching of the school of Luther into Sweden was the work, as I have implied, mainly of three men, the two whom I have mentioned, and Laurentius, the younger brother of Olaus Petri.

The two brothers were, like Melanchthon, sons of a smith. Their birthplace was Örebro, chief town of Nerike, whence Laurentius is often called Nericius, to distinguish him from his namesake and successor, Laurentius Petri Gothus. Their first teaching was probably at the Carmelite monastery in that place. Olaus seems to have been born in 1493, and Laurentius in 1499. Olaus took his degree as Master of Arts at the newly-founded University of Wittenberg in 1518, where he came into close relation as a student with both Luther and Melanchthon. It appears that Laurentius was also a student there, but his early life is but little known to us. He did not return from Wittenberg until 1527, and, when he did so, he seems to have worked quietly as schoolmaster (ludi magister) at Upsala. Olaus returned to his cathedral city in 1519, and was ordained deacon in 1520. He accompanied his bishop, Mathias Gregorii, to Stockholm for the coronation of King Christian II. He was a witness of the massacre in which the two bishops suffered, and describes it in some well-known pages in his chronicle.[1]

Mathias was the first executed, and Olaus remarked that no man had done so much for King Christian as Bishop Mats, and that without him he would never have succeeded in forcing his will upon Sweden, and that this was his reward. It is said that Olaus was in some danger himself, but was supposed by some of the by-standers to be a German. He was, however, soon to be the best known man in Stockholm, for Gustaf took both the friends with him to that city, where the experienced Laurentius Andreæ became his chancellor. Olaus, in 1524, became secretary to the city council of Stockholm, where his knowledge of Germany was at once valuable. He left memoirs of city affairs, besides his larger chronicle, which are very valuable as records of the inner life of the community. At the same time the king appointed Michael Langerben, another Wittenberg student, to the pastorate of Stockholm. Thus the promoters of reform leapt at once to a prominent position in the capital, and were known to be under royal patronage.

A certain check to their influence was, indeed, for a time given by the excesses of two Anabaptist preachers from Holland, Rink and Knipperdolling, to which Olaus and Langerben seemed to have given too much countenance. The king was absent; but, on his return, he showed his anger at the riot and iconoclasm which had taken place, and exiled the Dutch preachers. From this incident (coupled with the even worse experience of Germany) we may trace the abhorrence of Swedish Lutheran orthodoxy against the rougher and wilder forms of Protestant enthusiasm.

[1] *Svenska Chrönica* in *Scr. rer. Suec.*, I., pp. 346-7. The passage is one of those printed by Ad. Noreen and E. Meyer in *Valda stycken af Svenska Författare*, pp. 19-23, Stockholm, 1907. See above p. 179.

§ 3.—THE CHANCELLOR'S LETTER TO VADSTENA. NEW
IDEA OF THE CHURCH. THE KING AND HIS
MINISTERS.

The opportunity was taken by Laurentius Andreæ to publish in the king's name a long Latin letter, addressed to the Convent of Vadstena, from whom he desired a loan, describing the king's attitude towards the Church. It rested upon a theory of the meaning of the word. " By the name Church Holy Scripture did not meant the priests or prelates, or the church buildings, but the whole company of faithful men. Therefore, if we say ' the Church's money,' do we say anything else except the people's money? In the oldest times of Christendom the possessions of the Church were used for the good of the congregation. So ought it to be now. The superfluity of Church revenues ought not to go to stately buildings or fine ornaments, but to supply the needs of the people. Surely God has not more care for stocks and stones than for men for whom Christ suffered and died?"[2]

As regards the attitude of the king towards the new teaching, he writes as follows :—" The king hears with displeasure the report that he allows some new and uncatholic teaching to be disseminated throughout his kingdom. He wills and requires that you should abstain from such thoughtlessness yourselves, and not mislead the common people, remembering what is written, ' Prove all things: hold fast that which is good.' If a strange doctrine is found by you in some new books, whether by Luther or others, they must not be rejected before they are carefully examined. If something is found which varies from the truth, you may write books to refute such teaching through Holy Scripture. Though I am afraid that there is no one among you who is able or suitable for such a task. For, although I have little acquaintance with the new teaching, which some men call Martin's, yet from the little I have ascertained about it, Martin is too great to be refuted by us

[2] This is a summary, not an exact quotation. See Cornelius : *Hist.*, § 5. So also the next paragraph.

simple men, for he is armed with the weapons of Scripture, not with the writings of St. Birgitta or anyone else, but with those of divine Scripture " (Cornelius: *ibid.*).

But, though the king thus showed his intention of protecting the new teaching, he did not put forward any of its tenets.   Neither inclination nor policy led him to enter the theological arena.   He was not a learned man like Henry VIII., nor, even if he had had the desire to pose as a theologian, had he leisure for it.   A great political and financial burden rested upon him, especially in the absence from Sweden of any class of trained statesmen, or even officials capable of keeping accounts on a large scale.   He sent young men to be trained in Germany, as Upsala did not furnish them, and he tried in succession various ministers, to whom, in his impatience, irritability, suspiciousness and reluctance to give praise, he was a very hard master.[3]

The most successful perhaps was the first Laurentius Andreæ, who remained with him for about nine years till 1532.   When he retired he seems to have recommended his friend, Olaus Petri, who was, however, too much of an idealist for the practical needs of Gustaf, and too independent, straightforward and impetuous to be personally acceptable to him.   After two years of unequal partnership Gustaf dismissed him with the trying remark that he was as fit to be chancellor as an ass to play the lute, or a frisky cow to spin silk (Schück: *Olavus,* 56).   He was succeeded in the chancellorship by another learned man, Christopher Andersson, one of the students sent to Germany, with whom the king quarrelled badly.   Then came a German jurist, Konrad von Pyhy, or Peutinger, in 1538, who, in company with the Pomeranian nobleman, George Norman, introduced many novelties of administration from the Continent, including a good many borrowings from Roman civil law.   We shall have to speak later of the influence of Norman in the Church.   Von Pyhy was dis-

[3] See Lektor (now Riksarkivarien) E. Hildebrand: *Gustaf Vasa,* etc., pp. 17-25.

graced in 1543, after which the king returned to Swedish
ministers.   In the early period, with which we are at present concerned, the king had to work hard himself with
accounts and State papers; and, although it is easy to
criticise the exuberance of his style, and the indirectness
of his language (which somewhat remind one of Oliver
Cromwell's), we cannot but be astonished at his immense
diligence.   Indeed, he continued to exhibit this minute
diligence in affairs, small and great, until the end of his
life.

§ 4.—PRESSURE OF THE FINANCIAL SITUATION.   THE KING'S APPEAL TO BRASK.   HE RESUMES GRIP-SHOLM.

At the beginning of his reign the financial problem was
almost overwhelming, and it was this which, to a great
extent, governed the religious issue.   As an American
writer on this period has said [4]: " In Sweden more than in
almost any other land the Reformation was a political revolt.   Indeed, it may well be called a political necessity.
At the moment when Gustaf Vasa was elected king,
Sweden was on the verge of bankruptcy."   Then, after
speaking of the unsatisfactory device of debasing the currency which was tried, and found unworkable, he proceeds,
" When the new monarch ascended the throne it was evident that the treasury must be replenished in other ways.
The natural direction was that in which the greatest wealth
of Sweden lay—in other words, the Church."

The king's first inroads upon the revenues of the Church
were naturally rather tentative.   He obtained a good deal

---

[4] Paul   Barron   Watson: *The   Swedish   Revolution   under
Gustaf Vasa*, pp. 121-3, London, 1889.   This is a laborious
book, ending with the year 1528.   It is rather vitiated by the
final suggestion that Gustaf ought to have been a precursor
of George Washington, and have founded a republic instead of
a monarchy—a suggestion which seems to show a misconception of the practical possibilities of the period.   But the facts
are recorded (I believe) with accuracy and diligence, and in a
fairly attractive manner.

of voluntary help in the next years from the frequent assemblies which he summoned in order to deal with the pressing matter of his debts to the City of Lübeck, which had assisted him with mercenary soldiers and supplies. He also appealed for such help in person. Thus he made, as we have seen, an appeal to Vadstena. He also made a personal appeal to Hans Brask, Bishop of Linköping. Brask was a very able, and, up to a certain point, a resolute man, who, like our own Tunstall, knew the need of reform, and was a friend of the reforming pope, Adrian VI., who was for too short a time on the Roman throne (2nd January, 1522—24th September, 1523).[5] But he was a convinced supporter of the old Church. In this appeal the king asked Brask for a definite sum, and Brask seems to have done his best to meet the demands made upon him. Each, I think, tried at first to make the best of the other, but in time suspicion of Brask's loyalty on the part of the king, and fear on Brask's part that the king was bent on introducing a new religion, separated two men who might between them have done much to shape a policy of moderate reform for Sweden. Their letters to one another still remain, and present a vivid picture of the state of changing opinion at this period.

Another source of wealth was to be found in the resumption of estates recently granted to monasteries. Gustaf obtained the approval of the council of nobles for such a resumption on his part of the estate of Gripsholm, the Carthusian monastery of Mariefred, which had been founded quite recently (in the year 1493) by Sten Sture the elder. Gustaf, who was heir to the Sture property, through his maternal grandmother, Birgitta, Sture's sister, declared that his father had been forced into giving his consent to the foundation, and that he was, therefore, entitled to resume the estate. The Vasas had inherited the neighbouring lands of Räfsnäs, and, therefore, were naturally desirous of recovering Gripsholm. The Carthusians were

---

[5] Tunstall was provided to the Bishopric of London in 1522, apparently by Adrian VI.

persuaded to resign it, but this high-handed act aroused much criticism and suspicion. As Anjou says: " His enemies saw a judgment from on high in the events which made this place of Gripsholm a mournful witness of the fraternal hatred of his sons " (*Ref. in Sw.*, 147). The castle which the king built in 1537 is still preserved in the present palace, and is a place of pilgrimage for all who are interested in Swedish history.

§ 5.—THE SACK OF ROME (1527). THE RIKSDAG, RECESS AND ORDINANTIA OF VESTERÅS.

It was not, however, until four years after the election at Strengnäs that large measures of change were introduced in Sweden. During these years the war between Charles V. and Pope Clement VII. set at liberty the forces of the Reformation in Germany, and at the diet of Spires it was resolved, with imperial approval, that all the states of that country were free to choose their own religion. A similar freedom was felt in other neighbouring countries, and, after the sack of Rome by imperial troops in May, 1527, the power of the papacy was, for the time, brought very low. I may remark that Tyndale's English version of the New Testament was published in 1526, and that about the same time the validity of Henry's marriage with Katharine began to be publicly discussed. It was at midsummer in the year 1527 that the Church of Sweden was forced by a vote of the estates to take a new position towards the State. This was at the Riksdag of Vesterås, the most important moment of the Reformation of the sixteenth century, with the exception of the Upsala-möte of 1593. These two dates then, 1527 and 1593, are the most necessary for the student to bear in memory, and to group his recollections round them. At Vesterås a large measure of disestablishment and disendowment was carried after a struggle, and a general though indefinite liberty of preaching was conceded to the reformers, but no mention was made of Luther or Lutheranism. In this point the course of events was very different from what it was in Denmark, where, in August of the same year, the name Lutheran was distinctly adopted at Odense.   It was not until the Upsala-möte of 1593 that any Lutheran formula was accepted by the whole Church of Sweden, and the name " Lutheran," though in common use, is not official.

The Riksdag of Vesterås was attended by a large number of representatives, of whom the bishops especially concern us.   There was then in Sweden no archbishop.   Johannes Magni, a learned man, and a real lover of his country, but ambitious, fond of display, and weak in character, had come out in 1522 as legate of Pope Adrian VI., in order to settle the matter of the deposition of Gustavus Trolle.

Johannes was on good terms with the king, and was ready to ratify the deposition of Trolle, and, like Arcimboldi in 1518, desired himself to become archbishop in his place on election by the chapter.   Adrian VI. was not ready for this, though, if he had lived, he would probably have come round to it in time.   But his successor, Clement VII., was opposed to all reforms, and for some years paid little attention to Swedish affairs.

Johannes, for a considerable time, administered the diocese of Upsala, as archbishop-elect, and took upon him great state, going about with a large and burdensome retinue.   This offended the king, who knew the value of money, and the ill-feeling which such proceedings on the part of an archbishop occasioned.   The title of majesty was not yet known in Sweden, and, at a sumptuous banquet, the archbishop, who was host, called out to the king : " Our grace drinks to your grace."   The king rejoined : " Our grace and your grace have not room under the same roof," and, with these words, he left the table.   A breach arose, and, in the autumn before the Riksdag, Johannes was glad to leave the kingdom, and the king was happy to be quit of him.   Johannes left the administration of his diocese in the hands of Brask, who was thus the one strong hope of the old religion left in the country.

Four bishops only were present at Vesterås, Hans Brask of Linköping and Petrus Magni of Vesterås, who had both been consecrated after papal confirmation, and two others, who were as yet only bishops-elect. Petrus was a learned man like Johannes, but was somewhat weaker in character, though less fond of display, and, in fact, was a man of unpretentious temper. He had long resided at Rome as representative of Vadstena and as prior of the Birgittines there. His encyclopædic writings were of the most varied and technical character, and must have been valuable to his countrymen, but they were mostly translations or adaptations of foreign works. His best known book, the *Barnabok*, was an adaptation of Erasmus' *Institutio principis Christiani*.[6] In 1523 Petrus, called Sunnanveder, had been deposed for treason by the Chapter of Vesterås, and Petrus Magni was elected in his place—although he had voted against the deposition. He was confirmed and consecrated at Rome the 1st May, 1524, by authority of Clement VII.—a fact very important for Sweden since through him the " Apostolical succession " was maintained and transmitted at this critical epoch in its history.

The other two, who were at present only bishops-elect, were Magnus Haraldi of Skara, and Magnus Sommar of Strengnäs, who had been respectively chosen to take the place of the two Danish nominees, Slagheck and Beldenacke, who had been thrust into these sees by Christian II. in place of Vincentius and Mathias, whom he had so cruelly executed. There was no difficulty about their confirmation by the pope, except that he refused to give it until they had paid their fees, and in particular the usual contribution of annates, or first fruits. Probably they would have been willing to pay, but the king objected to so much money going out of Sweden, and he was also not sorry to represent the pope as acting meanly in selling the approval of the Church for money.[7] There was a precedent (as we have seen) for the remission of such fees in

[6] Schück : *Ill. lit. H.*, I., 159.
[7] See for the history of these negotiations Anjou : l.c., pp. 93-103.

difficult times, and if Clement VII. had been a more politic man he might well have waived his claim now (p. 159 n. 11).

Besides the four bishops, there were present four prebendaries, fifteen lords of the council, 129 nobles, thirty-two burgesses, fourteen miners and 125 peasants from nearly all parts of the kingdom. Only two or three came from the southern part of Dalarne, which was generally in a state of sullen revolt (*S. H.*[2], ii. 91). Deputies do not appear to have been summoned from Finland. The king gave a sort of warning to the bishops of the change which was imminent by seating them, at the opening banquet, below the councillors and the principal temporal nobles, instead of next to himself, as had previously been the custom, even when administrators ruled the kingdom (Anjou: 195). Before the public meeting of the Riksdag the bishops held a private conclave in the Church of St. Giles, at which, on Brask's proposal, they passed an anticipatory protest against any invasion of the rights of the Church, which they concealed under the floor, where it was found fifteen years later.

No detailed contemporary account of the Riksdag exists; and, although the description of it by Peter Svart, the king's historiographer, is peculiarly vivid and interesting, it was not composed till some thirty years after the event. The king's opening address was read by his chancellor, Laurentius Andreæ,[8] who was, of course, known to be a strong ally of the reformers. It is an able and striking document, which you will do well to study in the pages of Geijer or Anjou, if not in the original Swedish. I wish that I had time in this lecture to summarize it for you. It was particularly strong in denouncing the oppression of the papacy in money matters, the insolence of the bishops, and the excessive wealth of the priests and monks, convents and churches. The king requested the advice of the estates as to those who did not use their revenues for the good of the commonalty, and laid stress upon the needs of

[8] There is a fair account of this man s.v. *Anderson*, by Michelsen, in *P. R. E.*[2], which is not reprinted in *P. R. E.*[3]

the crown, which now spent every year two and a half times
what it received.   Turé Jönsson, the oldest member of the
council, put forward Brask to reply.   He spoke firmly and
temperately : " That he knew well indeed in what fealty he
was bound to his king, but he and his whole class were also
obliged to render obedience to the pope in spiritual things,
and could not without his sanction consent either to any
alteration of doctrine or to a diminution of the rights and
property of the Church.   Had worthless priests and monks
sought gain by encouraging superstitious usages, which
the heads of the Church themselves disapproved, such
practices might be abrogated and punished.''

The councillors and nobles generally agreed that this
was a fair answer.   Gustaf, with passion, declared he
would no longer be king on such terms.   He would sooner
leave the country and never return.   He left the hall in
tears.

This passion moved the assembly, particularly those
elements of it who had not yet declared their opinion.
Their feeling was voiced by Magnus Sommar, elect of
Strengnäs, who now acted in a contrary direction to Brask.
It is characteristic of Sweden, both that the assembly was
so swayed by real or seeming emotion (I hardly think that
it was *all* acting on the part of Gustaf), and that it should
so look to the bishops for advice first on one side and then
on the other.

The next day, according to the ordinary account—that of
Peter Svart—was spent in a disputation between Olaus
Petri, on the part of the reformers, and Peter Galle, on the
part of the Church.[9]   On the third day the nobles and the
clergy were obliged to yield to the tumultuous demands of
the burgesses and peasants, and the king was at last and
with difficulty persuaded to continue in the government on
the promise that his proposals should be accepted.   The
result, which appears to have been more than the king at

[9] Dr. H. Schück : *Olavus Petri*, p. 44, says the disputation
took place *after* the king's proposals were accepted, and, therefore, had no direct influence on the result.

first proposed, and perhaps more than he expected, was contained in the document called the " Recess of Vesterås." The word " recess," I may explain, was in use in Sweden and Denmark from about the middle of the fourteenth century (1354) for a protocol or minute of the proceedings of an assembly drawn up on its retirement (hence the name), to which the members or their commissioners affixed their seals in attestation of its accuracy. The important provisions are thus summarized by Geijer, in language which I cannot improve (p. 118) :—

" The bishops, who from this time were no longer summoned to the Council, briefly declared in a special instrument " that they were content however rich or poor soever his grace would have them to be."

The Recess of Vesterås contains :—

(1) A mutual engagement to withstand all attempts at revolt and to punish them, as also to defend the present government against all enemies, foreign and domestic ; (2) a grant of power to the king, to take into his own hands the castles and strongholds of the bishops, and to fix their revenues, as well as those of the prebends and canonries, to levy fines hitherto payable to the bishops, and to regulate the monasteries, " in which there had for a long time been woeful mis-government " ; (3) authority for the nobles to resume that part of their hereditary property which had been conveyed to churches and convents since the Inquisition (räfst) of Karl Knutsson in 1454, if the heir-at-law could substantiate his birthright thereto, at the Ting, by the oaths of twelve men ; (4) liberty for the preachers to proclaim the pure word of God, " but not," the barons add, " uncertain miracles, human inventions and fables, as hath been much used heretofore." Respecting the new faith, on the other hand, the burghers and miners declare that " inquiry might be made, but that the matter passed their understanding " ; as do the peasants, since " it was hard to judge more deeply than understanding permitted." The answer of the latter betrays the affection they still, for the most part, bore to the clergy, with the exception of the mendicant friars or sackmonks, of whose conduct they complain. Of the bishops' castles they say that the king may take them in keeping, until the kingdom shall be more firmly settled ; for the article respecting the revenues of the Church, they believe they are unable to answer it, but commit it to the king and his Council.

In that supplement to the statute, which is entitled the Ordinance of Vesterås, it is enacted, that a register of all the rents of the bishops, cathedrals and canons, should be drawn up, and the king might direct what proportion of these should be reserved to the former owners, and how much paid over to him for the requirements of the crown ; that ecclesiastical offices, not merely the higher, but the inferior, should for the future be filled up only with the king's consent, so that the bishops might supply the vacant parishes with preachers, but, subject to the reviewal by the king, who might remove those whom he found to be unfit ; that in secular matters priests should be amenable to the civil jurisdiction, and, on their decease, no part of their effects should devolve to the bishops ; finally, that from that day the gospels should be read in all schools, " as beseems those which are truly Christian."

§ 6.—THE KING USES HIS POWERS.   CORONATION 1528.
NEW BISHOPS.   COUNCIL OF ÖREBRO 1529.

The next few years saw Gustaf exercising the large powers thus put into his hands, as far as the insurrections with which he had to cope permitted him to do so. We must not suppose that all right and reason lay on the side of the peasants, and all injustice on that of the government and nobles. The Dalesmen and the Smålanders in particular had learnt that the power of warlike combination, of going out armed with cross-bow and poleaxe, was a convenient method of escaping taxation by whomsoever it was claimed. The Dalesmen were offended by the neglect with which they supposed their privileges and previous services to be treated. Then there was, at a later date, the still more important rising of the nobles and peasants in favour of the old religion under Turé Jönsson, in West Gothland, in which Bishop Magnus Haraldi was involved. Gradually, however, the king worked through his troubles. He already possessed three bishops' castles : he now took the others—Tynnelsö from Strengnäs, Leckö from Skara, and Munkeboda from Linköping. The monasteries were largely granted as fiefs to nobles whom it was prudent to conciliate, or they were restored to the private ownership of those who claimed them under the third article of the

Recess of Vesterås. The king himself found it possible to prove his relationship to a number of families besides that of the Stures, and where he claimed he was naturally regarded as having a strong case. Many of the inmates of the monasteries retired, more or less of their own free will, and many married. Nevertheless, the suppression of the monasteries went on with a comparative slowness, and the two Birgittine houses of Vadstena and Nådendal in Finland, and the Cistercian nunnery of Skokloster, south of Jönköping, survived for a number of years after the death of Gustaf, though in a state of decaying animation. Of Vadstena we read that in 1544 the king issued a letter permitting the monks and nuns, if they wished it, to return to a secular life. In the next year its chronicle ceased. " Yet " (says Anjou), " there were still eighteen sisters left in the cloister in the beginning of King John's reign, when, for a short time, it seems to have been again in bloom, until the stronger protestantism of Charles annihilated . . . in 1595 the last monastic establishment in Sweden " (Anjou: E. T., 234-4).

It should be added that a number of religious houses in Stockholm and other towns became hospitals under the government of the burgomaster and town council.

Hans Brask was satisfied with having made his protest at Vesterås, and left the kingdom in the autumn of that fateful year. He met Johannes Magni at Dantzig, but they had no great love for one another, and were unable to devise means for stemming the tide. Brask never returned to Sweden, though he wrote many letters to his flock and to the king. His latter days were spent in the monastery of Landa, in the diocese of Gnesen, in Poland, where he died about 1538. Johannes, the archbishop-elect, passed the rest of his life in Poland and Italy, particularly at Rome. He was confirmed and consecrated Archbishop of Upsala in 1533 (two years after the see was filled by Laurentius Petri) in the last year of Clement VIII., and died at Rome in 1544. His two books, the *History of the Kings of the Swedes and Goths* and *History of the Metropolitical Church of Upsala,* were edited by his learned brother, Olaus, who also became titular Archbishop of Upsala. Both John and Brask were good patriots, and may have been restrained by love of their country from attempting serious breaches of the peace. Brask was, however, much more practical than John in his attempts to serve his people. He was the first, as I have said, to conceive a plan for connecting Lakes Venern and Vettern by a canal, and he tried to establish a printing press at Söderköping.

As regards the official translation of the Bible, which the king requested the clergy to execute, Brask was at first critical of the undertaking; but, after a time, he seems to have become interested in it, and in 1526 the Chapter of Linköping was ready with its contribution—the Gospel according to St. Mark, and the two Epistles to the Corinthians.[10] But, though Brask was consistent in his principles, he had not the stuff of which to make a martyr, nor was Gustaf anxious to make martyrs. No one was put to death for his religion, either now or at any time in the following years.

In the autumn of 1527 the king prepared for his coronation, which was to take place in the following year. For this purpose it was necessary to have duly consecrated bishops. He, therefore, wrote in November to Magnus Sommar, elect of Strengnäs, to the effect that " the commonalty (allmogen) would hardly be content if they did not have anointed bishops; and, although that anointing was of little importance in itself, it was necessary for him, if he wished to proceed with his election, to have himself consecrated and anointed during the winter, only it must be before Epiphany. If he does not agree to this the king will not force him; but he will have to leave his bishop's seat, and the king will look out for someone else "

---

[10] Anjou (l.c., pp. 135-7) attributes the work to the precentor, Eric; but Holmquist inclines to think that it was Brask's own work: see *K. H. Årsskrift,* v. 247. Holmquist speaks of the work as still existing in MS.

(Cornelius: *Hist.* § 16). The result was that Magnus
Sommar, Magnus Haraldi of Skara, and a Dominican
friar, Martin Skytte of Åbo, were consecrated on the feast
of the Epiphany, 1528, by Petrus Magni of Vesterås, without papal confirmation, but evidently with the old ritual.
It is said that Petrus Magni only consented to perform the
duty on the promise of Laurentius Andreæ that the new
bishops should afterwards seek papal confirmation and
make an apology for Petrus to the Roman see (Anjou:
E. T., p. 244).

The coronation followed at Upsala on the 12th January.
It was noticed that the oath taken by the king was
shortened by the omission of the old promise on his part to
protect the holy Church and its persons. The coronation
sermon was preached by Olaus Petri, and contained some
remarkably free expressions of his thoughts on the position and duties of a king. The sermon was based on the
text of Deut. xvii. 15: " One from among thy brethren
shalt thou set king over thee: thou mayest not put a
foreigner over thee which is not thy brother." " The
king " (he says) " must not consider himself as lord over
his brethren, but should think on the fact that he and his
subjects have all sprung from the same root. He must
also remember that the reverence, the curtseying and bow-
ing, which is shown him by his subjects, is not for the
sake of his own person, but for that of his office, which he
has of God . . . and he should direct all the honour and
reverence which is shown him to God, giving Him the
praise which belongs to his office. For he is set to be a
ruler not over his own, but over God's, commonalty
(allmogen) and his fellow-brothers."

This democratic out-spokenness, as I have already said,
prevented Olaus from being a satisfactory minister of State,
and a practical politician, but it helped to endear him to
his fellow-countrymen, and to make them feel that some
of their best qualities were worthily represented in their
leading reformer.

About a year after his coronation the king wisely called

together a Church Council at Örebro (February 2nd-7th, 1529), which consisted only of spiritual persons, of whom about forty attended. Three bishops, Magnus of Skara, Magnus of Strengnäs and Peter of Vesterås, were there, but Laurentius Andreæ presided in place of the archbishop. We have no account of details, but we know its decisions, which are very important as evidences of the slow and cautious process of change in Sweden. The king's motto was: " Instruct first: reform afterwards." The first resolution was on preaching and teaching, the second on Church discipline, the third on ceremonies. Under the first head bishops were instructed to overlook the preaching of God's pure Word " as it is comprehended in the Scripture." In cathedrals there was to be a daily lesson of Holy Scripture, with a good explanation of it, which was to be attended by country clergy. The lower clergy of the cathedrals were also to attend. The town clergy were to be learned and to help to teach their brethren in the country, and to be ready to go out and preach for them. The old rule about repeating the Lord's Prayer, Creed, Ave Maria, and the Ten Commandments was renewed. The Ave Maria was, as I have said, in the same Biblical form as in England, not in the later Franciscan and present Roman form, which only crept in by degrees about this period into Southern Europe.[11]

As to discipline, scholars were forbidden to go about the country to collect alms—a re-enactment of a previous canon. The second article said: " As the law of the pope forbids some to enter into marriage whom God has not forbidden, it is determined to dispense with this law for honest reasons, provided scandal be avoided as far as possible." This was evidently a way of quietly repealing the law of celibacy as binding on the clergy, and probably all the prohibitions of marriage within the degrees of kindred or affinity, except those directly contained in Leviticus, or

[11] See my lecture, *The Invocation of Saints, and Article XXII.*, § 2, S.P.C.K., 1908. It does not appear in any Breviary before 1509, and then at Paris.

implied by parity of nearness. The bishops and chapters were apparently left in charge of this matter. Thus the course of legislation in Sweden in 1529 was not unlike that which was followed in England in 1533—1534, when the dispensing power of the pope was transferred to the Archbishop of Canterbury, except in cases prohibited by the " laws of God," with reservation of a reference to the sovereign or his council in unusual cases (25 Hen. VIII., c. 21). Whether Cranmer issued dispensations to the clergy to marry I do not know; but he had been himself twice married before he became archbishop.

As regards discipline over persons, the penitentiaries of cathedrals were allowed to " use any degree of severity with murderers and other heinous transgressors, as the worldly sword appears to be idle, and has not the force it ought to have."[12] The cloisters were put under the diocesan authorities. Monks were to show obedience to the bishops, especially in regard to preaching. Bishops, in their several dioceses, were to reduce the number of saints days, keeping our Lord's principal feasts, those of the Virgin Mary, the Apostles, and the local patron saint.

As regards ceremonies, there was no question of abolishing them, but only of explaining them as owing all their virtue to the work of Christ.

Thus it was laid down about anointing with oils or unction with chrism, that no other virtue was assigned to it, except that it was an outward sign of the inward unction which is given by the Holy Spirit. This explanation must have been intended to cover all kinds of unction—with oil on the breast in making catechumens ; with chrism on the crown of the head directly after baptism; with chrism at confirmation, in unction of the sick, and in consecration of bishops and perhaps of the hands of priests.[13]

---

[12] Anjou : l.c., 259.

[13] " Oelning eller Krismosmörjelse gifver ej annan magt utan det skall vara ett utvertes tecken till den invertes smörjelse, som sker genom den helige Ande." I cannot agree with F. N. Ekdahl (who quotes this passage, *Om Confirmationen*, p.

The Germans of Stockholm complained that so little progress was made in reformation, but it was too fast for many parts of the country. The result of the rising in West Gothland was that two more of the adherents of the old order, Turé Jönsson and Magnus Haraldi, Bishop of Skara, left the country, and did not return to it. The bishop's place was filled by the provost, Sveno Jacobi, whose election was confirmed by a council at Upsala in 1530. The see of Linköping was filled two years after Brask's retirement by a Johannes Magni, and that of old Ingemar of Vexiö, who died in 1530, by Johannes Boethii. Shortly afterwards the king agreed, after some reluctance, knowing how much mischief former archbishops had done, that the see of Upsala should at last be filled. He set aside the rights of the chapter, and held a large assembly of the clergy of the whole realm at Stockholm in 1531, of whom about 171 took part in the election of an archbishop. As many as 150 votes were given in favour of Laurentius Petri, brother of the reformer, and thus Sweden was, by God's providence, provided with its first reformed archbishop, who, wisely and faithfully, directed the course of the Church for the next forty-two years. The three first-named bishops were first consecrated at Stockholm the 13th August, 1531, and the new archbishop on the 22nd September of the same year. The consecration in both cases was performed by Petrus Magni and Magnus Sommar, who, however, met in Strengnäs on the 10th August, and compiled a protest against the Lutheran doctrine, the consecration of the new bishops, which they were forced to

9in., Lund., 1889) that this refers only to the use of chrism in baptism to cross the child's forehead and breast, and does not— as Staaff, I think, rightly concludes—include confirmation. It may be remarked also that the unction with chrism made by the priest after baptism, was not on the forehead and breast, but on the crown of the head—" *Hic fac crucem cum crismate in vertice infantis dicens* : Ipse te liniat," etc., are the words of the Skara ritual of 1493 ; and so Olaus *gör than itt kors pa thes hiessa medh chrismo och segher*, etc.

perform, the taxation of the clergy, the Swedish mass, etc. This was deposited with two members of the Chapter of Strengnäs, and does not seem to have been known to the king. Its object, we may presume, was to justify their action in case a change of government brought back the old order of things, and to escape punishment on account of it. Hans Brask had shown the usefulness of such a protest in regard to the case of Gustavus Trolle, and such a protest had been also made before the Riksdag of Vesterås.[14]

Petrus Magni shortly after this fell into disgrace by his indiscreet management of the unpopular call upon each of the churches to deliver up or redeem their largest bell, and to make other contributions to the necessities of the State, but he remained in office till his death in 1534. There was an even more serious breach between the king and his old ally, Magnus Sommar, and he was deposed in 1536, but afterwards pardoned and allowed to live in quiet retirement, while his place was taken by Botvid Sunonis, a friend of Olaus Petri.[15] Thus, by the year 1536, the various sees were filled by men who were in sympathy with the new teaching. The reformers had hitherto worked by influenc-

---

[14] On the contents of this protest see more in Anjou : *E. T.*, p. 282. He adds : " It was not drawn up to be made public, unless under a change of circumstances, which should render it necessary as a self-defence. It was another evidence of the moral laxity in the high places of the Church, which we have had more than one occasion to notice."

[15] The exact date and circumstances of the consecration of Bishop Botvid of Strengnäs are not known. He is an important link in the episcopal succession in Sweden, since he consecrated Paulus Juusten of Åbo in 1554, who in his turn consecrated Archbishop Laurentius Petri Gothus, 14th June, 1575. The fact, however, of Botvid's consecration cannot be doubted. See A. Nicholson: *Apostolical Succession in the Church of Sweden*, pp. 36-48, 1880. Up to 7th September, 1536, Botvid was only "electus." On 30th August, 1539, he ordained Olaus Petri priest (Nicholson, pp. 37 and 41). Unfortunately the records of Strengnäs have been destroyed by fire, or we should know at what date between those two days he was consecrated ; probably it was in 1536.

ing public opinion through the press and the pulpit, especially in Stockholm; they might now expect to be able to work more publicly and corporately upon the national life. But in 1539 the attitude of the king towards his old advisers was almost entirely changed, and the steady progress of the reformation in a Swedish Lutheran sense was checked by the introduction of an ultra-reforming and somewhat Calvinist regime under Von Pyhy and George Norman.

This, therefore, seems a fitting moment to say something of the literary activity of the first generation of reformers, especially of Olaus Petri, and to state what Sweden owes to him and to his brother, Laurentius.

§ 7.—WORK OF OLAUS PETRI.   FALL OF OLAUS AND LAURENTIUS ANDREÆ.

The main work of Olaus [16] was to popularize religious thought of a simple evangelical character among his countrymen, and to do this through the medium of books and popular preaching in their own language. The first printed book in Sweden came out in 1483, but that was in Latin. The first Swedish book was printed in 1495, and the second in 1514. There were not ten works printed in the language when the literary activity of Olaus began to be displayed in 1526. In this year appeared the Swedish New Testament, translated from Erasmus' revision of the Vulgate, with the help of Luther's early German version— a book which did much to form Swedish style, and to give it purity of language and a natural and logical syntax. The book bore no name, but, since the researches of Pro-

[16] See H. Schück: *Olavus Petri*, Stockholm, 1906, and J. E. Berggren: *Olaus Petris Reformatoriska Grundtankar* in Upsala Universitets Årsskrift, 1899, which draws its quotations from U. von Troils: *Skrifter och handlingar till upplysning svenska kyrko och reformations-historien*, Upsala, 1790—1791. Cp. H. Schück: *Våra äldsta reformationsskrifter och deras författare* in *Hist. Tidskrift*, 1894, pp. 97-130.

fessor Schück, it is now believed to be mainly the work of
Olaus.   Those to whom such questions are of interest
will do well to study Professor Stave's careful *Essay on
the Sources of the New Testament Version of 1526*, in
which the character and extent of the debt to Erasmus and
Luther are clearly explained.[17]   The Swedish New Testament and the chronicle of Olaus are considered as models
of what Swedish prose ought to be, although the style of
his brother Laurentius is even better.   Three other
Swedish publications of the same year, though anonymous,
are thought also to be the work of Olaus.[18]   Amongst them
was a Psalm-book, or hymn-book, which is unfortunately
no longer in our hands, which contained fifteen hymns,
some translations from Luther and others, and some
originals, of which several are still sung.[19]   The one on the
Nativity is full of life.

The following years saw a similar activity, and in these
four years Olaus printed twice as many books as previously
existed in Swedish.   These included the first catechism,
a free adaptation of Luther's greater catechism, useful
" postils " or explanations of the Gospels for the use of the
less learned clergy, the hand-book, or ritual, and the
Swedish mass.   The last two require special mention, and
we must be grateful to Dr. Oscar Quensel for making them
more easily accessible in his scholarly edition.[20]

The hand-book is not only the first collection of the
ritual services in Swedish, but it is the first book of the

---

[17] *Om källorna till 1526 års öfversättning af Nya Testa-
mentet*, af Erik Stave, Upsala, 1893.

[18] See H. Schück : *Olavus Petri*, p. 50, who puts the *Psalm-
bok* in 1526.

[19] Cornelius : *Hist.*, p. 45, assigns this book to the year 1530.
He refers to three hymns : (1) *O Fader vår barmhertig, god;*
(2) *O Jesu Krist, som mandom tog* ; (3) *En jungfru födde ett
barn i dag* as being still in use.   Probably the whole number
were reprinted in 1536, in the first Swedish hymn-book that is
still in existence.   It was reprinted in 1862.

[20] *Bidrag till Svenska Liturgiens Historia*, 2 parts, Upsala,
1890.   This also contains King John's missal and much other
illustrative material.

kind in any modern language.   It appeared first in 1529, and it contains the services for baptism, marriage, churching of women, visitation and communion of the sick, blessing of a corpse and burial of the dead, and visitation of prisoners.   In these services the old ceremonies were largely retained.

Thus baptism began with a short exorcism, followed by the " primsigning " (as it was called in Swedish), or crossing of the face and breast of the child, then laying hands on its head and blessing it, and a taste of salt put into the mouth.   Then came a further exorcism, another imposition of hands, whilst the priest knelt with the godfather and godmother to say the Lord's Prayer, a cross made with oil on the breast, questions as to the Creed, baptism with trine immersion, unction with chrism on the crown of the head, clothing the child, in the chrisom or white dress, and the light or font-taper put into the child's hands.

In marriage the ring was put first on the thumb, then on the index finger, and then left on the middle finger in the name of Father, Son and Holy Ghost.   It is now put on what we call the ring-finger, next the little finger.   The married pair were also covered by a canopy (pell or pallium) later in the service.

In the communion of the sick there was no consecration prayer, but the sacrament was administered in both kinds, apparently from what had been consecrated in church (l.c., i. 61).   Unction of the sick on eyes, ears, nose, lips, hands and feet was also provided (ibid. 65-6).

While these ceremonies were retained explanations of many of them were introduced in the form of long rubrics and exhortations, in accordance with the Council of Örebro.

There was, however, no form of private confession and absolution provided, except in the visitation of the sick and of prisoners.   But what naturally strikes an English reader as the greatest defect is the absence of any form of confirmation.   This is the more remarkable since Luther had already spoken favourably of some kind of rite of the

sort in a sermon preached in 1523. " We need not care
for confirmation as the bishops desire it, but every pastor
might examine children as to their faith, and, if it were
good and genuine, should lay on hands and confirm." [21]
Nothing, however, was prescribed in early Lutheran
books, except that when people came to communion they
should show that they had the requisite knowledge.
Evangelical confirmation in Germany appears to owe its
practical introduction to Martin Bucer, especially in his
struggles against the Anabaptists in Hesse in 1538, where
he found it a valuable protection of the custom of infant
baptism. It is generally said that it was dropped in
Sweden in order to maintain the supremacy of the two
sacraments ordained by Christ himself. But this explanation does not quite suit the previous and recent attitude of
Olaus, who, in his *Little Book about the Sacraments*, published in 1528, wrote that, as the sacrament of confirmation, considered as an act of unction, is not found in Holy
Scripture, it cannot be considered as necessary, " but it
can well remain as useful, when it is performed with the
intention which has just been mentioned, the intention
being to explain that the unction does not confer grace,
but is a reminder of the grace of baptism." I have already
quoted the similar resolution on oil and unction passed by
the Council of Örebro, held in the next year (1529). I
conclude, therefore, that Olaus, not being very clear or
keen on the subject, may have excused himself from not
naming it in his hand-book, because it was an episcopal
act, like ordination, and one performed by bishops at their
visitations, and for that reason was properly part of the
pontifical, not of the manual. It does not occur in the
Linköping, Skara and Åbo Latin services, which Freisen
has reprinted, and, of course, for this reason. We must

---

[21] " Confirmatio ut volunt episcopi non curanda, sed tamen
quisque pastor posset scrutari a pueris fidem, quæ si bona et
germana esset, ut imponeret manus et confirmaret," quoted by
G. Rietschel : *Lehrbuch der Liturgik*, II., § 24. On Bucer,
see the same section further on.

not, therefore, find fault with Olaus for not prescribing it; but, if we blame anyone, it must be his brother, Laurentius, of whose treatment of the subject in his *Kyrko-ordning* we shall speak later.   Its absence may have been made more natural by neglect on the part of the later mediæval bishops, a cause which I rather conjecture than am able to prove.

Certainly it is but rarely mentioned, and, as regards that worldly potentate, Archbishop Johannes Benedicti, we have the complaint made against him by his own chapter that his participation in secular politics and civil business led him to neglect his spiritual duties of visitation especially in the districts far from Upsala, so that confirmation (fermelse), which it was a bishop's duty to administer, was largely disused by a great number of persons.[22]

That the Swedish Church of the sixteenth century was in favour of episcopal confirmation of a sort I shall show when I come to speak of 1571.

The blessing of a corpse, whilst it is still in the house, contains a rather striking prayer, which appears to be mainly the composition of Olaus himself, though the last clauses in it are suggested by an older form.[23]   A very similar prayer also appears in the burial office.   The blessing of a corpse is as follows :—

" O almighty and merciful everlasting God, who on account of sin hast laid on man that he must die, and who, that we

[22] Ehdahl, l.c., p. 90, from A. W. Staaff : *Om Konfirmationens uppkomst och antagande i Sverige*, p. 46 n., Stkh., 1871.

[23] See the prayer : " Oremus patres charissimi pro spiritu cari nostri quem dominus de laqueo huius seculi liberare dignatus est : cuius corpusculum hodie sepulture traditur, ut eum pietas domini in sinu abrahe, ysaac et iacob collocare dignetur : ut cum dies iudicii advenerit inter sanctos et electos tuos eum in parte dextera collocandum resuscitari faciat," etc., in the *Manuale Aboense*, ed. Freisen, p. 230, Paderborn, 1904. It is found in Muratori : *Lit. Romana vetus*, Greg : p. 216, and in the *Leofric Missal*, p. 201.

should not for ever abide in death, hast laid death on thy beloved Son Jesus Christ, who had no sin, and hast so by thy Son's death transformed our death that it cannot hurt us, turn now thy fatherly countenance on us thy poor children and hear our prayer, that if our departed *brother*, whom thou through death hast called out of this painful life, is in such case that our prayers can avail to help *him*, thou mayest be to *him* gentle and merciful (O heavenly Father), keep *him* in Abraham's bosom, and at the last judgment raise *him* up in the resurrection of the just, through the same thy Son Jesus Christ our Lord. Amen.''[24]

The Swedish mass, according to the form now in use at Stockholm (then Svenska messan epter som hon nw holles i Stockholm medh orsaker hwar före hon så hollen vardher), was published with the name of Olaus in 1531, and probably represents the use which had prevailed for some six years in his church.   A mass had been first sung in Swedish at his wedding in 1525.   A vote also was taken on the question whether the mass should continue to be said in Swedish in the town council in 1529, which seems to refer to the form afterwards printed in 1531.[25]

More alterations and omissions were made in the liturgy than in the baptismal service.   Olaus seems to have followed most closely Luther's *Formula missæ et communionis* for Wittenberg, issued in 1523, and the *Nürnberger Messe* of Andreas Osiander and others of 1525. He was less influenced, if at all, by Luther's *Deudsche Messe* of 1526, and the *Malmö-Mässa* of 1529.[26]

[24] Dr. Quensel observes that this prayer is the foundation of one in the Prussian *Agende*.   This is true for the earlier part, but those German forms which I have seen turn the last clauses into a prayer for the living.

[25] Quensel : l.c., II., 21-2.   Among other complaints made by Turé Jönsson in 1529 was that the king had allowed the mass to be transformed into the Swedish tongue.

[26] Professor Carl Roland Martin has conveniently printed the *Nürnberger Messe*, the *Deudsche Messe*, the *Malmö-Mässa* and Olaus in parallel columns : see *Sveriges första Svenska Mässa med Jämförelser och Belysningar*, Upsala, 1901 ; but this does not contain the *Formula missæ et communionis*, etc., for which we must refer to Aem. Richter : *Die evangelischen Kirchen-ordnungen*, I., p. 4, Weimar, 1846 (or in the new edi-

The most remarkable point of contact with Luther's *Formula* and the Nürnberg mass was the introduction of the narrative of the institution of the Lord's Supper into the preface before the Sanctus—a novelty which Luther himself altered in his *Deudsche Messe* of 1526. We may, therefore, I think, date the composition of the first Swedish mass in the year 1525—1526, after Olaus had received Osiander's book from Nürnberg, but before he had seen Luther's *Deudsche Messe* of the latter year.   There is, therefore, some reason to believe that the form first used at the marriage of Olaus was that which continued in use at Stockholm until it was printed in 1531.   This, however, is only a conjecture.

The reason for which Luther adopted this arrangement clearly was in order that he might get rid of the prayers of the offertory and the canon of the Roman mass, and especially the element of sacrifice, which he viewed with abhorrence, and yet give the narrative of the institution a prominent place as part of the thanksgiving.   None of these German forms had a direct prayer of consecration, although such a prayer had appeared in the first Protestant form of service in the German language, that issued by Kaspar Kantz of Nördlingen in 1522.[27]   The Lord's Prayer was, no doubt, intended in some sort to supply its place in the Nürnberg and Swedish forms.

As to other less important points, Olaus seems to have

tion by Professor Sehling).   Luther's severe words about the "Canon missæ" may be recalled : "Octavo sequitur tota illa abominatio cui servire coactum est quicquid in missa præcessit, unde et offertorium vocatur.   Et ab hinc omnia fere sonant ac olent oblationem. . . . Proinde omnibus illis repudiatis quæ oblationem sonant, cum universo canone, retineamus quæ pura et sancta sunt."   Professor Martin considers the Nürnberg form to be the one which Olaus most closely followed in laying out the plan of the Swedish mass (l.c., p. 8).

[27] "Grant that this bread and the wine may become and be for us thy dearest Son's our Lord Jesus Christ's true body and sinless blood," leading up to the words of institution in the form of a prayer : see Martin : l.c., p. 8.

been rather careless as to the liturgical year, though he did not wholly overlook it.   He gives a general collect, and, as an alternative, "some other, according to the season." "After the collect" (he writes) "is read a chapter or half a chapter from St. Paul's, or some other Apostle's Epistles, the gradual (either 'the song at God's board,' or some other), then a chapter or half a chapter from one of the Evangelists, then the Apostles' or Nicene Creed."   He notes later that his idea is to read the Epistles and Gospels through continuously, but that the present system may go on till folk are better instructed.[28]

As regards the sermon, Olaus at first made no mention of one, perhaps because at first Luther himself inclined to put it before the introit, and to connect it with the matins, which preceded.   This, no doubt, was Olaus' own plan.[29]

As regards ceremonies, no mention was made of the mixture of the chalice (about which Luther was doubtful), but elevation was prescribed after the words of institution, both for the consecrated bread and the chalice—acts which Luther had allowed.

The rule was also laid down that there was to be a communion of the people at every celebration.

To turn now for a few minutes from the writings to the man.   Olaus was an attractive personality, and he had an active mind, but he was not a great theologian.   He had left the Lutheran University early in life, and he had few men of higher calibre than himself to associate with in Sweden.   It was, perhaps, fortunate for his country that he did not bring with him the atmosphere of the Protestant controversies which were developed in the latter part of

[28] Cp. Quensel : l.c., II., 32 foll., Martin : pp. 45 foll. 66, 84 foll.   The *Nürnberger Messe* had a fixed Epistle and Gospel, Rom. v., and S. John vi., 52-58, the *Malmö-Mässa* prescribes I. Cor. xi. 17 foll., or some other passage from the Old and New Testament for the Epistle, and a Gospel suitable to the season from the Evangelists.

[29] The fact that in the *Deudsche Messe* Luther took for granted that the sermon would be delivered during the Liturgy is another reason for the early date I give to the Swedish form.

Luther's life among the divines of his party. Olaus looked upon theology as a simple thing, and he had little sympathy with learned debates about it. It was to be "God's Word purely preached"; and although "God's Word" was not simply an equivalent for Holy Scripture, his teaching was intended to be entirely based on Scripture. When there was a difficulty it was to be overcome by comparing Scripture with Scripture. His business was to teach simple truth to simple people, and he did it in language such as we should nowadays largely address to children. His teaching was also very serious and solemn, and tinged with a strong sense of sin and of duty. Olaus had little of the geniality and enjoyment of life which made Luther so popular with his countrymen. In his later years he became disappointed and melancholy. He was disappointed with the king, who did not share his ideals, and rudely and ungratefully cast him aside and trampled on him, and disappointed with the men around him. He had indeed married before Luther did in the year 1525, a lady of good birth, called Kristina, five years older than himself, and, as I said, mass was for the first time said in Swedish on that occasion.[30]

But very little is known of her, and the event seems to have made little outward difference to his life, certainly nothing like that which Luther's marriage made to him. To Olaus marriage was a duty, as he describes it in a little book on the subject, and duty wore a somewhat stern aspect to Olaus all his life. There is no reason, however, to suspect that Olaus' marriage was an unhappy one, and

[30] So we read in Messenius' Rhyme-chronicle :—

> " On Master Olof's wedding day
> Our Lutherdom had made such way
> That mass in Swedish first was sung,
> So all men followed their own tongue.
> For so had Master Olof seen
> How things at Wittenberg had been ;
> There first at Carlstadt's marriage feast
> Was German mass sung by a priest."

they had at least two children, Elisabeth and Reginald.[31] His great outburst of literary activity in the two years after his marriage may also be taken as a sign that his life at this period was one of comfort, repose and hopefulness.

Olaus' principles as a reformer have been well expounded by ex-provost Berggren of Upsala. I will quote some sentences from the closing pages of this valuable essay (pp. 76-7):—

"It is no great art," says Olaus, "to punish or to break down, for a Turk or a heathen can do that; but it is an art to knock down what is wrong, and with reason and understanding to set up again that which is right and true." Olaus himself both broke down and built up, and he has proved that he understands how both one and the other ought to be done. He has broken down what needed to be broken, and built up what needed to be built, and his greatness lies not least in the latter. The most striking proof of this is in the *New Testament in Swedish* of 1526, *A Hand-book in Swedish*, *The Swedish Mass*, his postils, his catechism and his hymn-book. We cannot reflect without wonder on what he had so effected in a very short time, and under circumstances which were not the most favourable. Part of what he thus "set up" remains even now, after more than three and a half centuries, for the edification of the present generation. It is not pre-eminently through depth of thought, through wealth of great and original ideas that he distinguishes himself, but it is through the fresh, healthy, purpose-like element in what he proclaims; it is by virtue of his skill in producing just what the hour requires that he has his strength. It is a marked feature of his character that he only wills to *build up* through instruction, that he only wishes to work upon the feelings through the *understanding*. His reforming activity was not exhibited merely in combating one or more doctrines contrary to the Scripture, in removing the most injurious accretions, or false developments from the organism of the Church, in merely impressing life with the stamp of an external Churchmanship, in calling forth occasional pious thoughts and dispositions, but he aimed above

[31] *Biogr. Lexicon*, Vol. xi., p. 178. Elisabeth married a certain Ericus Petri in Stockholm, and Reginald took his degree as Magister Philosophiæ in Germany. The fullest account of the two brothers appear to be by J. G. Hallman: *The tvenne Bröder Oluff P. Phase och Laur. P. til lefverne och vandel beskrivne*, Stockholm, 1726. Laurentius does not seem to have taken the name *Phase*, which Olaus used.

everything to *renew and transform life from within*, and not merely the life of the individual, but that of the whole community."

Olaus was indeed a fine, strong, consistent character, to whom Sweden owes a great debt; but it owes an equal debt to his quieter and less democratic younger brother, Laurentius, who may be called the Cranmer of Sweden, as Olaus was its Luther. It is unfortunate that no modern life of Laurentius has been written, nor, as far as I know, is there even a good modern sketch of his life like Dr. Schück's sketch of Olaus.

At his consecration it is said that Laurentius received his bishop's staff from the king's own hand, who thus revived the old pretensions of the twelfth century sovereigns. The king had taken the possessions of the see into his keeping, but restored to Laurentius a considerable part of the temporalities of the see, and the right to ride with fifty attendants. The cost of the latter he generously converted into exhibitions to fifty young students. The first eight years of his episcopate were not eventful, but in 1539 the king turned bitterly against the two men whom he had trusted as his two former chancellors. Olaus had offended him by the freedom of speech which he used in the pulpit, where he called the king tyrant and miser, and also in a printed book denounced the habit of profane swearing in terms which were known to apply to the king. Gustaf wrote to the archbishop, 24th April, 1539: "Sermons ought to consist not in railings and invectives against ceremonies, but in the faith of Christianity, in the doctrines of brotherly love, godly living, patience in suffering and so on. Christ and Paul enjoined obedience to rulers; Swedish priests, on the contrary, preach contumacy, giving the king the blame of all the swearing in use, that the people may be offended. God's Word, however, teaches first to warn privately, and exhort to improvement; but here you commence with open maledictions, both from the pulpit and in print. As you, therefore, treat the matter so unwisely, we order that from this time no step is to be taken in the Reformation, nothing printed unknown to us; and you, archbishop, take you special heed to yourself if you wish to avoid disagreeables.''[32] After this the king appointed George Norman, who had come to him as tutor to his son Eric, by his first wife, Catherine of Lauenburg, to be superintendent of the clergy of the kingdom. Personal irritation, however, gave place to deeper suspicion in the king's mind when he discovered that his two former ministers had known of his German mintmaster's (Anders Hansson) intention of murdering him, but had kept it secret, because it came to them under the seal of confession. At the end of 1539 they were formally brought to trial at Örebro. The new chancellor, Peutinger, drew up the bitter indictment against them, which collected various indiscretions and freedoms of speech and writing, but nothing worse than the charge of not revealing treason. However, on the 2nd January, 1540, they were both condemned to death, without giving them time or opportunity to reply. The archbishop was one of the fifteen judges who pronounced the sentence, and, it is said, that he was forced to sign it. Whether he thought the sentence just we do not know, but it would seem that all the judges were expected to subscribe what the majority voted. The death penalty was remitted, but both were heavily fined.[33] Andreæ lost nearly all his property, while Olaus' friends in Stockholm paid for him.

[32] Fryxell, 2, 230-1. See the full text in Celsii : *Mon. polit. eccles.*, p. 32, and the quotation in the *Biogr. lex.*, xi., 175.

[33] The contemporary account of this trial by Erik Jöransson Tegels, in a MS. chronicle preserved in the Royal Library at Stockholm, was never printed until 1893, probably on account of the bad light in which it exhibited the conduct of the king. It may be found conveniently edited by Dean H. Lundström in *K. H. Årsskrift* for 1909, *Meddelanden*, etc., pp. 54-84. Lundström's own judgment on the archbishop's character as to this sad moment in his history, and other occasions on which he is blamed for weakness, may be found in the same review, vol. vi. for 1905, 204 foll. Lundström's defence on this point is that reservations on the part of minorities were not usual at that period, and, indeed, not until a much later date.

Olaus became again secretary of the city in 1542, and pastor of the Great Church in 1543, an office which he held till his death in 1552. Laurentius Andreæ lived in retirement, and died about the same time as Olaus.

§ 8.—PRESBYTERIAN TENDENCY OF THE KING'S POLICY. NORMAN'S VISITATION AND "CHURCH ORDER." DIVISION OF DIOCESES.

A great change in the attitude of the State to the Church occurred after the year 1539, when Laurentius Andreæ and Olaus Petri were condemned, and its effects continued during the latter half of Gustaf's reign. Their fall was largely owing to the influence of the two foreigners whom Gustaf trusted, who naturally viewed the Church from a German standpoint. The supremacy of the princes in Germany in their own States, and of Henry VIII. in England, and the absence of the episcopal order in Germany, and its transformation and subjection in Denmark, were precedents naturally brought to the notice of Gustaf. Henry VIII., in 1531, had received from the English Convocation " the title of singular protector and supreme lord, and, so far as the law of Christ allows, supreme head of the English Church and clergy." [34]   Gustaf now took the less arrogant title of " supreme defender of the Christian faith over his whole realm," and now appointed George Norman as his ordinary and superintendent. This man was (with the consent of a council and an assistant) to exercise the king's jurisdiction over bishops, prelates and all other spiritual persons. He was to put such persons in office in the king's name, and to hold visitations by his authority, with the duty of reporting to the king. Besides the superintendent and his assistant, there were to be local elders, seniores—who seem to have been clergy (not laymen as Anjou suggested), and a local conservator, probably a layman, to inspect places visited by the super-

[34] See R. W. Dixon : *Hist. of the Ch. of Eng.*, ed. 3, I., p. 64, 1895.

intendent. A council was occasionally to be summoned by the king to deliberate on Church matters, consisting of these various persons. Thus the authority of the bishops seemed entirely to be set aside, and nothing apparently remained for them but the duty of ordination. Norman and his assistant, the ex-Dominican, Bishop Henry of Vesterås, visited West Gothland, Vermland and East Gothland, and Henry alone visited Småland. The visitation was accompanied by a large confiscation of all valuables, except such as were supposed to be needed for the altered form of worship. A recommendation of the use of the new edition of the hand-book and Swedish mass of Olaus Petri went hand in hand with this visitation. These proceedings led to the very serious peasant revolt under Nils Dacke in Småland, where a civil war lasted for about a year (1542—1543). The plan of superseding the regular government of the Church was then gradually dropped, though Norman was not publicly cashiered. Norman appears to have been a good and able man, and a gentleman, and, therefore, superior to some of the persons used in England for similar work. But he had one great defect: he never learnt Swedish, and, therefore, remained always an outsider in the country, in the internal affairs of which he was called to interfere so invidiously and so minutely.

We possess Norman's " Church Order " both in Latin and Swedish, issued in 1540 and 1541.[35] It is an interesting document, showing less of a reactionary spirit than we might have suspected. It orders daily morning and evening prayers (Art. 2). It allows a daily mass, *i.e.*, without communicants, because all abuses cannot at once be removed (Art. 4). It lessens the number of saint days, but preserves the three great festivals of Christmas, Easter and Pentecost, and those of the Purification, Annunciation and

[35] The Latin was published by Otto Ahnfelt : *Tidskrift för teologi*, 1892, pp. 352-422, with notes and illustrations. See Janne Romson : *Om datering-en af Georg Norman's Svenska Kyrko-ordning* in *K. H. Årsskrift*, 1906, pp. 130-4.

Visitation of the Blessed Virgin Mary. It specially prohibits the superstitious observation of the Sabbath,
"which, with so much obstinacy, is kept up by many
country folk" (Art. 7). This is thought by Ahnfelt to refer to the mediæval usage of hallowing Saturday by a mass
to the Blessed Virgin (*Tidskr. för teologi* 3, p. 288). Other
saints days, including the Nativity of the Blessed Virgin
Mary, are retained for civil reasons, as being market and
fair days. But invocation of saints is to be preached
against (Art. 8). Bishops and seniors may celebrate
divine service in Latin on the chief festivals (Art. 10). On
such festivals organs and "cantica figurativa," that is, I
think, psalmody with measured music, may be used (Art.
12). Fasting on Fridays is commended as a memorial of
the Passion, but not as necessary (Art. 13). Freewill
offerings should still be made at the altar on the principal
feasts, to be divided into three parts for the Church, the
poor and the clergy (Art. 14). Preaching is to refer to
some article in the Catechism, which is to be gone through
four times a year, and people are to be taught the method
of prayer explained by Melanchthon (Arts. 15, 16). Stress
is laid on preaching our duty to magistrates, and explanation of the divine element in law. Unction of the sick is
not to be retained, and the writer doubts what he ought
to say on confirmation (Art. 17).

As regards matrimonial causes article 19 runs :—

"His Royal Majesty orders that matrimony may be con-
tracted in the fourth and fifth degree [*i.e*, between first cousins
and beyond that relationship], according to the laws and canons.
I say ' according to the laws and canons '—that is, in the first
place, that persons shall not be joined without or contrary to the
will of their parents or nearest relatives. For this is expressed
in the canon law and approved by the emperors.

"About divorces. Let not divorces take place except in the
case of adultery and under certain conditions as it is in the law
(in Iure). Further, his Royal Majesty wills that adultery, rape,
incest (adulteria, stupra, incestas nuptias) shall be severely
punished ; and in future before anyone shall be joined in matrimony his Royal Majesty orders that the banns be three times
proclaimed in the adjoining parishes before the marriage day.

" It shall be free to priests to contract marriage with modest and honest persons. The priests, that is the ministers of the Church, shall take care to live a life agreeable to the true doctrine, and, as Paul commands, to be ' husbands of one wife ' that is each content with his own spouse, etc."

It then goes on to order that weekly lectures in theology be given by prebendaries to young men who have had some knowledge in arts. A list of Latin books is given : " Grammatica, Dialectica, Rhetor(ica), Philippi; Poema Virgili, Ouidii, maxime in Eligiacis; Fabulæ Therentii; Epistole Familiares Ciceronis; In historiis commentaria Cæsaris " in sacred letters " Doctrina Cathecismi, Epistola ad Rhomanos." There is to be a scholastic disputation on Saturday in theology and ethics, and some instruction by the schoolmaster on Sunday.

Although the government by Norman and his body of officers did not very long continue, it would seem that the king's main line of policy was still persevered in. He wished to establish something like a German Presbyterian system, in which the bishops should be " ordinaries," or " superintendents," and the clergy " elders," and the king a sort of pope. He divided dioceses according to his own pleasure, so as to lessen the influence of the hierarchy— and, in fact, divided all except the little diocese of Vexiö, which was rather enlarged. The sub-division of dioceses was indeed a desirable piece of work, though the method and the personal aim were alike, unfortunate. It was a misfortune that the work was not undertaken in a proper ecclesiastical manner, as Sweden suffered and even still suffers from the unwieldiness of some of its dioceses. The occupants of the old sees called themselves " bishops," of the new ones " ordinaries." How far all these new officers received episcopal consecration is uncertain.[86] At

[86] Cornelius : *Hist.*, § 32, notes that both the bishops of Finland, one of whom was of the new class, were consecrated by Bishop Bothvid Suneson of Strengnäs. The word " ordi-narius " is found in earlier ecclesiastical Latin for a regular superior officer of the Church, *e.g.*, in *Sexti Decretales*, I., 16, *de officio ordinarii*, which follows *de officio legati*. Cp. the earlier title, *Decretales Greg. IX.*, I., 31, *de officio iudicis ordinarii*.

the same time the old chapters were gradually dissolved, and the priests yielded up their farms and became stipendiaries, receiving incomes from the two-thirds of the tithes now appropriated to the crown. On the other hand, the parish clergy for the first time became an estate in the Riksdag.[87]

§ 9.—LATTER HALF OF GUSTAF'S REIGN.   THE BIBLE OF
        1541.   PERSONAL RULE.   LAURENTIUS AND THE
        KING'S THIRD MARRIAGE.   HIS DEATH AND CHAR-
        ACTER.

The latter half of Gustaf's reign, at any rate after 1544, was, on the whole, quiet and prosperous. It was free to a very large extent from domestic tumults and foreign wars. Just half way through the reign, in the year 1541, was published that great treasure of the National Church, the Bible, in Swedish. It usually bears the king's name, but is the work particularly of the archbishop and his brother, Olaus. It is professedly based on Luther's German translation of 1534; but whether the Hebrew and Septuagint were also consulted does not seem to have been investigated.[38] It is rather characteristic of the country that certain selected books of the Old Testament were published five years before the rest (1536), namely, " Jesu Sirach's Book, Solomon's Wisdom, Solomon's Proverbs and David's Psalter." The Church of Sweden even now pays great respect to the Apocrypha, and is apt to criticize our British and Foreign Bible Society for not circulating it. The New Testament was generally different from that of 1526, at least in the order of the words. It was noticed that here and there were variations from Luther's rendering, e.g., that the Greek " presbyters," which Luther had rendered " eldermen," was translated " priests." Of the whole book it is said that the language was the purest and

---

[87] See for further details Anjou : pp. 322-7.
[88] See Schück : *Ill. lit. hist.*, I., p. 189 foll.

most beautiful that had as yet appeared in any Swedish book (Anjou: pp. 311-2).

The Riksdag of Vesterås, held in 1544, is memorable on two accounts, for the grant of hereditary right to the Vasa family, and for a new ordinantia in Church matters, which carried the Reformation some steps further, but imposed no new confession of faith.[39]   The organization of the Church was further regulated by the Vadstena articles put out in 1553, probably by the archbishop.

The king, however, took both Church and State into his own and almost sole hands, and ruled in patriarchal fashion, much after the manner that Queen Elizabeth affected in England, but in more minute detail.   The archbishop felt deeply the want of Church order and discipline of a spiritual character, and regretted the impossibility of having a Prayer Book put out by Church authority.[40]   His relations with the king were, on the whole, good.   He had a higher idea of kingly dignity and grace than Olaus had, and was doubtless better able to sympathize with the stronger and better side of Gustaf's character.   Their relations, however, were rather seriously troubled by the king's determination to marry his second wife's, Margaret's, niece, Kristina Stenbock.   The archbishop and most of the bishops thought, as Cranmer [41] and the English theologians and lawyers thought, that such a marriage, though not contrary to the letter of Scripture, was forbidden by inference from its other prohibitions.   The marriage was, in consequence, performed by the

[39] See for some details Anjou: p. 315, *E. T.*   On line 16, " consecration " should surely be " marriage " (vigsel).

[40] " Sjelf säges han år 1563 halfva yttrat, att han i mer än trettio år förgäfves sökt att få utfärda en Kyrdo-ordning." *Handlingar rörande Sv. Hist., Kyrko-ordningar,* etc., part I., p. xvii., Stk., 1872.

[41] Cranmer had so decided in 1536 : see my *Law of the Church as to the marriage of a man with his deceased wife's sister,* pp. 40-1, S.P.C.K., 1908.   The prohibition is contained in Archbishop Parker's *Table of kindred and affinity* (Nos. 29, 30) drawn up apparently in 1560, and put out in 1563.

" ordinarius " of Linköping, but Laurentius and others consented to crown the queen. Laurentius retained the same opinion twenty years later, when he published a tract on the prohibited degrees. He has been attacked for weakness of character in so far condoning the act as to crown the queen.[42] But the situation was a very difficult one for him to handle, owing to the absence of any detailed Church law in the country at this period, and the general impression that the king was a fountain of such law. He had, in fact, been used to give dispensation in marriage cases to others. Nevertheless, his own instructions, given through Norman, just quoted, only mentioned marriages in " the fourth or fifth degree " of the canon law, and marriage with a wife's niece is in the third degree of that law.

Gustaf died at Michaelmas, 1560—a man who would have been conspicuous in any age both for his personal virtues and for the skill which ensured his wonderful success. He was remarkable for the tenacity and consistency of purpose with which he pursued his ends, for the prudence which taught him when to give way or to hold his hand, and for the courage with which he used an advantage when the time was ripe for strong action. His early hardships and adventures had made him more familiar with the character and feelings of his countrymen in their solitary dwellings than any of their other rulers had been. I may, perhaps, apply to him the words of an English poet:—

> " Love had he found in huts where poor men lie ;
> His daily teachers had been woods and rills,
> The silence that is in the starry sky,
> The sleep that is among the lonely hills;"

and although these teachers did not quench all ambition in him, or soften away his natural roughness and impatience,

[42] He has been defended by Dean Lundström in the essay already referred to above, note 33, *K. H. Årsskrift*, 6, pp. 200-3. In England the archbishop was required to refer to the king or his Council in difficult cases of dispensations.

he kept throughout his life "in lofty place, The wisdom which adversity had bred." [48]

His insight into the course of events, his knowledge of what he could do and what he could not do, was extraordinary. He had a just idea of the needs of his country, and he measured correctly what he could do to meet them. He saw, from the time of his election as king, what a part religion might play in the liberation and development of his country, to which he devoted himself with an ambition that was not, as far as I can judge, in any high degree selfish. His private life and his life in his family was pure, temperate and affectionate. His court was bright and cheerful, and his intercourse with his guests of all degrees pleasant and familiar. His personal religion was genuine and consistent, though not that of a devotee or enthusiast, and his careful methods of education left a religious temper to his children and grandchildren, which was exhibited by all of them, though in very different ways. His treatment of the Church was, no doubt, that of a statesman rather than a Churchman, and required frequent apology. He looked upon the Church as an instrument to be used for the good of the nation, and one that required cautious handling, because of men's prejudices, rather than as a divine society controlling the acts of men, the welfare of which was an end in itself. His excuse may be that, in the age just before his own, intrigue and worldliness, violence and selfishness, had so intruded themselves into the high places of the Church, as to make it seem justifiable to use the powers of the Church in an arbitrary and politic, rather than in a sympathetic manner, provided the general welfare of the community were kept in view. In many points he is comparable both to Henry VIII. and Elizabeth of England. He had a simpler task, though, perhaps, not an easier one, than either of them. He found much less ability and intellect existing about him in the persons, either of his supporters or opponents, than they had. The

[48] W. Wordsworth: *Song at the feast of Brougham Castle*, written in 1807. The person referred to is a Lord Clifford.

temper of the Swedes was less strenuous and downright
than that of our countrymen.   Gustaf was fortunate in
the peaceable retirement of his principal opponents one
after the other, and in the comparative absence of Roman
intrigues against him.   But the people of Sweden were
obstinate and dogged.   They required to be treated with
patience and discretion, and they hated persecution in the
name of religion.   On the whole he gave the people what
they needed.   Gustaf was obviously a better man than
Henry.   I will not say that he was more admirable than
Elizabeth.   But he did more for his country—considering
the state of chaos which existed before his reign—and even
for the religion of his country, than either of those powerful sovereigns did for England.

§ 10.—THE REIGN OF ERIC (1560—1568).   HIS CAPRI-
    CIOUS CHARACTER.   CALVINIST AGGRESSION FORCES
    THE CHURCH TO DEFINE ITS POSITION AS
    LUTHERAN.   THE LIQUORIST CONTROVERSY.

The death of Gustaf brought a two-fold change in the
position of the Church.   He knew that his son Eric was
not strong enough for undivided rule, and he loved his
second wife and her children more than the first and his
eldest son.   He, therefore, followed Birger Jarl in making
his younger sons, John, Magnus and Charles, dukes with
hereditary rights, and a certain independence—a policy
which led to the same results of fratricidal war.   Eric was
just about to start on his voyage to England to court our
Queen Elizabeth, when his father's death delayed him.
He was twenty-seven years of age, " handsome, graceful,
eloquent, accomplished in manly exercises, a good
linguist, able to write well in Latin as well as in Swedish,
a poet, musician and painter, and skilled in astrology and
the mathematical sciences of his times.   But all these
advantages were marred by a strangely capricious dis-
position and by sudden and violent outbursts of temper,
which at times amounted to insanity " (Otté: p. 238).   He

went to war with his brother John, and imprisoned him at Gripsholm. Eric's folly, extravagance and changeableness were as unlike as possible to his father's carefulness, economy and perseverance, and he was both unable and indisposed to exercise the same personal domination in the affairs of the Church, though his religious temper, trained under the influence of Norman and Beurreus—a French Calvinist—was somewhat puritanical.

The Church thus recovered something of its normal independence, especially as the same wise archbishop continued to rule during the whole of Eric's eight years' reign. In the second place, during that reign Calvinism reached Sweden in a militant and aggressive form, and forced the Swedish Church to define itself as Lutheran. The championship of the Church against Calvinism was naturally undertaken principally, though by no means solely, by the archbishop, who issued tracts in defence of exorcism, and in opposition to the doctrine of the sacramentarians. He was clearly not in sympathy with certain decrees of the Council of Arboga in 1561, *e.g.*, that against the presence of images, which had been retained (as at Nurenberg) in some Lutheran churches. He was, however, no doubt in favour of the order that laymen should all communicate in both kinds, that there should be no mass without communicants besides the priest, and that neither mead nor water nor anything else should be used instead of wine. The questions how far wine is a necessary element in the chalice, how much water may be used and whether any substitute may find a place in it, have at various times exercised the Churches of the North, in which wine is a foreign liquor.[44] We have already seen a reference to them at the Council of Telje (Lect. III., § 12, 1279 A.D.). The dispute came to a head at a Riksdag in Stockholm in 1565, when the bishops and priests met separ-

[44] Thus Honorius III. wrote to the Archbishop of Upsala (*Perniciosus valde; Decretales*, III., 41, 13) that there was a bad habit of mixing too much water with the wine in his country.

ately, and condemned the usage of any other liquid than
wine.   Even John Ofeeg, Bishop of Vesterås, who had
taken the other side, subscribed this decree.   I may remark
that the opinion that when bread or wine is unattainable,
any other similar food or drink, by which our bodies are
sustained, may be employed to represent the spiritual food
of the Sacrament, was afterwards defended by Theodore
Beza (*Epist. theol.*, No. 2, p. 28, Geneva, 1573).

This and other controversies now decided the archbishop, to declare openly in favour of Lutheranism, which
he did in a tract, *On Church Ordinances (Stadgar) and
Ceremonies*, written in 1566, and published the next year.
King Eric, also in 1565, issued a strong mandate against
" distorted doctrines," by which Calvinism was intended
(Anjou: 360).   Laurentius expressed his opinions at
greater length, drawing attention to the diversity of
usages which prevailed in different countries and the necessity of a more settled order.   He ended as follows: " Each
province, each principality, in some places each city, has
its peculiar ceremonies and Church usages.   It is often the
case that the same custom is not long preserved, but
changes take place almost every month.   I know nothing
better to say or to advise, than that we assimilate with the
congregations who follow the doctrine of Doctor Martin.
For, as we have truly proclaimed that God of his special
grace has raised up that man to expose the hideous errors
of the pope, and show us the right way, and, as we have
received his doctrine as the truest, I cannot believe that we
shall find any better Church usages than they observe who
hold the same doctrines as we, that is, Doctor Martin and
Doctor Philip hold.   For this the special reason may be
assigned that we can easily and with least offence fall into
those customs, because between them and our own, as
hitherto practised, there is but little distinction or
difference " (Anjou: 366-7.   This is a fairly correct version
of the original fol. 61 B and 62, ed. Wittenberg, 1587).

§ 11.—THE REIGN OF JOHN III. (1568—1592). HIS
SCHEME OF REFORM ON A PRIMITIVE MODEL.
LAURENTIUS' KYRKO-ORDNING OF 1571. HIS
TEACHING ABOUT BISHOPS AND CONFIRMATION.

When Eric, who had occasional fits of passion amount-
ing to madness (as shown in particular by his murder of
the Stures), was deposed by his brother, John III., in 1568,
the Church acquiesced, but it incurred another danger.
John was a learned man, and had married a Polish Roman
Catholic wife, Katharina Jagellonica, who followed him
into captivity, and he spent much time of his imprisonment
in study, particularly of the Fathers and early Church history.   He was strongly under the influence of George
Cassander († 1566), and the party who desired mediation
between the old and new forms of religion.   At one time,
as we shall see, he actually entered into communion with
Rome, but, on the whole, his mind was set upon his own
scheme of moderate reform, which was to take as its model
the age of Constantine the Great.   It was, therefore, of
great importance for the future of Sweden that the old
archbishop was at last able before his death to put out his
own long-meditated Kyrko-ordning, or Directory for
public worship, in the year 1571, before the king's plans
had developed.   This epoch-making book is the foundation of all the successive Swedish formularies.   It was
issued at first with royal sanction, though not with that of a
Church council.   It was felt that it was too argumentative
and undecided to be of the nature of an absolute law.

The section which deals with the office of a bishop is of
such importance that the opening paragraphs of it must be
quoted at length :—[45]

[45] I have a copy of the rare original book of 1571 given me
by the great kindness of Professor Quensel. The reprint in
Kyrko-ordningar, etc., l.c., pp. 1-180, is so well and clearly
printed that the reader will probably prefer it for reference to the
original. The section on bishops begins p. 144, and is headed
*Ordning om Biscopar, hwilke pa Latijn kallas Superatten-
dentes, Ordinarii eller Ordinatores.*

"*Episcopus*, or *Superattendens*, is in Swedish rendered *Tillsynesman* (overseer), and for this reason every priest was also so called in the Scriptures, because he ought to have oversight or superintendence over those that are under his government, that things may go well and Christianly with them, as St. Paul says : ' Take heed unto yourselves and to all the flock in which the Holy Ghost has made you bishops, that is overseers.' For the distinction which now exists between bishops and simple priests was not known at first in Christendom, but bishop and priest were all one office, as we may observe in many places of St. Paul's writings ; yet before very long the distinction was so made that the man who had only one congregation in his charge kept the name of priest, while he who had government over several congregations, together with their pastors or priests, received the name of *Episcopus*.

"And the reason (according to St. Jerome) for this order was that at the period when Christianity began to grow and increase, so that even in one town were several congregations, everyone of which had its own particular bishop or parish-priest, it came to pass (as is generally the case under such circumstances) that variance and dissension arose between these bishops or church-priests, and so it sometimes happened that the same Christian congregations received notorious damage. But in order that this calamity might be stayed and stilled, the aforesaid congregations and their bishops and pastors came to an agreement that one bishop among them should be chosen, who should have superintendence over all the rest, and power to order and provide, both as regards the priests and their congregations, that things might go better and more correctly. And the man who was thus chosen retained the name of *bishop*, but the rest remained with the name *presbitter*, priest, etc.

" Therefore, since this ordinance was very useful and without doubt proceeded from God the Holy Ghost (who gives all good gifts), so it was generally approved and accepted over the whole of Christendom, and has since so remained, and must remain in the future, so long as the world lasts, although the abuse, which has been very great in this as in all other useful and necessary things, must be set aside. For, as regards the rightful office of a bishop, which consists in preaching God's Word and having oversight over them that are in his charge, so that they too preach aright, and behave themselves properly, this the bishops, who have been for a long while past, have let drop, and in its place have cumbered themselves with worldly things, yea and with things that serve for just no other purpose than mischievous misbelief, such as the manifold Jewish, and heathen consecrations (wixler), baptism of churches and bells, etc.

" So now must a bishop have oversight over all that are under his government, especially the clergy, that they may rightly and duly set forth God's word among the common men, rightly administer the sacraments, preach and hear the catechism at the proper season, hear confession when it is proper, exhort and bring the people to common prayers, visit and console the sick, bury the dead and faithfully and diligently perform all else that the ministry of the Church and the priestly office justly demands."

This passage is a good specimen of the simple style of Laurentius and of his persuasive method of putting his case.   An English Churchman would say that the case might have been easily improved by a reference to our Lord's institution of the apostolate, and by the inference which is thence drawn by many Presbyterians, as well as by ourselves, that He intended us to have a ministry created from above, and not from below, and that this should be an integral and permanent part of His system of Church government.

Further, we should have welcomed a statement of what is our own position and that generally of episcopal churches, that there is a certain connection between the apostolate, as the highest office in the primitive Church, and the episcopate, as the highest office in the sub-apostolic Church.   This, indeed, is an interpretation of history, rather than an absolutely certain fact of history, just as Laurentius' theory of the growth of the episcopate, drawn from St. Jerome's *Epistle to Evangelus*, is.   But the two interpretations naturally range together, as Richard Hooker shows in his seventh book, where he first says: " The first bishops in the Church of Christ were His blessed apostles " (*E. P.*, vii., 4, 1), and later : " The cause wherefore they under themselves appointed such bishops, as were not everywhere at the first, is said to have been those strifes and contentions, for remedy whereof whether [*i.e.*, either] the Apostles alone did conclude of such a regiment, or else they together with the whole Church (judging it a fit and a needful policy) did agree to receive it for a custom " (*ibid.* 5, 2).

But, as to the general conclusion of Hooker and ourselves, that the institution of episcopacy "had either
divine appointment beforehand or divine approbation
afterwards, and is in that respect to be acknowledged the
ordinance of God" (Hooker: l.c.), Laurentius is entirely
of the same mind as the Church of England.

As regards his final position that the episcopate is an
institution proceeding from God the Holy Ghost, and was
of universal acceptance in the early Church, and must continue to the end of time, we could not desire anything more
explicit.   In what follows also Laurentius refers to the
cases of Titus and Timothy, as examples of such oversight
over priests, as he here ascribes to bishops or *ordinarii*,
and in that way he recognizes the link between the
episcopate and the apostolate.

As regards election of bishops, he says: " In early times
it was the custom that the whole people should choose both
bishops and other Church ministers." Now dioceses are
too large, and there are many who do not know who would
best fill such an office.   Therefore, they should be elected
by some suitable persons of the clergy, and others who are
experienced in such matters.   A majority of votes should
prevail.   If votes are equal a lot may be drawn.   It is interesting, I may note, to observe this survival of the old
custom of resort to lots.   The elected bishop is to be confirmed by the sovereign.   The man so approved may be
openly ordained bishop with laying on of hands by some
other bishop, one or more.   There is no rule, as among
ourselves and elsewhere, that there must be three bishops
to consecrate another, nor is there any rule as to
confirmation by the metropolitan and comprovincial
bishops.   Dr. Holmquist tells me that consecration by a
single bishop was probably not unusual in pre-Reformation
times, where it was difficult to gather a number of prelates
together.   The three home-bishops (as we may call them)
of Upsala, Vesterås and Strengnäs could, of course, meet
with some ease.

The method of election here described shows that the

old chapters had now ceased to exist, or to be effective. Yet Laurentius desires that the bishop should have one or two capable clergy with him on his visitation, which ought to be annual, and that if he cannot visit in person he should do it by his official or provost with some other good men. He must also have his provosts in the country districts, whom he is to choose from among the priests of the neighbourhood (*Kyrko-ordningar*, l.c., pp. 147-8).

The subject of confirmation of children naturally arises in connection with the subject of visitation. Laurentius writes as follows (l.c., 150) :—

" The confirmation with oil (then olio-fermelse), which bishops have universally used under the pope, seeing that there is no commandment of God for it, and that it has also brought with it a very great superstition, shall no longer be at all used; but when a visitation takes places, they may have preaching and public prayers in the churches, especially for the young children, that God will strengthen them in the articles which were promised in their baptism, and afterwards do what is aforesaid (och sedan göra thet som tilförenne sagdt är). The same thing may be said of all other things which the bishops have taken upon them without God's commandment, such as are manifold consecrations of churches, churchyards, towers, bells, vestments, vessels, etc." The words " afterwards do what is aforesaid " are not clear. They seem to refer to a further action by the bishops which had been elsewhere prescribed. Was there such an action prescribed in the Vesterås ordinantia of 1544 or the Vadstena articles?

In a previous passage it is laid down that children should not come to communion before they are nine, or at least eight years of age (*Ordning medh Messonne*, p. 84). In the little book *On ordinances and ceremonies* (quoted at the end of § 10) he mentions the traditional practice of laying hands on those who have been baptized as one of those rightly received by the Church, like the canon of Scripture, baptism of infants, and a distinction of orders, etc. (l.c., fol. 19, ed. 1585). I am, therefore, inclined to think

that the words "afterwards do what is aforesaid" are a
reference to the absolution of children with laying on of
hands, after their first confession, which had been previously described (*Kyrko-ordning: Om Hemligh Scriff-
termål*, pp. 66-7).

Here we have the germ of an evangelical rite of confirmation, such as the course of the Reformation in Sweden
would naturally have developed, and did in fact develop
in the *Nova Ordinantia* of 1575. The service there set
forth was in full accord with the principles of Laurentius
(*Kyrko-ordningar*, etc., I., 226-9). No mention was made
in it of chrism. It was to be administered by the bishop, on
his visitation, or his deputy. It was very simple, consisting of a rather long but edifying prayer that the
children might be strengthened and receive the graces of
the Holy Spirit, followed by a laying on of hands and
blessing as follows:—

" God strengthen thee with the Holy Spirit in a right
faith, in knowledge of the Gospel and obedience to it, to a
Christian life, to the honour of God, to salvation for thy-
self, and to a good example and benefit to others, through
Jesus Christ our Lord. Amen." Then followed a hymn.

We shall see in the next lecture (vi., § 10) that Archbishop Laurelius continued to use this form of 1575 and
that Matthiæ introduced another similar to it, probably
under the advice of Comenius. I believe, indeed, that the
rite was never wholly dropped in Sweden: although, unfortunately, no reference was made to it in the Church Law
of 1686, and the form at last prescribed in 1811 was not
as good as that of the early precedents.

Dr. Ekdahl draws attention to the thoroughly Lutheran
character of this form and its likeness in particular to that
in the Waldeck Church Order of 1556.[46]

To add a few more words about the book of 1571.

[46] *Om Conf.*, p. 94.   Anyone who compares the German
prayer, on p. 44 (from the Brunswick-Wölfenbüttel *K.O.* of
1589) with the Swedish on p. 93 will see that they must have a
common origin.

Incumbents were to be elected by the parishioners, but examined by the bishop, who might declare the man chosen unfit, and put in another priest. Prayers, fasting and alms were recognized as religious duties. Severe and ignominious Church penalties should only be used for serious acts of vice, and those who defied the Church's discipline were to be punished by the secular power (Cornelius: *Hist* § 37). At a Church Council, held next year, at Upsala, the archbishop promised to issue a confession " after the pattern of the Confession of Augsburg," though he did not live to fulfil his promise. He had sufficiently shown his inclination towards the teaching of Melanchthon by recommending to preachers " the loci communes of Philip," to which he added the Swedish version of the *Margarita Theologica* (*K. O.*, l.c., p. 27). At this assembly it was agreed to maintain the ceremonies and Church customs which had hitherto been in use in the Swedish Church, and now were set out in the recently printed Church Order (Corn. § 38). Thus the archbishop's book received the approval of the Church, though it was not directly imposed upon it. He died 26th October, 1573, revered and honoured by all men, and mourned by the clergy as a father. Besides the Bible and the Church Order, Sweden owes to him its hymn-book of 1567, which is the foundation of all later books (*ibid.* § 38). His memory has been fairly honoured by an oration delivered by the poet, F. M. Franzén, before the Swedish Academy in 1842.

§ 12.—CHANGES IN OTHER LANDS. COMPARISON OF THE SOVEREIGNS OF ENGLAND AND SWEDEN. POSITION OF KING JOHN. THE *Nova Ordinantia* OF 1575. ITS PROVISIONS. THE LITURGY OF 1576. DISPUTES ABOUT IT.

In order to understand the events of King John's reign and the influence which it had upon the course of religion in Sweden, we must remember what had been taking place in Europe, and the changes which had come about in other

countries.[47]   The first energy of the reforming movement
had largely spent itself by the year 1546, when Luther
died, and much more so when Melanchthon died in the
same year as Gustaf Vasa (1560).   The Society of Jesus,
which was founded in 1540, had become a very large
and important instrument of the counter-reformation at
the time of its founder's death in 1556.   Lutheranism,
with its strongly personal and somewhat sentimental attitude towards religion, had been checked even in Germany
by the more democratic and theocratic and at the same
time systematic and logical teaching of Calvin and
Zwingli.   Lutheranism had a strong hold over great part
of Germany, but had not spread much beyond it.   Calvinism had established itself in the republican regions of
Switzerland and the Netherlands, and to a great extent in
Scotland.   It had obtained a considerable power in France,
and had been checked and put down in Italy and Spain.
The three northern kingdoms of England, Denmark
(which included Norway) and Sweden were all examples of
a different type of reformation.   In them the movement
towards a breach with Rome had come from the sovereigns
rather than, in any organized way, from the people,
though it was much more a popular movement in England
than in Sweden, and consequently was the occasion of
much more bitter strife.   In all three kingdoms the process
of change was comparatively slow, and followed the
changing attitude of the sovereigns who succeeded one
another.   In Denmark, owing to its proximity to Germany and other causes, the process was most rapid.   It
accepted the name Lutheran under Christian II. in 1526.
It accepted the Augsburg Confession and a Lutheran succession of bishops under Christian III. in 1536—1537.
In Sweden the change was much slower, and in England it
was slowest of all.   There was also considerable likeness
in the character, and even the external fortunes of the

[47] I have found in Karl Hildebrand : *Upsala-möte*, 1593, suggestions which have helped me in writing this section.   It was
published in Heimdal's *Folkskrifter* in Jubilee year, 1893.

sovereigns who led the various alterations in religion in
England and Sweden.

In England Henry's strength forced changes which followed his own changes of mind, as Gustaf tried to force
changes in Sweden. Under Edward VI. Calvinism for a
few years was in the ascendant. In Mary Romanism for a
short period violently triumphed. In Elizabeth we had a
moderate and politic ruler of the Church, who may also be
compared to Gustaf. The latter would have liked to be
like Henry, but he was forced by circumstances to be like
Elizabeth. In his bonhomie, his perseverance, his knowledge of the temper of his people, and in his politic treatment of the Church he was more like the two great Tudor
sovereigns than any other Swedish king, and he also
resembled them in the length of his reign. In Eric
Sweden had a man of Calvinistic education and sympathies, who had little force of character to carry out what
he may have personally desired. In John, Sweden had a
man who set himself to reconcile Catholicism and Protestantism in the spirit of Laud and the English High
Churchmen. Both in the character of his policy and in
the fact of his marriage to a Roman Catholic and its consequences, he reminds us more of our own Charles I. than
of any other of our sovereigns. In Sigismund, son of
John, it had a convinced Roman Catholic, who, like James
II. of England, lost his crown for his religion. In Charles
IX. it had another semi-Calvinist, who, like William of
Orange a century later, knew how to subordinate his own
prejudices, not from weakness, but from policy, to the
needs of the government of a country to rule which he was
called by a revolution.

John was, as I have said, of the school of Cassander, who
desired to find a *via media* between Romanism and
Lutheranism. In this he was fortified by his patristic
studies, and by the example of Ferdinand in Germany and
Elizabeth in England. Probably next to Cassander's
*Consultation on the Articles controverted between
Catholics and Protestants*, the proposals made by the

Emperor Ferdinand to the Council of Trent in 1562 were his model. But plans and suggestions made and rejected while the Council of Trent was still sitting were still less likely to meet with success after its dissolution in 1563, when the personal rule of the popes was reasserted.[48]

King John was also much influenced by a young man, Petrus Fecht, a scholar of Melanchthon, who inspired him with the romantic hope (like that in which our own tractarians have largely succeeded) of reviving " the Apostolic and Catholic faith of the primitive Church " (Cornelius : § 39).

The principal events of King John's reign may be briefly summarized. At a Church Council, held at Stockholm, in 1574, he put forward a sort of programme in which Fecht's principle was enunciated. He followed his father's method of electing to the vacant archbishopric at such a Council. Two candidates were nominated, of whom Olaus Martini, Bishop of Linköping, received the greatest number of votes. But the king preferred the other candidate, Laurentius Petri Gothus, a learned and much respected man, but of more pliable character. Before his confirmation and consecration he was required to sign certain articles which pledged him to support the king's plan of a return to primitive Catholicism.

In February, 1575, a clerical assembly consisting of four bishops and a few clergy, was held at Stockholm, which, after six weeks' deliberation, accepted the *Nova Ordinantia Ecclesiastica,* comprised in twenty articles.[49]   This book

---

[48] Cassander's *Consultatio* may be found in a little volume entitled *Via ad pacem ecclesiasticam,* edited by Hugo Grotius, anno 1642, containing the confession of Pope Pius IV., the Confessio Augustana, the Consultatio, with Grotius' notes, and certain poems by him, and a disquisition on " Pelagianism." Ferdinand's proposals in various forms, in which he had the help of his secretary, Frederick Staphylus, and others, may be found in J. Le Plat : *Monumenta ad hist. conc. Trid.,* v., pp. 212-268, Lovanii, 1785. Cp. Martin Philippson : *La Contre-revolution,* pp. 446-8, Bruxelles, 1884.

[49] It may be found in *Kyrko-ordningar,* etc., I., pp. 181-351.

was slightly shorter than Laurentius Petri's " Church Order." It was more of a theological treatise than a book of articles, and more of a book of articles than a Prayer Book, although it contained certain liturgical forms for confirmation, confession and the mass. It was, on the whole, in form more akin to the Augsburg Confession than to our Thirty-nine Articles. Its chief characteristic in comparison with similar books was the citation of many passages from the Fathers, especially in the two sacramental articles (2) *On sacraments in general,* and (7) *On the Lord's Supper,* which occupied nearly half the book. As regards the word sacrament, the book recognized the ancient broad use of the term, but named and discussed baptism and the Lord's Supper as the two principal sacraments of the New Testament. In one place (Art. 2, §, p. 206) it spoke of penance as one which might be added to them, and indeed as being a sort of quasi-baptism, or part of baptism. This treatment of penance as a sacrament was indeed very much in the line of the Augsburg Confession, in which it ranges with the other two in the series of sacramental chapters.[50]

The *Nova Ordinantia* was far from being an attack on the " Church Order " of 1571, and, in fact, it speaks of the late archbishop in laudatory terms. It was rather a development of part of it in the direction of patristic tradition, with a return in some degree to the old system of chapters and convents, in somewhat new forms. It spoke strongly against transubstantiation, the withdrawal of the cup, the sacrifice of the mass, compulsory private confession, and enumeration of all sins, and the cultus of the saints, while it recognized the marriage of the clergy (Art. 17). It restored (as I have said) the rite or ceremony of

[50] They are discussed in chapters 9, 10, 11, 12 of a series extending from 7 to 13 inclusive, and they are the only three which are discussed. In section 7 of the *Apologia Confessionis* we read: " Vere igitur sunt Sacramenta, Baptismus, Cœna Domini, Absolutio, quæ est Sacramentum poenitentiæ. Nam hi ritus habent mandatum Dei et promissionem gratiæ, quæ est propria novi Testamenti."

confirmation in a very simple form. As regards the saints, it asserted that, though they may pray for us, we ought not to pray to them. They should, however, be held in reverence, especially the Virgin Mary, "who, without doubt, was hallowed and purified in her mother's body by the Holy Spirit and afterwards ruled by the same Spirit in all virtues" (Art. 10, p. 332). Its article on the Lord's Supper was especially directed against the Calvinists or Sacramentarians, but it asserted (with Gelasius of Rome) the persistence of the substances of bread and wine (Art. 7, § 8, p. 291). It introduced a new preface, which really was a consecration prayer, and which, after a description of the intention of the Lord's Supper, continued: "Which supper we according to His command and ordinance desire to celebrate, bless with His Word [the] bread and wine, the gifts, which are set before [thee] that they in a right use may become thy Son's [true] Body and Blood." The words of institution and *laudes* were to follow the preface (Art. 8, §§ 7 and 8).

The book treated Church discipline at great length, and enumerated twenty-nine grievous sins or crimes which were still subject to Church punishment. Fifteen kinds of punishments are also recited, but of an ecclesiastical sort, not fine or imprisonment (Art. 6, §§ 2 and 3). In connection with this subject it created a *Consistorium ecclesiasticum* for the whole Church, consisting of bishops and old, God-fearing, learned and experienced men, to meet twice a year or oftener at Stockholm, to whom difficult cases might be referred by secular or spiritual authorities (*ibid.* § 14).

As regards the election of bishops, the plan adopted at the recent election to Upsala was generally sanctioned. The members of chapter were to announce the occurrence of a vacancy to the prince, who thereupon should call for the votes of the other bishops of the realm, and the most influential priests of the diocese. After the votes have been given the prince should "examine which of the candidates can be approved, and set him in office according to custom, so that the prince has the highest vote" (Art. 18,

§ 1). Prayer and laying on of hands suffice for consecration, but the use of mitre and staff have been of long time in
use, and are approved, though not of the substance of
ordination (*ibid.* § 2).

As regards the personnel of the Church the book provided in each cathedral learned priests to help the bishop,
having the following officers: A provost, to act as his
deputy; a dean, to overlook all schools, examine candidates and act as secretary to the chapter and keep the
records of the legal proceedings committed to it; an archdeacon, who may be also theological lecturer and public
penitentiary.   Besides these there should be a pastor,
schoolmaster and steward (œconomus) (Art. 12).   Their
chaplains were to sing daily evensong and mattins
(ottesång) in the cathedrals with the " deacons."

As regards the monasteries, it was decreed that, though
no life-vows were to be taken, convents which still existed
were to be restored as refuges for aged and incapable priests,
and for others who have no desire for the world, and for
old matrons and maidens who have no desire or suitability
for marriage.   The inmates of the cloisters were to live in
retirement and devotion, and should occupy themselves
with the education of children.   At least one cloister was
to be found in each diocese (Art. 20, pp. 348-9).

Nothing was said in this *Ordinantia* as to the use of
unction in the consecration of a bishop.   In fact, we are
told that it was one of the points proposed and rejected, together with extreme unction and prayers for the dead at
their burial (Anjou: p. 468).   But, in July of the same
year, King John (following the precedent of his father)
insisted upon it in the consecration of the new archbishop
and two others.   This was an arbitrary act which naturally
aroused suspicion of further changes in prospect, and suspicion was changed into conviction by the unfortunate
publication of the new Liturgy or Red-book of 1576, without any Church authority.   Had the king been satisfied
with the ground covered by the *Nova Ordinantia*, or even
introduced his Liturgy in a deliberate and ecclesiastical

manner, he might have contributed much more to the final
settlement than he actually did.   In that way the good
points of the *Ordinantia* might have been maintained.

But the Liturgy called forth the protest of his brother,
Duke Charles, who forbade its use in his dominions, and
that of many of the clergy in the king's own realm,
especially at Stockholm and Upsala, such as Abraham
Angermannus and Professor Petrus Jonæ.   Early in 1577
the king indeed put the matter before the estates of the
realm at a Riksdag in Stockholm, at which the laity seem
to have approved of, or assented to, the Liturgy, while the
clergy were silent, or, perhaps, absent (Anjou : 491).

I do not propose to analyse the Red-book in the same
detail as the *Ordinantia*.   The latter was carefully revised,
and had a certain degree of Church authority.   The
Liturgy was the work of the king and Fecht, and had practically no authority, except such as was obtained under
pressure ; nor is it a work of much liturgical tact and talent.
It retained the curious feature which Olaus had borrowed
from Luther's early *Formula* of introducing the words of
institution into the preface.   The preface was, however,
supplemented by a series of prayers, which, in a certain
degree, reflected the discarded prayers of the Roman
canon.   There was, however, nothing in these prayers that
could rightly offend a Lutheran, except the version of the
prayer *Unde et memores*, which, after speaking of our debt
to God for our Saviour's passion and sacrifice, went on as
follows : " The same, thy Son, His death and oblation, a
pure victim, a holy victim, a spotless victim, propitiation,
shield and protection set forth for us against thy anger,
against the terror of sin and death, we embrace with faith,
and offer to thy excellent Majesty with our most humble
prayers."   Here in the word " offer " was a point which
was eagerly seized on by the opponents of the Liturgy.
The two following prayers : *Supra quæ propitio* and *Sup-
plices te rogamus*, were moulded into one, which simply
asked that our prayers should be taken to the heavenly
altar, and that we who are partakers of Christ's body and

blood may be filled with heavenly benediction. There was
no attempt to introduce a definite consecration prayer like
that of the *Nova Ordinantia*, or even after the English
pattern. The words of institution were clearly considered
to have met the needs. There was also no reference to the
intercession of the saints.

This Liturgy then did not in itself deserve the bitterness
with which it was attacked. It certainly was not the work
of a Jesuit. The first of that society in Sweden was
Laurentius Nicolai, who was appointed theological lecturer at the Old Grey Friars, now the Riddarholm Church
in Stockholm, in August, 1576, at the suggestion indeed of
Fecht, but who had not been there many months. Fecht,
who had been to Rome in pursuance of the king's plan to
obtain a new succession of bishops, and was returning unsuccessful, was drowned in November of the same year
(*ibid.* 483). The king did indeed obtain an acceptance of
his book from the clergy in February, 1577, just about the
time that he carried out the death sentence against his poor
brother, Eric, which had some time been in suspense. But
it was not a genuine acceptance; and the further advances
of Laurentius or Klosterlasse (as he was called from his
place of lecturing), and more particularly of another Jesuit,
Possevin, produced profound unsettlement.

For a short time indeed the king actually embraced
Romanism, but always it would seem with the hope of
carrying out his scheme of reconciliation. He was not
only a religious enthusiast, but he desired the pope's mediation with the Catholic powers in his Russian war, and with
the Spanish Court in the matter of the maternal inheritance
of his wife, Catharine. When, therefore, Possevin returned to Sweden in 1578, with a declaration that Pope
Gregory XIII. refused nearly all the twelve points which
the king demanded, the latter gave up all real hope of success in the reconciliation scheme. Yet he did not cease to
work for a *via media*. After the death of the weak archbishop, Laurentius Gothus, in 1579, he kept the see vacant
for four years, whilst he looked about for some one to for-

ward his plans, and tried to force the adoption of his Liturgy by persecution, imprisonment and banishment. In 1583 he found a suitable instrument in Andreas Laurentii Botniensis, Bishop of Vexiö, who held the see for six and a half years, and who did his best by mingling cajolery with threatening to influence the minds of the teachers, who were imprisoned for their opposition, amongst whom were his two successors, Abraham Angermannus and Nicolaus Olai Botniensis.   The death of King John's queen, Catharine, in 1583, and his subsequent marriage to a young Swedish girl, Gunilla, of the family of Bielke, weakened his inclination towards Rome.   But King John had allowed his son, the Crown Prince Sigismund, to be educated by his mother in her own faith, in view of his probable succession to the Crown of Poland, and he had become a convinced supporter of the old order. He became King of Poland in 1587, and thus had to declare himself a faithful adherent of the Roman Church, and was obviously preparing to restore its domination in his native country whenever he should succeed to the crown of Sweden.

In the meantime the Swedish sees had been filled by new men who were in favour of the king's plans.   But his brother Charles strenuously supported the clergy of his dukedom in their opposition, especially those in the diocese of Strengnäs, and there was almost danger of a civil war. The brothers were reconciled in 1590, and a sort of modus vivendi was arranged.   But when King John died the 17th November, 1592, it was fairly evident that the work for which he had laboured so hard and hazarded so much was doomed to fall to the ground.   His death was, in fact, the prelude to a definitive triumph of Lutheranism by the adoption of the Augsburg Confession, which seemed to the great majority of the people the necessary way of proclaiming their final revolt from Rome and their resolution not to permit Calvinism to be taught in the country.

VI.

The great kings and the great bishops from the Upsala-möte to the death of Charles XII. (1593 A.D.—1718 A.D.).

LECTURE VI.

THE GREAT KINGS AND THE GREAT BISHOPS FROM THE
UPSALA-MÖTE TO THE DEATH OF CHARLES XII. (1593
A.D.—1718 A.D.).

§ 1.—CONSEQUENCES OF KING JOHN'S DEATH. DANGER
OF THE CHURCH. DAVID CHYTRÆUS AND
NICOLAUS BOTNIENSIS. NECESSITY THAT SWEDEN
SHOULD AT ONCE MAKE A FREE AND DEFINITE CHOICE
OF STANDARDS. CHARACTER OF DUKE CHARLES.
HIS GREAT SERVICE TO HIS COUNTRY.

The death of John III. in 1592 brought with it the complete and definite victory of Lutheranism in the form of an
acceptance by the whole of Sweden of the Confession of
Augsburg as presented to the Emperor Charles V. in the
year 1530. This confession was the work of Melanchthon,
and it was to Melanchthon's most zealous and beloved
scholar, David Chytræus, born himself in the year 1530,
that the later generation of Swedish theologians owed their
training. As professor at the University of Rostock,[1] near
Warnemünde in Mecklenburg, Chytræus was near enough
to keep up a constant correspondence with Sweden, and he
often was consulted on difficult questions, as, for example,
on Gustaf Vasa's third marriage. His history of the
Confession of Augsburg, published in 1578, no doubt was
in the hands of some of his former pupils. Foremost
amongst these pupils was Nicolaus Olai Botniensis, a
Hebraist and Biblical scholar, who had studied under
Chytræus for some four years (1578—1582), and taught at

---

[1] Two books by Krabbe are referred to Die Universität
Rostock im 15ten und 16ten Jahrhundert, Rostock and
Schwerin, 1854, and David Chythræus, Rostock, 1870. See also
A. M. Magnusson : Nicolaus Olai Botniensis, pp. 11-23, Upsala,
1898.

Rostock for some two years longer.   He had recently
(1586) become one of the professors of the college at Stockholm, now, of course, under new management, after the
retirement of Klosterlasse, who was banished in 1580.
He, with his brother professors, Eric Skinner and Petrus
Kenicius, was thrown into prison by King John in 1589,
thus sharing the fate which had befallen the professors of
the Upsala high school about nine years before.   In this
way King John had made enemies of all the most learned
men in Sweden, and had prepared the way for the reaction
against his life work, in which Nicolaus Botniensis was
now the principal leader.   The three professors had been,
it seems, released just before his death, but they had
pledged themselves in 1590 and later to permanent opposition to his liturgy, and especially to the sacrificial element
in it, to which I have referred.[2]

It was no accident that on Botniensis' tombstone,
amongst other pious texts, appeared in Greek:—" I will
have mercy and not sacrifice."[3]

[2] Magnusson : l.c., pp. 41 foll.   Cp. : Baaz, p. 484 :
" Probavimus autem manifestis demonstrationibus incruentum
illud sacrificium Missæ Pap(alis) in Liturgia contineri : hoc sola
vestra negatio non refutat.   Distinctio quam adfertis inter
" Sacrificare " et " Offerre " (offra och frambära) non excusat
factum Sacrificuli, offerentis in Missa Liturg(ica) Filium Dei
ipsi Patri Hostiam Sanctam, etc., ut verba Liturgiæ expresse
sonant, ex Canone Pap(ali) desumpta."   This letter was addressed to the Archbishop Andreas Laurentii Björnram, an
eager " liturgist," who died at the beginning of 1591.   Baaz's
accuracy as regards details of this correspondence is attacked
by Magnusson, but the sentence here quoted is not questioned.
At the Upsala-möte, during the session of the 3rd March,
Botniensis severely reproved Dr. Joachim, pastor of Upsala, for
his use of the term " sacrifice."   " Quali? dixit præses.   Pro
applicatorio et quidem per fidem, inquit alter.   Hanc nactus
occasionem præses acerbius in illum invehebatur, quod contra
usum ecclesiæ phrasin reiectam introduceret."

[3] For the inscription on his tombstone, in Upsala Cathedral
(which also contained a carelessly-cut text in Hebrew from
Psalm cxlii, 6, " My portion is the Lord in the land of the living," and St. John iii, 16 in Latin), see Rhyzelius, p. 64, who

Before his death King John had promised that there should be no more persecution on account of the liturgy, and that he would permit the summoning of a free Church Council. He died 17th November, 1592, and Charles took on the regency of the kingdom until his nephew, Sigismund, should appear in Sweden, drawing the Council of State, according to his abiding principle, into conjoint responsibility with himself.   The regency was confirmed by Sigismund, and was proclaimed to all the provinces of the country.   Charles at once began to make use of his power, and he saw that no time must be lost if the elements of religious freedom were to be secured before the advent of a Romanist as king.   The new union compact, under which Sigismund succeeded to a second crown, was even more dangerous than the old.   The counter-reformation was in full progress.   The conversion of Henry IV. of France was probably already known or suspected in Sweden, and the new pope, Clement VIII. (1592—1605), was busy in Poland with plans for the re-conquest of the northern kingdoms to the Roman obedience.   It was also essential to the stability of any settlement in religion that Sweden should now choose for itself, and not merely follow the lead of the government of the day and of the Council of State.   Such assent might, perhaps, have been obtained, but it would only have strengthened the habit of servility in matters of religion which had done much harm in the past, and might do immeasurable harm in the future.   The council, therefore, which was to be summoned, must be free; and it shows the sagacity of Duke Charles that he from the first insisted on this characteristic of the assembly which he at once determined to summon.   It must also choose for itself certain definite standards of doctrine and worship which could be set before the Romanist king for his acceptance, and as conditions of his recognition as

does not give the Hebrew, and Magnusson : l.c., pp. 180-1, who prints the Greek incorrectly.   But between the two the whole can be made out.

sovereign. These three conditions, rapidity of action and freedom and definiteness of choice, were met in the way which I will now describe.

There could indeed be no reasonable doubt what these standards would be, and reference was made to them early in the proceedings. All practical considerations—including the probability of an alliance of Sweden with the Protestant princes in Germany against Poland and the Empire —pointed to the acceptance of the Confession of Augsburg as one of these standards. On the other hand, the independent spirit of the country, and its attachment to the episcopal polity, and the higher consequent idea of the duties and position of the ministry, made it natural to fall back upon the Church Order of 1571. It was the mature work of the old archbishop, who had done almost as much for the Church unity of Sweden as King Gustaf had done for its unity in Government. These standards would secure that necessary *via media* between Romanism and Calvinism, which was secured to us in England by other means, but which there were no other means of securing in Sweden. Calvinism had proved a real danger under Eric: it was likely again to be so under Charles. The eminent service which the latter did to his country at this critical juncture was to suppress his own personal inclinations in the interest of the stability of the religious settlement.[4]

Duke Charles certainly possessed more of the good qualities of his father's character than any of his brothers, and

---

[4] The documents concerning the great Upsala-möte of 1593 are to be found in *Svenska Riksdagsakter*, III., 1., ed. Emil Hildebrand, Stk., 1894.   There is a good short account of it by Karl Hildebrand fil. Kand. in Heimdal's *Folkskrifter*, 1893. and in Magnusson, l.c.   Anjou's account of it is very full and interesting.   Geijer's is rather defective.   I may remark that there is a strange blunder on p. 607 of the E.T. of Anjou.   He is made to say, speaking of the Upsala-möte, of 1594 : "This hour, June 24, 1527, was of all others the most important and conclusive for the Swedish Church Reformation."   Obviously it should be : "This hour, *next to the day of Vesterås*, June 24, 1527, was," etc,

in some, he even exceeded him.   He is described as the least naturally able and the least widely educated of Gustaf's sons.[5]   But he must have had considerable training in theology.   Further, he had learnt much both in the way of experience and of self-restraint in his government of the duchy.   It had long been observed that as much industry, frugality and sagacity prevailed there as disorder and want of economy in the kingdom ruled by John (Geijer: p. 178; cp. p. 209).   In particular we may mention his colonization of the woodland province of Vermland by the Finns, his development of the mining industry there and elsewhere, and his foundation of Carlstad, now a bishop's see, the first town ever built in that province.   Of his brothers, Eric had long been on the borderland between sanity and insanity, and had never shown much talent for government.   His motto, "Magnos magna decent," showed the bent of his mind towards display, and to that habit of pose and acting which was not unknown to Gustaf.   Poor Duke Magnus was conscientious, but gradually became insane, and supposed himself to be loved by a mermaid.   John was like Gustaf in his perseverance and craft, and imitated his acts of arbitrariness, but he had little of his wisdom and prudence. Charles alone had both the perseverance and the prudence of Gustaf, and, perhaps, more than all his family, he had a genuine insight into the depth and seriousness of the Swedish character, and a sympathy with two of its marked tendencies—a desire that the whole community should be responsible for great changes and act together, and a dislike of persecution and compulsion in matters of religion.

[5] Fletcher: *Gustavus Adolphus*, p. 21.   See, however, Odhner: *Fäderlandets Historia*, p. 183.

§ 2.—The Upsala-möte, summoned January, 1593. Its
   composition and numbers. Its solemn opening, 1st March. Election of Nicolaus as
   president. It accepts the Augsburg Confession. Abraham Angermannus elected archbishop. Hand-book of 1571 confirmed. Other
   business. The Agreement of Upsala ratified
   20th March.

It was natural under these circumstances that the clergy
who assembled for King John's solemn funeral procession,
3rd January, 1593, should express a strong desire for a
council. It was agreed by the duke and Council of State
that one should be held at once, and letters of summons
were issued on 9th January for 25th February. They were
addressed to the bishops, who were bidden to bring their
best and most learned priests to Upsala, in order to determine concerning Church doctrine, ceremonies and discipline, and to elect an archbishop and other bishops.
They were to bring with them members of their chapters,
rural deans and some priests from each hundred. No
definite programme of agenda was issued, but it was
decided that, besides the clergy, the members of the
Council of State were to take part, and that other laymen
might be present. Between the summons and the meeting
Petrus Jonæ, one of the anti-liturgist professors, who had
in 1586 been elected Bishop of Strengnäs in Duke Charles'
dominions, was consecrated to that office (21st January,
1593).

The Council, as I have said, was to be free to do its own
work; and for this and for other reasons no official person
was appointed as its president by the duke and the Council
of State. The see of Upsala was still vacant, and none of
the four bishops who attended was suited to act as president. The Bishop of Linköping, Petrus Benedicti, whose
see was next in dignity to that of Upsala, was a weak man,
who had accepted the liturgy. Petrus Jonæ of Strengnäs
had Calvinistic leanings. The other two prelates who

filled the sees of Åbo and Vesterås were not men of great
mark, and had both accepted the liturgy. The choice of a
president was, therefore, to be made by election of the
members of the Council.

The number of priests who attended was 306, of whom
135 came from Upland, the nearest region. Some nine-
teen came from Norrland, also in the diocese of Upsala,
and from as far as Piteå, the home of Nicolaus Olai. The
other six dioceses were represented as follows: Linköping
by twenty-nine, Skara by fifteen, Strengnäs by fifty-one,
Vesterås by thirty-five, Vexiö by nine, and Åbo by thirteen.

To assemble such a body in the winter season from such
distant regions was a matter of obvious difficulty, and they
came dropping in rather irregularly. It was also convenient that those on the spot should get to know one
another's minds better, and have opportunity to prepare in
a less formal way for the great work which lay before them.
The solemn opening, therefore, did not take place till 1st
March. It was preluded by a speech from the high
steward, Nils Gyllenstjerna, in the name of the Government. The duke was careful to keep himself in the background so as to leave the assembly free to pass its resolutions, and himself free to criticize them. The steward
pointed out the dangers of disunion as seen in France and
the Netherlands. As regards the assembly before him, he
asked for (and received) an assurance that those who were
absent would feel themselves bound by the resolutions of
those who were present. He suggested that the clergy
should unite in some formulary of faith such as the Augsburg Confession and old Archbishop Laurentius' Confession in regard to doctrine and ceremonies. He ended with
the remarkable words : " If the king in Poland comes hither
he must not be lord over our faith and conscience, but we
must abide in that agreement as to doctrine which is here
determined. Whatever is here agreed on in accordance
with God's pure Word and will must be set forth in a
Christian manner, and be subscribed by all. Finally, I

pray that the living God may be the highest ruler in this Church Council, that He may govern all things in it, so that they may turn to God's praise and honour, and be a strong support and an eternal benefit to ourselves and our descendants." The election of an archbishop was deferred at the wish of the Government, but the assembly was invited to elect its president. Nicolaus, who received 196 votes, was elected. The Bishop of Linköping only received five, Petrus Jonæ of Strengnäs fifty-six, and the Bishop of Åbo one.

The articles of the Augsburg Confession were gone through one by one, and finally were accepted by all present, nobles, bishops and clergy, so that Nicolaus, as president, exclaimed in memorable words: "Now has Sweden become one man, and we all have one Lord and God." To the acceptance of this confession were joined requests against the open toleration of "Catholicism," that no Catholics should hold office, that all future priests and school teachers should accept the confession, and that the convent of Vadstena should be closed, and its revenues used for the support of students. The main business was, therefore, concluded on Tuesday, 6th March, in less than a week. But the council sat on till the 19th March dealing with personal cases, ratifying the Church Order of 1571, and the Hand-book of 1529,[6] and proceeding on the 15th March to the election of an archbishop. After the large majority of votes given to Nicolaus as president, it is somewhat surprising to find that Abraham Andreæ Angermannus, a former professor at Stockholm and Upsala, was now elected archbishop by an even larger majority. Abraham received 238 votes, Petrus Jonæ of Strengnäs sixteen, Nicolaus Botniensis thirty-eight and Petrus Kenicius three. This shows that the election was made by the whole body of clergy, and not only by those of the

[6] This appears from the detailed account of the session of 8th March (form C) in *Riksdagsakter*, p. 61, and Magnusson, p. 58. But there is no direct reference to the Hand-book in the final " agreement " of the Council.

diocese of Upsala. The reasons why Abraham was chosen rather than one of his more learned rivals, Petrus Jonæ or Nicolaus, seem to have been that he was older and more experienced, and had suffered considerably for his resistance to King John. He had been in voluntary exile in Mecklenburg for over ten years, and was known to be a man of great strength of will and purpose, and was, therefore, thought worthy of the dangerous honour of taking the leadership of the Church in the times of conflict which were evidently before it.[7]   The duke did not, however, confirm the election at once, but reserved to himself the right to approve one of the others, just as his brother John had chosen Laurentius Gothus, though another candidate had the plurality of votes.

On the same day as the election to Upsala new bishops were also chosen for Skara and Vexiö, but, after all, the bishops of those sees did not resign, but continued to hold them.

The remaining days were chiefly occupied in negotiations with the duke on the points in which he personally differed from the council—such as the use of certain ceremonies, and in particular, the retention of the exorcism, salt put into the mouth and lights into the hand in baptism, and the elevation in the liturgy, of all of which he disapproved.   At the end he gave way on most of the points, some smaller concessions being made on the other side.

The council insisted upon exorcism, apparently in connection with the doctrine of original sin, and upon " elevation " of the sacrament in the liturgy as a protection against Calvinism.   Finally, a question was raised as to the introduction of Calvinists and Zwinglians into the list

[7] The number of votes is given in *Riksdagsakter*, l.c., pp. 70 foll.   Cp. Magnusson, p. 65, for the reasons of the choice. Archbishop Abraham was married to Magdalena, the youngest daughter of Archbishop Laurentius Petri Nericius.   The elder, Margareta, was married in succession to two Archbishops, Laurentius Petri Gothus and Andreas Laurentii Björnram Botniensis (1583-91).

of heretics rejected. The president himself was against it as unnecessary and excessive, but the vehement party prevailed, and the duke at length allowed it with a rough jest.

To the decrees on faith and worship the council added sixty-three *Postulata* touching Church government, which, if granted, would have done much to secure reasonable freedom, but these were not so much decrees as requests, and they were neither accepted nor rejected.

In the end a general agreement (förening) was drawn up and accepted by those who were present, by the duke and the lords of the council and the nobility, and by the absent members of the estates to whom it was sent round for signature.[8]

After a preamble, describing the reasons for summoning the council in the disputes and disagreements which had prevailed especially as to religion, and mentioning the objects set before it, the following conclusions were set forth in detail :—

(1) Agreement to abide by God's pure and saving Word as it is contained in the writings of the prophets, evangelists and apostles, and to acknowledge its inspiration; and that it contains completely all that is necessary for Christian doctrine, faith and morals, and is a test to judge all disputes in religion, and needs no further interpretation by the Fathers or others.

(2) Assent to the Apostles', Nicene and Athanasian Creeds, and the oldest, true and unaltered Augsburg Confession of 1530; and to the religion held in the reign of King Gustaf and the lifetime of Archbishop Laurentius Petri Nericius, and set forth in the printed Church Order accepted in the year 1572. As regards certain ceremonies retained, such as salt and lights in baptism, the elevation in the Lord's Supper, movement of the mass book from one corner of the altar to the other, bell-ringing at the elevation, which are disused in most evangelical churches,

[8] It may be found pp. 86-90 of the *Riksdagsakter*,, and summarized in Anjou, pp. 622-4, and Cornelius, *S.K.H.*, pp. 107 foll.

parish priests, and bishops in their visitations, shall take care to explain them and prevent them being misused.   If it should be necessary that these ceremonies be abolished, the bishops, with some of their chapters and most learned priests, should take counsel how this might be done without scandal and disturbance.

(3) As regards exorcism at baptism, it was not indeed necessary, but, as it is so suitable as a reminder of the condition in which all men are who come to baptism and of what the power of baptism is, it may well be retained in our churches.   A slight change was to be made in the wording.   The council, however, did not wish to cast any slur on the foreign churches or " high personages here in the kingdom " who did not use it and yet accepted the same confession, or are one with us in faith.

(4) As regards the Liturgy which has caused so much unrest, and is proved by Scripture to be superstitious and very similar to the popish mass, which opposes and depreciates our Redeemer's work and leads on to other popish errors, the council rejects it and all its consequences in doctrine, ceremonies and discipline, and strictly forbids its use.   It also rejects all the errors of Sacramentarians, Zwinglians, and Calvinists, and also Anabaptists, and all other heretics by whatever name they are called.

(5) The council approves the discipline and order set forth in the printed Church Order, as tried by experience. Where circumstances require it additions may be made to it by the bishop's and chapter's joint agreement.

(6) While it is impossible wholly to exclude those who hold false doctrine and do not agree with us, they must not be allowed to hold any public meeting in a house or elsewhere.   Those who do so, or who speak against our religion, are to be suitably punished.

(7) These resolutions now agreed to are at once to be printed so as to be known by all men.   Those present express their determination to abide by what has been agreed, and commit their work to God's protection.

Then follow the attestations by signature and seal, the date being also given 20th March, 1593.

Copies of this resolution were sent to the different provinces, and we have the names and signatures of some 1,934 persons of distinction attached to the various copies which have been preserved.   Whilst they were being signed the document was in the press, but it was not completely printed or published until July of the next year, about the time of Sigismund's return to Poland.[9]   It contained a list of signatories not exactly agreeing with the MS. material, but this can only be accounted for by carelessness.

§ 3.—Immense importance of the " Agreement " of Upsala. Its unique character. Its effects. restoration of the University of Upsala.

It is scarcely possible to exaggerate the importance of this council as a turning point in the history of Sweden. The lay historians of the country have perhaps hardly realized its full significance and its unique character.   It stands out as evidence of what a national Church may do for the people when it is allowed to have a reasonable independence.   There are very few if any parallels to be found to it in the religious history of mankind.   The freedom and the unanimity of the action could only be possible in a nation so much accustomed to the idea and practice of self-government by a large popular assembly, and so ready to be swayed by enthusiasm in making great decisions at critical moments of its history.   No doubt this liability to be carried away by feeling is always apt to disguise to those present the probabilities of partial reaction, which may be ready to follow.   But, on the whole, the Swedes have shown a remarkable power, not only of

---

[9] It was printed at Stockholm by Gutterwitz.   It was edited by Johannes Thomæ Bureus.   The preface is dated 30th June, 1593.   The last page is dated July, 1594.   Cp. *Riksdagsakter*, p. 148.

making up their minds for themselves in a reasonable manner, but of adhering to their decisions arrived at in such moments of feeling.   It must be remembered that they had had seventy years of trying experience since the Riksdag of Vesterås.   Various methods had been set before them by various powers, and the result of following those methods had been subjected to a considerable amount of trial.   Personally, I do not think that what was good in King John's policy had been sufficiently tried.   He had spoiled its effect by persecuting his opponents with great harshness.   But, viewing the matter as a whole, a foreigner must, I think, judge that the Swedes took the wisest course that was possible to them under the circumstances, and one which their descendants of the same blood will view with satisfaction for generations yet to come. They accepted the most reasonable and uncontroversial Protestant confession of faith which was open to them, and they did this without revising it.   Had they attempted to revise it they might have disputed for a long period. But time pressed, and they took as a watchword the formulary which would best secure their general agreement at home, and unite them with their natural allies in Germany, allies in the struggle which was obviously imminent and obviously most serious.

In regard to the character of the Confession of Augsburg, I may quote what our own Hardwick says of it: " In the mildness of its tone, the gracefulness of its diction, and the general perspicuity of its arrangement, it is worthy of its gifted author; while in theological terminology it everywhere adheres, as closely as the truth permitted, to existing standards of the Western Church.   Melanchthon seems indeed to have been confident that he was treading in the steps of St. Augustine, and the Early Fathers; all his protests were accordingly confined to modern innovations and distortions by which sectaries and schoolmen had been gradually corrupting the deposit of the Christian faith." After giving an abstract of its articles, he says: " This meagre abstract . . . is enough to demonstrate that in presenting it to the imperial Diet, the reformers had been influenced by a strong desire to keep within the boundaries of the Latin Church, and to approximate as closely as possible to doctrines already received." Similarly Professor Richard, of the Theological Seminary of Gettysburg, Pennsylvania, has recently written of the framers of this confession that " it was their intention, by repudiating heresy, and by affirming the Catholic doctrine, to vindicate their right to remain in the Church." [10]   On the other hand, by adding to it the Church Order of 1571, the Swedes affirmed their belief that for themselves at least an episcopal polity was the best, and the one to which they were determined to adhere.

The wisdom of the first course was quickly demonstrated by the extraordinary call soon made upon Sweden to take the lead in the Thirty Years' War. Gustavus Adolphus, who was born in the year after the Upsala-möte, was undoubtedly the saviour of Northern Europe from forcible subjection to the papal monarchy, and he took that position in virtue of the work done at the council. The wisdom of retaining the episcopal polity, and with it the higher position of the ministry, could only be proved by longer experience. But there is one evidence of it which must occur to every student of Swedish history, the lead taken by the bishops in all literary and scientific pursuits, and educational and social projects, as well as in history and theology. Professor Schück's *History of Swedish Literature* bears remarkable testimony to the debt which the country owes them.

In this way Sweden was prepared for the advent of King Sigismund. Before he landed Duke Charles had received from the Council of State a promise to obey him in every-

[10] See Charles Hardwick's *Hist. of the Articles*, etc., pp. 16 and 25, Cambridge, 1859, and *The Confessional History of the Lutheran Church* by James W. Richard, D.D., quoted in *Journal of Th. Studies*, vol. 11, p. 591, 1910.

thing he should think fit to do for the maintenance of the
Confession of Augsburg. Sigismund came over with
twenty thousand crowns in his pocket from the pope towards the cost of the restoration of Catholicism in Sweden.
After some negotiation he accepted the "decrees of
Upsala" as a condition of his coronation, which took place
in 1594, at the hands of Swedish bishops, though his
enemy, Archbishop Abraham, was not permitted to set the
crown himself upon the king's head; and in his coronation oath he promised to preserve the Swedish Church.
He began, however, at once to break his promise, and to
try and rule Sweden through Polish ministers, and to treat
it as a dependency of Poland.[11]   The result may be easily
imagined; and step by step his hopes of success were
blighted by the resistance of three out of the four estates,
the clergy, burghers and peasants, although he had many
adherents amongst the nobles, who knew that their interests
lay in the weakness of the crown.   It was the transference
of the bishops and clergy as a body to the national side in
politics which made all the difference in the new struggle
against a Union sovereignty.   All Sweden owes a debt of
gratitude to them for their steadfastness, with few
exceptions, in this crisis.

The birth of Gustavus Adolphus in 1594 synchronized
with another most important event for Sweden, the restoration of the University of Upsala.   This was part of the
movement for the defence and propagation of the principles of the Reformation, and with it was joined the oversight of all the schools in the kingdom.   The charter,
dated 15th March, 1595, provided for the stipends of three
professors of theology and four of philosophy, for their
residence partly in old prebendal houses, and for a common
table for forty students.[12]

[11] Cp. C. R. L. Fletcher's *Gustavus Adolphus*, p. 12, G. P.
Putnam and Sons, London and New York, 1907.
[12] Cp. the *Postulata Clericorum* addressed to Charles and the
Council of State in 1595, Baaz, pp. 564 foll.

§ 4.—RIKSDAG OF SÖDERKÖPING (1595).   HARSH VISITA-
TION OF ARCHBISHOP ABRAHAM.   BATTLE OF
STÅNGEBRO (1598).   DIFFICULT POSITION OF
CHARLES.   ARCHBISHOP ABRAHAM IMPRISONED.
NICOLAUS BOTNIENSIS ARCHBISHOP-ELECT OF
UPSALA (1599—1600).   OLAUS MARTINI ELECTED
ARCHBISHOP AT THE RIKSDAG OF STOCKHOLM
(1602).   HIS CONSECRATION.

In the autumn of the same year Charles took a more
decisive step than before in convoking a Riksdag at Söderköping, not only without the consent of Sigismund, but
contrary to his previous prohibition (Geijer : pp. 190-1).
This assembly, in which Charles obtained his wishes by a
direct appeal to the people, decided that foreign dissenters
from the evangelical religion were to be exiled from the
kingdom, and this particularly concerned those at Stockholm, Drottningholm and Vadstena.   Swedes might remain, provided they did not cause scandal.   Vadstena was
to be closed as a convent.   Duke Charles was elected
governor of the realm of Sweden, thus securing his
superiority to the local governors, whom Sigismund had
left depending on himself.   Finally, two bishops were
elected, Petrus Kenicius to Skara and Petrus Jonæ
Angermannus to Vexiö.[13]

One of the results of the Riksdag of Söderköping was
the general visitation of all the dioceses in Sweden, undertaken by Archbishop Abraham under a commission from
the duke.   It was intended not only to punish offenders
against morality and Church discipline, but also sectaries.
It began in West Gothland in February, 1596.   The archbishop's procedure was stern and vigorous ; directly he had
pronounced his judgment on offenders they were seized by
his assistant " deacons," and punishment followed immediately.   The commonest punishment was birching with a

[13] See Baaz :   pp. 567-9.   The Commission to Archbishop
Abraham follows, dated Vadstena, 18th Dec., 1585 (pp. 571-2).
Then the Archbishop's letter to the clergy (572-5).

rod, followed by the deluging of the delinquent by so many
buckets of ice-cold water.   So severe was this treatment
that many of those who suffered it fell half dead.   Exceptional offences were punished with fines, which were partly
paid to the cathedral, partly to the parish church.   Whip-
ping in churches at this time and later was not an uncommon punishment, and the archbishop defended himself on
this ground against the charges of cruelty which were
naturally made to the duke.   But besides his severity, he
seems to have acted imprudently and inconsiderately in
regard to matters of marriage discipline, and to have been
needlessly puritanical in his abolition of old usages, and to
have also been the cause of much vandalism in regard to
old monuments.

From this time the Duke Charles and the archbishop
were on bad terms.

The duke was now in a position of direct resistance to
one whom he had acknowledged as lawful king.   He was
not easy in it until the end of his life, for he had great
reverence for his father's testament and for the hereditary
principle.   For himself he regularly took the title of
" hereditary prince and governor," and (at a later date),
when he allowed the publication of Christopher's land's-
law, he made a change in the article *de rege* asserting the
hereditary principle.   On the other hand, he felt the
necessity of resisting a government which brought back
all the evils and weakness of the old Union period, and
added to them the danger of a war of religion.   His way
was made clearer by the invasion of Sweden in 1598 by a
Polish army and the defeat of Sigismund at Stångebro,
near Linköping.   On this occasion, strange to say, Archbishop Abraham, who had long been at variance with the
duke, turned round to support the king.   In 1599 the
estates announced the withdrawal of their allegiance from
Sigismund as a papist, if he should ever return to Sweden.
The case of Abraham was gone into, but the clergy,
though ready to censure and suspend him, would not de-

pose him. He was, however, kept in prison, and in his
place his former rival, Nicolaus Botniensis, now first professor at Upsala, was elected, apparently by the estates
(6th February, 1599), to be archbishop.[14]   The election
was certainly irregular, and Botniensis did not live long
enough to be consecrated. A great deal of sympathy was
felt for Archbishop Angermannus, whose loyalist principles were stronger than his religious instincts, just as
Sancroft's were in 1688, and apparently he mistrusted the
duke's theological position. He remained in prison till
his death in 1608, supported in his sufferings by the
affection of the clergy of his diocese.

Botniensis died 18th May, 1600, being only about fifty
years old, and was a great loss to Sweden. Angermannus
was still in prison, but a new archbishop was chosen in the
following year at the Riksdag in Stockholm in the person
of another learned man, Olaus Martini.[15] He was son of
the Bishop of Linköping, Martinus Olai, King John's old
opponent, who had been roughly deposed by the king, and
took refuge under Duke Charles' protection. The new
archbishop had been himself a student at Rostock, like
Botniensis. He had preached at King Sigismund's coronation, and had for some years been pastor at Nyköping in
the duchy of Södermanland, and was, therefore, well
known to the duke. The Chapter of Upsala now accepted
this appointment, and Olaus was consecrated, as we learn
from his funeral sermon, on the 16th August, 1601, and,
as we learn from another authority, by Petrus Kenicius,
Bishop of Skara, who afterwards succeeded him in the
archbishopric. I am careful to state these facts, as doubt
was cast upon the reality of his consecration by Anjou, and
repeated by other Church historians, such as Norlin and
Cornelius.

I have myself had the opportunity of examining the
Chapter Acts of Upsala, which agree with the date given

[14] Magnusson : l.c., pp. 156 foll.
[15] See P. E. Thyselius : *Anteckningar om Olaus Martini*, 1880.

by the funeral sermon, and there seems really no doubt about it.[16]   As Petrus Benedicti, of Linköping, who was the senior bishop, had been the consecrator of Archbishop Abraham, it was perhaps natural that he should shrink from consecrating some one else during his life.

§ 5.—CHARLES BECOMES KING. HIS CHARACTER AND SCRUPLES. HIS SEMI-CALVINIST POSITION. HIS CONTROVERSIES WITH ARCHBISHOP OLAUS MARTINI. JOHN FORBES' DISPUTATION AT UPSALA (1608). PETRUS KENICIUS ARCHBISHOP IN 1609. DEATH OF CHARLES (1611).

Duke Charles became king in 1604.   He had waited to accept the title until his younger nephew, John, Sigismund's half-brother, son of Gunilla Bielke, had attained his majority.   Charles had offered him the crown in order to satisfy his conscience, but the young prince prudently

[16] We owe to Dean Lundström the clearing up of these points. See his *Skisser och Kritiker*, p. 118 foll., and *Kyrkohistorisk Årsskrift* I. p. 269 foll. (1900) and VII. p. 267 foll., 1906.   The funeral sermon was preached by J. Raumannus, and is still extant.   The day is also noted in Thomas Buræus' Diary for 1601. The name of the consecrator is given by E. M. Fant, *De successione canonica et consecratione episcoporum, Sueciæ*, p. 12, Upsala, 1790. The Chapter Acts quite agree as to the day. The entry for 11th July speaks of the consecration as future.   On a later day we read that the bishops who were called to the inauguration gave reasons for their not coming, and excused themselves.   The chapter decreed that " Dominus electus " may enter upon his office (*i.e.*, do such duties as a bishop-elect may do).   It was decided that the bishops should be excused for not being present, but they were to be admonished to come at another time.   The " inauguration " was fixed to take place " tempore S. Laurentii "—*i.e.*, in the week following August 10th.   On Wednesday, 19th August, there is a record of a divorce case, " Lata est sententia divortii a R.D. Archiepiscopo."   Evidently the consecration had taken place between the 10th and 19th August.   It was naturally on Sunday, 16th August, the tenth Sunday after Trinity.   The chapter met as usual the Wednesday after.

declined it.   He was content to hold a Swedish dukedom, of which the principal part was East Gothland (Baaz: v. 18).   Charles was crowned in 1607, and the crown entailed upon his heirs, being Protestants.   He published King Christopher's land's-law in 1608, and died in 1611.

Charles IX. was a man of restless energy, much of which he spent in theological controversy, and in plans for the revision of the catechism and the service book.   He was a moderate, not an extreme Calvinist, and he himself published a catechism based on the famous conciliation catechism of Heidelberg, which had been drawn up in the Palatinate in 1563 by representatives of the school of Melanchthon and Calvin.   Melanchthon himself, though he was strongly opposed to Calvin's doctrine of predestination, had strongly deprecated the dogmatism of the high Lutherans on the mysterious subject of the ubiquity of our Lord's human nature and on the nature of our Lord's presence in the sacrament.   The Heidelberg Catechism (as Hardwick says) " steered away as far as possible from all (such) speculative topics." [17]

Charles may have been drawn to this formula by his German connections,[18] and perhaps by the hope that the spirit of Melanchthon, who was so much honoured in Sweden, might help him to carry through his more liberal projects.

He was, like his brother Eric, a hymn writer, and a writer of prayers, though he did not venture, like King John, to compose a liturgy.   He was also anxious to revise the translation of the Bible.   But he was still more a controversialist.   He felt the Lutheran orthodox doctrine to be a heavy burden, especially its Eucharistic doctrine.

The teaching of the Heidelberg Catechism on this point

---

[17] It may be found in the *Sylloge Confessionum*, pp. 327-361, Oxford, 1804.   On its character see more in Hardwick : *Reformation*, new edition, pp. 160 foll., 1880.

[18] His second wife, Christina, was granddaughter of Philip the Magnanimous, Landgrave of Hesse.

is certainly different from the rigid Lutheran, and seems to suggest that there is a parallel but distinct spiritual feeding on the body and blood of Christ of which the feeding on the outward signs is symbolic.   How far there is a necessary connection between the two does not clearly appear, but it seems to be intended in one of the answers.[19]   In many ways and at many times Charles tried to get out of personal acknowledgment of the Augsburg Confession, and he resented the imposition of the agreement of the Upsala-möte as a new Church law.   In some respects he was before his age in the assertion of the duty of toleration and in his defence of the use of human reason in religious controversy.

These opinions brought him into conflict with the professors of Upsala, and especially with the new archbishop, who was destined to spend nearly his whole time in controversy with the king, who had been his father's friend and protector.   He was a strong self-controlled and able man, who replied with dignity to the king's books, and let nothing pass unanswered.   He is described as one of the finest figures in Swedish history, and to him is due the result that the unanimity of 1593 did not dissolve into chaos and unsettlement.   To the king appertains the great merit of refraining from the use of force in matters of conscience, although his hands were deeply dyed in the blood of his political enemies.

One of the controversies which were promoted by the king is more interesting to us than that in which Micronius,

---

[19] Q. 79 (pp. 346-7) asks why Christ called the bread His body and the cup His blood.   It is not only to shew us that His body and blood are the food and drink of our soul, " but much more, to certify us by this visible sign and pledge that we are no less truly partakers of His body and blood, by the operation of the Holy Spirit, than that we receive these sacred symbols, in memory of Him, by our bodily mouth : and, further, that His passion and obedience are as certainly ours, as if we had suffered punishment for our sins and made satisfaction to God ourselves.''

his Calvinist chaplain, was engaged in the early days of
Olaus Martini.   I refer, of course, to the disputation held
at Upsala, 17th November, 1608, in which the Scotsman,
John Forbes, was the champion.   He was a well-known
man of the family of the Lairds of Corse, and he owed his
invitation to Sweden probably to his brother Arthur, who
was a distinguished officer in the Swedish service in this
and the next reign, and afterwards became Earl of Granard
in Ireland.   John Forbes had been moderator of the Aberdeen Assembly of July, 1605, and had, in consequence,
been imprisoned and exiled by King James.   Since then
he had been pastor of an English and Scotch congregation
at Middleburg and Delft.   He was met at Upsala by the
archbishop and other professors in the presence of some
lords of the council, and a great multitude of students.   As
he entered the hall he might have conjectured the sort of
reception he would encounter, from a Latin epigram fastened to the lecture notice-board, in which his name was
punningly interpreted as " sheep-biter." [20]
For a whole day he contended against these odds with all
the courage of his family, his nation and his faith.   He
asserted that he did not come to convert Sweden, but to
explain and defend the religion of his own country.   But
he proclaimed the Calvinistic doctrine of absolute election
and reprobation without flinching, to the great scandal of
his audience.   The archbishop ended: " Irenæus records
that the old Germans closed their ears when they heard
abuse of God.   So we too confess that our ears are tired out

[20] See Baaz, lib. V., cc. 16 and 17.   The epigram was (p.
624) :—

> Forbesius præsto est : ne mordeat ille cavete
> Quos Christus sancta morte redemit oves.
> Forbesius nostrâ nam linguâ denotat illum,
> Balantem mordens qui vorat ore gregem.

I presume that the Swedish word intended is "får-bitare,"
" sheep-biter."   Ch. 16 contains the disputation, ch. 17 Forbes'
theses.   See also Th. Norlin : *Johannes Rudbeckius*, Bihang,
pp. 56 foll., Upsala, 1860.

with hearing the abuse of God which has been uttered by this stranger. Let us pray God that He may convert this misguided man." Forbes courteously replied, with undaunted pertinacity : " May God convert us all !" Forbes' ability was admired by the Swedes, but they were glad to find that he had no answer to one of Professor Peter Rudbeckius' arguments, and hence they sometimes use the proverb " Ad haec Forbesius nihil." [21]

The king, however, was not pleased with the crude Calvinism of his champion, and Forbes shortly afterwards left the kingdom. He returned with a union project in 1610, but it proved useless. He died in 1634.[22]

It is pleasant to contrast with this the delightful welcome given to one of our party, Dr. A. J. Mason, Vice-Chancellor of Cambridge University, by the professors and students of the same university of Upsala, when he came, not to convert Sweden, but to expound the position of the Church of England on 22nd September, 1909.

Olaus Martini died in 1609, only fifty-two years of age, the year after the disputation at Upsala. He was a diligent preacher, especially in his cathedral, and lectured regularly also to the students. He was succeeded by the Bishop of Skara, Petrus Kenicius (1555—1636), who had been one of the professors who suffered in the disputes about the liturgy. Charles IX. died in 1611, and the archbishop continued in office during the whole of the succeeding reign, that of Gustavus Adolphus, whom he crowned in 1617. He was a zealous and diligent man, and did much to stimulate the king's generosity towards the university ; but in his old age the diocese of Upsala fell behind those of his younger contemporaries. He died in 1636, having been archbishop for twenty-seven years, that is far the next longest period to Laurentius Petri Nericius.

---

[21] Norlin proves that this was not the famous John Rudbeckius (as Baaz and others have it), but probably his brother, Peter.

[22] Norlin, pp. 62-3, mentions the second visit. On Forbes generally see *Dict. of National Biography*, s.n. The article, strangely enough, contains no notice of this disputation.

§ 6.—The great kings and the great bishops. The Stormaktstid (1618—1718). Character of Gustavus Adolphus. Johannes Bothvidi and Isaac Rothovius. Rudbeckius and the humanists, Messenius and Stiernhielm. Rudbeckius and Gustavus Adolphus. Judaism in the diocese of Vesterås and elsewhere.

The most striking feature of the "Stormaktstid" of Sweden, that period of exactly a hundred years, from the outbreak of the Thirty Years' War in 1618 to the death of Charles XII. in 1718, to which its people naturally most readily turn back, and on which they dwell with lingering affection, is the eminence of certain of its leaders, and in particular its kings and its bishops. As regards the kings greatness may be ascribed to all of them—to Charles IX., the somewhat reluctant saviour of Lutheranism in Sweden, who, as it were, ushers in the period, and, above all, to his son Gustavus Adolphus, the saviour of Protestantism in Europe;[23] to Charles X., though he is less known than the others; to Charles XI., the reformer of the constitution, both of Church and State; and to Charles XII., the best known of all, next to Gustavus Adolphus. Their reigns make up the period when Sweden not only took the lead in the Thirty Years' War, which ended with the peace of Westphalia in 1648, but controlled the Baltic and extended its dominions to the widest area ever reached by it in historical times.

Let me, in reference to the greatest of these sovereigns, make my own some closing words of Mr. Fletcher's attractive biography of Gustavus Adolphus. After describing his fatal wound, at the Battle of Lützen, 6th (14th) November, 1632, and his last words to the cuirassiers who rode up to inquire the name of the fallen man: " I am the King of Sweden, who do seal the religion and liberty of the

[23] Prof. Harald Hjärne's *Gustav Adolf der Retter des Protestantismus* in Pastor Werckshagen's composite illustrated work *Der Protestantismus*, Vol. 1, pp. 141-168. It is translated by Kammer-Rat E. Jonas, of Berlin.

German nation with my blood," he recounts the extraordinary effort of his army to avenge their fallen leader. Then he sums up: "If I were asked to find a parallel to him among those who have controlled the destinies of the world, I should pitch upon Saint Louis, King of France —in whom also were combined the three greatest qualities of a ruler of men—justice, courage and devotion.   Saint Louis, being born out of due time, lacked the fourth great quality which was so largely displayed in Gustavus, a quality or virtue which is indeed in itself but a daughter of justice—tolerance.   The true glory of the King of Sweden was that he was the champion of Protestantism. Protestantism, though here and there it has been intolerant, and has used its triumphs unmercifully, has always led to freedom, and freedom to toleration.   And toleration has been the great—the only really great— achievement of the modern world." . . . "What was his character? . . . Simple, brave, passionate, truthful, devout; with the highest sense of his kingly dignity, and a yet higher sense of his great mission on earth, it is not unfair to say of him that he had a single eye to the work God had given him to do.   More cannot be said of any man."

"What were his aims?   This has always been a great problem.   But if any one may be supposed to have known his mind it surely was Axel Oxtenstiern, with whom, during his whole reign, he lived upon terms of intimacy so affectionate [as] to be very uncommon between great men of equal rank, but rare indeed between a subject and his sovereign.   And all Oxenstiern's utterances on the subject have the same ring: 'A great Scandinavian Empire if you will.   The Baltic and the Baltic coasts for Sweden. But NOT the crown of the Holy Roman Empire.'   Then he finely concludes as to the effects of his death on Germany.   'It sanctified a cause which the German princes themselves had only known how to betray.   He had been the first to set a bound to the tyranny which Germany was powerless to resist, and which would, if not resisted, have

spread far beyond Germany, even far beyond distant
Sweden. And for that reason Germany, Sweden and
mankind count him among their heroes.' "

For Sweden the whole century (1618—1718), of which
the reigns of Gustavus Adolphus and Charles XII. were
the epical or heroic periods, was a time of great expansion,
followed by one of serious depression and poverty—a century in which foreign wars and internal political changes
figure largely, and I can make no attempt even to trace
them in outline. But what I shall attempt to do is to give
some idea of the great bishops who were conspicuous in
this century, and who impart to it a very peculiar
character.

At the time when Charles IX. died the old and tried
leaders had passed and the stage was left clear, as when
Svante Sture died, about 1511, to men of a younger generation. Gustavus himself was only eighteen, and his great
minister, Axel Oxenstierna, was, at the age of twenty-eight,
a controlling power in European politics. The greatest
generals of the wars that followed were not yet thirty years
of age. It was so to some extent in the Church. The
archbishop was fifty-four years old; but Laurentius
Paulinus Gothus, Bishop of Strengnäs, was ten years
younger, and Johannes Rudbeckius, the greatest Churchman of the period, afterwards Bishop of Vesterås, was only
thirty.

The vigour of these young men, especially Rudbeckius
and Laurentius Paulinus Gothus, did much to help Sweden
to take the foremost place in the religious struggle which
followed. Gustavus Adolphus supported the Augsburg
Confession, and allied himself with the Church as he found
it. Johannes Rudbeckius was possessed with the spirit
almost of an Old Testament prophet, and he and two other
military chaplains (Johannes Bothvidi and Isaac Rothovius) were men of strong character, as well as great preaching power. They contributed not a little to form the spirit
of the Swedish army, which anticipated and probably ex-
celled that of Cromwell's Ironsides and the Scottish

Covenanters. You will not forget the close connection at this time between Great Britain and Sweden, which is exemplified in the life of Alexander Leslie, first Earl of Leven. He was one of many Scotsmen serving under the King of Sweden, who had at one time three Scotch and two English regiments in his army. Leslie, after thirty years' distinguished service abroad, returned to Scotland to be its most influential general and leader up to the time of his death in 1661. Nor will you forget that those remarkable books, *The Swedish Intelligencer*, and its companion, *The Swedish Discipline*, were two of the most popular books in England in the reign of Charles I.[24]

Of the three court and army chaplains whom I have named Johannes Bothvidi stood perhaps closest, and certainly longest, of all in the confidence of the king, for whom he had a great affection, and the king was sorry to part with him to the diocese of Linköping in 1631, the year before his own death. His work there was short, but valuable. He died in 1635.

Isaac Rothovius, son of a Småland peasant, had a longer and more striking career as Bishop of Åbo in Finland for twenty-five years (1627—1652). He came there as a stranger, and he ruled the diocese with a hand of iron, more like a military chieftain, it was said, than a bishop. But Finland needed discipline, and responded to it. Priests and people were both addicted to drink. Life and speech were very rough, and witchcraft largely prevailed. Rothovius' rules of discipline were severe. Whoever absented himself from church for three Sundays without necessity was fined three dollars. Whoever ate before divine service, one dollar. Priests who neglected their duty were subject to fine, or imprisonment in the chapter's prison, or finally to deposition.

[24] See C. R. L. Fletcher's *Gustavus Adolphus*, pp. 112-4. On page vi. he says : " In the library of the immortal Miles Standish the *Swedish Intelligencer* stood side by side with the Bible." This may have been so; but Longfellow, in his *Courtship of Miles Standish*, gives that honour to two other books.

On the other hand, Rothovius was a great and a powerful preacher, and he preached from Scripture. During his twenty-five years' previous pastorate at Nyköping he had preached more than 3,000 times (3,183), and had covered great part of the Old and New Testament. He was a founder of schools, and transformed the cathedral school into a gymnasium with six teachers in 1630. In 1640 he prevailed upon Per Brahe, who had been one of Gustavus' principal generals, and was now general-governor of Finland—a man of noble character—to found the University of Åbo. In the year 1642 the first printing press was established in Finland, and the Bible appeared in the Finnish language. When Rothovius died in 1652 he had learnt to love the people whom he had at first ruled so sternly as a stranger, and they had learnt to love him, and he was greatly mourned.[25]

But the most striking personality of all the great bishops was without doubt that of Johannes Rudbeckius, member of a strong family. Like the two reformers, he was born at Örebro, whither his father had migrated from Rudbeck in Holstein. He was professor of Upsala first of mathematics, then of Hebrew, then of divinity. At the University he had a terrible quarrel with a learned brother professor, John Messenius (c. 1579—1636), and both were wisely removed by the king from a place where they had troubled others as well as themselves by their discord. Rudbeckius became court preacher and Messenius was made head of the archives at Stockholm, where he was in his right place. Messenius is worthy of notice as almost the earliest antiquary in Sweden, where he was only just preceded by John Bureus (1568—1652), the first inquirer into the runes, and the first editor of an old Swedish manuscript, the *Konungastyrelse*. Messenius was the founder of the learned school of Swedish history and antiquities, and had something in him of our Archbishop Parker, our

[25] See Elis Bergroth : *Den Finska Kyrkans Historia*, pp. 103-9, Helsingfors [1892]. Rothovius' brother, Jonas Birgeri, was " superintendent " in Kalmar, 1618—1625.

Camden and our Dugdale. He was, like Parker and his own contemporary Bureus, a collector of old national manuscripts. Like Camden, he was a historian of his own country, and his *Scondia Illustrata* [26] rivals, and, perhaps excels, our *Britannia*. Like Dugdale, he was studious of the details of personal history and of ancient monuments, though he left nothing so important as the *Monasticon*.

His sympathies were doubtless with the old religion, of which he was suspected, with justice, of being an adherent, and which he openly professed before his death. But he was a critical and conscientious historian, and judged his predecessors and contemporaries without party spirit. Besides his antiquarian tastes, he was a dramatist of much repute in his own age. Both he and Rudbeckius had this in common that they were humanists and opposed to the revived Scholasticism, and Messenius won the affection of his undergraduates by teaching them how to act. His *Disa* takes its name from a legendary queen or goddess, whose yearly fair, the " Disting," is a marked event in the city of Upsala. It was a good play for acting, though he had little poetry or power of drawing character. Unfortunately he had an overweening opinion of his own talents, and wrote his epitaph in Swedish as follows:—

> " Here lie the bones of Doctor John Messenius;
> His soul's above : the world proclaims his genius." [27]

As I am speaking of humanist writings, I will just notice another much better poet, the Dalecarlian George Stiernhielm, whose life was also closely connected with that of Rudbeckius, but who stood in a much happier relation to him as a trusted teacher in his gymnasium. He was another of the encyclopædic minds of Sweden, being

---

[26] It was published long after his death by Peringskiöld, 1700—1705.

[27] Här under hvila sig Doctoris Johannis Messenii ben :
Själen i Guds rike; men ryktet kring hela verlden.

I am afraid that the first line is intended for an hexameter. Notice the rhyme in the pentameter.

famous as a mathematician, a lawyer, a philologist, a Platonist or Neo-platonist, as well as a poet. His quasi-epic poem of *Hercules* is written in a really good style, in well-turned hexameters, easy and flowing; and although it requires a glossary, much as Chaucer does, it can be read with great pleasure, and would repay translation into English. In it the old fable of the choice of Hercules is retold in an original way for the benefit of the young men of Queen Christina's and Charles X.'s court.[28]

The most prominent character, Pleasure (Fru Lusta), has three daughters, Lättia, Kättia and Flättia, whose allurements are described in a lively and sometimes comic manner, which shows something of Chaucer's power of local adaptation of an old theme. The praise of Virtue rings out strong and genuine, but it is not so vividly and dramatically expressed. Nevertheless her picture stands out before us as a bright ideal of womanhood, bred in the open air, according to the best traditions of Swedish home life, and worthy of a good man's lasting love. She is introduced as

> a faithful generous goddess,
> Modestly holding herself in gait, of worshipful presence,
> Weighty of speech, of earnest mien and noble in aspect,
> Brown under eyes and burnt with the sunshine, slight in her body,
> Pure in her dress, snow-white, all clad in glistering silver,
> Plain and clean and serene in the old-world fashion of honour.

But though Messenius and Stiernhielm deserve notice for their writings, Rudbeckius stands out above all his contemporaries for strength of action. He first showed Sweden what an active bishop who gave himself to his diocese could be like. In earlier life he did good service in the court and in the field, as Norlin shows in an excellent sketch of his life, of which I have been only able to obtain a

---

[28] It was printed apparently first in 1658, but had been read in MS. in 1648, and was probably then five or six years older. See *I. S. L. H.*, i., p. 322. There is an excellent selection from Stiernhielm: *Valda Skrifter*, ed. Fr. Tamm, Upsala, 1903, with glossary.

part.[29] His remonstrance with the young king (delivered
on 20th June, 1617), urging him to break off from the sins
of his youth, does honour to his courage as a court chaplain, and seems to have been well received by the king.[30]
In the same year Rudbeckius was named by him one of
the first four doctors of theology ever promoted in the
kingdom.

In 1618 Rudbeckius was sent by the king to inquire into
the Schism which existed at Vesterås, where the bishop,
Bellinus, was 103 years old.   This appears to have been a
kind of Judaism.   The accounts of this strange delusion,
almost unparalleled in modern Church history, remind us
somewhat of the condition of things presupposed by St.
Paul's Epistle to the Colossians.   The movement may
have arisen among the Jews at Archangel or in Poland.   I
suppose that it spread from Finland through Upper
Sweden and Dalarne, and down to the South as far as
Småland.   It affected many priests, as well as peasants
and citizens, and it consisted not merely in observance of
the Sabbath, but in a multitude of dreams and visions in
which revelations were given by angels.   Visions of angels
indeed had nothing necessarily heretical about them, and
readers of Bishop Svedberg's life may remember the

[29] *Johannes Rudbeckius, Biskop i Vesterås,* af Theodor
Norlin, Upsala, 1860.   The first half, down to his consecration
as bishop, 28th January, 1619, was published at Upsala, 1860.
The second half is in the *Nordisk Tidskrift* (1869), pp. 129 foll.,
but I have not seen it.   The life in the *Biographiskt Lexicon,*
signed P., is useful.   Cp. N. Söderblom in *Sertum philolo-
gicum Carolo F. Johansson oblatum,* pp. 70 foll., *Göteborg,*
1910, on the scarce *Privilegia Doctorum.*

[30] Mr. Fletcher (*Gust. Ad.,* p. 40) does not seem to have been
aware of this remonstrance, which is couched in general language, and recommends marriage.   It was perhaps caused
by the liaison with a Dutch lady, Margaret Cabeliau, who was
mother of Count Gustaf Gustafsson of Vasaborg, born in 1616.
But that liaison does not seem to have stood alone.   See
Norlin : l.c., p. 50.   Gustavus married in 1620 the daughter of
Sigismund, elector of Brandenburg.   He was not allowed to
wed Ebba Brahe, his own choice.

curious vision which he had when a young man of an
angel, who advised him what books to buy and study.
Such visions seem to be characteristic of Sweden. But the
Vesterås Sabbatarians were sadly led astray by theirs.
They rejected the New Testament, denied the Saviour, and
ridiculed the Sacraments and the Resurrection. The movement had appeared in Vesterås as early as 1597, when a
citizen and a peasant were put on their trial, and the latter
condemned to death.[81]

§ 7.—Rudbeckius in his diocese. His energy and
    success. Resists the king's plan for a
    Consistorium Generale.

This commission was Rudbeckius' introduction to the
diocese in which he was to spend the remaining twenty-
seven years of his life. He was consecrated Bishop of
Vesterås, 28th January, 1619, in Linköping Cathedral,
where the king had gone to attend the funeral of a sister.
Immediately afterwards the king ordered the bishops who
were present to inquire into the case of three Judaizers from
Vesterås, one of whom was handed over by the spiritual
court to the secular arm for suitable punishment, and was
put to death. Similar fanatics continued to appear at
various times until a much later date.

Rudbeckius did a wonderful work in the period of his
episcopate. He first turned his attention to the cathedral,
built by Birger Jarl about 1270, in the place of an older
one. It was now in a ruinous condition, and the new
bishop re-roofed it with copper. He founded and liberally
organised the first gymnasium or high school for boys ever

[81] On Judaism in Sweden see Baaz : *Inventarium*, lib. vi., c.
16, and vii., 7; Norlin : l.c., pp. 53-4 and *Kyrkans Hist. efter
Ref.*, 2, pp. 249 foll., and Cornelius : *Hist.*, § 140. For a cor-
rection of some mistakes about the subject see Otto Ahnfelt's
Tidskrift för teologi, 3, p. 288 (1893). He explains Article 7 of
the *Ordinantia* of 1540—1541, and Gustaf Vasa's often quoted
letter to the Finns for the 3rd December, 1554, as referring to
the cultus of the Blessed Virgin Mary, to whom Saturday was
particularly dedicated.

established in Sweden, and connected it with the University
of Upsala. It was not, however, merely a school for boys,
but contained provision for the training of clergy, and was
perhaps the first diocesan theological college ever instituted
in a Protestant country. He had indeed, I suppose, a
dream of founding a university of his own, and he may
have wished to emulate his old colleague, Rothovius, who
succeeded in getting such an institution established in
Finland.

He gave the gymnasium a library, and especially furnished it with musical books, which were, till that time,
rare in Sweden. He attracted to it good teachers, besides
Stiernhielm, of whom I have already spoken, many of
whom went out as head teachers into other parts of the
country. He founded a botanical garden. He set up a
printing press furnished with Hebrew and Greek, as well
as Latin and Swedish types. He established a girls'
school, with free education and board for the students.
The teachers were married ladies, who taught domestic
economy as well as other subjects. He also assisted in the
foundation of an orphanage, in which children were fed,
clothed and taught. But both of these institutions unfortunately fell into decay after his death. Many other
schools in the country and in the town of Fahlun owed
much to him. He rebuilt the hospital, or poor house, and
went into all the details of its economy himself. He also
rebuilt the consistorium or meeting hall for the clergy,
which is still called the Nya Kapitlet. He was not, however, by any means content with this creation of institutions and buildings. He was a law-giver to his diocese,
and established the system of Church registers, which has
now become universal in Sweden, and is one of the most
striking external features of Swedish clerical life. In
many ways indeed the diocese of Vesterås, under Rudbeckius, became a model to the whole country. During
his visitation journeys he made complete maps and topo-
graphical descriptions of all the parishes, and inventories

of all Church goods, possessions and revenues. He kept lists also of living persons, whether vicious or necessitous, unworthy or worthy, and was careful to direct the charity of others into good channels. He divided parishes and created a number of chaplaincies or district churches, and in all ways showed himself a good and laborious bishop. But his energy was not confined to his diocese. He was sent by the king to visit the continental provinces of Esthonia and Livonia, which were in an almost heathen condition, while polygamy and idolatry were practised almost openly. He went on this journey in 1627, but the consistorium and the town council in Reval, the capital of Livonia, so resisted him, on the grounds of their privileged independence, that he could do but little. In Sweden itself he attended all the seventeen Riksdagar that were held during his episcopate.

I have said that he was a member of a strong family. He was one of three brothers who survived the plague in which their father died. One of them, Petrus, was professor at Upsala, where he took part in the colloquy with Forbes; another, Jacob, was rector of the high school at Stockholm. He had himself fifteen children by one wife, of whom three became bishops, Nicolas of Vesterås, Johannes of Narva and Petrus of Skara. Another, Olaus, was a great botanist, famous in the history of the University of Upsala, author of the wonderful *Atlantica*. His son, another Olaus, was also an excellent botanist. The elder Olaus reckoned that his grandfather's family had increased to 397 persons in three generations.[32]

Such a man naturally had the support of the king, and he received much assistance in his great plans from him and from the nobility; but his personality and individuality were in the end too pronounced for co-operation with the king in his plans for the reform of the Church. The king saw the necessity of a stronger central government for the Church, since every diocese had its own usages, cere-

[32] Norlin : *Joh. Rudbeckius*, p. 6 n.

monies, prayer books and hymn books.   Each bishop with
his consistorium, or chapter, was a law to himself.   Those
who wish to trace the history of the revival and reconstruc-
tion of the Swedish chapters in the seventeenth century
may do so in a learned treatise by Professor Hjalmar
Holmquist, who, of course, draws attention to the German
influence which is implied in the word " Consistorium." [33]
In the time of which I am now speaking the lay element in
these revived chapters was small, and the principle involved in its presence was perhaps not perceived.

But the king wished to have a " Consistorium Generale "
for the whole kingdom, which was to superintend the whole
Church.   It was to be the court of appeal in all cases
between bishops and priests, to have the oversight of
academies, schools, hospitals, etc., to examine candidates
for benefices in royal patronage and others, and to watch
over the purity of doctrine.   It was to consist of twelve
members, the archbishop, and the bishops of Strengnäs
and Vesterås (that is the three whose see-cities were on
Lake Mälar, and, therefore, within easy reach of Stockholm), the chief court chaplain, the pastor primarius of
Stockholm, and the chief theological professor of Upsala—
and six laymen.   The latter were the high steward, two
councillors of state and three others.   It was to meet
every year at Stockholm.

This project was, however, stoutly resisted by Rudbeckius and the other bishops, especially Laurentius Paulinus
Gothus, Bishop of Strengnäs (1609—1636), and not less,
we may suppose, by those of the more distant sees.   On
the king's side, however, were many of the lower clergy,
led by Dr. Johannes Matthiæ, who, after a long residence
in England and Holland, had come to love the tolerance
which there prevailed.   In 1629 Matthiæ became court
chaplain, and followed Gustavus in the Thirty Years'
War.   The resistance, nevertheless, of the bishops was so

[33] See *De Svenska Domkapitlens förvandling till Lärare-
kapitel*, 1571—1687, Upsala, 1908, esp. pp. 54-62.

great that the king had to give way, and the plan was held in suspense.   The bishops took their stand on the rights of the spirituality, and urged that political persons had no business to intermeddle in the government of the Church. The king then tried another plan of excluding all bishops and having a council of thirteen priests from the city and neighbourhood of Stockholm.   But neither this nor another suggestion from the other side were agreed upon, and the matter was suspended.   The king's death left the government in the hands of the chancellor, Axel Oxenstierna, as regent on behalf of the young queen, Christina, and he had other difficulties to contend with.   The bishops did not deny that some central control was necessary, but they desired to find it in the separate meeting of the estate of the clergy at the time of the Riksdag, something like the Convocation in England, which was very much in their own hands.   This was called the " Consistorium Regni."

§ 8.—Laurentius Paulinus Gothus archbishop.   His synods and visitations.   Johannes Matthiæ. The Lapland Mission.   The colony of New Sweden.   Formation of new dioceses.

In the meantime the example of Rudbeckius' diocesan administration was being followed elsewhere.   He had unfortunately fallen out with the regency and the nobility on account of the hierarchical pretensions put forth in his *Privilegia Doctorum* (above n. 29).   So when old Archbishop Petrus Kenicius died in February, 1636, his candidature for the see of Upsala was not approved by the Government.   The clergy on the whole were in favour of Rudbeckius or the Provost of Upsala, Lenæus.   But, after various attempts at election, the Council of State took the matter into its hands, and declared that Laurentius Paulinus Gothus, Bishop of Strengnäs, was elected.   He was not indeed anxious for the place, and objections were raised by the clergy of Upsala and the other candidates. But, in the end, the choice of the Government prevailed, and just eighteen months after the death of Kenicius,

Laurentius made his solemn entry into the cathedral of Upsala (12th July, 1637).[34] In September of the same year he delivered a long oration on the principles on which he was about to govern the diocese, which had recently been much neglected. The two principal instruments were to be meetings of clergy and visitations. He introduced, that is to say, the methods which he and Rudbeckius had already used with so much effect at Strengnäs and Vesterås.[35] He determined to hold, and did hold, an annual synod of clergy, of which the records are preserved to us.[36]

Laurentius was also, like Rudbeckius, a great educator, and had founded the second gymnasium in Sweden in his old cathedral city. His *Ethica Christiana* in seven volumes (1617—1630) is a sort of encyclopædia on social, moral, and political questions. " From his biography," says Schück, " more than from anywhere else it becomes clear what an ineffaceable debt of gratitude Swedish culture owes to the Lutheran Church; not only our country's universities and schools, but the education of the lowest class grew up under the affectionate protection of that Church." [37]

Even greater work was done for popular education and catechizing by Johannes Matthiæ, the most eminent teacher in Sweden during the seventeenth century, the tutor of Christina and the friend of Comenius, the famous Moravian bishop. He was an Upsala professor, who became Bishop of Strengnäs in 1643, and lived on till 1670.

[34] See the full account of these proceedings in *Laurentius Paulinus Gothus, hans Lif och Verksamhet*, by H. Lundström, pt. 3, pp. 18-29.

[35] The heads of his address are given by Baaz: lib. viii., c. 10, and also the *Constitutions*, which he passed at his first meeting of the clergy, and sent round to other bishops as desirable to be adopted elsewhere.

[36] See *Svenska Synodalakter från Upsala Ärkestiftet, 1526—1800*, af H. Lundström, Uppsala, 1908, esp. pp. 35-37 These annual synods were continued by his successor, Provost Lenæus.

[37] Quoted by Dean Lundström in his Life of Laurentius, p 124, Upsala, 1893, which is full of careful detail.

I shall speak presently of the efforts for conciliation in matters of faith and doctrine which are so closely connected with his name.

But vigorous administration was not confined to the old centres. The mission to Lapland, where Charles IX. had founded several churches, was taken up with renewed energy in the time of Gustavus. It owed much to the statesman, Count John Skytte, founder of a professorship at Upsala, and a school at Ålem, north of Kalmar, who, in 1631, also founded and endowed an important school at Lycksele in the province of Vesterbotten, to which both Gustavus and Christina granted charters.[38]

The expansion of Sweden, which was so remarkable nearer home in the Baltic countries to the east and south, also now began in a westward direction, by the foundation of the colony of New Sweden on the Delaware River in the new world. Two Swedish vessels landed on the site of the modern Wilmington in 1637—1638, where Fort Christina was built, and a treaty made with the Iroquois Indians.

In 1643 Chancellor Axel Oxenstierna gave some remarkable instructions to Governor Printz, desiring him to treat the Indians with humanity and respect, and to try to convert them to Christianity and a good life. These instructions clearly were the basis of William Penn's wise policy a little later.

In 1646 the first Lutheran church was built near the site of Philadelphia, and somewhat later Luther's Little Catechism was translated into the Indian language. As the colony had to submit first to the Dutch and then to the English little was done for it by the Church at home. Charles XI., towards the end of the century, paid indeed some attention to this settlement, and so did Archbishop Svebilius, and more, particularly, Bishop Svedberg of Skara. Svedberg, who also had charge of the congregation in London, worked in harmony with Bishop Henry Compton, of London (1675—1713), who had charge of our

[38] See Johannes Schefférus' *Lapponia*, chap. 8, 1673. I have used the interesting English edition, Oxford, 1674, where both the charters may be found.

colonial churches. Thus we read in the diary of the Swedish pastor, Björk, of Wilmington : " We have always been counselled and instructed from Sweden to maintain friendship and unity with the English, so that we and the English Church shall not reckon each other as dissenters . . . but as sister Churches." Similarly, Andrew Rudman, founder of the old " Gloria Dei " Swedes Church at Philadelphia, which I visited with considerable emotion on the 23rd September, is described on his tombstone as " a Constant Faithful Preacher in the English, Swedes and Dutch Churches, eleven years in this country," where he died 17th September, 1708, aged forty. It is said that he " performed the functions of a clergyman of the English congregation for near two years during the absence of their own clergyman." [39]

Gustavus Adolphus had been beaten in his attempt to establish a centralized government of the Church, but the need of it did not cease.   Indeed, it was more and more felt because of the distant countries round the Baltic which were united to the Crown of Sweden, and which it was desired to attach to the Church, so as to make the union closer.   A number of new dioceses were, however, erected in this period.   Viborg, in Finland, in 1618; Göteborg as a superintendency in 1620, with a bishopric in 1665 ; Karlstad and Hernösand in 1647—first as superintendencies and later as bishoprics (1772).   Narva, in the Baltic province of Ingermanland, was a superintendency from 1641 to 1704, where several important Swedes—e.g., a Rudbeckius and a Gezelius—were bishops.   In 1645 the island of Gotland and the diocese of Visby were at last permanently attached to Sweden.   In 1658, after the successful war of Charles X., and the treaty of Roskilde which followed, Lund became a Swedish bishopric.   Its university was founded in 1666.

[39] For Björk see *Records of the Holy Trinity Swedes Church, Wilmington, Delaware, from 1697 to 1773*, p. 143 (Hist. Soc. of Del., 1890), and for Rudman see Prof. Kahn's *Travels* in Pinkerton's *Voyages*, xiii., 388, Lond., 1808.

§ 9.—MOVEMENT FOR AN EVANGELICAL CONFEDERATION.
DAVID PAREUS (1548—1622). HUGO GROTIUS
(1583—1645). GEORGE CALIXTUS (1586—1656).
JOHN DURIE (1596—1680). HIS CONNECTION
WITH ENGLISH BISHOPS, DAVENANT, ETC. HIS
VISIT TO SWEDEN (1636—1638). DAVENANT'S
LITTLE BOOK. DURIE'S ILL SUCCESS. QUARREL
WITH RUDBECKIUS. THE CLERGY DEMAND HIS
EXPULSION. AFTER-EFFECTS ON PRUSSIA.

We have now to turn our attention to a widespread
movement in Northern and Western Europe towards a
confederation in religious matters between the Evangelical
Churches, and especially towards a softening of the anta-
gonism between Lutherans and Calvinists, in which
Sweden was now invited to take a part. To many Statesmen and theologians in the seventeenth century such a
confederation seemed a most natural and necessary outcome of the struggle against the counter-reformation to
which the forces of Protestantism were called, especially
within the limits of the German Empire. Gustavus
Adolphus strongly favoured this movement during the
latter part of his reign, and his daughter, Queen Christina,
was imbued with the same ideas by her beloved tutor,
Johannes Matthiæ, who was the leader of the movement in
Sweden.

It is interesting to recall the names of some of the
eminent foreign theologians, who, following in the steps of
Bucer, co-operated at this time to urge German and
Swedish theologians to relax the stiffness of their Lutheran
orthodoxy. First I may name the gentle Heidelberg professor, David Wängler (1548—1622), who, according to the
fashion of the day, Grecized his name to Pareus. From
his residence in the Palatinate he had opportunities of making the acquaintance of the Princess Katarina, sister of
Gustavus Adolphus, who was married to his friend and
protector, the Pfalzgraf Johann Casimir. It was to
Gustavus that he addressed his *Irenicum: sive de unione*

19

et synodis evangelicorum liber votivus, in 1614, in which he recommended a general synod of all the Evangelical Churches in which the sovereigns of England and Denmark were to co-operate.

Next in order of time comes the famous jurist, scholar and statesman, Hugo Grotius (1583—1645), who had suffered much in his own country, Holland, for his defence of the Arminians against the Calvinists. In the latter part of his life he adopted Sweden as his country, and for eight years of the reign of Christina (1635—1643) he ably represented its interests as ambassador at the court of France. The next whom I shall name is George Calixtus, who was for forty-two years professor at the University of Helmstädt in Brunswick (1614—1656), where he studied under Caselius, the disciple of Melanchthon, and imbibed much of Melanchthon's temper and spirit. Calixtus, like many others (including Pareus), was influenced by his travels in England, where he rejoiced to meet his friend and model, Isaac Casaubon. His two proposed tests of reunion were the Apostles' Creed and the "consensus quinque-sæcularis" (agreement in the doctrine of the first five centuries after Christ). His principle was that agreement in fundamentals only was necessary, and that Lutherans, Reformed and Catholics were so agreed, and only differed in what was non-fundamental.[40] He influenced Sweden both through his writings and his pupils, especially Tersérus, of whom I shall speak presently.

Of even more interest to us than these great scholars and theologians, whose work in other departments of theology is recognized by those who care to explore the treasures of our old libraries, is a man of less commanding ability, who deserves recognition for the whole-hearted devotion with which he applied himself to the cause of re-union. I mean

---

[40] His *Iudicium de controversiis theologicis, quæ inter Lutheranos et Reformatos agitantur, et de mutua partium fraternitate atque tolerantia propter consensum in fundamento* and his *Desiderium et studium concordiæ ecclesiasticæ* were both published in 1650.

the Scotsman, John Durie, who gave up the last fifty years of a life of eighty-four years (1596—1680) to this work. From the year 1628 he laboured unceasingly in the North and West of Europe to promote the reconciliation, or at least to secure, the inter-communion and co-operation of the Evangelical Churches. He visited courts and statesmen, bishops and clergy, he attended synods, he held disputations, he entered into personal correspondence, he published elaborate treatises, in the interest of a confederation in which England and Scotland, and the Netherlands, and the reformed Churches of France and Germany, especially in the Palatinate, and Switzerland, were to co-operate with the adherents of the Confession of Augsburg.

The likeness of his work to that in which many in England and Scotland are now engaged, and that in more than one quarter of the globe, and its special bearing on the object of these lectures, may be my excuse for devoting several pages to an account of this remarkable man.[41]

John Durie was born at Edinburgh, but he was from his boyhood familiar with the Continent, and learnt to speak German like a native. He was brought up at Sedan, under his cousin, Andrew Melville, and at Leyden, where his father, formerly minister of Montrose, had settled. In 1624 he " sojourned " for a time at Oxford for the sake of the library.[42] In 1626 he was chaplain, as an independent minister, to a company of English merchants at Elbing in East Prussia, than under the rule of the Swedish king. Here he made the friendship of a Swedish privy councillor and judge, Caspar Godeman, and entered warmly into his

[41] Durie's life has never been fully written, though something may be found about him in most histories and biographical dictionaries. The fullest account I have found in English is in the *Christian Remembrancer* for January, 1855, Vol. 29, pp. 15-29, and in Swedish in Th. Norlin's *Sv. Kyrkans Historia*, 2, pp. 172-195, which is based on Carl Jesper Benzelius' *Dissertatio de Johanne Duræo pacificatore celeberrimo maximeque de actis eius Suecanis* delivered in the presence of Mosheim, Helmstad, 1744.

[42] Ant. A. Wood : *Fasti Oxon.*, i., p. 420.

project for establishing inter-communion between the Evangelical Churches, which seemed now more than ever profitable and possible. The well-known Sir Thomas Roe —whose co-operation with Cyril Lucar at Constantinople forms so interesting a chapter in another branch of the re-union movement—happened to come to Elbing as ambassador from Charles I. to Gustavus Adolphus, and warmly took up the project. Durie returned to England, and was well received both by Archbishop Abbot and by Laud, then the powerful Bishop of London. He returned again to Germany in 1631, bearing a recommendation signed by thirty-eight English divines, and he had a favourable interview with the king, then at the height of his glory, after the victory of Leipsic. This was at Würzburg, where he made the acquaintance of the army chaplains, Jacob Fabricius and Matthiæ. The king even offered to give him letters of recommendation to the Protestant princes, which Durie for the time declined. Various conferences of the Evangelical Churches were held, particularly at Leipsic and Heilbronn, in which Durie had a share. Gustavus' death at Lützen in 1632 unfortunately deprived him and the cause of his and its strongest supporter. When Durie was next in England, in 1633—1634, Laud, who had just become archbishop, encouraged him to be ordained in the Church of England. He was ordained priest by Bishop Joseph Hall, then at Exeter, 24th February, 1634. He was, however, not expected to reside in England; and he spent some months in procuring testimonials from bishops, with whom he had a large and a familiar acquaintance.

In particular Archbishop Laud addressed to him two letters expressing great interest in his work, both dated 10th February, 1634—one for use in dealing with adherents of the Confession of Augsburg, and the other, of a similar kind, for use in the Palatinate, Zweibrücken and Hesse.[43] His episcopal friends did even more for him. Bishop Edward

[43] Archbishop Laud : *Letters*, 98 (*Works*, A. C. L., vi., 410) and 264 (*ibid.* vii., 112).

Morton, of Durham, Bishop John Davenant, my learned predecessor; and Bishop Joseph Hall, his ordainer, all wrote Latin opinions for him on the method and character of the *Pax ecclesiastica* which they advocated.[44] The excellent Irish bishop, Bedell, the friend of Paolo Sarpi, and the editor of the Irish Bible, actually gave him an annual pension. In the spring of 1634 Durie was at Frankfort attending a great meeting of the ambassadors and divines from the Protestant states, and obtained from the latter a kind of circular to their brethren throughout Europe. He spent the winter again in England and Scotland, and, I suppose, at this time received his credentials from Archbishop Spottiswode.[45] In July, 1635, he was attending synods in the Netherlands, and in the same month, a year later, he found his way to Sweden.

Durie came into the country on the invitation of Johannes Matthiæ, whose acquaintance (as we have seen) he had made in Germany. He brought introductions from the Archbishops of Canterbury (Laud), St. Andrew's

[44] These three opinions were first printed in 1634, without name of place, under the title *De pacis ecclesiasticæ rationibus inter evangelicos usurpandis, et de theologorum fundamentali consensu in colloquio Lips. inito, trium in ecclesia Anglicana episcoporum Tho. Mortoni Iohannis Davenantii et Ios. Halli sententiæ Io. Duræo traditæ.* This is in the Bodleian. Another edition is entitled *De pace ecclesiastica inter evangelicos procuranda sententiæ quatuor . . .* the fourth being *ab ecclesiæ in Gallia Pastoribus, quibusdam eximiis.* At the end is a useful syllabus of writings in favour of ecclesiastical peace : Amstelodami, 1636. A third edition appeared in London, 1638. It was translated into English in 1641, and printed at Oxford under the title *Good Counsells for the Peace of Reformed Churches,* a book which contains also " The opinion of James Usher, Archbishop of Armagh, with some other Bishops of Ireland." Davenant's opinion was also printed in Latin (Cambridge, 1640), and in English (Lond., 1641), as an introduction to his *Ad fraternam communionem inter evangelicos ecclesias restaurandam adhortatio = An exhortation to brotherly communion betwixt the Protestant Churches.* I quote from the English, of which I possess a copy.

[45] Cp. Grubb : *Eccl. Hist. of Scotland,* Vol. 2, p. 371.

Spottiswoode) and Armagh (Usher), and the treatises of
Bishops Thomas Morton, John Davenant and Joseph
Hall, which he had reprinted at Amsterdam, together with
a fourth by some unnamed Gallican pastors.[46]   He had unfortunately not taken the opportunity of procuring a letter
from Gustavus Adolphus, but he was well known to the
great chancellor, Axel Oxenstierna, although the latter
treated him with a good deal of caution.   He came
certainly under much better auspices and on a more
prudent mission than his countryman, John Forbes.

You will understand that his connection with my predecessor, Bishop Davenant, who left a considerable mark
upon the diocese of Salisbury, is naturally peculiarly interesting to myself.   I may be excused if I take his opinion
as a specimen of the way in which well-informed and liberal
minded Englishmen approached the great subject.
Davenant had attended the Synod of Dort in 1618 in order
to watch the proceedings in the interests of our Church,
and he was familiar with the internal divisions of the
Netherlands.   He naturally attached much importance to
them, as well as to the larger divisions between the
" Saxon " and " Helvetian " Churches, as he calls them.
It is curious that he makes no mention of the difference
between Episcopalians and Presbyterians as being any
difficulty in the way of a project of brotherly communion.
The difficulties which he treats are those that divide the
Continental Churches, such as " Saxon " and " Helvetian " in different lands, or the Dutch among
themselves.

He seems to think with Calixtus that adherence to the
Apostles' Creed should be a sufficient basis of communion.
He notices that the difference between the Spanish and
Italian Churches on the one side, and the French on the
other, in their belief as to the papacy, does not interrupt

[46] De pace ecclesiastica inter Evangelicos procuranda sententiæ quatuor . . . eæ Johanni Duræo fuerunt ab Auctoribus
traditæ ad ecclesiarum reconciliationem promovendam, Amstelodami, 1636 (See note 44).

their communion, and commends this as an example to the
Protestant Churches.   The three points of difficulty to
which he specially refers are: (1) the doctrine of the presence of Christ in the sacrament, where he dwells upon the
identity of belief in the communion gift; (2) controversies
as to the omnipresence of Christ and the communication of
His properties; and (3) the doctrines of predestination and
freewill.   In regard to the last he presses the point that
what is really important is to attribute all grace and glory
to God's mercy; and to impute all the corruption of man's
nature, his obstinacy in sin, and the viciousness and servi-
tude of his freewill, and all that draws mortals to Hell, to
our own demerits, and to remove it far from God (pp. 27-8,
E. T.).   He takes it for granted that both the Saxon and
Helvetian Churches, *i.e.*, the Lutheran and the Calvinist,
" acknowledge themselves to have and desire to retain
brotherly communion with the English, Scottish, Irish
and the foreign Reformed Churches " (p. 33).   Why then
should they deprive each other of a like brotherly
communion?

That by " communion " he means joint partaking in the
sacraments, especially the Lord's Supper, is quite clear,
and he goes into the point at length.   For the purpose of
establishing it he recommends a conference of divines
chosen by the princes on each side rather than a general
council of Protestants, which would dispute for ever (p.
37).   Then a careful distinction of fundamentals from non-
fundamentals (p. 42), expressed in few words, according to
Tertullian's maxim, " Certa semper in paucis " (*de anima*,
c. 2, *ad finem*).   He deprecates bitter language, which
ought to be expunged from books of controversy, and
wishes " that those sirnames of *Lutherans, Zwinglians*,
and *Calvinists* were packed away and utterly abolished,
which are rather the ensignes of faction than badges of
brotherly union, and which never pleased the ancient
Fathers " (p. 46).   Generally his motto is to avoid all difficult controversies in public teaching and formularies.

" What make the subtleties of the schoolmen in the con-
fessions of the Church? All the salvation of Christians
consists in believing and worshipping, as of old it was
gravely said of great Athanasius " (p. 50). He points out
that by over-definition in articles of faith " many pastors,
learned, pious and peaceable, will be excluded and quite
shut out " (p. 51). He expresses the doctrine of the Lord's
Supper in a simple and beautiful manner. It consists of
union with Christ, and union among ourselves, and " that
as fellow-commoners we eate and drink the same living
bread and drink, to wit the flesh and blood of Christ to the
salvation of our soules " (pp. 51-2). Such is the main
purport of this " exhortation to brotherly communion " by
a former Bishop of Salisbury, of which Durie was now the
ambassador to Sweden.

Durie was kindly received, and he worked hard and in
a most sanguine temper to get his message a hearing in
Sweden, where Axel Oxenstierna, whom he specially regarded as his friend, had just returned from Germany.
He could not, however, obtain from the chancellor a general
letter of commendation to the Church, but the latter advised
him to turn his attention to the pastor of the Great Church
in Stockholm—Jacob Zebrozynthius, and his acquaintance,
Johannes Matthiæ, to the theologians of Upsala, and the
two strong Bishops of Strengnäs and Vesterås. Zebrozynthius and Matthiæ, seemed to him to fall in with his
plan. The Upsala professors received him with great
kindness and consideration, but they did not really encourage him, having different ideas of what was fundamental in
point of doctrine, and they pointed out that compromise
was unsafe and led to untruth on one side or the other. At
Vesterås Rudbeckius also received him very kindly, but
told him bluntly that his plan was unpractical. At
Strengnäs Laurentius Paulinus and his chapter agreed
with the professors of Upsala. Later he went for a journey
with the chancellor to his home, Tidö, in Westmanland.
He again visited Strengnäs, Vesterås and Upsala. He

was then invited to attend a prest-möte in Stockholm, where, instead of a pleasant reception, he was subjected to a severe examination. This took the form of inquiries as to the real union of the reformed theologians with the Lutherans on fundamentals, and then on the debated questions, including an inquiry into his own faith. At last it came to the point that Rudbeckius insisted on subscription to the Book of Concord, which, of course, was insisting on an impossibility even for liberal Calvinists.

The *Formula Concordiæ*, I may remind you, was merely an attempt to unite the followers of Luther and Melanchthon, and was, therefore, of no use in conciliating Calvinists.   Indeed, it was an exposition of developed Lutheranism, coloured by references to all the controversies of the day, and, therefore, more hard for Calvinists than the vaguer language of the original confession.[47]

Durie was advised to return home. He complained to the Chancellor of Rudbeckius, and the latter lost his temper with him.   Durie still held on, and put forward the opinion given in his favour by the famous six doctors of Aberdeen, dated 20th February, 1637. He made his last attempt at the Riksdag in Stockholm in 1638, but only to draw from the clerical estate an assertion that the difference between Lutherans and Calvinists was fundamental, and that not only the Augsburg Confession but the Apology for the Confession and the Formula Concordiæ must be subscribed by anyone who wished for union with themselves. They asked that he might be sent out of the kingdom.   The Government thought it best that he should go, but testified to the honesty, peaceableness and prudence with which he had pursued his mission. The chancellor was vexed at the incivility with which the clergy described his guest as a " transmarinus," but he gave way to the general dislike with which Durie was now visited.   The poor man was struck down with disappointment, and fell grievously ill,

[47] See Charles Hardwick: *H. of the Church during the Reformation*, ed. W. Stubbs, p. 163, Lond., 1880.

and was unable to leave before August.   During his illness
he vowed to continue his efforts to the end of his life, and
he did so; but with no immediate result.   His subsequent
subservience to Cromwell, his acceptance first of Presbyterianism and then of Independency, and other weak-
nesses of character led to his being called many hard names.
But he was a brave and persevering man, whose memory
is worthy of grateful record by posterity.

Almost his last attempt at conciliation was in the form of
a commentary on the Apocalypse.

Durie died at Cassel in 1680 (where the Princess Hedvig
Sophia gave him a comfortable retirement), almost despair-
ing of the cause to which he had devoted his life, but not
the least doubtful of its righteousness.   And as the broader
work of conciliation with Rome which Cassander and
Wicelius had championed, and to which Grotius in his
later years inclined, and which Calixtus had (at least in
theory) professed to desire, was carried on in Germany by
Molanus and Leibnitz, so the narrower and more obvious
project of uniting Lutherans and Calvinists was kept in
view in the kingdom of Prussia, and promoted also by
Leibnitz.   Here the house of Brandenburg had accepted
the reformed faith, while its subjects were mainly
Lutherans, and such a union was eminently reasonable.
The union, which was promoted and to a great degree
effected by Frederick William III. of Prussia in 1817, was
the outcome of the previous efforts in which Durie had
his share.[48]

---

[48] Cp. S. Cheetham : *H. of the Ch. since the Ref.*, pp. 423
foll., Lond., 1907.   I am glad to think that my friend, Archdeacon Cheetham, was able before his death to complete the
good work which Hardwick had begun of a short summary of
the whole of Church history.   Cheetham's first volume on the
Early Church, followed by Hardwick's two on the *Middle Age*
and the *Reformation*, and Cheetham's final volume, *H. of the
Church since the Reformation*, make up a compact series.
This last volume is a particularly useful one.

§ 10.—MATTHIÆ'S WRITINGS.   INFLUENCE OF COMENIUS.
CONFIRMATION   RE-INTRODUCED.   SYNCRETISM.
CHARLES X. SUCCEEDS (1654—1660).   FAVOURS
MATTHIÆ AND TERSÉRUS.   THEY ARE ACCUSED OF
HERESY AND OBLIGED TO RESIGN (1664).   ABSOLU-
TISM UNDER CHARLES XI. (1660—1697).   NEW
RELATION OF THE KING TO THE CHURCH.   NEW
CHURCH LAW OF 1686.   *Liber Concordiæ.*

After Durie's departure Matthiæ still continued to work
somewhat intermittently and cautiously in the same direction.   About 1641 he was cheered by a visit from the
famous Moravian bishop and educationalist, John Amos
Comenius (1592—1670), who had just been on a mission
from Poland to England.   Matthiæ received from him
suggestions on many practical matters, which he embodied
in his introductory address delivered at the first annual
synod of his diocese of Strengnäs, and published in 1644,
under the title *Idea boni ordinis in Ecclesia Christi*, based
on the usual text " Let all things be done decently and in
order " (1 Cor. xiv. 40).   The most interesting to us is the
section *De forma recipiendi Novitios.*   The form of receiving adults from another communion is first described.
They are to be examined as to their faith, to make promises
of obedience to God and the Church, to be admonished as
to perseverance, etc., and then to be admitted into fellowship.   Juniors are to be received before admission to holy
communion by reading of a suitable passage of Scripture,
with a very short explanation, by examination as to
whether they will renew their baptismal covenant with
God, and renounce Satan, the world and the flesh, and by
reciting the Apostles' Creed.   Then they are to say a
prayer for pardon, to be followed by an absolution, and a
permission to partake of the Lord's table, to be followed by
laying on of hands, and a further invocation upon them of
the divine name to strengthen their hope of heavenly
grace.[49]   The Swedish form, which has also been pre-

[49] The Latin description and the form that follows in Swedish
are given by F. N. Ekdahl: *Om Confirmationen*, pp. 98 foll.

served, giving more details, shows that the blessing which
accompanied the manual act was almost exactly that which
is so used in the English service to-day.   It was to be
administered by the bishop, or his deputy.[50]
We cannot doubt that Matthiæ introduced this rite
wherever it was possible in his own diocese, and it is interesting to know that in this he was in close agreement
with another eminent prelate of the orthodox party, Olof
Laurelius (1585—1670), who was Bishop of Vesterås from
the year 1647, where he continued the good work of Rudbeckius.   Like Matthiæ, he attaches the duty of confirming
to the bishop or his official, and that publicly in Church,
and he distinctly says the old term was " Confirmatio hoc
est fermelse," but now is " examination and blessing of
young people (ungdoms proffwen och welsignelse)."[51]
The rite consisted of the long " Collect " and blessing with
laying on of hands, taken directly from the *Nova
Ordinantia* of 1575, which has been already quoted (Lect.
V., § 11).[52]

---

[50] " Sedan skall biskopen eller hans fullmächtige låta barnen
falla på knä, läggia händerne på hvart och ett barn, och
therpå säga att the måge altidh bliva och dageligen tillväxa
uthi tin helga Anda, in till thes the komma uthi titt eviga rijke.
Amen." Ekdahl : l.c., p. 103.
[51] See H. Lundström: *K. H. Årsskrift*, vol. viii. (1907);
Meddelanden, etc., pp. 279—282, where the form is given.
[52] The form is given by H. Lundström in *K. H. Årsskrift*,
viii., pp. 280-1. It is, therefore, remarkable that there is no
reference to such a rite in the printed draft *Kyrko-ordningar*,
esp. in that ascribed to Laurelius, which is connected with the
work of the Committee of 1650. The seventh chapter *Om
Syndaboot, Skriftermål och Aflössning*, part 2, § x., speaks of
children or servants being sent eight days before they are admitted to the sacrament to the pastor or his assistant " that they
may well and perfectly know whether they are instructed in those
mysteries and strengthened in their faith," *K. Ordningar före
1686*, II., 1, p. 171. But in a variant form of this *K. O.*, quoted
by Ekdahl : l.c., p. 107, the parallel passage runs, " They shall
be publicly examined in the choir in the articles of their Christian
faith, and with laying on of hands with prayer they shall be re-

It is much to be regretted in the interests of the Church and of its hold over its young folk, that such good precedents were not authoritatively followed. The rite went on in some sort under Svedberg, and later under Hallenius in Skara (1753—1767), under Serenius in Strengnäs (1763 —1776), and in the Danish form in the diocese of Lund, and probably it was used elsewhere.

Matthiæ, unfortunately, laid himself open to suspicion by his treatment of the rite and doctrine of baptism in his *Idea boni ordinis*. He omitted the sign of the cross and exorcism from the rite. He had a curious doctrine about its celebration, which was at once rigorous and lax. He held that it could only be administered by a priest, but that it was not so necessary to salvation as to make its administration essential, and hence no layman could be allowed to baptize in case of necessity. This led to accusations of Crypto-Calvinism, or as it then shortly after began to be called, "syncretistic heresy." This peculiar word "syncretism" is a Greek term, which is only once found in ancient literature, in Plutarch's little treatise *On Brotherly Love* (p. 490, b.). He tells us that the native tribes in Crete, who were usually at war with one another, were wont to "syncretize" against a common outside enemy. Erasmus seems to have been the first to introduce it into modern literature in his *Adagia*, and he employed it in a flattering letter to Melanchthon, in order to describe their possible relations. Hence it passed into the language of the reformers, especially of a union among Protestants against Romanists. Later in the seventeenth century it was frequently used with a false idea, or a punning suggestion, of its derivation from another Greek root, of a " mixture," generally in a bad sense, of discordant ele-

ceived into Jesus Christ's body and Church (och med händers påläggning och bön inympas uti Jesu Kristi kropp och församling "). See more in G. Mott Williams : *The Ch. of Sw.*, etc., pp. 69-72.

ments of theology.[53]   It was, I presume, in the latter sense that Matthiæ's enemies used it in regard to him.   For the moment, indeed, the storm was stilled by the intervention of Queen Christina against the Chancellor Oxenstierna, on behalf of her old tutor.   At one time the hopes of the " syncretists " were raised by the calling of a conference at Thorn in Poland by the more tolerant king, Ladislas IV. (1632—1648), in the year 1645, in which the aid of Calixtus was invoked, though Lutherans were much surprised to see him leading the Calvinists.[54]   But the party of Calovius prevented the Lutherans from making any real concessions.   On the other hand, the strict Lutheran party could point to the danger of laxity of faith as leading sovereigns to be reconciled to the Church of Rome, and this was emphatically the case in Sweden in the person of Queen Christina.

Later in his life, in 1656, Matthiæ gave even greater offence by his *Rami olivæ septentrionalis*, but he was also protected by the new king, Charles X. Gustavus, who succeeded on Queen Christina's abdication in 1654.   He was the son of Charles IX.'s daughter, Katarina, and of the

[53] See the careful article s.v. *Synkretismus* in *P. R. E.*[3], Vol. 19, by Henke and Tschackert.

I find it used in titles of books, *e.g.*, "Davidis Parei notæ in Problema Theologicum, an Syncretismus fidei et religionis inter Lutheranos et Calvinianos, ideò iniri vel possit vel debeat ut antichristi tyrannis conjunctis viribus et studiis facilius et fælicius reprimi possit, a Leon. Huttero disputatum, apud Ion. Ros., 1616," and "Classicum Syncretismi Evangelici contra Papistas, 1631," and others of which the titles are given in the curious appendix or *Syllabus Scriptorum* at the end of Durie's little book (see note 44).

[54] See *Chr. Remembr.*, Vol. 29, pp. 36-43 for a good description of this conference between Roman Catholics, Lutherans and Calvinists, which lasted from August 28th to November 21st.   The writer says : "The best account of the Charitative Colloquy of Thorn is to be found in the *Historia Ecclesiastica* of John Wolfgang Jaeger, Vol. i., pp. 689-703. . . . Abraham Calovius in his *History of Syncretism* devotes no less than 360 pages to the Acts of the Colloquy."

Pfalzgraf, John Kasimir, whom I have mentioned as the patrons of the Heidelberg professor, Pareus, and he was, therefore, naturally in favour of the syncretism, which had its home in the Palatinate. He was long resident in Sweden before his coronation, and had been a persistent suitor for his cousin Christina's hand, and was much liked by her. His most permanent achievement for the country was the result of his invasion of Denmark in 1658, which had gone to war with Sweden during the king's absence in Poland. In this campaign nature helped him by freezing over the Great and the Little Belt so that his army was able to cross them. This was followed by the peace of Roskilde, by which the Southern provinces and Bohuslän were permanently united to Sweden.[55]

Matthiæ had an efficient allay in Johannes Tersérus, who had come under the direct influence of Calixtus, and was theological professor at Åbo, and afterwards at Upsala. He had done great service to the crown by his energetic leadership of the clergy at the Riksdag of 1650, when they joined with the burgher and peasant estates in their protest against the alienation of the crown domains to the nobility, and against various tyrannies and injustices exercised by the latter.[56]

Christina's word to him, " Now or never," is famous in history, and will always be associated with his name. Charles X. nominated him as Bishop of Åbo in 1658. This king died in 1660, and during the minority of his infant son, Charles XI., both Tersérus and Matthiæ had to suffer as " syncretistic heretics "—a sad outcome of their efforts which were made in so excellent a spirit. They were obliged to ask leave to resign their offices at the Riksdag of 1664. Matthiæ, before his death in 1670, expressed regret for what he had done. Tersérus lived on, and in 1670 he was promoted again to a bishopric, that of

[55] On the religious condition of these provinces, about the time of the Union, see A. Hallenberg in *K. H. Årsskrift*, Vol. viii., 193-228, and ix., 65-136 (1907—1908).

[56] See Geijer : p. 338.

Linköping, and recovered his reputation amongst his countrymen. He was naturally in favour with Charles XI., who assumed the government in 1672, and he was on the king's side in the initiation of his policy of " Reduction," by which he recovered to the crown the estates which had been lavishly granted away by his predecessors. Terśerus died in 1678, and he was, therefore, not responsible for the severity and sometimes injustice with which this policy was afterwards carried out, nor for the absolutism which followed.[57]

" These conflicts (says Dr. Holmquist) within the Church were to cost it dear. Absolute monarchy was introduced by Charles XI., and he was not willing that the Church should continue an independent factor within his kingdom. Through its own fault the Church was without any organized Government which could defend its interests. The bishops were now, in general, less important men. Not without the fault of orthodoxy, and in consequence of the state of constant warfare, a deep moral decadence, and increase of superstition had got hold of the people and the lower clergy. For instance, the epidemic of trials for witchcraft raged about the year 1670. The belief in witchcraft was defended by the clergy, and attacked by the famous physician, Urban Hjärne. Nowhere was there power to resist the king's pretensions. '

In 1686 a new Church law, in which the king had been much assisted by Dr. Haquin Spegel, now Bishop of Skara, was issued by royal authority. It was accepted by the cathedral chapters in 1687. In one respect it fulfilled the desire of the Church by making the *Liber Concordiæ* [58]

---

[57] There is a good popular account of *Karl XI.'s personlighet och lifsgärning* by Rudolf Fåhræus in Heimdal's *Folkskrifter*, 1897.

[58] These books are all conveniently printed in one volume by Dr. Karl August Hase, under the title of *Libri Symbolici Ecclesiæ Evangelicæ sive Concordia*, ed. 2, Lipsiæ, 1837. They are *The Confessio Augustana* (with the *Confutatio Pontificia* as an appendix necessary to understand the *Apologia*), the *Apologia*

that is the whole series of Lutheran books up to the *Formula Concordiæ* of 1580, a "confessional book," or formulary of the Swedish Church—not indeed on the same footing as the Augsburg Confession, but as an authorized explanation of it. The opening sentence of the first chapter of the Church law of 1686, which in substance is the law of Sweden to-day, runs as follows :—

"Throughout our kingdom and the countries which depend upon it all shall confess, jointly and severally, their belief in the Christian doctrine and faith as it is founded in God's Holy Word, the prophetical and apostolic writings of the Old and New Testament, and set forth (författad) in the three chief creeds—the Apostolic, Nicene and Athanasian, as well as in the unaltered Augsburg Confession of the year 1530, accepted in the Council of Upsala of 1593, and explained (förklarad) in the whole, so called, Book of Concord."

The Church Order that followed was based on two tentative drafts that had been published, one by Olof Laurelius, Bishop of Vesterås (1647—1670) and the other by Erik Emporagrius, pastor primarius of Stockholm, and Bishop of Strengnäs from 1664—1674. The Church Order of Charles XI. agrees (it is said) most with the work of Laurelius.[59] It contained, however, no section on confirmation. The general result was that the cause of orthodoxy triumphed, and the Church obtained a great deal more of unity and uniformity, but it lost its previous independence, and became a State Church, in which the superior power lay very largely in the hands of the king. Although the king never quite assumed the position of "summus episcopus," he had and has much more power of personal interference with the affairs of the Church in Sweden than the king has had in England since about the same period, the Revolution of 1688. It

Confessionis (1531), the *Articuli Smalcaldici* (1537), Luther's *Catechismus minor* (1529, etc.), his *Catechismus major* (1529, etc.), and the *Formula Concordiæ* (1580).

[59] Cornelius: *Handbok*, § 116. For Laurelius' draft see *Svenska Kyrko-ordningar*, II., 1. (1882), and Emporagrius' *ibid* II., 2 (1887).

is curious that at almost the same moment Sweden became
an absolute monarchy, and England a thoroughly constitutional one. The greatest point of difference in favour
of the Swedish Church is that the election of bishops and
clergy has been on a more popular basis, while in England
the same system of patronage has prevailed for both—the
king having the nomination of the bishoprics, with comparatively little check, and public and private patrons
having the nomination to benefices, also with rather
inadequate checks on the part of the instituting bishops.
Each nation lives under the system to which it is accustomed, and does not find its difficulties so great as men
of the other would imagine. To us the idea seems
strange that the king should prescribe texts for sermons,
while to the Swedes our system of election to bishoprics
appears very imperfect.

§ 11.—Imposing activity in Church matters. Church
    registers. Catechism and Prayer Book.
    Eric Benzelius (archbishop 1700—1709) edits
    the Bible. His family. Family system in
    parishes. New hymn-book. Jesper Svedberg,
    Bishop of Skara (1702—1735). His connec-
    tion with New Sweden and England. His
    form of confirmation. Haquin Spegel of
    Skara, Linköping and Upsala. His good
    work and patriotism. The two Gezelius' in
    Finland. Their "Bibel-verk."

The activity which prevailed in the Church just before
and after the year 1700 was indeed very imposing in its
achievements. The system of Church registers which
Rudbeckius had introduced was made universal in 1686.
The system of private catechizing in families, both by
bishops and clergy, was begun. In 1689 a common
catechism was produced, and an edict of 1695 ordered universal instruction in reading and in the catechism. In
1693 a new hand-book or prayer book was published, and

conformity to it was required. Both catechism and prayer-
book owe their form to the new Archbishop Olof Svebilius
(1681—1700). His successor, Eric Benzelius the elder
(1700—1709), was tutor to the Crown Prince, who succeeded as Charles XII. in 1697, and compiled for him a
manual of Church history. He edited the fine Bible
which was published in 1703 and known as Charles XII.'s
Bible. Benzelius is even more remarkable as the father of
three sons, who succeeded one another as archbishops (1)
Eric, Bishop of Göteborg (1726—1731) and Linköping
(1731—1742), and for a few months archbishop, who died
in 1743 [60]—a literary man of great distinction, editor of
Philo and Ulphilas, the friend and brother-in-law of
Emanuel Swedenborg, and father of Karl Jesper, Bishop
of Strengnäs; (2) Jacob, Bishop of Göteborg (1731), and
archbishop (1744—1747); and (3) Henrik, Bishop of Lund
(1740), and archbishop (1747—1757). Two of the elder
Eric's grandsons also became bishops, and five of his
daughters and granddaughters married bishops. This is,
perhaps, the most remarkable example of an episcopal
family in Sweden, but it is only an example of a tendency
towards the formation of a sort of clerical aristocracy which
we meet with in all periods of Swedish history, both in
mediæval times and more pronouncedly from the time of
Laurentius Petri Nericius onwards.[61]

A similar tendency is observable amongst the families of
the parish clergy, where it was very common for a new incumbent to be expected or even required to marry his predecessor's widow or daughter, the term " konservera "
being used for this act of respect for continuity. Svedberg
on one occasion allowed a priest of poor abilities to take a
benefice on the condition that he should marry his predecessor's widow. As a rule the country clergy were little

---

[60] There is a rather full life of Eric Benzelius the younger by
H. L. Forssell in *Svenska Akademiens Handlingar*, part 58,
pp. 113-476, 1883.
[61] See more in *the Ch. of Sw. and the Angl. Comm.*, pp. 62-5.

better than peasants; and, even in Spegel's diocese,
Linköping, which was probably one of the best, priests
were found who were entirely without books, even, for
instance, the Bible.[62]
Amongst the other books composed at the end of the
seventeenth century an important place must be assigned
to the new hymn-book, published in 1698, which was the
work of a commission in which Jesper Svedberg (afterwards Bishop of Skara) collaborated with Haquin Spegel,
bishop in succession of Skara (1685—1692) and Linköping
(1692—1711) and then archbishop (1711—1714), and with
the physician, Urban Hjärne, whom I have already named
as taking a wise and reasonable line in the trials for witchcraft.   Of these men Svedberg is well known as Bishop of
Skara for thirty-three years (1702—1735), where he did
much literary and educational work, and laboured ener-
getically in building and rebuilding after several disastrous
fires.   He was father of nine children, of whom one,
Emanuel, best known by the name of Swedenborg, is
deservedly famous.[63]   Svedberg is particularly interesting
to us from his connection with the colony of New Sweden
and the Swedish Church in London.   As vice-president of
the Chapter of Upsala, and its most efficient member in old
Archbishop Svebilius' days, he was entrusted by Charles
XI. with the oversight of the American colony, which had

[62] See *I. S. L. H.*, 1., p. 418 : " Den, som ville hafva ett
gäll, ansågs skyldig att . . . 'konservera ' (d.v.s. gifta sig
med) företrädarens enka eller dotter," etc.
[63] Svedberg's life has been excellently written by Bishop
Henry William Tottie of Kalmar, *Jesper Svedberg's Lif och
Verksamhet*, in two parts, Upsala, 1885—1886.   Svedberg's
autobiography exists in MS., of which a copy is preserved in
the library of the gymnasium at Skara.   Extracts from it have
been printed by Bishop Tottie in *K. H. A.*, 1., pp. 87-106.   A
good deal about this bishop will be found in the early chapters
of Wm. White's *Swedenborg : his Life and writings*. Lond.,
ed. 2, 1868.   Of the 482 hymns in the 1698 collection Svedberg
composed 16 and translated 20.   See Tottie : *Lif.*, part 1,
pp. 97 foll.   For Swedenborg see the next lecture.

been almost wholly neglected, and he continued to exercise
this oversight during the rest of his life.   Amongst the
priests sent out and encouraged by him was Andreas
Rudman, whose name I have already mentioned as taking
duty for the absent priest of the Church of England.   This,
no doubt, was with the goodwill of Bishop Svedberg, who,
since his visit to England in 1684 had been closely attached
to our Church.   He was one of the earliest members of our
great missionary society, " the Society for the Propagation
of the Gospel in Foreign Parts," and he much admired the
manner in which Sunday was kept in England.   His work
in New Sweden, and the good results which followed it, led
the Swedes in London to turn to him in 1710, when they
felt themselves obliged to separate from the Danish congregation, with which they had previously worshipped,
after Frederick IV. had declared war against their country.
The Church in London was treated, under royal authority,
and at its own request, as if it were a parish in the diocese
of Skara, and that not in a perfunctory manner.   Its most
important pastor in the eighteenth century was Jacob
Serenius (1724—1733), afterwards Bishop of Strengnäs
(1763—1776).   A letter has been preserved from Svedberg
to Serenius, in which Svedberg desires him to introduce
that form of confirmation into the London Church, which
he was already using in Sweden, on the ground that it was
even easier for him to do so, because that was a point of
contact with the English Church.   It seems to have consisted of public examination and blessing.[64]   Serenius'
own earnestness in reviving confirmation in the diocese of
Strengnäs is well known.

The last of the Caroline bishops whom I shall name are
Haquin Spegel and the two Johannes Gezelius'.   Spegel
was one of those who began his career as a court and
army chaplain, under Charles XI., when not yet thirty
years old.   He was Bishop of Skara in 1685, and Lin-

[64] Letter of 19th November, 1710, quoted by H. W. Tottie:
Lif., p. 266.

köping 1692, where he spent seven and eighteen years respectively of energetic and successful work. He was then archbishop for three years (1711—1714). He was Charles XI.'s chief adviser in passing the new Church law, and he had a considerable share in the other epoch-making books of the period besides the hymn-book.[65]   Of his hymns, as many as twenty-nine are retained in the present hymn-book, and they are still very popular.   On the other hand, he was well known as a philologist, and as the compiler of a *Glossarium Sviogothicum* and a *History of the Swedish Church*, which are both evidences of his patriotism—a patriotism which he showed in his readiness to make personal sacrifices in the straits to which Sweden was reduced by war.   He was of a less warm temper, and had less appearance of feeling than Svedberg, but he was a man of greater learning, good sense and piety.

The two bishops, Johannes Gezelius, father and son, were benefactors, especially to the Church in Finland. The eldest was Bishop of Åbo after Tersérus for twenty-five years (1665—1690).   He visited his extensive diocese seven times, and was in all respects a good bishop of the school of Rudbeckius.   Amongst other things, he set up the second printing press in Finland.   His son succeeded him, and remained in the see until 1713, when he had to retire before the Russian invasion.   Both were excellent officials, and useful to the Church, especially through their " Bibelverk," a text and commentary for preachers.   It appeared slowly, the New Testament after the death of the older bishop (1711—1713), and the Old after that of his son (1724 —1728).[66]   It was edited by David Lund, Bishop of Viborg, and then of Vexiö.

A third John Gezelius, son of the second, was afterwards bishop in Borgå, which took the place of Viborg (1721— 1733).

[65] Bishop Tottie has also written *Haquin Spegel såsom kateket och homilet*, 1890.

[66] For the Gezelius' see *Finska Kyrkans Historia*, pp. 114-121 and 136-148, Helsingfors, 1892, by Elis Bergroth.

§ 12.—CONCLUSION. MILITARY CHARACTER OF THE
    SWEDISH RELIGION IN THIS PERIOD. WHITE-
    LOCKE'S CONVERSATIONS. SVEDBERG'S CRITICISM
    OF THE FALSE LUTHERANISM OF HIS DAY.

Thus the external fabric of the Swedish Church was
completed, and the entire victory of Lutheran orthodoxy
seemed secure. " Pure doctrine," without much freedom
of thought or even feeling, was triumphant, and Luther's
subjective teaching about the individual soul's justification
by faith was turned into an intellectual assent to certain
rather abstruse theological propositions, under the pressure
of authority. Even these propositions were not developed
with any originality within the country, but accepted from
teachers mainly in the German Universities. It is impossible not to admire those who had built up this fabric.
They were men of undaunted energy, of deep piety and of
thorough devotion to duty. They loved their country, and
hated its enemies. Many of them had been court chaplains
and field preachers in the army. They knew, and loved,
and honoured their strong kings. They dreamt of a permanent Swedish hegemony in Northern Europe. They
hoped to spread Swedish Lutheranism all round the Baltic.
It is impossible not to see the strong military spirit which
was, through them, infused into the Church. The character of mind thus fostered in the high places of the Church
is well illustrated by some remarkable conversations which
Bulstrode Whitelocke, Cromwell's ambassador to Sweden
in 1653—1654, reports as taking place between himself and
Archbishop Lenæus and the prince, afterwards Charles X.

Whitelocke suggested to Lenæus that his Church went
very near to claiming infallibility, and the archbishop came
very near to acknowledging it. Karl Gustaf dwelt very
much on the danger to the State of disunion in matters of
religion. But neither of them showed any signs of admir-
ing the toleration which existed (or was supposed to exist)
in England. Svedberg, who outlived the Caroline age,
and had all through his life something of the visionary

spirit of his famous son, was, however, a severe critic of
the idea that justification by faith alone meant faith without
good works.   To him faith was rightly a matter of the will
and the heart, very different from the " fides historica "
which many Swedes of his day regarded as a sufficient substitute for it.   Of such persons he wrote: " I sigh and
lament at heart, as often as I think of it, how ill most
Lutherans understand Luther's doctrine, how ill they
understand what faith in our Saviour the Lord Jesus Christ
is." . . . " If they go to Church, and at certain times in
the year to the Lord's Supper, and at the same time live in
all sorts of sinful works of the flesh—it's no matter : ' sola
fides,' strong faith, shall do their business for them.   No
one shall say that they are not good Lutherans and
Christians, and shall not be saved without any contradiction.   My God, who hast called forth and equipped
Luther with Thy spirit of freedom in order that he should
restore the Christian doctrine about faith, raise up another
Luther, who, with like freedom and blessed effect, may
again restore a Christian life! " [67]

But, true as this is, it may be doubted if Svedberg and
others of his generation sufficiently understood the real
meaning of faith, as trust in the person of the Lord and
intimate fellowship with Him.   A more intimate and
mystical faith was needed in order to break into the hard
ground of the Swedish character.   It was not a reconciliation between faith and works, but the exchange of a hard
faith for a living loving faith that was needed.

The period that follows will show Sweden making many
attempts in this direction, of which I shall endeavour to
give some account in my next lecture.

[67] For Whitelocke's conversation with Lenæus, see his
Swedish Ambassy, Vol. 1., pp. 410-8, Lond., 1772 ; for that
with the Prince, *ibid.*, 2, pp. 209-13.   From the first it also
appears that the diaconate was then recognized as a degree
leading to the priesthood.   Svedberg's own reflections are in
his MS. *Lefvernes Beskrifning*, p. 137, and are quoted from
H. W. Tottie's : *Lif*, pp. 28 foll., and his article in *K. H.
Årsskrift*, i., p. 90, 1900.   Cp. Schück, *I. S. L. H.*, i., 416-7.

VII.

THE TIME OF FREEDOM AND THE PERIOD OF NEOLOGY (1718—1812 A.D.).

LECTURE VII.

THE TIME OF FREEDOM AND THE PERIOD OF NEOLOGY (1718 A.D.—1812 A.D.).

§ 1.—CONSEQUENCES OF THE NEW TERMS OF SUBSCRIPTION IN SWEDEN. PARALLEL MOVEMENTS ON THE CONTINENT AND IN ENGLAND. ENGLAND FORTUNATE IN NOT ACCEPTING THE LAMBETH ARTICLES.

In my last lecture I explained how the dangers of indifference and disintegration apprehended from syncretism led to a tightening of the terms of subscription in the Church of Sweden, and to a narrowing of its whole system by what we should call a strict Act of Uniformity. It seemed inevitable at the time that the "Book of Concord," including the "Formula Concordiæ," should become a standard of the Church, though happily it was not set on the same level as the Augsburg Confession. But, none the less, this tightening of the system was in many respects a misfortune. It was part of a tendency which was felt almost equally by Lutherans and Calvinists, and in England as well as on the Continent—a tendency to measure the soundness of the position of a Church one-sidedly and almost exclusively by the supposed "purity" of its doctrine, and to think comparatively little of the fruits of the Spirit as a test by which it should be tried. Men were apparently unable to distinguish between the truths of revelation and those which were acquired by laborious and hazardous inference, between the dogma necessary to the existence of a Church and the doctrine which might be advisable or permissible in catechizing, lecturing, or preaching; nay, they were apt—as the Roman Church had so disastrously done in the case of the doctrine of

"transubstantiation"—to confound the speculations of
the schoolmen with the just requirements for Church communion.   The result of the adoption of the "Book of
Concord" was to emphasize the tendency to contempla-
tive intellectualism and a barren Lutheran scholasticism
both in Germany and Sweden.[1]

In the Reformed or Calvinistic Churches the same tendency to over-definition was apparent in the Dort decrees
of 1618; which drove out the Arminians, although,
happily, these decrees were not received by all Calvinistic
bodies.   A similar movement had been made in England
in the attempt to enforce "The Lambeth Articles" of 1605.
It is true that Archbishop Whitgift took from them their
most Calvinistic extravagances, and replaced them with
Augustinian propositions,[2] but, happily for our Church
and its position in the world, this movement met with such
resistance that the Thirty-nine Articles, with their
moderate and restrained statements, remained without
any authorized appendix.   If we have, as I believe, a Pro-
vidential call to be a mediating and reconciling body in
Christendom, it is because our formularies do not err on
the side of over-definition.   The promoters of syncretism
in England in the seventeenth century saw this advantage;
but the time was not then ripe for more than a strong
appeal for peace abroad and simplicity of doctrine at home,
an appeal which could be afterwards remembered and enforced.   It is important in this connection to recollect that
the Church of Denmark and even more that of Norway have
retained the simpler position which Sweden left in the reign
of Charles XI., and may, therefore, in that matter, co-
operate with ourselves in days to come.

[1] Cp. I. A. Dorner : *Hist. of Protestant Theology*, E. T., i.,
p. 383, Edinburgh, 1871.
[2] One of our clergy, the Rev. W. D. Sargeaunt, of Stoke
Abbot, Dorset, has recently done good service in calling attention in detail to this point, to which Hardwick had given a general
reference in his book on *The Reformation*, chap. iv., p. 241,
n. 4, and details for comparison in *Hist. of the Articles*, App. v.

Both in Germany and Sweden the strictness of Lutheran orthodoxy led to the appearance of frequent movements of protest in favour of the rights and duties of the individual, and in defence of a truer conception of faith, and of an emphasis on the need of hope and love in the Church as a whole. The first and the most far-reaching of these movements was that of Pietism, to which all that have followed have been more or less indebted.

§ 2.—MOVEMENTS OF PROTEST AGAINST ULTRA-ORTHO-
DOXY. PIETISM. SPENER AND FRANCKE. UNI-
VERSITY OF HALLE. THREE OBJECTS OF PIETISM:
REGENERATION OF THEOLOGY BY STUDY OF HOLY
SCRIPTURE; REGENERATION OF THE CHURCH, A
HIGHER CALL FOR LAYMEN IN HOME AND FOREIGN
MISSIONS; REGENERATION OF MORALS. PIETISM
IN SWEDEN. FRIENDLY ATTITUDE OF SVEDBERG,
ERIC BENZELIUS JUN., AND RYDELIUS. MURBECK,
TOLLSTADIUS, NILS GRUBB. OPPOSITION. DE-
CREES AGAINST CONVENTICLES.

The first leader of Pietism in Germany was a very good, wise and moderate man, Philipp Jakob Spener (1635—1705), an Alsatian, who was one of the leading Lutheran clergy of Frankfort-on-the-Main from 1666 onwards, and afterwards worked in Dresden and Berlin. In his youth he was not only much influenced by the writings of Johann Arndt, especially his celebrated book, *True Christianity*, but also by those of some of the English puritans, such as Richard Baxter, Lewis Bayly (Bishop of Bangor), author of a very popular book, *The Practice of Piety*, and one or both of the brothers, Daniel and Jeremiah Dyke. Pietism lay, historically as well as spiritually, between the early puritanism of England and the evangelical movements in our own country—both in its principles and in many of its outward forms and expressions. It began in private meetings for devotion and discussion, which were attended by like-minded persons who were dissatisfied with the dryness of the Church life of the day—the so-called *collegia pietatis*. It exhibited itself especially under its second great leader, August Hermann Francke, at Leipzig, in a renewed study of the Bible, in the so-called *collegia philobiblica*. It obtained for itself a refuge, and something more than a refuge, from the ill-will, and, indeed, persecution from which its adherents suffered, in the newly created University of Halle, in the electorate of Brandenburg, of which Spener may almost be called the founder. It set before itself three noble objects: the regeneration of theology, the regeneration of the Church, and the reformation of morals.[3]

Let me say a few words upon each of them.

The first of these objects, the regeneration of theology, was to be mainly effected by a return to Holy Scripture, and by the requirement of a new spirit in theological teachers. It was held that they must themselves be regenerate in order to have a saving influence on others. There was little or no attempt, at any rate at first, to alter the current doctrines of Lutheranism. It is clear, however, that these two principles, admirable as they are in themselves, might easily become mischievous in the hands of conceited or narrow-minded men. Bibliolatry was one danger of Pietism; cant, hypocrisy and rash judgment another. Even in the hands of more cautious and humble-minded men restriction of theological study to Holy Scripture might be injurious to the proper claims of reason, history and science, which assuredly are also channels of revelation by which God makes himself known to man. Conformity to Scripture is the test of truth, but all truth open to men is not in Scripture.

The second great object of Pietism, the reformation of the Church, was of even greater moment, and led Churchmen into paths of hope which will extend before them to the end of time. It restored much of the spirit of primi-

[3] See esp. I. A. Dorner: *Hist. of Prot. Theol.*, E. T., ii., pp. 203-227.

tive Christianity, and led men to dwell on the world-wide mission of the kingdom, and on Christ's second coming. Hence it was in many minds connected with Chiliasm,[4] a doctrine of some sort of millennium.

The new idea of the Church was that of an active body of believers, all of whom were alive to their duty, all in conscious possession of the Holy Spirit, each feeling it right to take part in spreading the kingdom of God. Hence arose, as I have said, the first interest in home and foreign missions in the Protestant Church of Germany, and the call to laymen to take a much more prominent part in Church affairs than they had been used to do amongst Lutherans. According to the teaching of Pietism, says Dorner, " the abyss between clergy and laity must become simply a distinction between those who teach and have the care of souls entrusted to them, and their brethren who are to be, or who have already been, instructed in practical Christianity, that they may be their fellow-workers. The Christian laity possess not only the right of offering to God the sacrifice of prayer, both for themselves and others, they may also exercise their priestly office, whether at home or among friends, may help to edify the Church in their house, have the right mutually to edify each other —especially under the direction of their minister—from

[4] Cp. I. A. Dorner : *System of Christian Doctrine*, E. T., iv., p. 392, Edinb., 1882 :—" As there was no thought of a new world-historical mission of the Evangelical Church [in the 16th and the first half of the 17th century], so especially there was no thought of the conversion of heathens and Jews, despite the words of Christ and His Apostles. It is sufficient, the Dogmatists thought, if only a sample is saved from every nation. . . . A different tone of thought has prevailed in the Evangelical Church only since Spener's days. In his case, Evangelical *faith*, inspired with new life, advanced, as in early Christian days, to *hope*; and since hope sketches for itself ideals of the period of consummation, this hope kindled the mind for the world-historical mission of the Church, and, as in the beginning, the Christian spirit turned from eschatology to the Church's work of love in the earth, to Foreign and some also to Home Missions."

the Word of God, and to open their mouths, both in question and answer, in devotional meetings."[5] Nothing, you will observe, is said as to the ministering of the sacraments, or as to preaching in Church. Spener was apparently too orthodox a Lutheran to think of that. But the germ of much that followed both inside and outside the Church is here in principle.

The new impulse given to foreign missions by Pietism is also most important. For reasons, which I have not time to explain, neither Luther nor Melanchthon, nor, on the other hand, Calvin or Beza, felt the call to follow the example which the Roman Catholic Church, to its credit, had never wholly ceased to set. On the contrary, they were rather cold and critical towards such efforts, when they did not actually oppose them. Happily, the founders of our English colonial empire were not of this mind, and the Elizabethans, at any rate, were in favour of carrying the Gospel with them, both for the sake of their own explorers and the natives to whom they came. The names of " Maister Wolfall " and Thomas Harriott— the latter very remarkable as a mathematician and astronomer—do honour to the voyages of Martin Frobisher and to Sir Walter Raleigh's first settlement of Virginia.[6]

It is also specially interesting to members of the Anglican Church to observe that perhaps the earliest defence of the principles of foreign missions, from the pen of a Protestant theologian, came from the excellent Adrian Saravia, the friend of Hooker, who was naturalized in England, and who dedicated his book, *On the Divers Degrees of Gospel Ministers*, to the English bishops in 1610. He first defends the thesis that "the form of apostolic government was not brought to an end by the

---

[5] *H. of Prot. Theol.*, E. T., ii., pp. 209-10.

[6] See *Digest of S. P. G. Records*, p. 1 (1893), and Hakluyt's *Voyages*, ed. 1588, pp. 760-1 for Harriott, and p. 816 for Sir W. Raleigh's endowment, when he assigned his rights to others. Raleigh was never himself in Virginia, though he had been in Guiana.

death of the Apostles and Evangelists " (c. 16), and then " that the command to preach the Gospel to all nations continues to bind the Church . . . . and that apostolic authority is necessary for it " (c. 17).[7]

It is noticeable how naturally these principles were associated with the episcopal polity which Saravia found and admired in England. The same spirit, however, continued during the time of the Commonwealth in which our first missionary society was founded, generally called " The New England Company," a society which still exists and administers a small income. In Sweden the missions to Lapland and Finland and the work done in the colony of New Sweden, both early in the seventeenth century and at its close, are interesting parallels. How far either country directly contributed to foster the missionary spirit of the pietistic movement in Germany I cannot say, but certain it is that some of the leading continental Pietists were associated with the missionary movement in England at the end of the seventeenth century. That movement arose from the " Religious Societies of London and Westminster," which were founded in 1678, and the " Societies for Reformation of Manners," founded in 1691, which must surely have owed some part of their impulse to Spener's *collegia pietatis*. These societies were the direct antecedents of our first great comprehensive society, " The Society for Promoting Christian Knowledge " (S.P.C.K.), founded in 1698, and its offshoot, the more distinctly missionary society, "The Society for the Propagation of the Gospel in Foreign Parts " (S.P.G.), founded in 1701. The " Religious Societies " were more closely allied to the Church than those for the " Reformation of Manners " and were of more abiding value. The latter became offensive because of their inquisitorial spirit and the encouragement given by them to informers.

Amongst the earliest corresponding members of the

---

[7] See Saravia's *Diversi Tractatus Theologici*, pp. 171-178, London, 1611.

Christian Knowledge Society were Professor A. H. Francke, of Halle; the much-loved pastor, John Frederick Osterwald, of Neuchatel; the great scholar, Dr. John Ernest Grabe, who became a clergyman of our Church, and Dr. Brinck, a Danish minister of Copenhagen.[8] The connection of England with Denmark in evangelistic work was very close, especially through B. Ziegenbalg and C. F. Schwartz, who worked in the Danish colony of Tranquebar in India, but were supported also from England. We do not, I think, know of Swedes who worked in distant missions at this date, but Svedberg was much struck with the missionary zeal of his friend, Edzardus,[9] at Hamburg, and I have already noticed that Serenius was an early member of the S.P.G.   None of those who came within the Halle circle of influence could fail to be aware of the missionary activity which flowed from that centre.   Probably the first Swede to propagate mission work in India was Johan Zakarias Kjernander.   As a student he had been sent away from Upsala for some fault and migrated to Halle, whence he went out to Calcutta in 1758.   He married there and acquired great wealth in commerce, which he used to good purpose (Cornelius: *Hist.*, § 193).

The third great object of Pietism was the regeneration of morals.   It was here, perhaps, that greatest effort was needed, but here also that it was most easy to go wrong and to excite criticism, jealousy and opposition.   Though Spener was a wise and circumspect man, many of his followers were not so; and Pietism soon became identified with a narrow code of morals, in which strict rules as to dress, expenditure and amusements and a forced distinction between the " world " and the Church, seemed to take the place of moral principles.   It was also found to be narrow in its range of studies and narrow in its sympathy with art and science, and even in its enjoyment of natural beauty.   These were the extravagances of the movement, but, on the whole, it was an incalculable blessing to the

[8] See *Hist. of S. P. C. K.*, p. 2, Lond., 1898.
[9] See H. W. Tottie: *Jesper Svedberg's Lif.*, etc., i., p. 40.

whole Church, to be sent back to the devotional study of Scripture, to be reminded of the duties of individual piety and corporate missionary activity, and to have the idea of self-denial restored to its proper place in Christian life. Sweden profited not less than Germany by its endeavours to attain these objects.

At first Pietism was rather favourably received in Sweden. Light is thrown upon it by a study of Bishop Svedberg's life, to which I have already referred, and, although he did not work directly with it, he recognized what was good in it. It entered Sweden in force about 1702. Its new hymn-book, "Songs of Moses and the Lamb," first printed in 1717, and often since republished, gave the Pietists a bond of union which was very useful to them, though it excited some contempt from the simplicity of its language. A new element was introduced into the movement on the return of the Swedish prisoners of war taken in Charles XII.'s unsuccessful war in Russia, especially from Siberia, about 1721. Francke, personally, had done much to soften their painful existence in captivity, and his spirit had taken great hold of the troops, though even there it was not wholly welcome to the military chaplains who were among them. In Sweden itself, however, it was at first rather encouraged by the two greatest religious leaders of the age, Eric Benzelius, junior (1675—1743), Bishop of Linköping, and then archbishop, and Professor Andreas Rydelius (1671—1738),[10] the first independent philosopher of Sweden, who died after a four years' episcopate as Bishop of Lund. Rydelius was particularly friendly to Peter Murbeck in Skåne (1708—1766), who has been called "the Francke of Sweden," though he was a harder man than Francke.[11] At the same time Eric Tollstadius was working effectually in Upper

[10] There is a short and interesting biography of Rydelius, by J. A. Eklund (Bishop of Carlstad), Stockholm, 1899.
[11] There is a sketch of Murbeck's life and work in Hjalmar Lyth's *Ropande Röster*, Stockholm, 1908. A fuller treatment of the life is published by Rydberg.

Sweden, especially in Stockholm (†1759). On the other hand the Pietists were in many places subjected to great suspicion, and even to persecution, of which Tollstadius had a considerable amount to suffer, as well as the excellent Provost Nils Grubb, of Umeå, farther north.[12] The general feeling, which was voiced by Gustaf Adolf Humble (1674—1741), who became Bishop of Vexiö in 1730, was against the movement, and the edicts against Conventicles of 1706, 1713, 1721, and especially the severest of all, that of 1726, were intended to check and suppress it. We must remember, however, that these were government edicts, not laws freely passed by the Church. The last of these, forbidding all public gatherings for worship except under the parish priest, was not repealed till 1858.

§ 3.—OFFSHOOTS OF PIETISM.   SCHOOL OF BENGEL AND THE MORAVIANS.   SALUTARY INFLUENCE OF THE MORAVIANS IN SWEDEN.

Pietism gave birth to two other very important movements—the revival of the Church of the Moravian Brethren by Count Zinzendorf at Herrnhut, and the theological school of John Albert Bengel, whose *Gnomon of the New Testament* is a classic even in England, and who is recognized as the founder of textual criticism of the New Testament in Germany. Of these two Dorner says that they agreed in their rejection of the real defects of the older Pietism, and in their appropriation of those genuine elements of Churchmanship which it had neglected to adopt. They resembled each other also in their full appreciation of Christian liberty and of the loveableness of Gospel truth, and their intense perception of its creative originality. Where they differed was in this: Zinzendorf founded a Church, with something of the defects which

[12] There is an extensive life of N. Grubb in *K. H. Arsskrift*, by E. Wermcrantz, Vols. 4, 5, 6, 7 for 1903-6. On Bishop Humble see Cornelius : *Hist.* § 157.

cling to a small community, however large-hearted and free from sectarianism.   Bengel only founded a school which penetrated and elevated a larger body, to its great advantage.[13]

In reading the pages of Dorner on the Church of the Brethren,[14] in which he writes with unaccustomed warmth and almost unstinted praise of their belief and worship, I cannot but be carried back to days long past—forty-five years ago—when J had the privilege of some acquaintance with this honoured leader of theological study at Berlin, when I attended with him on one or two occasions the services of the Moravian Church, where, I believe, he found his own most congenial home of worship.

Moravianism had a very early connection with Sweden. When Zinzendorf founded his community at Herrnhut in 1727 he had a fellow-worker in Assessor C. H. Grundelstierna, who was also of use to himself in his own religious development.   Through him and through other Swedes the Church of the Brethren was introduced into the country in the years 1739—1744, when two centres were established, one in Stockholm, and one in West Gothland.   Its influence was great, salutary and opportune, for Sweden was at this period disturbed in many quarters by fanatical separatists and mystic visionaries.   Moravianism itself was for a time drawn into some of these extravagances, but it recovered about 1760, and continued to be a rallying point for those who did not find the established Church sufficiently warm in its life and its attitude towards our Lord and to His religion.

[13] I. A. Dorner : *Hist. of Prot. Theol.*, ii., pp. 226-7.
[14] L.c., pp. 245-8.

§ 4.—NEW LIFE IN THE CHURCH IN THE SO-CALLED " TIME
    OF FREEDOM." POLITICAL RESULTS OF THE
    DEATH OF CHARLES XII. WEAK REIGNS OF
    FREDERICK OF HESSE (1718—1751) AND ADOL-
    PHUS FREDERICK (1751—1771). NEW LIFE.
    SVEN BÄLTER. JAKOB SERENIUS. ANDERS
    NOHRBORG. ANDERS ELFVING IN SKÅNE. PER
    FJELLSTRÖM AND PER HÖGSTRÖM IN LAPLAND.
    IRREGULARITIES IN ORDINATION BY SUPERINTEN-
    DENTS AND OTHERS.

The death of the heroic Charles XII. in 1718, at the
early age of thirty-six, made a very great change in the
political situation. Sweden, from being one of the leading powers of Europe, sank back exhausted to take a lower
place. It lost in a short time nearly all its new possessions,
and only retained the southern provinces, which it had recovered from Denmark, and Swedish Pomerania, which
it kept until 1815.[15]   Finland, an older possession, also
remained in great part Swedish up till 1809, when the
necessity of an alliance with Russia against Napoleon
forced the cession of the Grand Duchy and the island of
Åland, right opposite Stockholm, to that powerful neigh-
bour.

The death of Charles not only left Sweden without a
king and leader, it left it without a proper heir to the
throne.   This was an opportunity for the nobility, or
rather the Council of State, to regain something of the
power of which Charles XI. had deprived them.   They
made a compact with the younger sister of Charles XII.,
Ulrica Eleonora, the younger, that she and then her husband, a Hessian prince, should reign in the place of the
dead elder sister's (Hedvig Sophia's) son, another German

---

[15] Cp. *Betydelsen för Sveriges utveckling af 1600-talets
Krigspolitik* af Ellen Fries, Fil. Dr., in Heimdal's *Folkskrifter*,
1898. This is an interesting sketch which I wish I had room
to quote.

prince.   This was a natural arrangement under the circumstances, since Ulrica had been practically regent, in
her brother's absence in Russia, Turkey and elsewhere,
and was the only adult member of the family resident in
Sweden.   She had, however, to give up her hereditary
right, and submit to election, and the government, during
the whole reign of her husband (Frederick of Hesse)
(1718—1751), and that of another German prince, Adolphus Frederick of Holstein-Gottorp (1751—1771) — a
period of over forty years—was in the hands of an oligarchy.   The return of Sweden to an elective monarchy on
these two occasions is, of course, a very important political
fact.   It facilitated the change of dynasty by which the
present royal family came to the throne in the early years
of the last century.

The period was one of humiliation for the crown and of
great political unrest within, but, on the whole, it was a
time of growth both for literature and science and for the
Church.

Even in these lectures it seems right to take some
notice of the general progress of culture in Sweden,
and I cannot omit to draw your attention on the one hand
to Olof Dalin, as a representative of literature, and on the
other to the great botanist, Karl von Linné or Linnæus
(1707—78), founder, with others, of the Swedish Academy
of Science, such as the astronomer, Anders Celsius, and
the chemist, Torberg Bergman, and his pupil, Scheele.
Dalin's *Swedish Argus*, which appeared in 1732, was produced when he was quite a young man, aged twenty-four.
It had the same objects as Addison's *Spectator* and other
similar periodical essays, the improvement of morals and
style; but it was also intended to spread useful information.
Dalin himself wrote much better and more naturally than
his predecessors, and was popular both as a poet and a
historian.   Of his *History of the Kingdom of Sweden* it
was said that he had brought down history from the book-
shelves into the hearts of the people.   His little poems
were sung all over the country, and it was his greatest joy

to hear them trolled from the lips of a postillion or hummed by any youngster in the streets.[16]

Linnæus touches Church life more closely, as he was the son of a country curate and never forgot his home and its teaching. He was first a student at Lund, and then for many years a teacher at Upsala, where his influence was most wholesome and inspiring, especially to his pupils. His whole life was, as it were, a song in praise of the beauty of nature and of the wisdom of the Creator. The opening sentences of his great book, the *Systema Naturæ*, reveal at once his simple and reverent character :—

"I saw the back of the infinite, all-wise and all-mighty God as He went from me—and I was appalled. I traced out His footsteps over the field of nature, and I remarked at every extremity of it an infinite wisdom and power. I saw there how all animals are nourished by plants, plants by the earth, how the earth-ball is turned night and day round the sun, which gave it life, how the sun with the planets and the fixed stars are held up in their empty nothing by the motive and director of universal existence, of all causation, this world's Lord and Master. If one should call Him *Fate*, one is not wrong, for all things hang on His finger. If one should call Him *Nature*, one is not wrong, for from Him all things have come. If one should call Him *Providence*, one speaks rightly too, for all things are done according to His will and pleasure."

Over the door of his bedroom was written in his own hand : " Live without reproach ! God sees thee !" [17]

There were no very great men in the Church in this period, but there was no lack of good ones. The Pietistic and Moravian movements, and others of more local origin, stimulated the energies of the Church within, and a remarkable succession of bishops and clergy adorned the Swedish Church in the middle of the eighteenth century. We may mention first Sven Bälter, Provost of Vexiö (1713—1760), a great and attractive preacher, whose book on " Church ceremonies amongst the first Christians and in the kingdom of Sweden " is indispensable for our

---

[16] C. Grimberg : *Sveriges Historia*, p. 394, Stkh., 1908.
[17] See Grimberg : l.c., p. 405.

subject.[18] With Bälter it is natural to associate the name of Andreas Rhyzelius, Bishop of Linköping from 1743 to 1761, whose lives of Swedish bishops and description of Swedish monasteries are of no slight value to the historian.[19] Jakob Serenius (1700—1776), Bishop of Strengnäs from 1763 to his death, has been already incidentally named as having been pastor of the Swedish Church in London, and as having done much to introduce confirmation into Sweden, after the English and Danish manner. His residence in England also led to his writing two important philological works, an English, Swedish and Latin dictionary, and a dissertation on the early relations between the Sveogoths and the Angles. He was zealous for order and education in his diocese, and had something, I suppose, of the masterful spirit of Rudbeckius. The court preacher, Anders Nohrborg (1725—1767) is best known as the author of that most popular book of postils or sermons, entitled *The Way of Salvation for fallen Man*, which for many Swedes has come next to the Bible and the hymn-book as a help to devotion.[20] It is remarkable as being the work of a strict Churchman, and one opposed to all sectarianism. In this way it did much to maintain the position of the National Church. An even more popular preacher in his own life time was Anders Elfving (1745—1772), "the man with the spirit and power of Elias," on whom Murbeck, the Pietist, had

---

[18] *Historiska Anmärkningar om Kyrko-ceremonierna så wäl wid den offenteliga Gudstjensten, som andra tillfällen, hos de första Christna, och i Swea Rike ; i synnerhet efter Reformationen*, etc. It was published first in 1762. I have used the third edition " with appendix and alterations in accordance with the Hand-book of 1809," by Professor A. E. Knös, Örebro, 1838.

[19] *Episcoposcopia Suiogothica*, two parts, Linköping, 1752, *Monasteriologia Suiogothica eller Kloster-beskrifvning*, 1740.

[20] *Den fallna menniskans salighets ordning*, published after his death by his brother Daniel, in 1771. The 17th edition appeared in 1877.

exercised an abiding influence.[21]   Although he died at
the age of only twenty-eight, he had made an immense
impression on the people, especially in Kalmar and Skåne,
and legends of him, like the legends of the saints, were
still current a short time back in places where he worked.

For instance, it is said that a servant in his household
determined to find out whom Elfving had to help him in
preparing his sermons, inasmuch as he spoke so much
better than other priests. One Saturday night this man
laid himself under Elfving's bed, knowing that his master
had been so much occupied during the week as to have
been unable to prepare his sermon. When Elfving came
into the room he sat down to write like anyone else, but
he was not satisfied with what he had written. He then
knelt down and began to pray aloud, at first in a faltering
voice, but in the end with such a burning torrent of words
that his auditor under the bed was deeply moved. When
all was still, he crept out and saw an angel standing by his
master's side, and whispering to him what he was to
write.[22]

It is also a happy thing to notice that mission work
among the Lapps was carried on vigorously and affectionately by Per Fjellström (1697—1764) and Per Högström
(1714—1784). The former produced a grammar and
dictionary of their language as well as school books and
Church books; the latter was a great traveller and observer,
as well as a translator of useful books, and a benefactor in
many ways to the people of the North, especially in the
town of Skellefteå in Vesterbotten, where he worked as a
pastor for nearly forty years.

Although on the whole the so-called period of freedom
may have been favourable to the progress of the Church,
it witnessed certain irregularities which are accounted for
by the weakness of the crown. The most important of

[21] There is a sketch of Elfving's life in Hjalmar Lyth's
Ropande Röster, Stockholm, 1908, which also contains sketches
of P. Murbeck, Lars Linderot, and P. L. Sellergren.
[22] *Ropande Röster*, p. 42.

all would be, if it could be proved, an irregularity or failure in the consecration of Johannes Steuchius, Archbishop of Upsala (1730—1742). He had previously been Superintendent of Carlstad (1723—1730), and was then appointed Bishop of Linköping, where, however, he does not seem to have resided. It has been remarked that no mention of his consecration to Carlstad, Linköping or Upsala is made in his funeral sermon, and it is known that superintendents were not always consecrated. But since Rhyzelius, who was Provost of Linköping (1720—1743) and then bishop (1744—1761), asserts that he was consecrated to Linköping by Bishop Jesper Svedberg at Skara, 15th November, 1730 (the archbishopric being then vacant by the death of Steuchius' father, Mathias), there seems every reason to believe the statement. It is also to be noticed that the learned Eric Benzelius the younger, who succeeded Johannes Steuchius both at Linköping and Upsala, left in manuscript a treatise on the Apostolic succession, still existing in the diocesan library at Linköping, in which there is no reference to any anomaly in the case of Steuchius. Nor is there any reference to it in the dissertation *On the Canonical Succession and Consecration of the Bishops of Sweden* by the historian, E. M. Fant, published at Upsala in 1790. This difficulty may, therefore, be dismissed.

The serious irregularities that are known are generally of the nature of royal permissions given to superintendents and deans to ordain priests on account of distance, and the difficulties which candidates had of attendance on a bishop—as, *e.g.*, in the army, in the colony of New Sweden, and during a vacancy, etc.[23] Such irregularities

[23] The following are the instances kindly furnished to our Commission by Dean Lundström (21st September, 1910) :—

1 (1703—1706).—Superintendents of the Forces ordained priests at Jarislov (outside Sweden) according to Olof Wallquist (*Eccl. Coll.*, 2, 131).

2 (1709—1721).—General Superintendent Norberg, when a captive in Russia, ordained two ministers at Moscow, 13th March, 1713 (*ibid.*, p. 130).

were due, not to the desire of the crown to increase its prerogative, but to its weakness and inability to resist the pressure put upon it by influential persons. This laxity ceased on the restoration of personal government under Gustavus III., who wrote on 25th June, 1786, to the Dean of Upsala refusing to give him liberty to ordain, saying: "We have found that ordination belongs to bishops alone." A similar refusal was made to Olof Celsius of

3.—Jakob Serenius, when chaplain in London, obtained permission from Bishop Svedberg of Skara to ordain for him a minister for New Sweden. It is not known whether he acted on it (Letters of E. Benzelius, jun., at Linköping).

4.—The Dean of Upsala, Matthäus Asp, at the request of the Chapter, obtained a letter from King Adolphus Frederick, during the vacancy of the see after the death of Archbishop Henricus Benzelius († 20th May, 1758), under which he ordained twenty priests, 20th June, 1758 (Bälter, p. 678, ed. 1838).

5.—Similarly, Lars Hydrén, Dean of Upsala, obtained the "jus ordinandi" from the same king, under which he ordained sixteen priests, 16th December, 1764, during the vacancy caused by the death of Archbishop Samuel Troilius († 16th January, 1764). [I do not quite understand the date, as Beronius, Bishop of Kalmar, is said by Hollander to have become Archbishop 26th June, 1764. Perhaps he had not been enthroned.]

6.—The same dean held a similar ordination of thirteen priests under similar circumstances 21st July, 1775. Beronius had died 18th May, 1775.

The ordinations of Hydrén seem to have been limited to these two cases in 1764 and 1775: see Archbishop U. von Troil's *Life of Lars Hydrén*, p. 64, Upsala, 1890.

I may add under this head that about 1700 the three Swedish pastors of the Delaware, Rudman, Björk and Sandel, ordained Justus Falckner, a Halle student, to the priesthood. When this act was cited as a precedent for presbyterian ordination, twenty-four years later, "the four Swedish pastors disclaimed the authority to ordain, and explained the ordination of Falckner upon the ground that Rudman had been made by ' the Archbishop of Sweden ' ' suffragan or vice-bishop ' " (H. E. Jacobs : *The Evangelical-Lutheran Church in U.S.A.*, p. 97, ed. 1907). A similar commission, not carried out, was given by the archbishop, and consistory of Upsala, 7th November, 1739.

Lund, who wished his dean to ordain for him on account of his old age, in a royal letter of 31st August, 1792, "as both the Church law and the dignity of such a ceremony demands that it ought to be performed by a bishop."

None of the persons so irregularly ordained became bishops.

I must now turn from these details to draw a picture—however slight—of a single person, whose career and character exhibit something of the same restless and audacious genius in exploring the mysteries of the unseen world, as that of St. Birgitta in the mediæval period—I mean, of course, Emanuel Swedenborg.

§ 5.—EMANUEL SWEDENBORG (1688—1772).[24] HIS EARLY LIFE. FRIENDSHIP WITH CHARLES XII. HIS DISAPPOINTMENT IN MARRIAGE. TWO GREAT WORKS ON INANIMATE AND ANIMATE NATURE. ANTICIPATIONS OF MODERN THEORIES. TRANSITION TO THEOSOPHY. MUGGLETON. DIPPEL. STRANGE CONDUCT IN 1743—1744. HIS GNOSTIC AND SABELLIAN THEOLOGY. THE LAST JUDGMENT IN 1757. THE "NEW CHURCH." HIS CREDENTIALS. CRITICISM.

One of the most striking figures in the whole history of Sweden, and particularly in the religious history of that country in the eighteenth century, is that of Emanuel

[24] There is a good and popular biography of Swedenborg by James John Garth Wilkinson, M.D. (1812—1899), a surgeon and physician, a homœopathist and anti-vaccinationist, himself a mystic and a disciple of Swedenborg, an admirer of Blake, and a friend of R. W. Emerson—1st ed. 1849, 2nd ed. 1886. Wilkinson translated as many as eleven works of Swedenborg into English ; for the list see *D. N. B.*, s.n. *J. J. G. Wilkinson.* His presentation of Swedenborg won the praise of Emerson. Less sympathetic and somewhat vulgar, but much fuller and more critical, is the life by William White : *Emanuel Swedenborg : his Life and Writings*, 2 vols., London, 1867, 1 vol., ed. 1868. Cp. the review of it in the *Christian Remembrancer*, Vol. 54, pp. 305-25, 1867, and Wilkinson, ed. 2, p. viii. E. Paxton

Swedenborg (1688—1772). He was third child and second son of the famous Jesper Svedberg, Bishop of Skara, already several times mentioned, and his first wife, Sara Behm. He inherited from his father the visionary temper, which had such strange manifestations in the last thirty years of his long life. But this was only one side of his character. Both father and mother came from the Stora Kopparberg, the mining district of Dalarne, and Swedenborg inherited from his mother and maternal grandfather, not only mining property, but in all probability his remarkable interest in and intelligence of all matters therewith concerned. Swedenborg is certainly one of the most extraordinary combinations of the speculative, and the practical, the visionary and the materialist characters that the world has ever seen. He is the greatest of the encyclopædic geniuses produced by his native country, or as one of his admirers calls him, " the most grandly superficial writer who had then arisen—a rare qualification in its good sense " (Wilkinson : p. 53).

For the first ten or twelve years of his life he had marked religious instincts, and he was happy to remember in his

Hood : *Swedenborg : a Biography and an Exposition*, London, 1854, is wordy and diffuse, but rather interesting. I have not seen Tafel's works. The other books I have consulted are the article in *P.R.E.*[3], Vol. 19, by W. Köhler, and older articles in biographical dictionaries; Schück and Warburg : *I.L.S.H.*, ii., 234-9 ; and particularly Hjalmar Holmquist : *Swedenborgs första Verksamhet-s period* in the *Bibelforskare*, February, 1909, and Alfred H. Stroh : *Grunddragen af Swedenborg's Lif*, Stockholm, 1908. I have used Dorner's *H. of Prot. Theol.*, E. T., ii., 240-5, as a criticism of S.'s theological position. R. W. Emerson's essay on *Representative Men*, provides criticism of another kind.

Of Swedenborg's own works I have *The true Christian Religion, containing the Universal theology of the New Church* (translated from the Latin published at Amsterdam, 1771), London ; *Swedenborg S. B. and F.*, 1890, and Rev. Augustus Clissold's 4 vols. : *Spiritual Exposition of the Apocalypse*, Lond., 1851. William White's analyses are sufficient for most purposes. I quote the second edition of both White and Wilkinson.

latter years that his parents talked of him as a child through whom angels spoke. Angels were doubtless often the subject of conversation in Swedenborg's home, and the father may have often spoken of his own intercourse with them. Bishop Svedberg, however, left his son's mind free from the theological conceptions of orthodox Lutheranism which he indeed himself freely criticized. "I knew of no other faith or belief," wrote Swedenborg late in life, "from my fifth to my twelfth year than that God is the creator and preserver of nature; that He endues man with understanding, good inclinations and other gifts derived from these. I knew nothing at that time of the systematic or dogmatic kind of faith . . . and had I heard of such a faith it would have been then, as now, perfectly unintelligible to me " (Wilkinson: p. 5). As a young man Swedenborg had some inclination to literature, but his taste was directed to mathematical and scientific studies by Eric Benzelius the younger, husband of his beloved sister Anna, and then the influential librarian of the University of Upsala, who was dearer to him than his own brothers.

After assisting his elders in founding a learned society at Upsala—the "Collegium curiosorum"—Swedenborg travelled for five years (1710—1715), the first two of which he spent in England. Here he made many friends and acquaintances, especially the great trio, Isaac Newton, John Flamsteed and Edmund Halley. But he was taking in on all sides the influences of the great men who adorned the latter years of the reign of Queen Anne (Holmquist: l.c., 12-19). He then passed through Holland, where the Congress of Utrecht was in session, and he had the assistance of the Swedish representative, Palmqvist, in making use of his opportunities. He spent some time in Paris, where he met the astronomers, Delahire and Varignan, and Germany, where he made the acquaintance of Leibnitz and the mathematician and physicist, John Christian Wolff. He returned to Sweden in July, 1715. His head was full of ideas, and plans, and projects, particularly of a mathe-

matical and mechanical nature, amongst which we observe
a submarine vessel to be used in war, a system of locks for
canals, a universal musical instrument and a flying
machine (Holmquist: p. 22). He then published the first
scientific periodical ever issued in the country, the
Dædalus Hyperboreus, in which he co-operated with his
elder friend, Christopher Polhem, a great engineer, whom
he named the Archimedes of Sweden. This periodical
attracted the king's notice, and further acquaintance
ripened into friendship between himself and Charles XII.,
who aspired, among other things, to be a mathematician.
The king, who recognized his powerful genius, made him
an assessor of the College of Mines—the board of directors
who governed this side of Swedish industry—an office
which his mother's father had held. The king employed
him with Polhem in the construction of the docks at Carls-
crona, in the development of the salt industry, and in the
project for a canal through the lakes across the peninsula,
which Hans Brask had suggested long before, as well as in
the usual mining operations. Swedenborg's mechanical
genius enabled him even to help the king directly in his
campaign against Norway in June, 1718. The direct
approach to Fredrikshald and the fortress of Fredriksten
up the Svinesund was blockaded by the Danish and Norwegian fleets, supported by English vessels. Swedenborg, who was at Strömstad with the Swedish fleet on the
coast of Bohuslän, either accidentally or summoned for
the purpose, devised machinery by which a number of
vessels were drawn across the mountains of Bohuslän,
some fifteen to seventeen English miles, to the upper end
of the Idefjord, where they served to draw the pontoons on
which the artillery was placed, and to set it in the
desired position against the fortress. But this siege was
destined to be the end of the friendship with the king,
which promised so great a career for Swedenborg. On
the 30th November, 1718, the king was shot down by an
unknown hand as he was inspecting the works on the east
side of the Fredriksten. Swedenborg, in one of his later

books, makes this striking reference to him.[25] Speaking
of courage in man, he writes: "We may see genuine
courage illustrated in the person of the dead King of
Sweden, that hero of the North, who never knew that
which others call fear, nor that fallacious courage and
boastfulness which is excited by intoxicating drinks; for
he touched no other than water. Of him we may say that
he lived a life farther removed from death than others, and
that he had in reality lived more than other men."

This death not only closed a period in Swedenborg's
life, but it was followed shortly after by another blow, his
disappointment in the only love affair which is known
to have seriously touched his heart. He was greatly
attracted by Emerentia Polhem, his dear friend's younger
daughter, and Polhem made her promise in writing to
marry Swedenborg. But the young lady could not disguise her sorrow and distress, and Swedenborg was forced
to give her up, and swore that he could never think of
another woman. Thus it came to pass that one who wrote
more warmly than anyone else of the honourable estate of
matrimony, and who afterwards taught as a matter of revelation that it was (in a spiritual manner) to be part of
human life in another world, was himself debarred from
entering it.[26]

[25] In his *Œconomia regni animalis*, quoted by Holmquist,
l.c., p. 38.

[26] Swedenborg's own moral character is a matter of debate.
On the one hand (1) his writings shew a coarse habit of mind,
and a great familiarity with vicious thoughts, and (2) in his
moral teaching he allowed great laxity to men, especially in
the unmarried state. He seems to view woman chiefly from the
man's standpoint, and to have had no ideas of the elevation
which she then so sorely needed. On the other hand, the actual
lapses of conduct attributed to him do not appear to be made
out. Holmquist, l.c., p. 39 n., criticizes the story that he had
an älskarinna in Italy. On the coarseness of his diary in 1743—
1744, see White, chapter xi., and *Chr. Rembr.*, l.c., p. 318. On
the laxity which he allowed to men, either unmarried or living
apart from their wives, see White, pp. 554-62, and Wilkinson,
pp. 180-1. His works are in parts anything but pleasant

In 1719 the Svedberg family was ennobled and took the name of Swedenborg. The bishop died in 1735. His son, who inherited some fortune from both his mother and his stepmother, was able to live comfortably and to travel largely and spend much money in printing books which did not sell.

Shortly after his father's death Swedenborg began to publish his great works on natural philosophy, in which the critics see the influence of Descartes and Newton, Leibnitz and John Christian Wolff (1679—1754).

The first of these was the collection called *Opera Philosophica et Mineralia* in three folio volumes, published at Dresden and Leipzig (1738—1741). The first and most important volume contained the *Principia*, or cosmogony, the fundamental position of which is that the groundwork of nature is the same as the groundwork of geometry—the point or infinitesimal atom. The most perfect motion is that of the spiral, a thought apparently borrowed from the " vortices " of Descartes. The other volumes are of a more practical nature, and include Swedenborg's personal experience of mining, smelting and metallurgy.

His second great work was one on animate nature, the *Regnum Animale*, which dealt with anatomy, physiology and biology, the first two parts of which were published at the Hague in 1744, the third in London, 1745—that is, just at the time of his great change.

In these printed books and in the large mass of manuscript material, which contains corrections and developments of great extent, scientific men of our own day have noticed amidst much that is prolix, diffuse and fanciful, a wonderful anticipation of later and modern theories and discoveries. For instance, Swedenborg gave currency to the following notions: (1) That the planets of our solar system have their origin in the material of which the sun is made;

reading. Emerson says of him: " Except Rabelais and Dean Swift nobody ever had such science of filth and corruption." *Representative Men*, p. 102 (Temple Classics).

(2) that the earth and the other planets have gradually separated themselves from the sun, and, therefore, have acquired a gradually lengthened orbit; (3) that the earth's period of rotation has gradually increased; (4) that the solar systems are arranged round the Milky Way, in the central line of which they lie most closely; (5) that there is an even greater system in which the milky ways are arranged together (A. H. Stroh: l.c., p. 40). In his "animal kingdom" modern physiologists are particularly struck with his anticipations of recent conclusions as to the anatomy and functions of the brain. In the first place, they say, he had the courage to defend the coincidence of the movement of the brain with that of the lungs in respiration, on the ground of observations made by himself and with reference to experiments made by others on animals. He was also the first to make clear that the cortex of the brain is the seat of the higher psychical activity, the point of contact between soul and body. Swedenborg also recognized that the grey substance of the cortex of the brain is connected with the will and with the voluntary motions which the will originates. He further postulated the existence of different motor areas in this part of the brain, and their connection with the activity of different muscles (*P. R. E.*[3] 19, 182). It was unfortunate for Swedenborg's reputation as a man of science, in his own day, that the great change took place in 1743—1745, which turned him from an inquirer into a seer, from a philosopher and man of science into a theosophist. The change was indeed an immense one, and he seems to have quickly lost almost all interest in his previously absorbing studies. The change was, however, not wholly unnatural. He had worked up from inanimate to animate nature, from mathematics and physics in its different branches, from geology, chemistry, and astronomy to physiology, biology and psychology. He was in his last book busy with the question of the relation of soul and body, of the infinite and the finite, and with the thought of God. "I have gone through this anatomy (he

writes) with the single end of investigating the soul.   It
will be a satisfaction to me if my labours be of any use to
the anatomical and medical world, but a still greater
satisfaction if I afford any light towards the investi-
gation of the soul " (Wilkinson: p. 48).   He had
started from geometry and mechanics, and he had, like
Comte afterwards, found the highest sphere of nature in
man.   But, unlike Comte, he felt that the presence
of something higher was postulated by the phenomena of human life and thought.   He was an evolu-
tionist, like Darwin afterwards, but his evolution led him
to *The Worship and the Love of God*, the title which he
gave to the book, which was the expression of his highest
thoughts in his period of transition.   What influences
were exercised on him in his religious development have
not, I think, been clearly investigated.   In some of his
speculations, particularly in his anthropomorphic idea of
God, he had a predecessor in Ludowicke Muggleton (1609
—1698), who, like himself, circumscribed the God-head in
the person of our Lord Jesus Christ and retained the
human form in heaven.[27]

He seems to have met that strange restless being,
John Conrad Dippel (1673—1734), the so-called Demo-
critus Christianus, on the occasion of his visit to
Sweden in 1729, where he was invited to cure the king.[28]
Dippel was a physician of considerable ability, but he was
also an alchemist, an astrologer, and a charlatan—a sort of
eighteenth century Paracelsus.   His interests were largely
theological, and especially in the direction of the less
worthy forms of Pietism.   In his *Papismus Protestan-
tium vapulans* (1698) and his *Vera Demonstratio Evan-
gelica* (1729) he attacked the prevailing orthodoxy.   He
substituted a divine inward light for the revelation of Scripture ; he denounced the teaching of the wrath of God, whom

---

[27] Cp. White, l.c., p. 704.   See also *D.N.B.*, s.n. *Muggleton*.
[28] Holmquist : l.c., p. 45.   On Dippel, see Cornelius : *Hist.*,
§§ 165-6, Dorner : *H. of P. Theol.*, ii., 262, *P.R.E.*[3] 4, 703-7,
art. by F. Bosse.

he described as entirely love. God (he says) needed not to
be reconciled to us, but we to Him. Christ came into the
world not to make satisfaction for our sins and to earn
salvation for us, but to lead us from love of the creatures
to love to God. He is our example rather than our Redeemer. His death was not an atoning sacrifice, but an
encouragement to self-sacrifice. Dippel also attacked the
orthodox doctrine of the Trinity.

It is easy to see the points in which Dippel's theology
coincides with that of Swedenborg, and probably Dippel's
pretensions to supernatural power were not without attractions to the young Swede. There is, however, I think, no
evidence that they met in later years, and the great religious crisis in Swedenborg's life occurred much later, in
the year 1743, when he was in London. What the nature
of that crisis was is not exactly known.

According to the narrative of Brockmer, with whom he
was then lodging in Fetter Lane, Brockmer was called up
one evening by Swedenborg, who had gone to bed, and
found him in a very wild state, in fact quite insane.
Swedenborg, who was foaming at the mouth, and spoke
with difficulty, confided to him that he was the Messiah,
that he was come to be crucified by the Jews, and wished
Brockmer to go with him to the synagogue on the morrow
to be his interpreter. According to this account he did
many other wild things at this time, and had to be taken
care of in another house.[29] Details of his outer life are
otherwise wanting for this period.

Swedenborg (perhaps naturally) gives no such account
of what happened to him, but relates many dreams, sometimes quaint, strange and irreverent, and sometimes coarse
and vulgar, which befell him about this time. He
describes in particular the way in which he was able, by
holding his breath, to enter into close relations with the
invisible worlds. I believe that in this he had a supposed

[29] See W. White : l.c., ed. 2, pp. 129 foll., also quoted in *Chr.
Remembrancer*, 54, 315-7.

experience parallel to that of many Indian ascetics.[30]
There is no doubt that long practice in holding the breath
does enable a man to hypnotize himself in a certain degree.
The physical account (suggested to me by a medical friend,
Dr. Donald Coles, now of Haifa, who has paid much attention to such subjects) seems to be this: Restraint of
ordinary breathing deprives the lungs of the amount of
oxygen which they need to purify the blood. The blood
sent to the brain becomes darker, and is in an impure condition, being overcharged with carbonic dioxide, and this
produces a state of coma or trance—sometimes ecstatic,
sometimes passive, in which a train of thought already
begun may be carried on, or a suggestion be received from
the outside and developed without the control of the reason. It was in such a condition as this that Swedenborg
received the revelations which have filled his later books—
revelations only differing from those of other seers in their
fulness and in a certain degree of power and grandeur,
such as the man's large and active mind would lead one to
expect, but thoroughly tinged with his own passions and
prejudices, and suffering from the limitations of his
religious experience.

He also described his special call to a holy office in a
vision of the Lord Himself, which apparently took place
in London in April, 1745 (Wilkinson: p. 77). Some of
the Lord's words were: " I am God the Lord, the Creator
and Redeemer of the world. I have chosen thee to unfold
to men the spiritual sense of Holy Scripture. I will myself dictate to thee what thou shalt write " (l.c., 75-6).
Certainly it would appear from his diary that he was in a
very strange and excitable condition during these years,
assailed by manifold inward temptations and with a brain
working beyond its natural activity. We have to think of
one who had made intense efforts to understand the problems of the universe, and that apparently with an increasing moral purpose. With a mind of extraordinary pene-

[30] See for a fuller account of this method of breathing or
not-breathing, Wilkinson, l.c., 77-83. Cp. White, 150-1.

tration, yet without the control of dogmatic belief or strong Christian experience, he had surveyed the whole of nature, and in his own mind brought it into unity.

Everything in his past experience moved him to seek and expect to find some solution of spiritual problems which would be of something the same nature as his previous solutions of natural problems—in one word something simple, and, if I may use the word, geometrical. He has had sufficient success in life to take a comfortable view of the universe. He has had money, friends, honour and recognition. Though tempted inwardly he has been able to struggle against temptation, and he is thoroughly imbued with the Pelagian view of morals: free-will can do anything, and a man's destiny is what he makes it. He has now come to that point in his inquiries when he must be either an atheist or a theist. The former alternative seems to have no attractions for him, and it is contradicted by the whole tendency of his childhood to expect and to attend to visions. He recurs to the habit of dreaming, and he carefully observes and cultivates it, by holding his breath in expectancy of entrance into the spiritual world, a habit which quickly develops into one of seeing waking visions and hearing angelic or other voices. He begins to study the Bible, as if it were a new book, and he expects to find in it help towards the solution of the problems of existence, though he is far from thinking of taking it in its literal sense.

His attitude towards Holy Scripture is a peculiar one. He uses grand language about it, but he deals with it very freely after the manner of the ancient Gnostics. Like Marcion, he has a canon of Scripture of his own : roughly speaking, it contains the historical and prophetical books and the Psalter, the four Gospels and the Apocalypse. But he drops the Hagiographa, the Acts and the Epistles of St. Paul, and the other Apostles,[31] which seemed to him

[31] " The following books are the present Word : The five books of Moses, the book of Joshua, the book of Judges, the two books of Samuel, the two books of Kings, the Psalms of David,

wanting in the spiritual sense. Indeed, he puts both David and St. Paul among the lost. Holy Scripture, according to his teaching, is divine, and, in fact, an Incarnation of the Son of God. But, starting with this principle, he rejects from it all that does not seem to him divine—that is, all that does not fit in with his theory of the other world. The human instruments who convey it are not necessarily important people. This theory is made further possible by the doctrine of the spiritual sense of Scripture, and by that of correspondences which teaches that everything on earth has its counterpart in the other worlds. This, of course, has its partial justification in our Lord's parables and in the teaching of the Fathers as to the mystical sense of Scripture (Cp. *True Christian Religion*, §§ 199-207). The *Memorable Relations* with which Swedenborg illustrates the larger sections of his book indeed often remind us of the *Similitudes* of Hermas.

As might be expected from the manner in which he approaches his subject, that is from the pursuit of unity in nature, his doctrine is essentially monistic or pantheistic and also rationalistic. He is by his own showing a hater of philosophy, and declared that the more a man had of it the blinder he grew. He trusts then not really to Scripture or to any definite system of scriptural interpretation, or to any system of philosophy, but to his own visions, which, according to the long habit and bent of his mind, give him the image of an invisible kingdom or kingdoms of the same sort as the kingdom of nature. It is conceived, like the vision of Dante, in a thoroughly concrete form and under geometrical figures.

" He represents the universe of being " (says Dorner: l.c., p. 243) " under the figure of three concentric circles,

the Prophets " (4 and 12), " and Lamentations " . . . " and in the New Testament, the four Evangelists . . . and, lastly, the Apocalypse (Wilkinson, 145)." But Job and the Acts are not infrequently quoted, and some of the other books of the New Testament. Cp. Köhler, *P.R.E.*[3] 19, *Swedenborg*, p. 189 for the canon.

in the innermost of which is the Lord as *love*, surrounded
by the various orders of that world of exalted spirits of
whose actions love is the spring. In the second circle the
Lord appears as *Divine truth*; and this circle also is a
realm of spirits, but of those whose characteristic is
thought. The visible sensible world, including our
nature, forms the third circle."

But these circles, though concentric, are not in the same
plane. They are best conceived in the form of a cone, the
apex of which is the love of God, the source of all existence. From this apex a downward movement takes place
through the circle of knowledge and truth to that of nature.
This movement begets by emanation the inhabitants and
other contents of the surrounding and subordinate circles.
In this way God himself advances from being (esse),
through development (fieri), to existence and reality
(effectus), until He at last is adequately realized in man.
The likeness of this thought to that of Hegel is obvious.

Besides this very Gnostic theory of the universe the
chief peculiarity of Swedenborg's theology is the position
which he (in company with Muggleton) assigns to our
Lord Jesus Christ. As is well known, he has what is
called a Sabellian, or Unitarian, doctrine of the Trinity.
But to him the only God is God becoming man in the person
of our Lord. Christ is the true one Man in whom dwells
the true Trinity—God as divine existence, the idea of God,
and the sensible reality. We may, perhaps, find in this
peculiarity the special attraction which this doctrine has
had for a number of persons. It certainly enables the
followers of Christ to differentiate themselves from the
followers of all other religions, and to regard them as purely
heathen.[32] Yet this is a philosophical rather than a theological notion. He has but little reference to or interest in
the historical Christ, the Christ of the four Gospels. He
rejects as unnecessary the Atonement and the principle of

[32] See Nathan Söderblom : *Vater, Sohn und Geist unter den
heiligen Dreiheiten und vor der religiösen Denkweise der
Gegenwart*, pp. 63-4, Tübingen, 1909.

mediation. Christ appears and disappears. He cannot
descend to earth again, and his place is taken by the
Word, an idealized revelation, of which the Bible is a sort
of symbol, the reality being found in Swedenborg's interpretation of it after he has rejected what he holds to be
unspiritual from it.

The whole character of Swendenborg's religious system
is rationalistic. It deprives everything as much as
possible of mystery. God has no fulness of life apart
from creation. As there is no Trinity of persons there
is no interior life of love in the God-head. God necessarily
finds Himself in man. The invisible world is as much
as possible—after the old Scandinavian Valhalla tendency
—an extension of the present life with marriage, society,
houses, gardens, entertainments and discussions. Angels
and demons are good and bad spirits of departed men.
They may be said to make their own heaven and hell by
their characters, choosing their associates and living apart
from one another with like-minded beings. The "last
judgment" prophesied in Scripture is not a great and
awful assize to which we are to look forward, a magnificent consummation which is to shake heaven and earth,
but it is a transaction in the invisible world which took
place in the year 1757, of which nobody but Swedenborg
was aware (Wilkinson: pp. 104-111).

This was a sufficiently startling anti-climax. It culminated in another which was even more remarkable, the
declaration that "the Church of the New Jerusalem" was
about to descend from heaven. Swedenborg does not
seem to have supposed that it was established before his
death, which took place early in 1772, and in London,
where his previous revelations had begun. The "New
Church" gradually came into being, and with very little
observation. Swedenborg's doctrines were accepted by
many Methodists, some Quakers, and some members of
the Church of England, especially by the Rev. John
Clowes, long Rector of St. John's, Manchester. The
"New Church" was, however, actually founded by

Robert Hindmarsh, a Clerkenwell printer, in 1782. It was joined by the sculptor Flaxman, and had some influence on William Blake. Its formation as a community was discouraged by Clowes, and it is very doubtful whether Swedenborg himself would have desired it. It exists chiefly as an English and American sect, and is more common in Lancashire and Yorkshire than in any other part of England.

Swedenborg's credentials, besides the general effect of his writings, are certain cases of telepathy and thought-reading. We cannot explain how he came to know of the fire which took place at Stockholm while he was at Göteborg in July, 1759, or how he discovered Marteville's fire insurance receipt, or the secret about which the Prince of Prussia had written to his sister, Queen Louisa Ulrica of Sweden, just before his death.[33] But we are more accustomed to such strange phenomena now than people were in the last half of the eighteenth century, and we have no reason to think that any persons who seem to possess such powers are necessarily more acquainted with the really important secrets of the universe than others. Indeed, it is not unfair to say that the apparently successful "spiritualist" is almost the last person to whom an inquirer after truth would look for aid in attaining the knowledge of God.

Swedenborg is interesting as a man rather than as a seer. There are beauties in his writings and there are grave defects, especially their occasional coarseness, their frequent triviality and their abundant tediousness. His theology is only explicable and in a measure defensible as a reaction against the sterile orthodoxy of his day. It may help the Church historian to understand the better Gnostics of the primitive Church, and so to obtain a juster view of a long past period by the aid of a recent and familiar experience. But it has clearly no future inside Christendom itself. Swedenborg has no poetry, no

[33] See White : l.c., pp. 343 foll.

music, no humour, no sympathy, though he tells us that he delighted in children. He tells us that he walked and talked with angels, but their conversation was usually somewhat trivial. Emerson well sums up his characteristics: " Swedenborg is disagreeably wise, and with all his accumulated gifts paralyzes and repels " (l.c., p. 111). He is naturally compared with his contemporary, Linnæus, who died six years later. The contrast is sad and striking between the selfish self-centred theosophist, who had reduced heaven and hell to commonplace, but had never found a home on earth, and the warm-hearted, joyous and reverent man of science, surrounded by loving pupils and a happy family, and looking with mingled awe and gladness at the footprints of the Creator in the field of nature.

§ 6.—Gustavus III.: his double character. Progress and degeneracy. The period of neology. Foundation of the Vasa-order (1772) and the Swedish Academy (1786). Bishop Olof Wallquist (1755—1800). Contrast between Gustavus IV. and his father. His hatred of Napoleon and support of England. Deposed 1809. Charles XIII. (1809—1818). Marshal Jean Bernadotte (Prince Karl Johan) adopted as his heir and successor. Political changes in Finland, Pomerania and Norway. The Church of Finland.

Swedenborg's death in 1772 coincided with the *coup d'état* by which the young king, Gustavus III., the nephew of Frederick the Great of Prussia, brought the period of freedom to an end, and restored personal government. Unlike his father, Adolphus Frederick, he was himself born in Sweden, and his talents and his imaginative powers, his openness and ease of manner, and his hard work to restore his country to a high place in Europe, made him at first deservedly popular. He thought of himself as one of the old Vasas returned to lead his people on a triumphant progress.   Many valuable internal reforms took place in his reign.   Torture was abolished.   Laws affecting punishment, especially the death penalty, were made milder.   Freedom was given to the press.   An attempt, though a very blundering one, was made to deal with the prevalent vice of drunkenness. The stringency of the old rules of the trade-guilds was relaxed.   The currency was put on a better footing and commerce prospered, particularly during the time of the war between England and her North American colonies.   Finally, foreigners professing another faith were allowed to exercise their religion, and Jews were permitted to settle in three Swedish towns and enjoy certain civil rights (Odhner : pp. 342-3).   On the other hand, the young king was vain, frivolous, profligate and deceitful.   " The king with two faces," [34] as he has been called, had a French education, and brought much of the pleasure-loving, pleasure-making, festive atmosphere of the French court into Sweden, especially into society in Stockholm.   Here and in his numerous country seats amusement was made a regular business.   He was also an apt pupil of the infidel and rationalistic school which had spread from England, France and Germany over Northern Europe; and his reign of twenty-one years (1771—1792) ushered in what has been justly called the "period of neology."   " Two things (he used to say), love and religion, are free in my kingdom," and infidelity and libertinism were indeed widely propagated by the bad example of the court, especially among the higher classes.   Yet superstition also prevailed.   The king, who mocked at his son's confirmation, used to spend hours of the night in the Riddarholm Church at Stockholm in the hope of obtaining omens from the graves of his ancestors, while his

[34] This is the title of the late Miss M. E. Coleridge's remarkable novel (3rd. ed. 1897).   The writer acknowledges her debt " to Mr. Nisbet Bain's most interesting work, *Gustaf III. and his contemporaries.*"

brother, Duke Charles, promoted the secret societies of
Illuminati, Freemasons, Rosicrucians and the like which
spread largely over Europe during this period. [35] The doctrines of Swedenborg also made a number of converts, some
of them men of piety and ability. But no Swedenborgian
society was recognized in Sweden until the year 1885, and
only a small one now exists.   The period of neology
was nevertheless also a time when, not only law and justice, but art and literature made considerable progress.
There was a spirit of chivalry as well as of frivolity, of
research into, as well as of superficial interest in, the great
problems of life.   It was a time also of foundation in two
directions. The orders of knighthood, like those of the
Garter and the Bath in England, do not appear to be very
old in Sweden.   The statutes of the orders of the Serafim,
of the Sword and the Northern Star date from
1748.   Gustavus III. dignified them by giving them
an Ordens-Biskop as their chaplain.   To these older
orders he added the Vasa-order in the year of his
coup d'état (1772), for the useful purpose of rewarding
merit of a more civil character "in regard to agriculture,
mining, fine arts and commerce, or through writings
which have done eminent service to the State in these
directions."   There can be no doubt that there was a
revival of something more than mere romanticism, which
might have led to much greater things if the king's character had not been perverted by evil influences around
him.   The latter part of his reign saw the foundation of
the Swedish Academy, in imitation of that of France, in
the year 1786.   Its motto, "genius and taste" (snille och
smak), shows that it was intended to be literary rather than
scientific; in fact, it was designed mainly to concern itself
with languages.   But it has been of great service to
Sweden, though the taste which it promoted in its early
years was not always the best.   It has, unlike English
institutions of the same kind, administered a considerable
income, which is used for the encouragement of literature.

[35] See *Sv. Hist.*[1], VI., 284-307, *Gustaf III.'s hof.*

The most prominent ecclesiastic in this and the next reign was Olof Wallquist (1755—1800), Bishop of Vexiö, a politician and a financier, who, when scarcely more than thirty years old, became leader of the Riksdag and the Church. Under him a new office was created, the " Ekklesiastik expedition," intended to prepare all Church business for the consideration of the king. It did not last very long, but it paved the way for the ministry of public worship which was afterwards created. Wallquist, who was a man of literary ability and piety, an effective preacher of the school of Bälter, was an opponent of neology. He died worn out with hard work at the early age of forty-four in the year 1800. His autobiography has been published, and gives the picture of a very modern mind.

When Gustavus III., who had made himself absolute in 1789, and had thereby earned the hatred of the nobility, was assassinated at a masked ball in 1792, he left his brother, Duke Charles, as regent for his young son, Gustavus IV. Gustavus III. was naturally a supporter of the Bourbons, and was preparing to go to war to restore them to the throne. Duke Charles entirely changed this policy. He favoured the French Republicans. He also at first sought an alliance with Russia by agreeing to betroth his nephew to a young Grand Duchess. But when the hour arrived the young king was absent, and the reason was given that he was unwilling to allow his future bride a chapel for her own religion, which was one of the articles of the contract. But the stronger reason was, I presume, a political one.

Gustavus IV., when he became responsible for the government, was a great contrast to his father. He was simple in his tastes, averse to extravagance, and upright in private life. But he was narrow, obstinate and barren in conception and initiation, and dreamy in his religion. His great principle was hatred of Napoleon, whom he regarded as the Beast of the Apocalypse.

Englishmen have reason, indeed, to speak and think

well of Gustavus IV. You will remember how, in 1807,
Napoleon fascinated the young Emperor of Russia,
Alexander I., and, by the peace of Tilsit and the secret
conventions that accompanied it, appeared to have reduced
the whole Continent of Europe to obedience to his single
will. You will remember how the supreme necessity of the
situation justified Nelson's attack on Copenhagen, which
prevented Denmark from joining in the so-called " Continental system," Napoleon's plan for excluding all British
trade with the rest of Europe. Sweden, under Gustavus
IV., in the extreme north, and Portugal, in the extreme
west, were then our only allies, for Prussia was humbled,
and Russia was bribed by hopes of extension to the east
and in Finland. You will not, then, be surprised that I
recall with pleasure the tribute paid to the last sovereign
but one of the Vasa line by a contemporary poet, William
Wordsworth, who wrote two sonnets in his praise in the
series of *Poems dedicated to National Independence and
Liberty.* The second and finest of them thus begins:—

> Call not the royal Swede unfortunate
>   Who never did to Fortune bend the knee;
>   Who slighted fear; rejected steadfastly
> Temptation; and whose kingly name and state
> Have " perished by his choice and not his fate."

Unfortunately the King of Sweden had no military
genius, and, when the Russians overran Finland, and both
Russians and Danes were ready to invade Sweden, his
countrymen deposed him in 1809, and gave the crown to
his uncle, Charles XIII. Charles was an old man, and
had no children. A successor was chosen in the person
of a young and popular prince of Augustenburg, who
died quite suddenly in the next year. Then, happily for
Sweden, and indeed for Europe, under circumstances
which read like something out of a fairy-tale, the choice
fell upon one of the bravest and most successful of
Napoleon's generals, Marshal Jean Bernadotte, Prince of
Ponte Corvo, from whom the present royal family is
descended. Napoleon made some difficulty in granting

his consent, and at last gave the required permission with the ominous words " Go, then, and let us fulfil our several destinies." His former general, under the title of Prince Karl Johan, quickly became a Swede both in religion and in sympathies, and soon felt it necessary to renounce the conflict with England, to which Napoleon had pledged him, and to enter into an alliance with Russia and Germany, which involved, of course (at this time), a war with his old master. The prince won the affections of the people in an extraordinary manner. All the young men of the nation were enrolled as soldiers. The prince formed the plan of campaign for the allied forces, and took command of the northern army. He defeated Napoleon's troops in two engagements at Gross-Beeren and Danewitz, south of Berlin. Then the two other armies concentrated, with the northern army, on Leipzig, and the terrible and prolonged conflict there in 1813 led up to the final freedom of Europe. The result was, in the end, that Finland, which for 600 years had been united to Sweden, had to be ceded to Russia, while Pomerania, the only continental province which remained of all the conquests of the Stormakstid, was sold to Prussia for a sum of money which was rightly used to pay foreign loans. On the other hand, Norway was disjoined from Denmark in 1814, and united to Sweden, under a constitution, which lasted until the bloodless revolution of 1905 in our own day.

The loss of Finland, though it was perhaps not very important politically, was a considerable one to the Church. It had given the Church a wider and broader outlook, and a variety of experience, and a number of valuable public men. The succession of bishops continued for many years, but unfortunately a time came when there was a break, and the Russian government did not permit a succession to be renewed from Sweden. In 1869 the Church of Finland ceased to be a State Church, and received its constitution as the free Church of the people. The office of bishop is preserved, and the chapters continue, but without the professorial element which is so strong in the

23

Swedish chapters. There is also a general council, which meets every ten years, the first being held in 1876.[36] The experience of the disestablished Church of Finland may, some day, be valuable to the Mother Church of Sweden.

§ 7.—UNFORTUNATE REVISION OF THE PRAYER BOOK AND CATECHISM IN THE TIME OF NEOLOGY (1772—1818). ARCHBISHOPS UNO VON TROIL (1746—1803) AND J. A. LINDBLOM (1746—1818). THE REVISED PRAYER BOOK ISSUED IN 1811. A CONFIRMATION SERVICE PRESCRIBED. ITS CHARACTER. NEW FORM OF 1894. UNFORTUNATE CHANGE IN THE ORDINATION OF PRIESTS. IMPROVEMENT IN 1894. FORMS OF CONFIRMATION IN U.S.A.

It was a great misfortune for Sweden that the self-importance of the period of neology and the bad taste which accompanied it led at this time to a revision of the Prayer Book and Catechism. For in it taste, liturgical knowledge and Church feeling were all at a low ebb. This revision was carried out under the direction and with the imprimatur of two archbishops, first of the learned historian, Uno von Troil, and then Jacob Axelsson Lindblom, the stately and popular Bishop of Linköping, afterwards archbishop (1805—1819). The Prayer Book was altered, notwithstanding the protest of the pious and influential Upsala professor, Samuel Ödman, who pointed out the danger of tampering with forms venerable by their antiquity. The revised Prayer Book, which had been in preparation since 1793, was, however, issued with royal sanction in 1811. It had one improvement, namely, the introduction of a service for the first communion for young people, which was regularly known by the name of confirmation. This form did not adhere so closely to tradition as some of those which had been practically, though not compulsorily, in use in the seven-

[36] E. Bergroth : *Finska Kyrkans Historia*, pp. 270-1.

teenth and eighteenth centuries. It contained no imposition of hands, and it was to be administered by the pastor with no reference to the bishop or his visitation, and the blessing was not at all specially appropriate. It had, however, a touching and suitable prayer to our Lord to keep His children in dangers and temptations. Even as it was it met with considerable opposition.

The most recent form of this rite, adopted in 1894, is certainly better. It has the following appropriate scriptural benediction before the Lord's Prayer: "The Father of our Lord Jesus Christ give you according to the riches of His glory that ye may be strengthened with might through His Spirit in the inner man and filled with all the fulness of God." A prayer based on the one I have already mentioned follows the Lord's Prayer. The form is, therefore, clearly sufficient. It has, however, no imposition of hands. I am informed that in some dioceses at least a commission to confirm is contained in the letters of priests orders, and, therefore, it may be said that priests perform this duty as deputies of the bishop. Laying on of hands is also used by some priests just before they administer the first communion. I am inclined to think that in one or two dioceses the rite is still administered occasionally by bishops.

But the greatest blot upon the new Prayer Book of 1811 was the alteration which it made in the service for the ordination of priests. Happily, the service for the consecration of a bishop was not essentially changed. It was called "How a bishop shall be set in his office" (Huru en Biskop i Ämbetet skall inställas) and the word consecration was not used. But it was clearly a service for consecrating a new bishop not merely one for his enthronement. It was taken for granted that consecration to a bishop's office is coincident, as it generally is, with his entrance into a particular see. That an act of primary appointment is in question is shown also by the fact that the person to be "set in office" appears first clothed only in a surplice or rochet. He does not receive the pectoral cross and staff, and is not vested in the cope, until after the office of bishop is formally committed to him just before the laying on of hands and the Lord's Prayer. The Prayer Book of 1811 was, I believe, the first in which the pectoral cross was mentioned.

For the ordination of a priest, however, we unfortunately find the phrase " Invigning till Prediko-Ämbetet," substituted for the old title " till Prest-Ämbetet ": that is to say, " consecration to ministerial office," instead of " to priestly office." On the other hand, it is right to remember (1) that the intention to make a priest is clearly shown by the use of the chasuble, in which the ordinand is vested after the delivery of the office and before the laying on of hands and the Lord's Prayer; (2) that the word " priest " is found continually in the other services of this Prayer Book; for instance, in those for baptism, holy communion, marriage, burial, etc.; (3) that the sections in the Church-law referring to the priesthood remained unaltered, and that in Swedish literature, dictionaries, etc., the words are considered to be synonymous, and to connote the ministry of the *Word and Sacraments*, and not merely the ministry of the *Word*. The " ministry," as described in the Augsburg Confession and other symbolical books, is never restricted to preaching. This blot has happily been removed in the Prayer Book of 1894.

The modern form of ordination of a priest is as follows: After an introductory hymn and prayers and the recitation of the names of those to be ordained, certain passages of Holy Scripture bearing on the office are read, and commended to the attention of the ordinands. Then a confession of faith is made in terms of the Apostles' Creed, and certain questions are put, including the following, which refers to the special formularies of the Swedish Church:—" Will you, according to your best understanding and conscience, purely and clearly proclaim God's Word as it is given to us in the Holy Scripture, and as our Church's confessional writings witness thereto?"

Then comes the act of ordination: " May God Almighty strengthen and help you to keep these promises! and according to the power which in God's stead is intrusted unto me by His Church (af hans församling) in this behalf, I commit unto you herewith the office of priest, in the name of God the Father, and of the Son and of the Holy Ghost. Amen."

Then follows a hymn to the Holy Spirit, during which the bishop gives the ordinands their letters of orders, they are vested in their chasubles, and kneel down to receive the laying on of hands from the bishop and the assistants, and then the bishop says for each of them separately the Lord's Prayer, which, in Sweden, is applied with special intention to each of the sacramental or ritual acts. Then the bishop says a prayer towards the altar beseeching God to look graciously on those His servants, who now are consecrated to His service in the holy office of priesthood, and to give them His Holy Spirit, and to strengthen them to fight for His kingdom and to perform the duties of their calling. An English Churchman will naturally miss here a reference to the ministry of the Word and Sacraments, though, I believe, that this is referred to in the letters of orders, as it is in the Church-law, as well, of course, as in the Augsburg Confession. In any case the sufficiency of the form at present used cannot be doubted.

We must be thankful that the recent revision has gone as far as it has done in its return to ancient models. I am glad also to know that some Swedish congregations in the United States have admitted the English confirmation blessing which was used in Sweden by the well-known Bishop of Strengnäs, Johannes Matthiæ (1643—1664).[37]

[37] See F. N. Ekdahl: *Om Confirmationen*, p. 103, Lund., 1889, quoted Lecture VI., § 10, note 50, and *Kyrko-handbok för Sw. Ev. Luth. Kyrkan i Amerika*, see p. 261 of the English part of this interesting book, ed. 2, published by the Engberg-Holmberg Publishing Co., Chicago, 1893, and drawn up by a committee of Lutheran divines in that city. After the ques-

The Augustana Synod permits, though it does not enforce, the laying on of hands which has long been in use in Denmark.

It is also to be noticed that in the Apostles' Creed the Prayer Book of 1894 translates " Catholic " by " universal " (all-männelig) as the agreement of Upsala in 1593 had done. In 1811 the word used had been " Christian."

tions, " *The candidates then all kneel around the altar, and the minister proceeds to lay his hand solemnly on the head of each, saying*: Defend, O Lord, etc. (printed at length).   *Or* The Father, of mercies ever multiply unto you His grace and peace, enable you truly and faithfully to keep your vows, defend you in every time of danger, preserve you faithful unto the end, and bring you to rest with all His saints in glory everlasting. Amen."   Or they may be admitted with the right hand of fellowship.   There is no direct prayer for the gift of the Holy Spirit.   The Augustana Synod, since 1895, has naturally to a large extent adopted the Swedish revised book, but it has not prohibited this one.   In the book now authorized by it the following rubric is inserted after the Lord's Prayer and prayer for protection : " Where laying on of hands is in use the priest lays his hand on every child's head and pronounces a suitable sentence of Scripture, for example the apostolic benediction." See *Kyrko Handbok för Augustana-Synoden, Antagen, 1895,* Rock Island, Illinois, p. 80.

VIII.

THE MODERN PERIOD (1812 A.D.—1910 A.D.).

LECTURE VIII.

THE MODERN PERIOD (1812 A.D.—1910 A.D.).

§ 1.—DEVELOPMENT OF CHURCH LIFE. THE (OLD) READERS (1760—1780). REVIVAL OF PIETY WITHIN THE CHURCH. SAMUEL ÖDMAN (1750—1829) AT UPSALA AND HENRIK SCHARTAU (1757—1825) AT LUND. STRONG AND WEAK POINTS OF SCHARTAU.[1]

The period of neology, which was described in my last lecture, with its claim to freedom of thought and opinion, naturally gave an opening to the development of Free Church life among the older sects of Moravians and Pietists. It also saw the appearance of a new sect, that of the Readers (1760—1780), in the northern provinces. They were so called from their private meetings to read the Bible, the writings of Luther and the postils of Anders Nohrborg, " The way of salvation for fallen man " (Cp. Lect. VII., § 4). From Herjedal, on the Norwegian frontier, this revival, which had in it something of a much needed temperance movement, passed to Helsingland and then to the south to Småland. But it largely degenerated into fanaticism, especially at its wild nightly meetings. The readers were often seized with epileptic fits and convulsions, and, like our own ranters, often gave vent to deep sighs and groans, which were taken as signs of the presence of the Holy Spirit.

[1] In writing the following sections, I have made special use of Bishop Fr. Nielsen's article, *Der Protestantismus in den Nordischen Landen*, in Werckshagen's *Der Protestantismus*, Vol. II., pp. 997-1003.

The Church was naturally stimulated to oppose such excesses and to supply something better in the way of religious zeal and fervour. The two university cities of Lund and Upsala were, in this period, as in many others, centres of healthy reaction in the persons of the two contemporaries, Henrik Schartau (1757—1825) and Samuel Ödman (1750—1829). The latter was a professor of theology and an eminent naturalist, a pupil of the celebrated Linnæus. He wrote much, but he exercised an even greater influence by the bright example of his patient teaching from his sick bed, on which he lay for about forty years. He lectured in his little bedroom to generation after generation of students. Schartau,[2] though he wrote unceasingly, published nothing during his life, and he, too, exercised an immense personal influence, but over a much wider circle than Ödman. He was a pastor whose chief work was at Lund, not a university professor. The great merit of his teaching was that it was strong and spiritual, and without the defects of Moravian or Pietistic sentimentality. Unlike the preachers of these schools, he held his head high, and looked you well in the face. He had a strong instinct of command, which he found it difficult to check. To personal humility he added a deep sense of the dignity of his vocation and of the importance of asserting it in his great business of guiding souls. His thought was clear and definite, and when he gave advice he expected it to be obeyed. He was as powerful in his own study, where he spent long hours in ministering to the anxious and the penitent, as he was in the pulpit or the choir, preaching or catechizing. The latter was one of his strongest points. He impressed at once learned professors and simple country folk, who thronged the cathedral from all the district round Lund. Many of his spiritual letters have been preserved and published since his death.

[2] Besides Nielsen, I have made use of an interesting and life-like sketch of Schartau, by Dr. N. Söderblom, in *Ord och Bild*, pp. 514-27, 1907. See also Edv. Rodhe: *H. Schartau såsom predikant*, Lund., 1909.

They may be compared, I imagine, to those of Fénelon in France and Keble and Pusey in England, especially to those of the latter. He had something of the character of Dr. Pusey in his relation to those who consulted him, but, in his position at Lund, and his general influence, he was perhaps more like his English contemporary, Charles Simeon (1759—1836), at Cambridge. He set himself to develop strength and reverence apart from sentimentality, and in this way he separated himself from the Pietists, and he valued the Church, and the sacraments and ordinances of the Church, in a way that they often failed to do. His conversion, if we may call it so, came to him in hearing the absolution pronounced by a very ordinary priest in the communion service, and the powerful ministry of this rite in public or private was one of the most characteristic features of his own career.

His fault, which was exaggerated by his followers, was a certain constant reference to the forms and divisions of logic and to the inward state of the soul—in other words to psychology. This led to a curious and anxious introspection, to a balancing of motives and convictions, and to the requirement of a conscious ascent through certain stages of progress, which was not altogether healthy. In his followers these characteristics have produced a certain dryness and tediousness, and, it is said, too great a dependence on the " direction " of the chosen spiritual guide. But there can be no doubt of the depth of the influence of Schartau and his best disciples. And this influence, being deep, is also abiding, though popular favour is no longer strong for the system which he inaugurated.

§ 2.—E. G. GEIJER (1783—1847), THE HISTORIAN, AND HIS
    CONTEMPORARIES. HIS SERVICES TO RELIGIOUS
    THOUGHT. FRANZÉN, BISHOP OF HERNÖSAND
    (1772—1847). ESAIAS TEGNÉR, BISHOP OF
    VEXIÖ (1782—1846), AND J. O. WALLIN, ARCH-
    BISHOP (1779—1839). HIS GREATNESS AS A
    PREACHER AND HYMN WRITER.

Almost as important as the work of Schartau for the regeneration of Swedish religious thought must, I think, be
set the influence of one who was not by any means
primarily a theologian, Eric Gustaf Geijer (1783—1847).
His essay *On False and True Enlightenment in Relation
to Religion* marked an epoch in the religious revival. It
was published as early as 1811, and had an immense
influence over the whole of the rising generation of intellectual men, which was beginning to look for something
better than the free thought of the French Revolution. Of this essay H. Reuterdahl, the most important
theologian in Sweden of the first half of the nineteenth century, wrote : " It was this treatise that thirty years ago
attracted a great part of the younger generation of Sweden
to inward and spiritual things. It was as important to
Sweden, though in a somewhat less degree, as Schleiermacher's speeches about religion for Germany. Acquaintance with this treatise was for many (as for myself) the
cause of their passage from an unconscious to a conscious
and riper life." [3]   Geijer was not only the greatest historian
of Sweden, but he wrote in a philosophical and imaginative spirit which has been too often deficient in the literary
men of his native country. He was a poet, orator and
musical composer, and, therefore, found many points of

---

[3] Quoted in *P.R.E.*[3], 18, p. 39, s.v. *Schweden*, article by
Gustaf Aulén. The same writer has published an important
monograph, *H. Reuterdahl's Teologiska åskådning med särskild
hänsyn till hans ställning till Schleiermacher,* Uppsala, 1907.
He speaks there also of Geijer's influence, pp. 14 foll., but shows
that Schleiermacher's was greater.

contact with his three famous contemporaries, **F. M.**
Franzén (1772—1847), the pious and sympathetic Bishop
of Hernösand; Esaias Tegnér (1782—1846), Bishop of
Vexiö, the most popular poet of Sweden, and the still more
important Johan Olof Wallin (1779—1839), at first bishop
in connection with the Order of the Seraphim, and then
Archbishop of Upsala.

Geijer was a man of a good Austrian family which can
be traced back to the thirteenth century. Two members of
this family were invited into Sweden by Gustavus
Adolphus in 1620, in order to direct the work of mining, to
which he rightly attached so much importance.

It cannot be doubted that this fact inspired Geijer with
an interest in the past, and that his German extraction enabled him more readily than his contemporaries to take an
independent point of view. He was familiar with foreign
literature, and passed from youthful admiration of
Rousseau and Schiller to that of Shakespeare and Goethe.
A journey to England, where he spent a year (1809—1810)
as tutor to a young Von Schinkel, had a great effect in
enlarging his mind and developing his principles as a
thinker. The greater part of Geijer's life was passed as
professor at Upsala, and he was wise enough to refuse a
bishopric which was twice offered him, saying: "You
might perhaps get a blameless and mediocre bishop, but
all would be over with Eric Gustaf Geijer." He was never
in holy orders, though he had once seriously thought of
it as a career. In the essay already referred to he fought
with weapons taken from German philosophy and
especially from Schelling against the conception of religion which prevailed in the period of rationalism. In
philosophical language he asserted that the fundamental
fact of experience is not the ego and the non-ego (I and
not I), but "I and thou"—the "two self-luminous beings" to which John Henry Newman referred in a famous
passage of his *Apologia*. His principle was that history
was a continuous manifestation of God founded on religion, and "only for a religious person is there a

history." He was a most inspiring lecturer on this subject. All the persons about whom he read and their actions became living to himself, and he conveyed this sense of life to his hearers. He did not create the taste for history in Sweden which had long existed, and which Dalin had done something to improve, but he profoundly modified the conception of what true history is, and induced many to take an interest in it who would otherwise have regarded it as dry and tasteless.[4]

Geijer was not exactly orthodox either as regards the Bible or the Church, and some of his followers, such as K. P. Wikner (1837—1888), went further than he did, epecially in his book *Thoughts and Questions in the Presence of (inför) the Son of Man*—a book which attracted many readers and raised much controversy.

Of the bishops of this period Wallin is undoubtedly the most important. His speech as a young man at the first anniversary of the Bible Society in 1816 made almost as much impression as Geijer's essay, yet it was only on the text which, to us, seems so natural, that it is wrong and irrational to put " the Supreme Being " in the place of the living God. As a preacher, according to his contemporary, Tegnér, he was unrivalled. His power of speaking was enhanced by an original method of delivery, into which he introduced an accent different from that in common use, while his language vibrated with poetry.[5] His powerful voice sounded like a message from another world. It roused the sleeping conscience; it seemed to compel obedience. As a poet he is best known by the new hymn-

---

[4] The reader may remember an often quoted passage in which Geijer describes his early life. It is translated in Mary Howitt's book, *Literature and Romance of Northern Europe*, *II.*, pp. 366-9. He wrote in secret for the Academy's prize, an eulogy on Sten Sturé the elder, and complained that he had only access to Dalin's crabbed pages—but he won the prize.

[5] See Howitt's *Literature and Romance of Northern Europe*, Vol. II., p. 339 foll. On Tegner, see H. H. Boyesen, *Essays on Scandinavian Literature*, 219-288.

book which is at present still in use. It was brought out by him in 1819, and contains five hundred hymns, of which a hundred and fifty were written or translated by himself. Of his single poems " The Angel of Death "—a majestic and terrible poem, written at the time of the cholera, but ending with a hopeful note—is the best known. Wallin died himself in harness. He had once experienced a delightful time of quiet work in an irresponsible position in his first pastorate, and had often longed for similar repose from the responsibilities and conflicts of his high office. But only death brought release from them. The following quatrain from his great poem is his epitaph :—

> Earth's unrest ends,
> Sure peace remains ;
> Death makes all friends,
> Heaven all explains.[6]

§ 3.—EVANGELICAL MOVEMENTS OF THE NINETEENTH CENTURY DERIVED FROM PIETISM. LARGELY ORIGINATE IN NORTHERN SWEDEN. THE " NEW READERS " OPPOSE THE BOOKS OF 1810—1811. BECOME ANTINOMIAN AND SEPARATIST. LARS LEVI LÆSTADIUS (1800—1861) IN THE EXTREME NORTH. HIS LEGALISM. CHANGE AFTER HIS DEATH. ERIK JANSSON (1808—1850) IN HELSINGLAND. HIS COLONY, BISHOPS HILL, IN U.S.A. DOCTRINE OF SINLESSNESS. ROSÉNIUS (1816—1868). SKETCH OF HIS LIFE BY BISHOP NIELSEN. P. P. WALDENSTRÖM (b. 1838). THE " SVENSKA MISSIONS FÖRBUNDET " FOUNDED 1878. ITS WORK.

I must not attempt to give details of all the movements of religious thought in Sweden during the nineteenth century, especially of those of more recent years. It will

---

[6] See Carl Grimberg : *Sv. Hist.*, p. 574. The original is :—

> Jordens oro viker
> För den frid som varar.
> Graven allt förlikar ;
> Himeln allt förklarar.

suffice to indicate the main directions, both of those which may be called evangelical and social and those which are more distinctly ecclesiastical.

The evangelical movements may be considered as more or less derived from the Pietism which, as we have seen, entered Sweden after the Church law became more stringent under Charles XI., and especially in company with the returning soldiers who had been taken prisoners in the wars of Charles XII. It is a striking fact that these movements, like many older ones in Sweden, were generally initiated in the northern provinces, and often by men of northern birth. This is the case with the " New Readers," with Lars Levi Læstadius, with the prophets of Helsingland, and with Rosénius and Lektor Waldenström. They took, however, different forms, and it is necessary to distinguish one from the other.

The earliest of these movements, that of the " new readers," took at its beginning the form of a protest against the Catechism and Prayer Book put out by Archbishop Lindblom, and prescribed by authority in the year 1810 and 1811 respectively. It arose in Norrland, particularly in the neighbourhood of the coast towns of Piteå and Skellefteå. The " Old Readers " had not separated from the Church, but the new sect, after a time, were eagerly desirous to do so. About the year 1848 they began to administer their own sacraments. They professed to be enthusiastic for " pure doctrine," as against the unorthodoxy of the State Church, and they pressed justification by faith to an antinomian extreme. For instance, a soldier from Piteå, who became one of their leaders, asserted that a man could have saving faith, even when sin and a love of this world were ruling in his heart; while John Roström, a peasant preacher (who died in 1868), denounced the clergy of the established Church as false prophets.

The movement which is connected with the name of Lars Levi Læstadius (1800—1861) was, at any rate in its inception, of a very different character. He was a learned man and an eminent botanist,[7] skilled above all other men of his age in the power of distinguishing certain forms of northern vegetation, such as those of the "salices" or willow-tribe. He was sent as pastor to the northernmost corner of Sweden, beyond Haparanda, where he found the people sunk in vice, especially that of drunkenness. He preached the law, therefore, rather than the Gospel. He strongly inculcated public confession of sin, and he used largely the methods of absolution and excommunication. He strove also to make sin loathsome by his cynical descriptions of its effects. But his realistic language while it touched the common people was very distasteful to the educated. His preaching proved for a time very effective; but his revival was connected with the strange outward manifestations in which fanaticism has so often expressed itself—convulsive movements of the body, loud cries and groans, ecstatic embracings, dances, fainting fits and the like.

Excesses arose into which it was necessary to inquire, and the visitation of the good Bishop of Hernösand, Israel Bergman, the successor of Franzén, did justice to all that was healthy in the movement and its much-loved chief. Læstadius died in 1861, and his followers than turned round from the legal view of religion to a kind of hyper-evangelical belief, and to a close sectarianism, according to which salvation was limited to their own body. The cries, which at first were occasional, became a regular accompaniment of public worship, and took the form of wolf-like howls "hih! huh!" from which the popular name "Hihuliter" has been derived. Nevertheless, as the Læstadians are not officially registered as a sect, there is some hope of their restoration to the National Church.

[7] The *Biographist Lexicon* and the *Nordisk Familjebok* practically only recognize him as a botanist. The Church histories, of course, describe his religious work, and there is a full account in Cornelius : *Hist.*, § 226-32. There is also a larger life by J. A. Englund : *Lars Levi Læstadius : en Kyrklig tidsbild* (extracted from the *Teologisk Tidskrift*), Upsala, 1876.

Doubtless Bishop Bergman's gentleness will have done much to contribute to this result if it be achieved.

Erik Jansson (1808—1850) was himself born in the province of Upsala, but he found acceptance as a prophet in Helsingland, north of Dalarne. At first he was in spirit a "reader;" that is, he spent his time and that of his followers in reading the Bible and the writings of Luther and the Pietists, Arndt, Nohrborg and Murbeck. But, after a time, when he had adopted the doctrine that all true Christians are sinless, he threw over all his teachers, and declared himself the real prophet of the faith: "I am the only true preacher since the Apostles' time" (Cornelius: *Hist.*, § 236). The community which he formed transferred itself to the United States in 1845—1846, where the colony of "Bishops Hill" was founded near Galesburg, Illinois, receiving its name from the founder's birthplace, Biskopskulla. A system of communism was introduced, over which, however, the prophet had financial control to the detriment of the society. He was shot dead in 1850 by one of his followers, who was jealous of his interference in his domestic concerns. In the next ten years the sect broke up. It is interesting as one of the earliest Swedish settlements in North America in the last century, but it appears to have had less root than almost any of the other religious movements of which we have been speaking.

The last of these movements which I shall mention is that of Rosénius (1816—1868), who was, like Læstadius, born in Vesterbotten in the diocese of Hernösand. In 1840 he allied himself with the English Methodist, Scott, in Stockholm, and worked there till his death. This movement is of great importance, as it approached much closer to normal Christianity, and was free from the excesses of the other sects. It also paved the way for the most important of modern Free Church movements in Sweden, that of which Lektor Waldenström is the leader, in the "Swedish Missionary Covenant" (Svenska Missions Förbundet), founded in 1878.

I shall, therefore, extract some pages from an excellent essay by the Danish Bishop Nielsen on the modern history of *Protestantism in the Northern Lands,* from which I have already drawn some material.

Karl Olof Rosenius was son of a clergyman in Piteå [in the diocese of Hernösand]. The father was a friend of the "Readers," and the young Rosenius was early introduced into the circle of the "awakened" or converted laity. Already, as a student in Hernösand, he gathered into his room a circle of such comrades. During a visit to his home, he made the acquaintance of Maja Söderlund, a remarkable woman, who had gained a great name by her Bible classes in the neighbouring country. She became, as it were, his priest and the confidant of his soul. In 1836, at the age of twenty, he began, with Bishop Franzén's dispensation, to preach in his native town, but his course of study in Upsala went on slowly. The worldly life of the students did not please him, and poverty, as well as illness, hindered his work. In 1839 he accepted a place as tutor in the house of a nobleman, but there he fell into doubt and temptation. He was ashamed to open his heart to his friends, but rather sought for comfort and help in the Methodist preacher, Georg Scott, in Stockholm. With the assistance of this man he overcame his doubts, and soon began to preach again, filled with depressing experiences of his own misery and his own littleness, but also supported by a strong faith in the unmerited grace of God. Scott saw the young man's ability; but instead of advising him to complete his studies, and become a preacher in the established Church of Sweden, he drew him into a situation as a free-preacher in the Church which had been formed by his own numerous friends. . . . . Rosenius confessed to Maja Söderlund that the reason why he had given up all thoughts of taking Holy Orders was that it only seemed to be good for those who wished to be "dumb dogs."

From 1840 he worked in Stockholm as a lay-preacher, without being ordained. He gathered many round the pulpit in the new Methodist Church, and in 1842, he began, together with Scott, to publish the periodical called *The Pietist,* which soon found 5,000 subscribers. The name of the periodical was, properly speaking, an erroneous one, for Rosenius was no Pietist. The powerful sermons, which were preached by him and by Scott, excited great commotion in the town, and on Palm Sunday, 1842, a crowd of people pressed into the church and drove Scott down from the pulpit by throwing stones; in particular they accused him of speaking contemptuously about

Sweden and the Swedes. The church had to be closed for the time, and Scott left Stockholm secretly, so that Rosenius was now sole leader of the revival in the Swedish capital.

In the following ten years he contented himself by holding religious assemblies in private houses, and in hired rooms; then his friends bought Scott's church for him, and called it "Bethlehem Church," and there Rosenius worked till his death as lay-preacher, joined by many from all directions. His light and manly figure, his honest and grave expression, his deep feeling and his lively imagination brought great crowds when he preached of "the pure unmerited grace in Christ Jesus" and summoned individuals to seize that grace, saying "Come entirely as you are." Many were prepared for such a sermon by the "Readers," and the simple and gentle spirit which reigned in the services of the Bethlehem Church, exercised a powerful attraction on many who had not felt satisfied by the stiff sermons of the Pietists and Schartauans. Soon Rosenius' congregation obtained their singer in "Oscar Ahnfeld," whose hymns with tunes, easy to sing, became known in the three northern kingdoms.

The circle which generally gathered to hear Rosenius' sermons about "free grace" and "the sweet Gospel," stood in a very loose relation to the established Church. Rosenius himself did not secede from the established Church, and did not advise his followers to do so, but he had no good words for the "External Church," and for the preachers of the established Church, who were for the most part, hirelings in his sight. "The little flock," the conventicles, were enough for him, but he always desired the Holy Communion in the established Church, and also had his children baptized there. He died young, exhausted by spiritual work, and his followers did not separate. The lay preachers continued his work and spread the gospel of "unmerited grace" and his other hyper-Evangelical doctrines. His writings, especially his voluminous *Commentary on the Epistle to the Romans*, and his *Family Prayer-book*, seemed to many in the three northern kingdoms, the best reading for quiet hours, next to Holy Scripture. The *Family Prayer-book* alone had a circulation of 30,000 copies in Denmark and Norway. Through Bornholm, Rosenius' ideas found entrance into Denmark, and the neighbouring parts of Germany; and Denmark, as well as Norway, have also some "Bornholmists" who are as slack in relation to the Danish and Norwegian Church, as Rosenius to the Swedish. . . .

After the death of Rosenius, the publication of the *Pietist* was taken over by Lektor Paul Peter Waldenström in Gefle (born at Luleå in 1838).[8] He preached at first at Bethlehem Church in Gefle as a decided follower of Rosenius. But the way in which Rosenius' disciples spoke of the expiatory death of Christ "for all" excited him to contradiction, and in 1872 he came forward with a subjective doctrine of atonement. This caused a rupture between him and part of Rosenius' friends, but Waldenström found new followers just because of his rejection of the old doctrine of atonement.

At first he was averse to "Communion guilds," which the awakened laity had formed in order to be able to "Break the Bread" at home in their houses. But when once his request to hold Holy Communion for his friends in a church of the town was refused [by Archbishop Sundberg] he accepted the "free Breaking of Bread" as part of his own programme. Upon that his followers collected 22,000 signatures to a petition in favour of a free celebration of the Lord's Supper, as well as of freedom in spreading the Word; but it was refused. In spite of the refusal, the assemblies for Holy Communion increased in number and in strength, and in 1878, Waldenström succeeded in uniting the greatest part of the free Church Swedes into the so-called "Swedish Mission Covenant," which built chapel after chapel everywhere in Sweden—just as the Home Mission in Denmark built mission houses. But while the discord continually increased between the free Church Swedes and the Swedish established Church, the Home Mission of Denmark has, up to the present time, generally been on friendly terms with the National Church of Denmark and her preachers, owing principally to William Beck's firm hold over ritual and his consistent Lutheranism.

On Sunday, 26th September, 1909, I visited Lektor Waldenström, the Wesley of Sweden, at his new mission house in Lidingö—a pretty island suburb of Stockholm. He has a remarkable face, broad and strong, and smiling, and a fresh colour after 72 years of life. His head is large and his hair thick, while the eyelids droop obliquely from the nose and partly cover the eyes. He received me very courteously, and readily answered all questions that I ventured to address to him. His society is still nominally within the Church, that is to say its members have not officially registered themselves as separatists, and they

8 I owe to the kindness of my friend, Rev. Mats Åmark, a copy of *Paul Peter Waldenström en teckning af hans lif af en Samtida*, Stockholm, Fredengren, 1900

continue to pay their Church dues.   In consequence of this he is an elected member of the Representative Church Council.   What will be the future of his society it is not easy for a foreigner to prophesy.   He has a large following of about 100,000 members or adherents, and 1,200 to 1,500 chapels or prayer-houses (Bön-huser) scattered over every part of the country.

He or his son (I forget which) was good enough to tell me something of his experiences in Norrland, where he learnt to preach in the style of Luther by continually reading aloud to the people in Umeå and its neighbourhood. He found that this was what still interested them more than anything else, to hear Luther's commentaries and postils read aloud for hours together.   The mission house is an excellent building, and it prepares men and women both for home and foreign missions.   The society has stations in the Congo State, in the Hu-peh province of China (on the Yang-tse Kiang), and at Kashgar in East Turkestan and elsewhere.[9]

It has thus, like the Moravian brotherhood, a strong missionary activity to keep it sweet and to save it from the narrowing influences which have beset sectarian bodies everywhere, and, not least of all, in Sweden.   An English Churchman cannot but pray that some place may still be found for it inside the National Church, and that the reconciliation may not be too long delayed.   I have not heard that Lektor Waldenström has any very clearly-marked successor to whom he would naturally bequeath the direction of his society.

---

[9] See *Något i ord och bild om Svenska Missions förbundets Mission*, Stockholm, 1909, a report on *The Congo Mission of the Swedish Missionary Society* (1909), and *The Mission Field in Russia and Chinese Turkestan* (for Edinburgh M. Conference, 1910).

§ 4.—SOCIAL PROGRESS. THE TEMPERANCE MOVEMENT
AND DR. PETER WIESELGREN (1800—1897). HE
BEGINS AS A 'SCHOOLBOY. HIS WORK AS A PASTOR.
THE MOVEMENT BECOMES POPULAR. LAW OF
1854. NEW TEMPERANCE MOVEMENT, c. 1880.
MOVEMENT FOR THE EMANCIPATION OF WOMEN.
FREDERICA BREMER, THE NOVELIST. NEED FOR
WOMEN TO FIND WORK OUTSIDE THE HOME.

With these evangelical movements it is natural to connect the movements for social reform, with which many of
them have been in a measure connected. The work of
Lars Levi Læstadius was, as we have seen, largely directed
against drunkenness in the North. But the general temperance movement in Sweden had its origin in the person
of Dr. Peter Wieselgren, son of a peasant in Småland
(1800—1877), a learned man, who was successively a
teacher and librarian at Lund, a pastor in that diocese, and,
lastly, for twenty years Provost of Göteborg Cathedral.[10]
But temperance work was the main business of his life.
As a schoolboy at Vexiö he was struck by the sight of a
fine-looking young man, sitting crouched up in the window
of his cell in the county gaol, reading the Bible. He found
that this was a man of good character, who, in a drunken
fit, the first he had ever indulged in, had murdered his
much-loved young wife, and so was condemned to death,
and destined to make his children both fatherless and
motherless. The young man was beheaded, after writing
a poem of warning against the use of brandy, which
Wieselgren had printed. Thus his career in life was fixed
by this tragic experience.

The evil against which he had to fight was immense and
of long standing. Brandy had come into use in Sweden
in the Russian wars of Gustavus Vasa, whose soldiers
thought of it as a sort of charm used by their foreign opponents to give them courage. From that time it became the

[10] See Cornelius : *Hist.*, § 275, *De S.K. inre Misson* and Grimberg : l.c., pp. 551-6. There is also a short biography by
Sigfrid Wieselgren, Stkh., 1907.

deadliest enemy of Sweden within. Every foreigner who visited the country noticed it. Amongst others, I may name our countryman, Bulstrode Whitelocke, who had the moral courage to decline absolutely to drink the healths to which he was almost forced at the various State banquets and private dinners to which he was invited. Frederick the Great of Prussia once said that the Swedes for centuries had been trying to work their own ruin by their drunkenness, but, strange to say, had not yet succeeded. It was one of the projects of his nephew, Gustavus III., at once to promote sobriety and to increase the revenues of the crown, by stopping the multitude of private stills, and making the sale of brandy a crown monopoly. Unfortunately his agents pushed the second part of the project so vigorously that drunkenness on " crown brandy " became a sort of evidence of patriotism, and the evil was worse than before.[11]   Much secret distillation took place, and the crown lost rather than gained in revenue, while Gustavus himself owed his final unpopularity very largely to this ill-considered project. The monopoly was given up and the evil went on as before. Up till 1830 the consumption of brandy was enormous, that is to say, at last it rose to forty litres per head of the population per annum, and, of course, enormously more than this for every full-grown man. It was no uncommon thing to see a drunken judge and drunken officers deciding in court the fate of unhappy prisoners. The average of human life fell to thirty-five years, whereas now it has risen to fifty.

It was with such a gigantic evil as this that Wieselgren felt that he was called to struggle, and he had prepared himself for it by a boyish spirit of adventure—climbing the highest fir trees that were to be found, and wandering far afield, in the hope of losing his way and having to find it again. Thus the boy was father to the man. He formed a society for total abstinence from all spirituous liquors with five of his school-fellows, and thus the first temperance

[11] See Grimberg: l.c., p. 439 foll.

society in Sweden was started by a schoolboy. But his real power of leadership came to him in his parish of Västerstad. One incident of his ministry may be mentioned as an example of his experience and courage. A peasant, who was being punished for his evil life by the Church Council, resolved to kill his pastor. He sent for him to come to his house on the pretext that his wife was dying. Wieselgren was warned, but went all the same. He first commanded the pretended dying woman to rise from her bed, and then turned to her husband, who stood axe in hand behind the door, and said: "Lay down your weapon." The man obeyed; but when his pastor urged him to change his evil life and ask God for pardon, the man answered scornfully: "There'll be time enough for that when one lies on one's sick bed." The priest's answer came back like lightning: "You'll never lie on a sick bed." A few days after the man fell down his own well in a drunken fit, and was drowned, and Wieselgren's influence was stronger than ever. In time his parishioners saw that temperance was for their own good, and his reputation spread far and wide. Prince Oskar, afterwards Oskar I., who succeeded King Karl Johan in 1840, took up the movement, and so did the great chemist Berzelius, and the physician Huss. From them proceeded the familiar physiological arguments, which explain the action of alcohol on the human body, and on the descendants of drunkards, as well as on drunkards themselves. Wieselgren himself travelled over the whole country from south to north, and at length the nation was ready for the great reform of 1854, when private distillation was forbidden, and a heavy tax put upon brandy. But, though the results were great, it was found after a time that beer drinking had become a national danger, and the new temperance movement of 1880 and the following years was inaugurated. The various societies are supposed to number about a quarter of a million members.

I regret to learn from the bishops' charges, which will

be quoted in section 10, that the influence of the temperance societies is by no means always favourable to religion.

Temperance reform is thus specially connected with one name, that of Peter Wieselgren. The emancipation of women in like manner owes much to a single lady, Miss Frederica Bremer.[12] To some of us who remember her early stories, which had much of the quiet wit of Jane Austen and Maria Edgeworth, it may be almost a surprise to know how great a spirit of almost political enterprise lived within this accomplished writer of clever domestic chronicles. There is a pleasant English book by Margaret Howitt, *Twelve Months with Frederica Bremer*, which is worth reading by anyone who wishes to know the manner of her later life. She had long rebelled against the dull confinement of her childhood and early youth, and had found vent for her energies in fiction, but a journey to the United States in 1850, and a visit to its schools and institutions for women, opened her eyes as to what was needed for others in her own country. The result was the foundation of the high schools for girls, which have changed the whole condition of women in Sweden, and opened the universities and the higher professions to them, as well as many other walks of life.

The legal changes which have accompanied this movement began in 1845, when sisters acquired an equal right of inheritance with brothers. Then followed the resolution of parliament, which allowed unmarried women to come of age and to act for themselves at the same time as men. The need for such legislation lay in the fact that there was no longer so much work for women in the home, as in former days, when each house gave employment for all the family in domestic arts, which now are much more cheaply carried on in workshop and factory. Sweden still has many remains of this hem-slöjd, more probably than England, but it was not enough for all as in old time. This

[12] See Grimberg : l.c., pp. 546-51, from whom I have freely borrowed.

emancipation of women from the home naturally met with great opposition from old-fashioned folk, who saw beauty in the gentle dependence of woman, regarding her in Tegnér's words as :—

> "A tendril, withering if unsupported,
> A creature unto which the half is wanting."

It was fortunate for the women of Sweden that they were led by so essentially womanly and refined a lady as Frederica Bremer.

Whether the wisdom of Swedish legislators will carry the equality of the sexes still further and emancipate married women as entirely as their unmarried sisters, and give one or both of these classes votes for parliament, and further opportunities for public duty, I cannot venture to prophesy. There is a fundamental difference in the sexes as well as a fundamental equality, and for the sake of women as well as of men, and of the future of the race, it is important that home should have more claim on the one, and the world more claim upon the other, and that laws should recognize the difference.

§ 5.—MOVEMENTS WITHIN THE CHURCH: FOREIGN MISSIONS. PETRUS LÆSTADIUS IN LAPLAND. PETER FJELLSTEDT (1802—1881). THE "SWEDISH CHURCH MISSION" (1873—1874). THE "EVANGELICAL NATIONAL INSTITUTE" (1856) BECOMES MISSIONARY IN 1861. OTHER SOCIETIES. SEAMEN'S MISSIONS. MISSIONS TO ISRAELITES.

In my last two sections I have dealt with popular movements, religious and social, which were partly within the Church and partly without it, but which did not specially use it and its ministers as instruments, or definitely increase its power of organization—nay, in some cases tried to break it down and diminish it. Happily there have been others which directly tended to strengthen and build up the Church as a society.

Both Denmark and England felt the responsibility of their foreign possessions as a call to mission work among the heathen in a way that Sweden, which had few such possessions, could not be expected to do. Work among the Lapps did, indeed, as we have seen, begin early, and produced much fruit. The good work of Fjellstedt and Högstrom in the eighteenth century was continued by Petrus Læstadius, a younger brother of Lars Levi, who was active in Piteå from 1826 to 1832 and later. The result of his and others' work was an attempt by the government to concentrate the education of the Lapps into four schools, but the nomadic spirit of the people was too strong, and the clergy who minister to them still have to follow their wanderings.

After Kjernander, of whom I have already spoken, who stands almost alone in the eighteenth century, the first important Swedish missionary and promoter of missions to distant lands was Peter Fjellstedt (1802—1881), son of a peasant in Vermland. In 1829 he entered the service of the English Church Missionary Society, and served for four years in the Tinnevelly Mission in Southern India. After that he was employed in Asia Minor at Magnesia, near Smyrna, for another five years, especially in distributing the Bible in Turkish. The rest of his long life he spent for the most part in his own country, zealously serving the same cause in other ways, especially as editor of the *Lunds Missionstidning*, and as a preacher for the Basel Missionary Society.[18] He was a great linguist, and kept up a correspondence with missionaries in many parts of the world. A school was founded in his honour, which bears his name. It is now in Upsala, and most of the pupils become clergy in Sweden or America, while some go out as missionaries to India and Africa.

Fjellstedt worked hard, but it was some time before the

[18] The latter part of Fjellstedt's life is described in *Peter Fjellstedt : hans verksamhet i fosterlandet mellan åren 1843-81*, af Emilia Ahnfelt-Laurin, Stockholm, 1881.

Swedish Church maintained missionary work on its own account.

The first missionary society [14] in the Swedish Church began its work in 1835, in connection, however, with other foreign societies. The first independent society was that of Lund, founded ten years later, in order to work in China; but this, too, had soon to ally itself with another, that of Leipzig. It was not till after the first meeting of the Representative Church Council, in 1868, that the Swedish Church took up the project of an official mission to the heathen. As a result of the second meeting, in 1873, a royal letter was issued in 1874, appointing the archbishop *ex-officio*, and six members of the council chosen by itself to act as the governing body of the " Svenska Kyrkans missionstyrelse." A royal letter had been already issued earlier in the year, appointing an annual collection with missionary sermon on a particular day to be made in every church throughout the country.

The main work of this society lies in South Africa, especially in Natal, Zululand and Rhodesia, where it has nine Swedish priests and one African, besides ladies and other subordinate native workers. It also has work in South India in connection with the Leipzig Society at Madura, and also in Ceylon at Colombo. In these stations there are seven Swedish and two native priests. Besides this, the society has an important seamen's mission with stations at Copenhagen, Stettin, Kiel and Wismar, London and Hartlepool, Calais and Dunkirk. This Church society has made admirable progress in recent years under its energetic secretary, or " missions direktor, Pastor K. A. Ihrmark.

This official society does not, however, by any means exhaust the missionary energies of the Swedish Church. A larger amount of work is done by the earlier " Evan-

[14] There is a good short account of all Swedish mission work in *De Svenska Missionerna*, 1904, *utgifven af Uppsala kristliga Studenten-förbund.* See also *P.R.E.*[3], 13, pp. 146, 183, 185.

gelical National Institute" (Evangeliska Fosterlands-
stiftelse), a society founded in 1856 for work by lay evangelists at home, which remains within the Church, but
stands in a free relation to it. In 1861 it took up the work
of heathen missions, and in 1862 it founded a missionary
college under the direction of Dr. W. Rudin, the much
loved and honoured Upsala professor, at Johannelund,
near Stockholm. Its stations are found in Northern East
Africa, more particularly in the Italian "Colonia
Erythræa," Abyssinia, and the neighbouring regions,
where it has fifteen Swedish and four native priests. It
works also in the " central provinces " of India, with seventeen Swedish priests. It has also a seamen's mission, with
stations at Lübeck, Hamburg and Bremerhaven, Grimsby
and Liverpool, at Marseilles, at Boston U.S.A., and
Melbourne in Australia. The income of the society has
grown from 383,317 kr. in 1900 to 597,509 kr. in 1909. It
has ninety-seven European and 204 native agents, and
twenty-three stations.

In addition to this, besides the Free Church work of
the Waldenstromians, which I have already mentioned,
there is the " Swedish Mission in China," which works in
concert with the English "China Inland Mission," and
has eight stations; the Free Church " Helgelse förbundet,"
which works in Natal and China, and the " Scandinavian
Alliance Mission," part of the "Christian Missionary
Alliance" of New York. The latter has its Swedish centre
in Jönköping. It works in Tibet and North-West India,
in China, Japan and South Africa, but its workers are few.
There is also a Swedish Baptist Mission, a Swedish
Women's Mission to the women of North Africa, which
has a school at Bizerta in Tunis; a Swedish Jerusalem
Union, founded in 1900 by Bishop von Schéele, which has
a school in the holy city and a medical missionary at
Bethlehem; and, lastly, a " Union for Mission to Israelites," which was founded in 1875 in Stockholm by Pastor
A. Lindström. This appears to be one of the most active
of the smaller societies.

Considering that most of this activity belongs to the last fifty years, the result is considerable. It is obvious that an alliance between our Church and that of Sweden might be very beneficial to both, especially in South Africa and India, and that the seamen's missions of both churches might be made use of by the mariners of both countries wherever there was no station belonging to their own people. The number of Scandinavians in our own mercantile marine is great, and they are much valued.

§ 6.—DIFFERENT CHARACTER OF THE UNIVERSITIES. E G. BRING'S EXPERIENCES AT BOTH, ABOUT 1832 A.D. THE THEOLOGICAL FACULTY AT LUND. THOMANDER AND REUTERDAHL. THEIR SUCCESSORS AND THE *Swedish Church Times* FROM 1855. E. G. BRING AND A. N. SUNDBERG COMPARED. BISHOP BILLING'S ACCOUNT OF THE MAIN PRINCIPLES OF SWEDISH HIGH CHURCHMEN. MOVEMENT AT UPSALA. DR. SÖDERBLOM'S ADDRESS TO STUDENTS. THE LUND PROFESSORS BECOME BISHOPS: BRING OF LINKÖPING (1861—1884); SUNDBERG OF CARLSTAD (1864) AND ARCHBISHOP (1870—1900); FLENSBURG OF LUND (1865—1897).

It is difficult for a foreigner to estimate and compare the debt which Sweden owes to its two universities—the older and larger at Upsala, with 1,800 white-capped students, men and women, and the smaller at Lund, with some 800. There is, of course, greater possibility of variety of life at Upsala, both from its own resources in the larger number of professors and students, and the greater collections of books and apparatus, and from its nearness to the capital and consequent closer participation in much that goes on there. In both the students are classified as belonging to thirteen so-called " nations," each incorporating the young people from one or more of the twenty-four provinces or " län " into which the kingdom is divided. But while each of these nations has its own club house, sometimes a fine building, at Upsala, there is only one at Lund, which is shared by all. On the other hand there is, I think, a larger hostel for students living together at Lund, and, therefore, more opportunity for the training of the future clergy in a definite manner.

It would not, perhaps, be wrong to say that there are more opportunities for general culture at Upsala, and for the study of philosophy and history, while life is more intense at Lund, and that dogmatic theology and classical literature were more at home there than at the Northern University. Certainly this appears to have been the case in the first half of the nineteenth century, according to the interesting notes made by Bishop Ebbé Gustaf Bring (1814—1874) of his own student life at both Universities.[15] He left Upsala in 1832, after three years spent there, and migrated to Lund, where he took his degree as Master or Doctor in Philosophy in 1835, though only twenty-one years of age. In comparing the two universities he speaks of the " Phosphorists," the leaders of the new romantic or Gothic school at Upsala, as having grown to maturity, and having lost their faults and developed their strong points; and of the interest for philosophy, æsthetics and poetry, which was, therefore, naturally much greater at Upsala than at Lund. Among his teachers at the former he mentions with gratitude " Geijer, Atterbom, Grubbe, Boström, Kolmodin, Lundwall, Törneros " as examples of valuable influences which all would recognize. But, above all, he speaks with gratitude of the companionship of his young friend, Ernst Kjellander, a poet, who died a few years later in Italy. On the other hand Lund had its advantages in the interest for classical Latinity awakened by Lindblad, in the provision there made for the study of natural science, and in the strength of its theological faculty, then led by Ahlman, Bergqvist, Reuterdahl and Thomander. Schartau had died in 1825, but his strong spirit still swayed the University, and Thomander (1808—1865) was taking

---

[15] *Biskopen M. M. Ebbe Gustaf Bring, några minnesblad,* af Gottfrid Billing, pp. 10 foll., Lund, 1886.

his place as a preacher. He is described as very impressive in his boldness and assurance, and Bishop Nielsen says of him: "Sweden never had a greater speaker." In his youth he had a strongly-marked period of æstheticism, in which he was an enthusiast for Aristophanes, Shakespeare and Byron, and he remained a Liberal in politics and theology.[16] He became Provost of Göteborg in 1850, and Bishop of Lund in 1856.

Beside Thomander, the best known of the Lund professors of that date was Henrik Reuterdahl (1795—1870), who worked there as a University teacher and professor for thirty-five years. He edited the *Theological Quarterly* (Theologisk Quartalskrift) for many years, in company with Thomander, produced an *Introduction to Theology*, which was long a text book for students, and, not only edited many documents appertaining to Swedish Church history, but produced the best existing history of the Church up to the year 1533—the middle of the reign of Gustaf Vasa. His writing appears to us of this generation somewhat dull and wanting in ideas, but it is clear and full and accurate, and based on independent study of ancient documents, and, therefore, indispensable to the student. His work may naturally be contrasted with that of his younger contemporary, L. A. Anjou (1803—1884), a Upsala professor for ten years, and Bishop of Visby from 1859 to his death. We can see in Anjou the influence of Geijer, from which Reuterdahl is almost free. Anjou is interesting, but rather diffuse, and occasionally obscure, and it is difficult to know where to find the facts one needs.

In 1852 Reuterdahl was called by King Oskar I. to be head of the ecclesiastical department of State, and three years after became Bishop of Lund. He was, therefore, in that city at the beginning of the period of which I am now to speak, but he was called to the archbishopric in 1856, and held it till his death in 1870. I shall mention later his relations with Bishop Whitehouse, of Illinois.

[16] See Nielsen in *Der Protestantismus*, p. 1003.

After the departure of Reuterdahl and Thomander, in the middle of the last century, the University of Lund had a professoriate of exceptional brilliance, especially in its chairs of theology. The faculty consisted mainly of four "High Churchmen," H. M. Melin, Bring himself, Anton Niklas Sundberg and Wilhelm Flensburg. Of these men the best known to the outside world are Bring and Sundberg. Bring had been brought up at home as a boy, and chiefly by kind-hearted women. This training developed his gentle and sensitive nature, but it was joined to a great passion for righteousness. He was older than Sundberg, and succeeded earlier to his professorship, and this was an advantage to the movement which they were to lead, since he was more considerate of opponents and entered more into their point of view than Sundberg. Both were alike in this that they experienced no great crisis in their spiritual life, and developed harmoniously and happily. Yet both were distrustful of self, and of a somewhat anxious temperament. Bring appears to have had much more of a distinct call to the priesthood, and to have had the finer nature. He was much valued as a pastor, and attached great importance to the prebendal system by which pastoral charges are assigned to the theological chairs. He was selected to prepare the young princes for confirmation and first communion—a duty which he performed both on this occasion, and generally with extreme carefulness and fulness. Sundberg, however, was the more imposing personality, and was an acknowledged chief both in Church and State. It is a striking evidence of his capacity as a leader that he was especially acceptable in his relation to the University of Upsala, of which he was officially vice-chancellor. This is brought out very clearly in Bishop Billing's memorial discourse before the Swedish Academy.[17]

[17] *Minne af A. N. Sundberg: inträdes-tal i Svenska Akademien*, 20th December, 1900, af Gottfrid Billing: pp. 50 foll., Stkh., 1901.

These two able and popular men, in company with Wilhelm Flensburg, inaugurated a Lund movement, as we may call it, which was almost as important for Sweden as the Oxford Movement some twenty years earlier had been for England. Strange to say, Cornelius does not mention it in his *History*.

In their hands the vague ideal of the glory and the beauty of the Church which Reuterdahl in his youth had caught up from Schleiermacher, passed into a clear and definite conception, in which they were much aided by the new Lutheranism of Germany. They also absorbed the higher conception of the ministry to which Schartau had given currency, and added much from their own studies of ancient Church history. They not only set themselves against open unbelief and materialism, and so-called un-dogmatic Christianity, but against the separatist spirit, which was now showing itself largely within as well as outside the Church, and which had an able champion in their own colleague, H. B. Hammar, editor of the *Evangelical Church Friend*, and head of the tract distributing committee in Southern Sweden.

The Lund movement specially set itself to correct tract distribution and Methodism.

The *Evangelical National Institute* for home missions was founded in 1856 by Hans Jakob Lundborg, who had been much influenced by what he saw during a visit to Scotland. It worked through " colporteurs " and tract distribution, and promoted evangelistic addresses given by laymen, who were desired first to obtain the leave of the clergy. It wished to remain, and has remained within the Church, like our " Church Army," but its principles at first gave great offence to many of the clergy, who disliked to see laymen intruding, as they thought, into their office. They appealed against it to the fourteenth article of the Augsburg Confession " That no man must teach publicly in the Church or adminster the sacraments unless rightly called. '

I have already spoken of the more distinctly separatist work of Rosénius, and I may add that in 1854 he prevailed upon his friends to build for him a chapel or prayer house at Gefle, the second only at that time in Sweden, the first being in the North at Umeå.

It was in order, then, to check these ardent individualists and to bring to mind great principles that had been, as they thought, overlooked, that Bring, Sundberg and Flensburg became co-editors of the *Swedish Church Times*, which from its foundation, in 1855, and for about ten years afterwards, exercised almost as great influence in Sweden as the *Tracts for the Times* had done in England. The editors worked in such complete harmony that they did not distinguish their articles by signatures. In the first article, which is known to have been by Bring, mention was made of the Mecklenburg theologian, Kliefoth, whose *Eight Books on the Church*—of which only four were published—made a considerable impression at that time in Northern Germany. The critics of the day said sarcastically that the *Kyrko Tidning* "did not stand on its own foot (fot), but on Kliefoth." The question, however, was: "Was its teaching right and in harmony with the doctrines of the Church of Sweden?" Its main principles are thus summarized by Bishop Billing of Lund in his affectionately but judiciously written sketch of his father-in-law's life (pp. 54 foll.). They certainly had good ground for claiming the authority of the first German reformers.

In the first place the *Church Times* strongly accentuated the truth that the Church is an organized society, not merely a sum of individuals. In opposition to those who were agitating for the entire freedom of the individual and urging that the Church should abolish everything that offended any individual conscience, or hindered anyone from any religious action to which he felt called, the editors of the *Kyrko Tidning* attempted to awaken and stimulate a consciousness of the divine origin of the Church and its right to be respected as a society. It is a society founded by the Lord Himself, introduced into the world through the outpouring of the Holy Ghost at Pentecost, and continuing the same through all centuries. Its traditions are of great importance, and no change in them can be welcomed which cannot show that it is an organic development of some of the already existing fruits of Church life; and, further, no Christian life can be wholesome which does not keep in close touch with the life of devotion which exists in its full strength within the community.

The second great principle is contained in the answer to the question: "What is the Church?" All Swedish Churchmen would answer with the seventh article of the Augsburg Confession: "The Church is the congregation of the saints in which the Gospel is rightly taught and the sacraments are rightly administered." But the question is, Which of the two limbs of this definition stands first in the conception? In answering this question I may remark that the editors, or at any rate the author of this article in the *Church Times*, seems to have passed unconsciously from the definition "congregatio sanctorum" to that of the next article of the confession "congregatio sanctorum et vere credentium," and to have, in accordance with Swedish practice, laid more stress on the "vere credentium" than the "sanctorum." The question as it presented itself to them was: "Which is first, right faith or the means of grace?" They answered: "The means of grace, as being the Lord's own institution and the source of faith. Not only the functions discharged by the ministry, but the ministry itself is an office instituted by the Lord. Whoever does not receive his office in an orderly way has no right to minister the means of grace; if he does so he not only breaks a human but a divine ordinance."

As to the difference between this teaching and that which contemporaneously prevailed at Upsala, and was expressed in the *Theological Journal* (Teologisk Tidskrift), Dr. J. E. Berggren puts it concisely and epigrammatically in his memorial of Archbishop Sundberg (p. 8) :[18] "The Lund

[18] Read at the Prest-möte at Upsala, 5th August, 1902.

theology emphasises more strongly the objective element in the life of Christendom, the Upsala lays more stress on the subjective. The Lund theology is penetrated by the conviction that false subjectivism is the greatest danger of Protestantism. Upsala theology recognizes that true subjectivism is the necessary condition of Protestant life." In other words, the theology of Upsala was, during the last century, much more of a philosophy, in which the idea of the Church was tolerated rather than loved. Dr. Söderblom, who has written some interesting pages on this subject, in a brilliant address to the *Student Volunteer* meeting at Huskvarna, in 1909, entitled *The Individual and the Church*, expressed himself as follows:[19] " Attachment to the Church was not a leading feature of Upsala theology, still less did it create enthusiasm. Rather was it felt as a burden. An inspiring conception of the Church, penetrated with enthusiasm, was manifested later on by S. A. Fries, evidently in connection with (the philosopher) Boström's *Ideal of an Established Church*, and by J. A. Eklund (Bishop of Carlstad) in the form of the ideal of a national Church, which he assigned to the period of our political greatness." The idea, therefore, even then, was not a general one like that of the Lund theologians, of an eternal world-wide society, founded at Pentecost, and embracing the best efforts of all men, but a partial and patriotic one of narrower scope and compass. The two may, of course, be united, as they are to-day by the professors of Upsala, in an attempt to define what the Church of Sweden may do as a constituent part of the universal Church, and to encourage men to labour to realize this in action as its contribution to a united offering of service to our Lord and Master Jesus Christ (Söderblom: l.c., pp. 25 foll.).

Before the *Church Times* had been in existence ten years the editors were called upon to separate. Bring became

---

[19] *Den Enskilde och Kyrkan* af Nathan Soderblöm, föredrag hållet vid Studentmötet i Huskvarna, 1909, p. 20, Uppsala, 1909.

Bishop of Linköping in 1861, where he remained till his death in 1884. Sundberg became Bishop of Carlstad in 1864, and archbishop, as Reuterdahl's successor, in 1870, himself dying early in 1900. Flensburg became Bishop of Lund in 1865, and thus was able to continue the tradition in the centre from which it originated up till 1897. It is also still happily and worthily represented by the present bishop. Thus Bring and his colleagues, including their friend, Genberg, who had been professor of philosophy for a short time, and then head of the ecclesiastical department, and finally Bishop of Kalmar (1852—1875).[20] spread the principles of the Lund theology all over Sweden, and were especially valuable to the Church in the critical time of the foundation and first assembly of the Kyrko-möte, or representative Church council, which met in September, 1868.

§ 7.—THE CHANGE IN THE RIKSDAG FROM FOUR ESTATES
    TO TWO CHAMBERS (1865). THE FORMATION OF
    THE KYRKO-MÖTE (1863). CHURCH AND STATE IN
    SWEDEN. POSITION OF THE KING. RELATION OF
    THE KYRKO-MÖTE TO THE RIKSDAG. ITS CON-
    STITUTION AND METHOD OF ELECTION. ITS
    BUSINESS.

The first meeting of the Kyrko-möte was historically connected with one of the greatest changes in the civil constitution of Sweden, a change carried out on the initiative of the Prime Minister, Baron de Geers, in the year 1865. This was the transformation of the Riksdag from an assembly of four estates—nobles, clergy, citizens and peasants—to a parliament with an upper and lower house, with no class restrictions as to the composition of either. It was easy to see the defects and cumbrousness of the old system, and since the *coup d'état* of 1772 the house of

[20] Genberg was not a priest in 1852 when chosen bishop, but he was ordained priest before his consecration, as I learn from my friend, the present Bishop of Kalmar.

nobles had ceased to have special powers or duties besides its position as a branch of the legislature. But it was otherwise with the house of clergy, which had been accustomed to special discussion of Church questions, and to take the lead in them without much interference from the other estates. The question of a separate Church council had constantly been mooted, and it now naturally became a question of pressing importance. It must, however, be noted that the formation of a general Church council had been determined at least two years before the four estates adopted the project of law proposed by De Geers. The " royal ordinance " creating the Church council is dated 16th November, 1863; the law affecting the Riksdag was not passed until December, 1865. But it is possible that if the new parliament had not been created the Kyrko-möte would not have been summoned.

I regret that I am unable to tell you what were the influences which decided the method of the formation of the Kyrko-möte which now took its place as a constitutional body representing the national Church side by side with the Riksdag. But I will take the opportunity of sketching the relation of Church and State in Sweden as it now exists, making use of Professor Holmquist's article already several times quoted, and other authorities.

" The King of Sweden " (writes Dr. Holmquist) " is at the same time the highest earthly ruler of the Swedish Church. Therefore, he must always profess ' the pure evangelical doctrine, as far as it is accepted and explained in the unaltered Augsburg Confession and in the Resolution of the Upsala Council of 1593.' Further, the king, in the exercise of his power in the Church, must always ' seek for information and counsel ' from a separate minister for Church affairs (Ecclesiastik Minister) and from the whole Council of State, all members of which must make profession of pure evangelical doctrine. And in respect of Church legislation his power is limited both by the Riksdag or parliament and the Kyrko-möte or re-

presentative Church council.   According to the Swedish
fundamental law ' the Riksdag, in conjunction with the
king, has the right to pass Church laws, to alter them, or
to repeal them; but for this matter the consent of a general
Kyrko-möte is requisite.' Inasmuch then as the Riksdag
consists of two independent chambers, and the Kyrko-möte
need only be summoned by the king every five years, the
danger of hasty legislation is avoided, but, on the other
hand, the adoption of reasonable reforms is made difficult.
It is easier, however, to obtain changes in the sphere of
those Church matters which are within the administrative
competence of the king.   To this sphere belong questions
which concern a new translation of the Bible, the Hymn-
book, the Gospel-book, the Church Hand-book and the
Catechism.   In regard to these purely ecclesiastical
matters it is not necessary to consult the Riksdag, but only
the Kyrko-möte, and in this last body two-thirds of the
members must agree in order to pass a resolution.''

The Kyrko-möte [21] consists of sixty members (to which
four will be added when the new diocese of Luleå is in being), half of which, as I have said, are clergy and half are
laymen.   All the twelve bishops are officially members of
the body, and so is the pastor primarius of Stockholm.
Then there are four professors of theology, two from
Upsala and two from Lund, and thirteen elected clergy,
one from each diocese and one from Stockholm.   The lay
element is exactly equal.   Each diocese is represented, but

---

[21] I have made use of the *Memorandum on the Constitution
of the Ecclesiastical Council of Sweden*, which I printed as an
appendix to the *Report of the Joint Committee of the Convocation of Canterbury* '' *On the Position of the Laity*,'' of which
I was chairman (ed. S.P.C.K., 1902, pp. 89 foll.).   It is drawn
from copies of the *Royal Ordinance* of 16th November, 1863,
establishing this council, and of the *Working Order*, adopted
5th September, 1868, and amended 6th October, 1873, which
were kindly supplied to us by Bishop Von Schéele, of Visby.
See also Dr. Holmquist's article *Schweden*, p. 37, and
Cornelius : *Hist.*, § 284.

by a somewhat different number of persons in proportion to its importance. All clergy entitled to perform duty are electors of the clerical representatives, and the election is direct. The election of lay representatives is indirect. Members of the parish vestry or Kyrko-stamma elect the electors. The electors vote by ballot, the returning officer being appointed by the chapter. The electoral areas are fixed by the king.

A deputy is chosen to take the place of every member of the council (whether clerical or lay) in case he is not able to attend. At the meeting of the council the archbishop presides, or, in his absence, a bishop appointed by the king. The lord chancellor and the minister of ecclesiastical affairs may be present and join in the discussion; but they may not vote unless they are elected representatives.

Business introduced by the king takes precedence of other business. As we have seen, there is a distinction between measures which come up from the Riksdag and purely ecclesiastical matters, which are within the administrative competence of the crown, such as changes in the Prayer Book. No change can be made in these matters unless two-thirds of the members present accept it. With regard to other business, the council regulates its own procedure. Every member of the council has one vote, and voting is by ballot. The expenses of the council and its members are paid by the State.

In the *Working Order* it is provided that the number of clerical and lay members on a committee must be equal (sec. 14). All general meetings of the council are public (sec. 26). The president appears to have little power, and has not even a casting vote. If votes are equal a lot is practically cast to determine the issue.

§ 8.—THE TASK NEARLY COMPLETED. ATTEMPT TO DO
JUSTICE TO THE DEPARTED WHOM WE HOPE TO MEET
IN A NEW LIFE. DUTIES THAT REMAIN. SPECIAL
SUBJECT: THE SWEDES IN U.S.A. ATTRACTION
OF THE NORTHERN STATES OF THE MIDDLE WEST.
WHAT U.S.A. OWES TO SWEDEN. MODERN
SETTLEMENT BEGINS WITH UNONIUS (1841).
BISHOP WHITEHOUSE, OF ILLINOIS (1851—1875):
HIS ACTS OF INTER-COMMUNION: (1) ADMITS BRED-
BERG; (2) INTERCOURSE WITH REUTERDAHL; (3)
ORDAINS MR. ALMQUIST. BISHOP WHIPPLE, OF
MINNESOTA (1859 ONWARDS). THE " AUGUSTANA
SYNOD ": ESBJÖRN, HASSELQUIST, NORELIUS.
ITS GREAT WORK IN FIFTY YEARS. VISIT TO ROCK
ISLAND, 19TH OCTOBER, 1910. QUESTIONS BEFORE
IT: LANGUAGE, SECRET SOCIETIES, ORGANIZATION.
THE " MISSION COVENANT ": WORK OF TWENTY-
FIVE YEARS. VISIT TO NORTH PARK COLLEGE,
CHICAGO. OTHER BODIES. ACTION OF THE
SWEDISH BISHOPS AND THE LAMBETH CONFERENCE
NO STRANGE THING.

I have now come to the conclusion of the main portion of
the task which I had so audaciously undertaken. I have
sketched in rough outline the course of Church history in
Sweden from the earliest dim traces of religious life in the
Stone Age to our own times. I have attempted to indicate the influence and to draw the characters of a certain
number of the remarkable men and women who have enriched and ennobled the annals of the country. In doing so
I have naturally felt the responsibility which a Christian
must acknowledge when he remembers our Lord's words to
the Sadducees, explaining the divine title " God of Abraham, Isaac and Jacob." " God is not the God of the dead,
but of the living," and the persons whose lives we record
in our Church histories are living brothers and sisters in
Christ, whose fellowship will, we trust, one day be ours in
actual personal intercourse. I remember Dean Stanley,

after he had finished the last volume of his history of the Jewish Church, saying in his deep voice and quaint abrupt manner: " I have tried to do justice to Judas Maccabeus: I hope he will some day thank me for it." I have tried in a much humbler way to be just to the men and women of the Swedish Church, whose lives fall within the compass of this volume. I undertook the task partly, I must confess, with the feelings of a traveller who desires to explore a new and interesting country. But my chief attraction to it was the sense that the task must, under the circumstances of the times, be undertaken by some one, and my wish was that it should be handled by a sympathetic English Churchman. I began it with sympathy. I prepare to leave it with much greater sympathy. But before I say farewell to it and you, I have still two duties to discharge, the first special, the second general.

The Swedes in U.S.A.

My special duty is to turn away from the lakes and forests of the Scandinavian peninsula to the new regions of this great country, and especially to the lakes and forests of Wisconsin, Illinois, and Minnesota, and the other States of the Middle West. They offer scenes very like those of Sweden itself, but with greater freedom and fertility, and they have had for the last seventy years, since Unonius landed in this country, a marked attraction for the Swedish people.[22] The subject is full of interest, and there are plenty of materials in my hands for writing about it, but as it is not the main subject of my lectures, I will ask your indulgence for very slight treatment of it. Over one million immigrants from Sweden have landed in this country since 1841, most of them young and middle-aged

[22] On the reasons for this attraction see Grimberg: I.c., pp. 560; such as love of adventure, desire for greater freedom, introduction of manufactures into Sweden displacing labour, poverty at home, overplus of population about 1880, national tendency to overvalue what is foreign, brilliant pictures of success sent home by settlers, etc.

people in their best years, and what Sweden has thereby lost and this country has gained may readily be, in some degree, apprehended.[23]

The United States owes very much to its Swedish immigrants and settlers. The Swedes in this country, who now number, perhaps, two millions, are everywhere recognized as a peaceable, industrious, capable, honest and religious element, of great value to its development. The debt began, as we have already seen, in connection with the settlements at Wilmington and Philadelphia in the reign of Gustavus Adolphus. Two traditions were impressed upon them, both of great value—fair treatment of the Indians, and friendship with England and the English Church.[24]

Relation between the Swedish Church and the Episcopal Church of U.S.A.

It was, therefore, quite in the natural order of things that, when fresh ministers were no longer supplied from Sweden, the congregations of Delaware and Pennsylvania should unite themselves permanently with the American Episcopal Church.

So also when the Swedes begun again to enter the country as settlers from the year 1841 onwards, and to arrive in parties of colonists, it was natural that the same policy should be pursued both by the Church of Sweden and the Church in this country. I shall proceed to give some instances of this policy which especially concern the diocese of Illinois, in the see city of which it is my happiness to be invited to lecture.

In the early part of the last century the few Swedes who

[23] See below, Appendix B, at the end, p. 449.
[24] See above, Lecture VI., Section 8, p. 287-8, and cp. A. E. Strand : *Hist. of Sw. Americans in Minnesota*, i., p. 60, 1910, and Lars P. Nelson : *What has Sweden done for the United States?* p. 11, 1903.

came to America came as individuals.[25] The sea passage
was generally made in sailing ships, and was often very
long, tedious, painful and dangerous.   The individuals
who most concern the history of religion were Erik Alund,
who came in 1823 to Philadelphia, and the brothers Olof
Gustaf and Jonas Hedström.

Both of the latter were Methodist preachers, and they
came over in 1826 and 1833 respectively.   But the first
regular settlement of Swedes was that led by Gustaf
Unonius in 1841.[26]   This remarkable man was born in
1810, and, at the age of thirty, had already had a varied
career.   He had been an army cadet, had taken a degree
in law at Upsala, and had served with distinction as an
emergency physician in a cholera hospital.   He was recently married to his twenty-year-old bride, Carlotta
Margareta Öhrströmer, who evidently shared his adventurous spirit.   There was something of the old Viking love
of wandering which led him and his few companions, men
of education and refinement, to take the seven or eight
months' voyage to America, and to attempt to settle in what
was then the extreme west.   It was unfortunate for them
that they did not bring skilled labourers with them to their
first home, Pine Lake (Tallsjön), in Wisconsin.

Here Unonius and his wife laboured hard, both physic-

[25] The opening chapters of E. Norelius' *De Svenska Luterska
Forsamlingarnas och Svenskarnes Historia i Amerika*, Rock
Island, 1890, treat in detail of the early settlements.   I have
also to thank a learned friend, Dr. Tofteen, of Chicago, for
valuable notes on the same subject.   See Appendix B to this
lecture.   E. W. Olson's *The Swedes of Illinois* contains many
details about early individual settlers as well as later colonies.

[26] For Unonius I have used an article in the Swedish paper
Idun, reprinted (in English) in *The diocese of Chicago official
paper*, Vol. xiv., for March, 1902, entitled *Unonius, Chicago's
senior priest*, and Ernest W. Olson's *The Swedes of Illinois*, I.,
p. 185 foll., and p. 414 foll., Chicago, 1908.   I have not seen
Unonius' *Memoir of Seventeen Years' Residence in North-
West America*, but I have seen the Appendix to it (*Bihang*,
Stkh., 1896), in reply to Esbjörn.

ally and morally, and he did what he could as a layman to keep the settlement religious. In a very short time his neighbours asked him to become their regular pastor, and he consented to do so. Having consulted the leading men of the Swedish Church in regard to his plans for the future, he decided to affiliate himself to the American Episcopal Church, and he became a student at the recently-founded Seminary of Nashotah. After three years' study in that quiet and beautiful spot he came out as its first graduate, and was ordained in 1845 by Bishop Kemper. He remained in Wisconsin till 1849; but the Swedish element in Tallsjön was gradually dwindling, and when Frederica Bremer visited it in 1850 but few families remained. A number of them had moved to Chicago, which was becoming a considerable Swedish settlement, and Unonius had naturally received a call thither. Thus he became the first pastor of the newly-founded Church of St. Ansgarius, which had its origin in the church in which I am now speaking (St. James). But, before he moved to Chicago, his letters to Swedish newspapers had induced other Swedes to come to U.S.A., and especially a company of fifty persons from Haurida in Småland, who came also to Wisconsin—first to Sheboygan.

Unonius worked hard to obtain money for the building of his church, and travelled much for the purpose, evangelizing his countrymen wherever he found them. He was very successful in raising money in Delaware and Pennsylvania, and he also received considerable help from the great Swedish singer, Jenny Lind, on her American tour. One of her gifts, a valuable and beautiful silver communion cup, is still in use in St. Ansgarius' Church.[27] She also gave 1,500 dollars to the Rev. Lars Paul Esbjörn,

---

[27] It is figured in *The Swedes of Illinois*, p. 418, and bears the inscription : " Gifvet till den Skandinaviska Kyrkan St. Ansgarius i Chicago af en Landsmaninna, A.D. 1851." It was happily in safe custody at the time of the fire in 1871. I saw it 29th October, 1910, the day on which this lecture was delivered, by the kindness of Pastor Lindskog.

who had come over in 1849, and helped to found the colony at Andover, Illinois. Her gift was sufficient to build a church there, and also a frame church at Moline, adjacent to Rock Island, in the same State.

Work of Bishops Whitehouse and Whipple.

These gifts were made in 1851, the year in which Bishop Henry John Whitehouse, the second Bishop of Illinois, became co-adjutor to Bishop Chase (20th November). His episcopate continued till his death, 20th August, 1874. Bishop Whitehouse was a remarkable man, and did more than any other bishop of this period, except Bishop Whipple of Minnesota, to maintain and develop those relations of inter-communion with the Swedish settlers which had begun in Wilmington and Philadelphia. In these acts of inter-communion Bishop Whitehouse was only continuing the policy of Bishops Henry Compton, of London, and Svedberg, of Skara, to which I have already referred, and, in more recent years, that of Bishop Charles James Blomfield (1828—1857), to which we may add that of Bishop Archibald Campbell Tait, afterwards Archbishop of Canterbury. In 1837 Bishop Blomfield asked Bishop Wingård, of Göteborg, to confirm for him some children of members of our Church. Bishop Wingård obtained permission from the king, Karl XIV., to do so, using the Swedish ritual, but adding to it " the laying on of hands considered essential in England." [28]

Unfortunately no life of Bishop Whitehouse has been published, but three points in his Swedish work are known and must be recorded here. The first is his admission of the Rev. Jacob Bredberg, a Swedish priest, who was ordained in that country in 1832, to be Rector of St.

[28] See *Sveriges Kyrkolag af 1686*, ed. A. J. Rydén, p. 14, Göteborg, 1864. The king's letter given in full in Anjou's *Reformation*, E. T., p. 641 and in an article in the *Church Quarterly Review* (Vol. 70, pp. 270-1) for July, 1910, *Reunion and the Churches of Scandinavia*, by Rev. G. C. Richards, Fellow of Oriel College, Oxford.

Ansgarius' Church in this city. Unonius had resigned his cure in 1857, and left this country in 1858, and placed his work for the time in the hands of the Rev. Henry Benjamin Whipple, then rector of a parish in this city, afterwards the beloved and famous Bishop of Minnesota, whose friendship with myself is a delightful recollection of past years. He thus writes of this period: " One of the three services which I held every Sunday was for the Swedish congregation. In my work for them I became deeply attached to the Scandinavian race for their love of home, their devotion to freedom, and their loyalty to Government and God." Thus he was prepared for his after-work in this field in his own diocese.[29]

I do not know the year in which Mr. Bredberg actually began his work, but it was probably in 1860. Bishop Whitehouse thus spoke of him in his address to the Convention of 1861 :—

" Among our clergy entitled to seats in this Convention is the Rev. Jacob Bredberg, an ordained minister of the Church of Sweden, whom I have recently received on his letters of orders and other papers from the Bishop of Skara.[30] In this I have, of course, formally recognized the validity of the episcopate in that venerable Church : guided in this act by the best-informed judgment of the English Church and that of my brethren in the episcopate here, whose opinion was favourably, though informally, expressed in answer to my own request for it during the last session of the House of Bishops in Richmond. This referred to the giving of Letters Dimissory to the Swedish bishops as well as the reception of ministers from there as regularly ordained. Mr. Bredberg succeeds the Rev. Mr. Unonius in ministering to the Swedes connected with the Church of St. Ansgarius, Chicago, and there is a prospect that through him I may be able to extend the use of our services into some Swedish settlements accessible by railroad."

[29] *Lights and Shadows of a long Episcopate*, p. 434, Macmillan and Co., 1902.

[30] Mr. Bredberg's name appears on the *List of Clergy* on p. 3 of the *Journal* containing the Bishop's address. On his case see Bishop G. Mott Williams, *The Ch. of Sw. and the Anglican Communion*, p. 103 foll. He writes : "Other Swedish clergy have officiated under license without seeking or obtaining membership in the Convention. The most notable case is that of Professor Mellin of the General Theological Seminary."

Unonius, as I said, returned to Sweden in 1858, and in 1859, he received a gift of 3,000 crowns, voted by the Riksdag in recognition of his long and useful services to his fellow-countrymen in U.S.A.   It was, I believe, on account of the king's death that he did not receive, as he had expected, a position as pastor of a parish in his native land, but he continued to do occasional duty, while he earned his living in a civil office.   He died at Hacksta 14th October, 1902, much respected, at the great age of ninety-two (Olson : l.c., 420).   He may justly be held in honour here as one of the founders of modern Chicago.

Mr. Bredberg laboured on till his resignation from ill-health in 1877.   In his time the present church of St. Ansgarius was erected, largely by gifts from Bishop Whitehouse, the first having been destroyed by fire in the disastrous year of 1871.   Bredberg translated our Prayer Book into Swedish, and many of our psalms and hymns.[31] It is important to recollect that Bishop Whitehouse's successor, Bishop William Edward McLaren, who was consecrated in 1875, accepted Bredberg without question as a priest of his diocese.   On his death, in 1881, Bishop McLaren spoke of his reception in 1861, saying :—

" This act was a formal recognition of the validity of the episcopate of that venerable (Swedish) Church, and was taken by my predecessor after consultation with the House of Bishops. Mr. Bredberg succeeded in enlarging our work among the Scandinavian population of Chicago, and was for many years esteemed for his fidelity and earnestness " (*Convention Journal*, 1882, p. 59).

Other Swedish clergy have from time to time been licensed or permitted to minister in our American churches, the most notable being Dr. Mellin, one of the Professors of the General Seminary of New York, in Bishop Henry Potter's time.   Dr. Flodin, on his visit to this country, also officiated in the same way, and his services were very welcome.

[31] Bishop Whitehouse's address to the Twenty-Sixth Annual Convention, *Journal*, p. 16, 1863.

The second remarkable act of Bishop Whitehouse's was
his journey to Sweden in the winter of 1865, when he visited
the English congregations in Denmark, Norway and
Sweden, under commission from Bishop Archibald Campbell Tait, of London. This visit was marked by the establishment of very close personal relations between himself
and Archbishop Reuterdahl, of which he thus writes in his
address to the diocese in 1866 :—

" At Stockholm I was favoured by affectionate intercourse
with the venerable Swedish Church. The presence there of
many of the bishops in attendance on the Diet, exercising for
the last time the important legislative functions which they have
enjoyed for 600 years, afforded me an opportunity which could
only thus occur. The special courtesy and Christian sympathy
of His Grace the Archbishop of Upsala, assisting at our services, partaking at our altar, and folding me in many relations
of confidence and love—the correspondent action of several of
the bishops—the legislative action in the pastoral letter com-
mending their emigrant members to our bishops and clergy,
have enlarged the personal intercourse into a real fellowship
between the Church of Sweden and our own in the United
States." [32]

The " Pastoral Letter " here referred to was decreed by
the estate of clergy at the last meeting of the Riksdag, of
which I have already spoken. Clergy were directed to use
it when any of their parishioners emigrated to U.S.A. It
runs as follows :—

Ministerial Certificate (Attest). That N.N., belonging to
N.N. Church (församling) in N.N. diocese in the Kingdom of
Sweden, who now intends to emigrate to the United States in
North America, receives herewith the following certificate :—

He (or she) was born the   18 , is
confirmed, etc.   In case that he (or she) shall come to settle
in a place, where access to a Swedish Evangelical-Lutheran
congregation (menighet) is wanting, he (or she) is recommended to the Right Reverend Lord Bishops and Reverend

---

[32] *Journal of 29th Annual Convention*, p. 123, 1866 : Bishop Whitehouse had
with him as his chaplain an Englishman, Dr. F. S. May, who laboured
long and vigorously in the same cause, as a corresponding member of the
" Anglo-Continental Society," now the " Anglican and Foreign Church
Society," of which I have the honour to be president. Cp. *Journal of the
30th Convention*, pp. 41 foll. 1867.

Presbyters of the Protestant Episcopal Church in the United States of North America for the reception of such spiritual and bodily care as he (*or* she) may desire, and as may be found needful for him (*or* her).

N.N., the   18   ,

N.N.,

Minister in N.N. Church.

This important document is dated 22nd June, 1866, and signed by H. Reuterdahl on behalf of the estate of the clergy, and countersigned S. H. Almquist.[88]

It was natural to suppose from Bishop Whitehouse's language, that the form of this document expressed all that he desired, and I venture to ask my Swedish hearers, especially any that belong to the Augustana Synod, to observe that the certificate is only for use " where access to a Swedish Evangelical-Lutheran congregation is wanting." The idea is clearly that of such an alliance, or "fellowship," as he calls it, as is now contemplated by some of us, a co-operation intended to supplement other natural opportunities of Christian fellowship, not an attempt to substitute membership of the Episcopal Church for membership of one more like the National Church of Sweden.

It is difficult, of course, to draw the line in practice in such things, but it is hard to think that any Swedish clergy who may warn their compatriots—isolated from their brethren—to have nothing to do with the Episcopal Church can have realized either the true conditions of religious life in this country, or the policy of their own national Church in past days.

A third act of Bishop Whitehouse's, in 1869—1870, which deserves to be recorded, is his ordination of the veteran, P. A. Almquist, who is still living at Minneapolis, and with whom I have recently had some delightful intercourse, under commission from the same Archbishop Reuterdahl.

[88] The original is given by Unonius : *Bihang*, pp. 8-9, Stkh., 1896.

Bishop Whipple began his work in Minnesota on 13th October, 1859, and carried with him his love for the Scandinavians, and especially of the Swedes, which had grown up in Chicago.   About 1871 he said in a Convention address :—

" The position of the members of the Church of Sweden in this State (Minnesota) has long been of deep interest to me. With a valid ministry, a reformed faith and a liturgical service they ought to be in communion with us.   For lack of their own episcopate as a bond of union between them they are becoming divided, and are losing their distinctive character as members of the Church." [34]

I must not attempt to give any detailed account of the Swedish work of Bishop Whipple at Litchfield, Cokato, Minneapolis, St. Paul and elsewhere, nor of that in the East at Boston, Providence, New York and Yonkers.   As regards Litchfield (Minnesota) and some other places, I may observe that the movement for union with the Episcopal Church seems to have originated with the Swedes themselves.   Many of the educated Swedes perceive the similarity between our Church life and that of their native country, and naturally fall into fellowship with us. According to the canons of the American Episcopal Church, a bishop can license the use of a foreign liturgy, and I found the Swedish book of 1894 in use at St. Ansgarius, Chicago.   Confirmation is naturally administered in the English form.

Work of the Augustana Synod.

On the other hand, those of the peasant class have often, in their own homes, resented the secular and official side of the national Church life and its ministers, and desire at once greater freedom and more of spiritual discipline.   It is the merit of the work of the Augustana Synod, to which I must now turn, to have done something which largely satisfies these aspirations, and yet does not fall into mere

[34] *Lights and Shadows of a long Episcopate,* by H. B. Whipple, D.D., p. 434, 1902.

separatism or congregationalism. It is, therefore, generally and naturally, recognized, both in Sweden and in the U.S.A., as a " daughter Church," although it has not yet acquired the full polity of its mother, and is, as some one has said, " a daughter which has not quite finished her education."

I need not go into the details of the laborious and self-denying efforts which have built up this great institution, which has just kept its first jubilee at the close of fifty years. It will be inseparably identified with the names of Lars Paul Esbjörn, Nilsson Hasselquist and Erik Norelius. The first of these came over from Gestrikland, as I have said, in 1849, and founded churches at Andover, Moline, Princeton, and Galesburg, all in Illinois. Hasselquist, a priest from the diocese of Lund, came over to Galesburg in 1852, and was a highly qualified man, and has a conspicuous position as founder of the Augustana College at Rock Island in 1871. Dr. Norelius, who is still living, is well known as the historian of the community and as president of the synod.

It was with great pleasure that the Bishop of Marquette and I visited the college at Rock Island on Wednesday, 19th October, 1910, where we were hospitably received by the president, Dr. Gustaf Andreen, Dr. C. S. Lindberg, Professor of Theology, and the other Professors of the College. We had some frank and friendly conference with them for about three hours, and, I trust, removed any misconception which might have been previously felt as to the objects aimed at by the Commission appointed by the Lambeth Conference of 1908, and by my own visit to this country. We were impressed by the zeal, both for truth and education, expressed by the members of the faculty with whom we had the opportunity of conference. The following statistics seem to be the last (1909):—

Communicants	163,473
Baptized Members	254,645
Ministers	611

Congregations	1,092
Churches	965
Value of Property	8,077,862 dollars.
Annual Contributions (1908)	1,607,201 dollars.

There are also ten colleges or collegiate institutions.

These are remarkable figures for fifty years of work.[85]

The synod is associated with the "Lutheran General Council," but it is quite independent in its internal management. Indeed, the congregations affiliated to itself are much more independent, and the whole polity is much more congregational, than is the case in Sweden. This appears clearly in the jubilee publication, from which the above figures are taken (pp. 50 foll.), and in the *Proposed Constitution of Evangelical-Lutheran Congregations*, which we also obtained at Rock Island. Nothing is said in this *Constitution* about ordination, but it is clear from the *Kyrko Handbok*, accepted in 1895, that the Augustana Synod has the same corrected form of ordination to the priesthood as the National Church of Sweden has had since 1894. The ordainers are the president of the synod and other priests, but, in other respects, the form is clearly valid and sufficient. The confession of faith is also practically the same as that of the Mother Church.

The Augustana has adopted the office of deacons from the Presbyterians and Congregationalists, but, in the sense of a lay office, elective every three years. They form the board of administration of a congregation, together with the pastor and the trustees.

There are three questions which are of some consequence to the present policy of the Augustana Synod—the language question, the question of membership of secret societies, and the question of the episcopate.

(1) On the language question there is a very interesting paper by the Rev. Julius Lincoln, pastor of an important

[85] *The Augustana Synod*, 1860-1910, p. 203. We received copies of this interesting book by the kindness of President Andréen.

parish at Jamestown, in the State of New York, in the jubilee volume already quoted (pp. 198-212). This paper contains some remarkable statistics, showing that of 1,659,467 persons of Swedish birth or parentage (according to the census of 1900), only 457,973, or considerably less than one quarter, are registered members of any church (p. 206). It is argued that this does not mean wholesale irreligion on their part, but an unwillingness to be bound by any ties implying special nationality. The residue are, in fact, gradually becoming Americanized. Many belong to congregations, but not to organizations.

In connection with this it has been remarked that there has been a falling off of Swedish immigration into this country since the year 1903, when the influx was very large, and that in 1908 (the year of industrial depression) it was much smaller than in recent years. I do not, however, attach much importance to these figures, and, when the totals for the decade 1901-1910 have been made up, I believe they will surpass those of the previous decade.[86]

But what is to be remembered here is the fact that every year the proportion of the influx, in relation to the great mass of Swedes already in this country, will be less and less important. It is also clear that the rate of Americanization is becoming more rapid. If, therefore, the Augustana is to maintain and increase its work, it must become more and more an English-speaking body. It has already gone a long way in this direction. It has an authorized English Prayer Book, and a good English hymnal. Instruction at Rock Island is usually in English, and its daily prayers (which we were very glad to attend) were in that language.

(2) I do not think it wise to speak at length on the policy of rejecting from the Church those who are members of secret societies. I venture to say, however, that it seems to

---

[86] See details in Appendix B at the end. On the growing rapidity of Americanization see E. A. Steiner's *The Immigrant Tide : its Ebb and Flow*, New York, 1909.

require a closer and more generous definition than it has as yet received. Further, it seems a great anomaly that a congregation should exclude or excommunicate a member whom the synod has not excluded or excommunicated—as sometimes is said to be done. Membership of a professedly " infidel " society—such as the synod constitution refers to—is one thing. It is a justifiable cause for exclusion. But it is quite another thing to exclude as "infidels" men who belong to such lodges of the Freemasons as now exist in the British Isles and in Sweden, or to some benefit society which admits to its privileges men who are not all of necessity Christians. If a man is bound by any unholy tie or rite he ought not to remain a member of any such society. But if the religion is true and pure, as far as it goes, it is hard to insist upon it. I think, however, that the custom of inducing a man, when he joins a society, to promise in writing that he will allow himself to be buried by it, is much to be reprobated. Such services give the society too much the character of a Church, or a substitute for the Church, and it is right to warn a man not to give such a pledge. I do not say that he is to be excommunicated because he has done so.

(3) The third question, that of introducing the Swedish episcopal polity, or some form of it, into the Augustana Synod, is evidently one on which there is a difference of opinion in the body. Many fear to relax or forfeit their associations with other Churches affiliated to the " Lutheran General Council," which is said to have a total of 900,000 communicants. But, if the much talked of " Lutheran freedom " of Church organization means anything, it must mean that it is quite as open to any Church to organize itself on the basis of traditional episcopacy, as in Sweden, as it is to organize itself on that of episcopal Superintendency as in Denmark and Norway, or of Superindency in Germany, or of Presbyterianism with synods and presidents. Melanchthon, as I have indicated, wished to retain the degrees of order in the Church. Three of them were long retained in Sweden, and the two most important

are still retained. I have shown the value of traditional or historical episcopacy to Sweden itself in many pages of these lectures, and I do not think any reasonable historian will doubt it. I believe that episcopacy would be equally valuable to the Augustana Synod in U.S.A. as a bond of internal unity, a guarantee of faith, and an instrument of equal and impartial discipline. Its introduction need not weaken the synod's existing alliance. It would certainly strengthen its ties with the Mother Country, and be a protection against any supposed tendency to aggression on the part of the American Episcopal Church, as well as a link of fellowship with it.

The Mission Covenant and other bodies.

The next largest Swedish Church to the Augustana in this country is the "Evangelical Mission Covenant," otherwise called, I believe, the Mission Friends, which has its origin in the Waldenstromian movement in Sweden. It differs, however, considerably from the native society. It has adopted ordination—on the Congregational plan—it has a Prayer Book partly in English, and it is not, I believe, generally so lax on the doctrine of the Atonement as in Sweden. I have to thank an unknown friend in Minneapolis for two books which describes its history and present position.[87] The Bishop of Marquette and I were mostly kindly received at North Park College, in the suburb of Edgwater, Chicago, by President Hjerpe and the other professors when we visited it on Wednesday last (26th October, 1910). The Covenant has, I believe, about 23,000 communicants, and about 280 organizations, and an ordained ministry of some 200 pastors. It is clearly

---

[87] *Sv. Evang. Missions-förbundets i Amerika Årsberättelse*, 1909-1910, Chicago, 1910, and *Missions-förbundets Minneskrift*, 1885-1910. The title of the Prayer Book is *Pastoral Handbok, utarbetad af Pastorerne E. G. Hjerpe, A. L. Anderson och A. P. Nelson, utgiven*, 1901. It may be obtained from the New Eastern Weekly Publishing Co., 274, Main Street, Worcester, Mass. (price 1½ dollars).

a body which deserves to be better known by our clergy, and to be treated with friendliness and respect.

There is also a Swedish Evangelical Free Church with some 6,952 communicants, which clings, I believe, to the baptism of adults, and has its Theological School at Minneapolis. And there is a Swedish Methodist Church, which has no very large number of members, but is of good standing and influence.

Conclusion.

I have, I think, made it clear that neither the visit of the Bishop of Kalmar, who bore a letter from the Archbishop of Upsala to the Lambeth Conference of 1908 and himself addressed the conference, nor the action of the 240 bishops of the Anglican Communion, which was based upon it, is a strange event. They were rather part of a series of movements towards an alliance between our respective Churches, which have their origin far back in history, and have from time to time, though somewhat intermittently, come into prominence. The increased means of locomotion and correspondence which now exist, and the juxtaposition and intercourse of our countrymen in many lands, and particularly in our foreign missions, make such an alliance as is in contemplation much more natural and opportune than it ever has been before. It will be a great joy to me if I have in any way contributed to this result, either by personal visits and correspondence, or by the delivering and publication of these lectures.

§ 9.—THE GENERAL SUBJECT: SUMMARY OF IMPRESSIONS.
FUNDAMENTAL DIFFERENCES BETWEEN ENGLAND
AND SWEDEN. THE NOBILITY ALOOF FROM MUCH OF
NATIONAL LIFE. THE CLERGY AND THE KING CON-
TROL RELIGION. TWO-FOLD RESULT: (1) THE
CHURCH RELATIVELY INDEPENDENT OF THE STATE;
(2) IT HAS CLOSE CONNECTION WITH THE UNIVERSI-
TIES. NEED FOR MORE SPIRITUAL TRAINING OF THE
CLERGY. THE DIACONATE. VALUE OF THE EPISCO-
PATE TO SWEDEN. DIVISION OF DIOCESES AND
CLOSER RELATION TO THE PEOPLE NEEDED.

Having said thus much on the special subject, I must now
attempt a short general summary of the impressions which
I have formed from a study of this history.

I have several times remarked upon the difference
between England and Sweden in certain fundamental social
and political conditions which have affected its history in
the past, and still continue to do so. Sweden, unlike
England, was a settled rather than a conquered country.
Its civilization is founded on a community of small freeholders. Like England, it never accepted Roman law,
but, unlike England, it never had a feudal system. The
result has been that the nobility have formed a body with
interests easily detachable from, and often in opposition to,
those of the rest of the community. They have been
naturally prominent in time of war, just as they were in
the Viking Age, but in time of peace they have tended to
stand somewhat apart from the general development of the
country. Where they have governed, as in the Union
period and the "time of freedom," things have not pro-
gressed favourably. There have, of course, been frequent
and striking exceptions of public-spirited noblemen, and
the names of Per Brahe, founder of the University of
Finland, and Jacob Gustaf De La Gardie, founder of many
Bell and Lancaster elementary schools and a normal school
for teachers [88] in the first quarter of the last century, and

[88] See Cornelius: *Hist.*, § 291.

others, belonging to other great historical families, Wrangel, Sparre, Skytte, and the like, will occur to your memory. But, as a rule, the nobility has not mixed so freely in the life of the country as it has in England, and this has been a misfortune for all parties, and not least in matters of religion.

At the time of the Reformation the Swedish nobility, like the English, was enriched with the spoils of the Church, and was in that way bribed to consent to a change which it did not heartily approve. But the practical management of religion has been left mainly in the hands of the king and the clergy. The clergy, being largely chosen by the people themselves, have been, on the whole, men of the people. But they have been distinguished from the clergy of many other lands by their close connection with the universities. The bishops have, at any rate since the Reformation, been very frequently themselves university professors, and the clergy have represented the standard of culture and attainment which has prevailed at the universities.

The result of this position of the clergy has been two-fold.

On the one hand it has enabled the Church to acquire and maintain a strong position of relative independence, which is very honourable to it, and strikingly distinguishes it both from the neighbouring Church of Denmark and the other Churches on the Continent which accept the Augsburg Confession, and, indeed, from all the other Protestant Churches of Germany. The maxim, *Cuius regio eius religio*, which worked such havoc with the public conscience in the German States, has never prevailed in Sweden, and those of you who have followed my fifth lecture on the Reformation period will have been struck with the unique spectacle which it affords of a popular change of faith gradually overcoming the wayward efforts of a line of able kings who desired to enforce the continental maxim. The peculiar force of character thus engendered gave cour-

age to the bishops of the Stormaktstid, and helped the
armies of Gustavus Adolphus to fight for their faith with
no " transient heroism." [39]

In order to illustrate this point I cannot do better than
quote some words of that great champion of the Church,
Johannes Rudbeckius, spoken at the Council of State on
the 22nd June, 1636:—" Ever since the Reformation our
religion has been ill-treated in Germany. As the prince
has gone, so the province has had to follow. But, thanks
be to God, we have here stood well hitherto. If the government (magistratus) has desired to have something done
which it ought not to have desired, the clergy have kept
the government back. The government for its part has
kept the clergy in its eye for the last hundred years. . . .
We must not adopt German manners if we wish to escape
their ill-fortune and avoid the peril in which they are." [40]

The result is that Sweden has at this moment an
established Church which has a better theoretical and in
some ways practical relation to the State than any except
perhaps the established Church of Scotland, and which
surpasses that Church by its greater hold upon primitive
order and certain elements of worship.

On the other hand, the peculiar circumstances of the
Church, to which I have referred, working themselves out
as they did under Rudbeckius and others in the struggle
with the crown, which ended with Charles XI.'s Acts of
Uniformity, have produced a certain stiffness and narrow-
ness of orthodoxy, which have led to constant reaction ever
since the time of Pietism. Rudbeckius' own voluntary
activity became a hard type, which was impressed upon
the clergy by law, and has made them in certain departments of their work seem to others, and often perhaps to
themselves, more like government officials than Christian

---

[39] Cp. a fine passage in Professor Söderblom's address: *Den
Enskilde och Kyrkan*, p. 26.

[40] This passage is quoted by H. Lundström: *Laurentius
Paulinus Gothus*, Part III., p. 15.

pastors. Nor has the close connection with the universities and university chairs been altogether beneficial.   It
has, indeed, been so in great measure.   It has certainly
kept the occupants of those chairs, who have also had
pastoral duties to perform, closer to the tradition of the faith
than has been the case in the continental universities.
We have seen, for instance, how strongly Bishop Bring
felt this at Lund.   This close connection has also secured
a high standard of intellectual attainment, which may be
compared with that of the Church of England, of the
established Church of Scotland, and our own sister Church
of Ireland.   Probably the official requirements of the
Church of Sweden are somewhat higher than those of the
Church of England.   Yet just as we in England have
long been feeling the need of a more devotional and pastoral training for our own clergy, and have become dissatisfied with the restriction of training to what the
universities can give, so it has been, I believe, in Sweden.
Nor can I fail to point out the misfortune which the Church,
in our eyes, has suffered by its disuse of the diaconate.
The clergy come too soon into the plenitude of official
responsibilities and powers.   They have too little opportunity of having their mistakes corrected and their shortcomings supplied.   They do not become accustomed to a
severe discipline of routine, nor do they acquire that
veneration for the character of an experienced pastor set
over them, and a desire to be like him, which our clergy
have so often the chance to gain.   The disuse of the
diaconate is all the more remarkable, inasmuch as it was
clearly dropped, without any definite order, since the
middle of the seventeenth century.   When Cromwell's
ambassador, Whitelocke, visited Sweden in 1653, and
talked with Archbishop Lenæus the diaconate was clearly
in use as a degree of order leading up to the priesthood.[41]
So also it was used by Rudbeckius in the same generation.
Nor can it truly be said that the principles of the Swedish

[41] See above, p. 312, note 67.

27

formularies are against it. For although the ministry, as defined by the Augsburg Confession, is " the ministry of the Word and Sacraments," that must be taken to be a generic rather than a specific description. And just as this description does not exclude the episcopate as a practical institution for the well-being of the Church, and particularly for the oversight of this ministry (as all Swedish Churchmen consider it), so it does not exclude the diaconate as a sphere of training for this ministry, and an opportunity for exercising subordinate functions in connection with it. That this was Melanchthon's opinion is, I think, evident from the seventh article of the *Apologia Confessionis*, in which he writes as follows. He is dealing, of course, primarily with the episcopate, but his words cover the whole subject :—

" We have often asserted that we are exceedingly desirous to preserve the ecclesiastical polity, and the degrees (gradus) in the Church, even these created by human authority. For we know that it was with good and useful intention that ecclesiastical discipline was constituted by our fathers in the way which the ancient canons describe."

This is surely one of the instances in which parts of the Book of Concord are valuable as explanations of the Augsburg Confession.

I am, of course, aware of the partial substitutes for the diaconate that exist in Sweden ; yet I cannot but hope that the sense of the practical value of the old institution, of which we have a long and convincing experience in the Anglican Church, may lead to a revival of what Lenæus and Rudbeckius found useful in the seventeenth century. The archbishop's words to Whitelocke were : " When one is presented for that calling (of minister), if he is found in learning and abilities fit for it, the bishop doth first ordain him to be a deacon, and in that office he makes trial of his gifts for preaching, and so continues until he be admitted to a benefice, and upon such admission he is made a priest " (*Swedish Ambassy*, Vol. i., p. 415, ed. 1772).

As regards the other great point in which Sweden and England agree and differ from the generality of the Reformed Churches, the maintenance of the historic episcopate, almost every section of my lectures, after the first, bears witness to its practical value to the country. Even before the Reformation, when the episcopate was sometimes pursuing selfish aims, it was a valuable link with the culture of other lands, and by its councils and the internal discipline of its dioceses it made men at least dimly conscious that the kingdom of God was a reality. It filled Sweden with beautiful churches, it established a parochial and ruri-decanal system which still covers the land, and it secured to every man participation of the sacraments and other rites of the Church which bring grace, dignity and consolation to our fallen human nature. Though the standard of discipline was somewhat low, the corruptions of indulgence-mongering were little known, and the national spirit was not wounded by the frequent intrusion of foreign ecclesiastics.

I have already spoken of the unique escape of Sweden in the sixteenth century from royal tyranny in matters of faith. This was due, under God, to the Archbishop Laurentius Petri Nericius, who laid the foundations on which all his successors have since built. It is true that at the time of the Upsala-möte of 1593 the lead was for the time in the hands of the professors of the university and of Stockholm, but this was exceptional.

Since the Reformation the bishops have again and again been the centres of revived activity in education and literature, and very rarely the opponents of progress. They have been hampered obviously in various ways, as by the multitude of their secular duties, by the excessive area in many cases of their dioceses, by the difficulties of locomotion, and by the disuse of the ministry of confirmation as an episcopal act. These difficulties have, perhaps, been particularly evident in the case in the immense diocese of Upsala, the archbishop of which has had an unusual share of concurrent duties, but it is impossible for anyone to read the able and detailed reports of the present archbishop and other bishops to their dioceses without perceiving the extraordinary value of the constant and laborious oversight which they reveal.

At this point I cannot but express my regret at the difficulties which are thrown in the way of the Church in carrying out the much-needed division of dioceses, which is even more necessary in Sweden than it is in England. To make it a condition of the establishment of the new diocese of Luleå in the North, that Kalmar and Vexiö should be united in the South, is to inflict a grave injury on the efficiency of the Church, and to destroy local traditions of great value and dignity. In England we escaped from such a humiliating bargain, which proposed to reduce the number of dioceses in Wales, in order to found new ones in England, about the beginning of the reign of Queen Victoria. I trust that it may be so also in Sweden. The reason why the episcopal office is not so popular and so highly valued among Swedes as it ought to be is because bishops are so little seen and familiarly known. If they became again the ordinary ministers of confirmation, and were brought into personal touch with the young people in every parish, they would be welcomed with a new enthusiasm. The bishop would be turned from an Inspector into a Father in God.

§ 10.—CONCLUSION. FOUR QUESTIONS PROPOSED: (1)
WHAT WILL BE THE FUTURE OF THE SWEDISH
CHURCH? DISESTABLISHMENT AND DISENDOW-
MENT IMPROBABLE. DOCTRINE; (2) HOW FAR HAS
IT LOST GROUND? EVIDENCE FROM U.S.A.
SPECIAL DIFFICULTIES. BISHOP'S CHARGES—
UPSALA, KALMAR, STRENGNÄS; (3) WHAT ENCOUR-
AGEMENTS ARE APPARENT? I. IMPROVEMENTS IN
TASTE AND WORSHIP. 2. NEW MOVEMENTS AMONG
YOUNG PEOPLE AND CLERGY. STUDENT MOVE-
MENT. DIAKONI-STYRELSE. SVENSKA KRYKO-
FÖRBUNDET. MEETINGS AND ASSOCIATIONS; (4)
WHAT DEVELOPMENT MAY BE EXPECTED? SWEDEN
NO LONGER ISOLATED. ENLARGEMENT OF THE
LUND CONCEPTION OF THE CHURCH. TRAINING
FOR THE PRIESTHOOD. GREATER FULNESS OF
WORSHIP. GREAT POSSIBILITIES OF AN ALLIANCE
WITH THE ANGLICAN COMMUNION.

Finally, I would venture to propose the following
questions:—

(1) What is the probable future of the Swedish Church
as regards its relation to the State and nation, and as to its
doctrine?

(2) How far has it lost ground, and what are the chief
difficulties and anxieties reported by its own representatives?

(3) What are the encouraging features of its present
condition?

(4) What line of development may we hope and expect
that it will take, and what may be its main contribution to
the progress of the Kingdom of God and to the life of the
Catholic or Universal Church?

Such questions are easier to ask than to answer; but
merely to ask them may help to stimulate thought and tend
towards the creation of that ideal which all institutions
need to set before themselves if they are to respond to
God's design.

(1) The question, *What is the probable future of the Swedish Church?* suggests at the outset the probability of some changes in its relation to the State. We in England are familiar with such changes in detail, and I cannot doubt that Sweden will also become more familiar with them. The Church, indeed, might welcome legislation which freed its clergy from official business, even though they might lose some secular prominence and leadership thereby. Many of the clergy, like Bishop Ullman of Strengnäs, whom I shall presently quote, resent this charge upon their time and strength. But, as to prospects of final disestablishment, the only recent precedents, those of Ireland and France, are so thoroughly dissimilar that they scarcely need mention. I notice also the absence of any sympathy inside the Church with the disestablishment proposals of Mr. Waldenström, proposals which he has repeatedly brought before the Kyrko-möte and renewed this year. If, indeed, the Church of England or Scotland were disestablished, or that of Denmark, the probability would be greater. Even if the Church of Sweden were disestablished it need not, I think, dread disendowment, since its constitution is so popular and so broadly based, and it has no rival of any size to profit by its weakness or to rejoice in its spoliation. I think, therefore, that the future of the Church of Sweden as a national Church, whether formally or practically, is fairly secure, and this is a very real reason why its own people, as well as foreigners, should take an interest in its welfare. It is a body which has a future before it, and a future which will continue to link it to a great and noble nation.

As to its doctrine, I do not expect to see any important formal change, but I do expect a much greater comprehensiveness in practice, such comprehensiveness as may attract again into the Church those who have been alienated from it, or at least win their respect and admiration. This may well come about through the reflex action of Swedes in U.S.A., and to some extent from greater intercourse, not only with Germany, but with England and other non-

Lutheran countries. Bishop Ullman's charge, quoted below, throws some light on this point, and shows his desire for an acceptance of "modern positive theology" in the place of the old stiff orthodoxy.

(2) *How far has the Swedish Church lost ground, and what are its chief difficulties and anxieties? Difficulties in U.S.A.*

Looking at this matter first from the American point of view it is impossible not to come to the conclusion that the Church has lost hold of the population in many districts. This is evident from the fact that three-quarters of the immigrants to U.S.A. have drifted away from Swedish, and, indeed, from all Lutheran associations. Something is doubtless due to the attractions of material comfort, and to the satisfaction which is felt by many new settlers in home life, and political and business life, apart from Church life. Yet I do not think that alienation from Church life is due mainly to materialism and irreligion. It is due rather to the fact that the adhesion of the Swedish peasantry to the Church has (as in England) meant too often submission to law or custom, and is not the result of affection or religious conviction. The glory and the beauty of the Church has not got a hold of their imaginations. In making these comments I am quite aware that they largely apply to Anglicans and Anglicanism, both at home and in foreign countries, and in our colonies and dependencies.

Difficulties in the Mother Country.

The loss of ground in the Mother Country may be illustrated from the recent charges of Swedish bishops, three of which have come into my hands from the dioceses of Upsala, Kalmar and Strengnäs. They contain also (especially the two latter) hints and notes of encouragement, but on the whole the picture is discouraging.

This is particularly the case with the careful statistics collected by the Archbishop of Upsala for the years 1902—

1907, contained in his charge to the Prest-möte of 1908, a charge which must, I feel sure, have given him great pain to deliver.[42]   I count it an honour to have him for a friend, and, should he read this book, he will believe that I recall his observations with the deepest sympathy.   The general result described is that the Church is unpopular in many parts of the great diocese which he is called to administer; that the attendance at its regular services is more often poor than good, or even fair; that the communicants are in very many places few in number; that the number of persons confirmed is declining; that there is a great decay of faith and a growth of Socialism and infidelity; that the relations between employers and employed are often uncomfortable, and that there is a lamentable laxity of morals among the young people.   There are also important signs of encouragement.

We are accustomed from time to time, and, at all times, in different parts of the country, to observe such phenomena here in England, and I suppose that they are evident in all regions of Christendom.   They are due, generally speaking, to the spread of an independent democratic spirit, which reacts everywhere against custom, tradition and authority.   They have to be met, and are met elsewhere by a restatement of Church doctrine and principles in a manner suited to the age, and by a frank acceptance of new conditions, and especially by using the principle of voluntary association, and enlisting the services of laymen, young as well as old, in their propagation.   This, as I shall show, is being done with considerable enthusiasm in Sweden.   But there are several special difficulties there which ought to make English Churchmen patient and sympathetic, if the efforts of the Church to counteract this spirit, and to turn it into proper channels of new life, do not develop and mature so fast as we could hope.   I will try to summarize them at the risk of some repetition of what has already been said in the last section.

[42] *Tal och Föredrag*, etc., Wretman's Boktryckeri, Uppsala, 1908.

First, I should place the lack of that leadership and support on the part of landowners and gentry to which we are so well accustomed in England. Secondly, I should call attention to the curious tendency of the Swedish character to depreciate its own institutions and generally to under-value what is native and home grown, and to over-value what is new and foreign. Thirdly, I must refer to the frequent rivalry and even hostility of the Free Churches, which have, I fear, been too much influenced by English, Scottish and American teachers. Their opposition has too often given their well-intended piety a bitter, contemptuous and self-righteous flavour. Fourthly, I am constrained to suppose that there is a want of spirituality and initiative, and a defective intelligence of the new conditions of life on the part of a considerable proportion of the clergy. There is certainly, as Bishop Ullman shows, a great depression of energy caused by external conditions. Further complaints of a somewhat dull officialism on their part seem to be so frequent that I am constrained to believe them in some measure true. These complaints must, however, be discounted by consideration of the other three causes to which I have referred.

Statistics of the Diocese of Upsala.

With this preamble I will summarize the Upsala statistics published in 1908, reminding you that, though the archbishop performs episcopal acts in and for the city of Stockholm (340,000 inhabitants), it is not part of his diocese, but is a sort of " enclave " administered by the " pastor primarius " and his consistory. To a stranger this appears a cause of weakness, and some change in the arrangement seems desirable.

The number of congregations in the diocese proper is, I believe, 235, though in many cases two or three of them are under one pastor. The number of incumbents is 162, and of com-ministri or assistant curates 81 ; while the whole body of clergy in the diocese is about 300.[43] The congregations are grouped in twenty-eight rural deaneries or contrakter "—one of them containing the congregations in London and Paris. The rural deanery is, therefore, a smaller unit as to number of congregations than with us (about 5-10), though the average population of the parishes throughout the country (1,700) is rather large, as compared with those of most English dioceses. There are no archdeacons, and a bishop's work of oversight is very heavy, particularly as he is expected to be at home in his cathedral city every Wednesday to preside at the weekly chapter. The population of the diocese is 552,550, and its area is very large. It is the bishop's duty to hold a meeting of his clergy (Prest-möte) at least evety seven years, and to visit every year as many parishes as possible, in a manner prescribed by law.[44] These parochial visitations are not generally part of a tour, but are special visits, taking a long time, so that even an active bishop may never be able to carry out the duty of visiting every parish during his incumbency. A meeting of rural deans (Prost-möte) is held yearly.

About thirty of the churches stand in need of repair or restoration. Two new ones have been built, and there seems to be a good spirit in this matter. There are only 115 fonts, and baptism is frequently or generally administered in private and out of church. The number of clergy has decreased by twenty in the period. Two churches have to be in some cases worked together by one clergyman, and a service taken by a layman on alternate Sundays—a sort of Bible Class in the afternoon. The services of the lay preachers of the " Evangelical National Institute " are acknowledged as valuable in such cases

[43] I take some of these figures from the useful *Statistik matrikel öfver Svenska Kyrkans Prästerskap*, 1909, by Håkan Th. Ohlsson, published in Lund.

[44] For the Prest-möte see *Sv. Kyrkolag*, ch. 25, and for the bishop's visitation ch. 24, §§ 6 foll. The rural deans also visit and hold their own meetings (*ibid.* § 19).

(pp. 42-3). Besides the legal services, most parishes (all but fifteen) have these *Bibel-förklaringar*. Children's services are held in about sixty of the larger town and country parishes. There are only twenty-five Church Sunday Schools, but fifty Free Church ones, and one Socialist. Services of preparation for holy communion are not popular. Generally what we should call "mission services," held outside the churches, seem more popular than those in church, even when the man who conducts them is the same. It is suggested that the sermons preached in church are too long. Probably also both heating and lighting are imperfect. The attendance in church is poor in one hundred cases, fair or tolerable in eighty, and satisfactory in fifteen. In only ten is an increase observable (p. 61). There is a serious decline in the number of communicants, and not eight per cent. of the qualified adults come to communion. Yet there are some cases of very large numbers. Monthly communion is, I believe, the ordinary rule.

Of other services, the churching of women has been generally given up. It is, perhaps, retained only in twenty parishes (p. 66). Baptism in church appears to be confined to forty parishes, and that chiefly in summer time. Yet, on the whole, children are usually baptized. In more than fifty parishes there is a number of persons, more or less, who are not confirmed, and yet still belong to the Swedish Church (p. 67). This would seem to be remarkable since, until lately, confirmation was a legal requirement. Apparently the clergy have often failed to seek out personally those who did not send in their names, and have required too high an age (fifteen years complete) for confirmation (p. 67). Clearly a transformation of the approach to confirmation into a personal act of the will instead of a legal requirement is very much needed. Preparation for confirmation is, indeed, more elaborate and thorough than is usual in England, and there seems no reason why the rite should not be restored to its proper place in public estimation. The confession of faith in it is fuller also than with us, and is a really impressive feature of it. Private catechizing (husvörhör) has also been a remarkable feature of Swedish Church life ever since it was prescribed by law in 1686.[45] It is part of the regular pastoral work of an incumbent, and is also in use to some extent at a bishop's visitation. It has naturally been rendered more difficult by the new spirit of independence. But an active pastor who will take pains to hold it in the homes of single families may still do much with it. Family prayer is rare, though less rare among Free Churchmen. Private devotional reading is more common, but the Bible is too often set aside for less valuable religious reading. The observance of Sunday is much infringed upon, not only by diversions, but by agricultural and other labour.

Adherents of various sects are spread over the whole diocese, and there are only about thirty parishes in the diocese which has not some kind of meeting house (bönhus). One sect, that of the Swedenborgians, has disappeared since 1902. The smaller enthusiastic sects, like "Eric Janssenism," are reduced in numbers. The members of the "Mission Covenant" (Waldenstromians) have increased, and there are smaller active bodies of Baptists and Methodists and of the Salvation Army. The latter has recently thrown off a small Swedish independent force. Of these sects the Baptists seem to be the least aggressive, and they are active in Sunday School work. In one place they claim to have the gift of tongues (p. 71).

The relation of the Church to dissent seems to vary in different localities very much as it does in England. In some places dissent is very friendly, and even helpful, in others very critical, suspicious and contemptuous. The archbishop has carefully avoided anything like harsh language about it, and there seems great possibility of reconciliation in many places. I think we English bishops might advantageously study his method of reporting progress under these heads.

[45] *Sveriges Kyrkolag af* 1686, ch. 2, § 9.

The report of moral conditions is unsatisfactory. Besides the old sins of bad language, drunkenness and unchastity, there are reports of dishonesty and untruthfulness. A bad relation between farmers and labourers is said to be common. Labour contracts are broken, and the farmers' families sorely put to it to do their own work without proper hands. In forty parishes the vice of bad language is decreasing, and the example of North America is quoted as showing how public opinion may be used to check it (p. 75).

Temperance societies are doing good work in many places, but in some parishes they are rather conspicuous for the amusements which they foster, and the temptations to neglect " keeping the Sabbath " which they create, and the political and Socialistic agitations with which they are connected.[46] In about ninety parishes intemperance has diminished; in some in a high degree. In others, however, it has increased. In 200 parishes from which statistics are given more than twelve per cent. of the total births are illegitimate. In three cases the proportion rises to from thirty to thirty-three per cent. In one place half the girls of twenty years of age have illegitimate children. Marriages also, in which the rite has been anticipated, are naturally extremely frequent, so that this may be considered in many places a social custom (p. 76).

Other Diocesan Addresses.

I might illustrate many of the foregoing points from a similar address of the Bishop of Kalmar [47] at his clerical synod of September, 1909, held just before our visit to Upsala. But the statistics are not given with much fulness. I gather, however, from its tone that the condition of Church life is more encouraging than in the diocese of Upsala. Thus the practice of bringing children to be

[46] Bishop Ullman also notices this, p. 4.
[47] *Tal och Föredrag* af Bishopen, Doktor H. W. Tottie, Kalmar, 1910.

baptized in church is growing (p. 51), and many societies of young people who have lately been confirmed are being formed (ungdomskretsar eller ungdoms föreningar, p. 61), answering, I suppose, to our communicants' guilds. This movement is, I may note, supported by a popular fortnightly periodical, *Sveriges Ungdom*, which has a circulation of 30,000 in the present year throughout the kingdom.

Notwithstanding this, even in the diocese of Kalmar, no return from any parish states an increase in the number of communicants, and several state a decrease. It is worth noticing that the bishop does not much press for the establishment of Sunday Schools or children's services, holding that Sunday ought to be made a day for the union of parents and children in religious life (pp. 40 and 71).

The charge of the Bishop of Strengnäs (Dr. U. L. Ullman), *The present condition of our Swedish Church*, has been printed as one of a series of useful tracts (*Svenska Kyrko-förbundets Skriftserie*) in the current year (1910). In the form in which it has reached me it is general rather than particular in its contents. All the first part is a lament over the opposing tendencies of the age. The bishop deeply regrets the separation of the schools from Church influence, even though the clergy are expected to give religious instruction. Children in them are instructed rather than educated, and are not introduced into the living fellowship of the Church (p. 13). He complains of rationalistic school books in the gymnasia. As regards the clergy, he declares that the State has exploited them for its own purposes by laying on them ever increasing burdens, treating them as clerks for the preparation of statistic, economic and military details, in a way which is unknown elsewhere in the world, and using their services to save the public purse without any acknowledgment (pp. 18-19). Many, too, of the clergy are so poor as to have no joy in life, and no heart for their vocation (p. 19). He speaks sadly of the growth of unbelief and Socialism, of the neglect of Sunday, and of the increase of acts of murder and bitter revenge, and of cases of divorce and suicide (pp. 20-21). He then mentions the old Schartauan movement and the new student movement, of which I shall speak presently, as helps to better things (pp. 23-27). He recommends careful attention to the popular movement so as to make it really educational, and mentions various books for confirmands and confirmees, including two of his own (p. 28). A new priesthood is needed, not merely new priests. Also a new style of theology. The choice does not lie between the old orthodoxy and rationalism, but between rationalism and " modern positive theology " (p. 35). He illustrates this last by the names of many German professors—some well known in England like Von Orelli of Basel, Zahn and Caspari of Erlangen—and others less known whom we may be glad to hear of (p. 38). In this connection he mentions with approval the series of *Bibliska tids- och strids-skrifter*, edited by Professor Adolf Kolmodin. I have only touched on a few of the salient points of this spirited charge, which has more life and fire in it than is perhaps usual in such documents.

(3) *What are the encouraging features of the present activity of the Swedish Church, and in what directions do they need to be supplemented?*

The encouraging features of the present condition of Church life in Sweden revealed by the three charges which I have been examining may be referred to two principal heads : (1) Those which show increased interest in church building, church music, church services and the like, and (2) those which express a new spirit of freedom and activity in religion, especially in young people and the clergy. I am glad to be able to add something of importance under both heads. It is quite clear that there is much more of encouragement in popular movements at work in Sweden than would be gathered from these charges if read by themselves.

(1) *Improvement in taste and interest in church building, church music and church services generally.*

Much attention is being paid to the fabrics of the churches. Fine new churches have been built in Stockholm and Göteborg. The finest example of church restoration is said to be that of the Cathedral of Strengnäs, and I also saw a good one at the important town of Falun. An exhibition of church arts was held at the time of the re-opening of Strengnäs Cathedral, of which the attractive catalogue lies before me. Much is being done for church music by the "Friends of Church Song," an association that has branches in different dioceses, which aims at the restoration of the old melodies. They have re-edited the old tunes of the chorales in their ancient rhythmic form, which had been obscured by the German, Höffner, about a hundred years ago, when he harmonized them in a very popular manner.[48] This ancient music is making great progress, and there is also a liturgical movement spreading "the music for the Swedish Mass." Many churches have voluntary choirs (men and women) in western galleries, but not every Sunday.

The vestments prescribed by the Church—which are red and black chasubles, with heavy gold and silver ornaments, worn over plain white albs—are being used more regularly than in former years. Forty years ago there was a prejudice against their use on the part of some Evangelical clergy, but this is now rare. They are, I am told, not worn every Sunday (except in some cathedral churches), but on festivals and at celebrations of Holy Communion—which, apparently, are generally once a month. This importance lies, of course, in the evidence of the continuity of Church life which they afford. We were much struck with the reverent and full attendance at two "liturgical evensongs" at which we were present in

---

[48] *Svensk Koralbok i reviderad rytmisk form*, published by Gleerup, Lund (price 4 kr. 75).

Upsala Cathedral, and at the beauty of the singing there and at Lund.

(2) *Movements among young people and among the clergy.*

The most important of these signs of hope is the " student movement," which has attracted much atention in the last few years. It began twenty-six years ago by the foundation of the " Student Mission Association " at Upsala, 1st February, 1884—a year famous for a like initiative in our own University of Cambridge. A similar association at Lund was founded two years later. In 1890 the first Scandinavian Students' Mission Conference, fired by the enthusiasm which was wafted over from America, was held at Hilleröd in Denmark.   Seven such united conferences were held up to 1903, after which the Swedish students thought it best to meet alone. Two memorable assemblies were held at Huskvarna, near Jönköping, in 1907 and 1909. Among the leaders who spoke at the last Bishop Eklund of Carlstad (" de ungas Biskop "), Professors Nathan Söderblom and Einar Billing and Mr. Manfred Björkqvist stand out as particularly influential.[49]

Among the addresses delivered at Huskvarna that of Professor Söderblom on *The Individual and the Church*, already quoted, is full of interest for our subject.   This movement, which is confined to university students, has done much to send actual missionaries into the field, though not so many as was first hoped. It has also done even more for Sweden itself.   Under the title of " Kyrkliga Frivilligkår " (the Church Volunteer Corps) it has become a somewhat close organization within the

[49] See *Från den Kristliga Student rörelsen* : *Huskvarna mötet*, 1909, Norblads Bokhandel, Uppsala, and *The Student Movement in Sweden* by Dr. Söderblom in *The Student World* for October, 1910, published at 124, East 28th Street, New York. I have also received valuable letters on the matters dealt with in this section from Bishop Billing, of Lund, and my younger friends, Revs. S. Gabrielsson, jun., of Venjan, and Mats Åmark, of Norn, both in the diocese of Vesterås.

student movement at Upsala. Its watchword is " Sveriges Folk ett Guds Folk," and a spirited fortnightly journal called *Vår Lösen* (" our watchword ") has been published this year as the organ of the movement. Its editor is Mr. Björkqvist, and it has already a circulation of 3,000 copies. It aims at making the national Church the great instrument of national religion, and to create enthusiasm for this idea. It desires also that it should take its part in the task set before the universal Church. The recent salutary action of this Church Volunteer Corps has shown itself not only in the Huskvarna conferences, but in the lectures on the Church and Church history which it has arranged. These lectures were given this year at the Public School or College of Lundsberg in the diocese of Carlstad, a school after the English type, of course during the school holidays, and attended by about 150 persons, men and women. Similar lectures have been promoted by the student association of Lund.

The students have also organized " crusades " against infidelity, which they have prosecuted with great enthusiasm during their vacations. In the spring of this year 800 parishes were visited at the request of the clergy.[50] About 400 students, or one-eighth of the whole of Swedish University students, are members of these associations. They have their battle song in a fine hymn, *Fädernas Kyrka i Sveriges land*, written by Bishop Eklund of Carlstad, the leader of this work among the bishops, which is sung to a catching tune by Docent G. Aulén, of Upsala, who has himself done much to popularize a knowledge of modern Swedish Church history.

Next to this I may mention the foundation at the Kyrko-möte of last year (1909) of the *Svenska Kyrkans Diakoni-styrelse*, which is due to the energy of Bishop

[50] A bright account of the experiences of some of the " crusaders " of 1909 is given by Pastor Axel Lutteman in *Julbok för Wästerås Stift*, 1909, pp. 126-144, which particularly describes their discussions with " young Socialists " in Bergslagen in Southern Dalarne.

Lövgren of Vesterås. This institution is not to be confounded with the training house for deacons (*Diakonanstatten*), which also owes much to the same bishop. The *Diakoni-styrelse* is intended to be a sort of counterpart for home missions to the "Church Missionary Institution," which also owes its foundation to the Kyrko-möte (1876). As far as I can understand it, the *Diakoni-styrelse* will be something like our "Society for Promoting Christian Knowledge," and be specially occupied with the diffusion of religious literature. The archbishop is the president. Its work, of course, lies in the future. One of its designs is to publish a *Swedish Church Year Book*, which will be of great value to Churchmen. It will probably occupy itself very much with providing the text books and hymn books which will be needed for the Sunday School organization already determined upon by the *Allmänna Svenska Prest föreningar* (A.S.P.).[51]

The committee of the *Diakoni-styrelse* are half priests, half laymen.

A somewhat earlier voluntary association (*Svenska Kyrko-förbundet*) was started in 1909 by Regements-Pastor Schröderheim of Stockholm and others, and it has done good service by the publication of the series of tracts, in which Bishop Ullman's charge is printed. Its object is the spread of knowledge about the Church and Church history, the introduction where possible of daily services, improvements in liturgical matters, etc. The first number is an attractively illustrated and pleasantly written comparison of *English and Swedish Church life* recording Pastor Schröderheim's very kindly impressions of two visits to England in 1908 and 1909. This little book will, I hope, do much to interpret what is good in English Church life to Swedish readers.

Besides the permanent institutions I may mention the

[51] Pastor Gunnar Ekström, of Falun, has been a great promoter of Sunday Schools. See his *Är tiden inne för den Svenska Kyrkan att på sitt program upptaga Sondagsskolverksamhet?* Västerås, 1907.

" Mösseberg Conference " of clergy held in the autumn of 1908, at a watering-place in West Gothland.   It lasted a week, and was attended by 150 priests, and was the first of its kind in Sweden.   Its object was mutual edification, and those who took part in it lived a common life for the time. I presume it was somewhat of the nature of the Keswick Conference, but that it also had something of the character of a " Retreat " for clergy.

Further great *Kyrkliga-möter* or Church congresses have recently been held in some of the cathedral cities, attended by, perhaps, 1,000 members from different parts of the country.   The first was in Stockholm (1908); the second in Skara (1909); the third in Hernösand (1910). The questions discussed seem to have been very much like those brought forward at our own congresses.

It would be easy to add to these details by the description of more local efforts.   Probably the many " mothers' meetings " which are being held will in time develop into a society like our " Mothers' Union," the work of which I should like to commend to any of my Swedish readers who may be interested in the maintenance of Christian family life.   Our English society has a membership *in the Empire and elsewhere* of 316,990, and 6,359 branches (*Ch. Y.B.*, 1910, p. 74).[52]   Quite as important for Sweden, if it were possible to introduce it, would be an association like the " Girls' Friendly Society," the need of which is shown so sadly by the Upsala statistics.   Our G.F.S. was founded in 1875.   It has, *in England and Wales alone*, a membership of 180,396, with 37,004 associates; and it works in 7,000 of our parishes (l.c., p. 73).[53]   It is also,

[52] The objects of the " Mothers' Union " are : (1) To uphold the sanctity of marriage ; (2) to awaken in mothers of all classes a sense of their great responsibility in the training of their boys and girls ; (3) to organize in every place a band of mothers who who will unite in prayer and seek by their own example to lead their families in holiness and purity of life.

[53] The objects of the G.F.S. are : (1) To band together in one society women and girls as associates and members, for mutual help (religious and secular) for sympathy and prayer ;

like the Mothers' Union, extended throughout and beyond the Empire.

I have already mentioned the " Evangeliska Fosterlands förbundet," and the value of its lay missionaries. I do not know what its present strength is, or how far it employs working men, but I think it might be well worth while for some Swedish Churchmen to study rather closely the merits and defects of our English " Church Army." I have often spoken of the immense debt which we owe to this latter body.

The " Church Army " founded in 1882, shows how some 500 evangelists, of strict loyalty to the Church and splendid devotion, may be drawn from the ranks of working people. I pass over the myriad other agencies which give fibre and blood to our corporate life. I only quote these as evidences of what may be done voluntarily by men and women who are in earnest, working within the Church and in strict subordination to authority, to put new spirit into an old institution.

There seems absolutely no reason why similar movements should not succeed in Sweden (where the " Salvation Army " has already made great progress), and in a short time bear fruits worthy of our admiration and emulation. Its freedom of self-government enables it to move solidly and safely, and its home and foreign missions are evidently growing fast.

(4) *What line of development may we hope and expect that the Swedish Church will take, and what may be its main contribution to the progress of the Kingdom of God and to the life of the Catholic or Universal Church?*

The position of the Church of Sweden is a very remarkable one as an intensely national and rather isolated

(2) to encourage purity of life, dutifulness to parents, faithfulness to employers, temperance and thrift; (3) to provide the privileges of the society to its members wherever they may be by giving them an introduction from one branch to another.

Church, which has seen, in the last fifty years, an immense part of its population transferred to entirely new conditions of freedom and contact with other Christian bodies across the Atlantic. The closest parallel to its position is that of the Roman Catholic Church in Ireland, which has experienced something of the same fortune. Even Irish Romanism, with its insular political scheming, is gaining a somewhat broader outlook by this experience. It cannot but be much more so in the case of an enlightened country like Sweden. Our own Church has gained very much more by the new experience of its colonies and dependencies, and its world-wide organization, but that has been a matter of slow development, and we must not expect Swedish experience to ripen all at once. The country will, however, inevitably acquire a much wider conception of the Church, while it learns to value, even more than before, its own national office and character. It will become, as we should say, more " catholic " in its character, using the word in its proper sense of consciousness that it has a share in the life of the universal Church of Christ.

What are the duties of a national Church so shaken out of its isolation? They are, I conceive, in general terms, three.

In the first place, every Church, and in particular every national Church, ought to feel its duty to bring the blessings of Christian life to every soul within its borders, and to co-operate with others in preaching the Gospel to the world. In the second place, every Church needs to feel its way to continuity with the whole past of Christendom, through and beyond the Reformation and Mediæval periods, right up to primitive and apostolic times, and so to the foundations laid by Christ Himself. There must be no gaps in its consciousness of its previous history, no leaps over periods of its past experience as barren and unfruitful. Further, it ought to feel an instinct of brotherly sympathy with all other Churches. It ought to regard their work with interest, whether it be faulty and imperfect, or noble and strenuous, or, as is usually the case, a mixture of both. It should try to make its own work supply the defects on one side, and co-operate with the triumphs of goodness on the other.

Such an ideal might have seemed a mere picturesque dream a few years since. But increased means of locomotion and intercourse, and an increased sense of the brotherhood of mankind and of the dangers of a divided Christendom in the face of common enemies, have made it the natural longing of millions of our fellow-Christians. Both in the British Isles and in Sweden we must escape from our provincialism. Mere Anglicanism, mere Presbyterianism, mere Lutheranism are provincial and out of date.

The Church of Sweden both already possesses the general conception, and has gone far along the process of realizing it.

Much was done by the Lund movement to give form to this higher conception of the Church. All that is needed seems to be to drop from it the coercive and negative features, which encumbered it, and to enlarge it in three directions. The idea of the Church must surely be that of a divine society inspiring all its members, clergy and laity, men and women, old and young, with a desire to participate in (1) home missions; (2) foreign missions; (3) the spirit and work of the universal Church—a Church having both the beauty of holiness and the voice of the Lord's living authority.

What means are needed, besides those already in use, to realize this broader conception?

In looking at the evidence before me of the feeling at present existing in Sweden on this subject, I am much struck by Bishop Ullman's remark that it needs a new priesthood as well as new priests. We in England are trying to obtain such a general elevation of the priesthood by arranging for our clergy both university training and special training. The latter hardly exists in Sweden, although something is done by the " Studentenhem " at the universities to give more of religious family life to

serious minded students, a class which naturally includes
candidates for Orders.   But surely the latter require a
time of special discipline of their own.

After their university course they need at least a year's
devotional and spiritual training, with some practical instruction in preaching.   Just as Moses was prepared for
his mission on Sinai, Elijah on Horeb, and St. Paul in
Arabia, so should each priest, who is to be a prophet to his
generation and a builder of the City of God, have a time of
retirement and communing with God :—

> So separate from the world his breast
> May duly take and strongly keep
> The print of heaven, to be expressed
> Ere long on Sion's steep.[54]

I have ventured also to express my strong feeling as to
the blessings which might follow a revival of the diaconate
as a period of probation for the priesthood, and of the custom of episcopal confirmation—both of them Swedish
institutions, dropped only in a time of torpor.   Whatever
may be said against the *necessity* of adopting such ancient
usages, I venture to think that there can be little doubt as
to their *expediency*.   I should press them on this ground
on the attention of my dear friends and colleagues in
Sweden.

I also confidently expect that the increased interest in
the conduct of public worship will develop almost universally as it has done in England.   This has gone on
among us hand in hand with the development of associations for the promotion of a Christian life on Church lines.

We began with greater attention to worship, from about
1840, coupling with it the first tentative efforts at organization.   The level of worship among us has been raised in
an extraordinary manner, *pari passu*, with the growth of
these organizations.   A weekly celebration of holy communion is now the rule, and less frequent celebration the

---

[54] John Keble, *Christian Year* for Thirteenth Sunday after Trinity, comparing Hebrews viii. 5—"See that thou make all things according to the
pattern shewed to thee in the mount."

exception. Although the ritual of our Churches has been in some cases carried to an extreme or even a dangerous point, such cases are not common. But everywhere the value of the mysterious and the beautiful elements in religion is recognized. Everywhere we see surpliced choirs of men and boys, largely voluntary; and reverent and joyful services both on Sundays and week days. We cannot rival the congregational singing of Sweden, at any rate in the South of England, but participation in worship is general and hearty. What has been possible in England is surely equally possible in Sweden—and without any legislation. We may look to its cathedrals to set the precedents, especially Upsala and Lund.

I believe then that the Swedish Church, which has a history so like our own, will develop in a manner like our own—no doubt with its own idiosyncrasies, and, very probably, profiting by observation of our mistakes. I am not inclined to propose our example as at all perfect or complete. I merely suggest that our experience is so parallel as to be valuable to a sister Church. If this be so the two Churches together may look forward to making a joint contribution to the life of the Church universal, which will be of immense value. First, each may strive to rival the other in all that concerns the self-denying ministry of a national Church to its own people and so set an example which others may follow. Secondly, we may co-operate in countries like the United States and Canada, where our own people dwell side by side. Thirdly, we may co-operate in our foreign missions, especially since the missions of the Swedish Church (though not those of the " Mission Covenant ") are largely within the British Empire. Lastly, an alliance, such as I venture to hope for, would be the natural link between the (estimated) thirty-two millions of Anglicans and the (estimated) seventy millions of Lutherans.[55] The isolation of

[55] This estimate of Anglicans or Episcopalians is given in Whitaker's *Almanack*, p. 427, 1909, and that of Lutherans by Dr. Lenker, of Minneapolis, a well-known authority on Luther and Lutheranism, and the translator of Luther's works.

Lutheranism is, I know, hard to break down, but one of the most hopeful roads, at present, is through Sweden. Conceive what power such an alliance might possess, both in strengthening inward faith and discipline, and in influencing the world outside! Even if it extended at first only to England and Sweden it would be a magnificent instrument in the hand of God. May He who gives His servants the power to see visions also help us to make them realities.

SIT · SOLI · DEO · GLORIA.

APPENDICES TO LECTURE VIII.

A.—ROUGH LIST OF BOOKS BEARING ON THE HISTORY OF THE SWEDES IN U.S.A.

1.—THE SWEDES IN DELAWARE AND PENNYSLVANIA.

Thomas Campanius Holm(iensis) : *Description of the Province of New Sweden*, translated by Peter S. du Pouceau, Philadelphia, 1834. [The author was grandson of John Campanius, who accompanied Governor Printz to America as his chaplain in 1642, and translated Luther's *Little Catechism* into the language of the Lenni, Lenape or Renappi. The author was never himself in America, and has introduced some strange stories.]

Israel Acrelius : *Description of the former and present condition of the Swedish Churches in what was called New Sweden*, etc., Stockholm, 1759, translated with notes by W. M. Reynolds, D.D., for the Historical Society of Pennsylvania, Philadelphia, 1876.

The Records of the Holy Trinity (Old Swedes) Church, Wilmington, Delaware, from 1697 to 1773, translated by Horace Burr, with an abstract of the English records from 1773 to 1810, published by Hist. Soc. of Delaware, Wilmington, 1890. [This contains Pastor Björk's valuable diary quoted above.]

Benjamin Ferris : *A History of the Original Settlements on the Delaware from its Discovery by Hudson to the Colonization under Wm. Penn, to which is added an account of the historical affairs of the Swedish settlers and a history of Wilmington to the present time*, Wilmington, 1846.

Otto Norberg : *Svenska Kyrkans Mission vid Delaware i Nord-Amerika (i f.d. Kolonien Nya Sverige), Akademisk Afhandling*, Stockholm, 1893.

The most recent work is by Professor Amandus Johnson, of Philadelphia : *The Swedish Settlements on the Delaware, their history and relation to the English and Dutch, 1638-1664, with an account of the "South," the "New Sweden" and the "American" Companies and of the efforts of Sweden to regain the Colony*, two volumes, Pennsylvania University, Philadelphia [1910?]. [I have been unable to see this book.]

2.—NEW SWEDEN IN MAINE.

The Story of New Sweden, as told at the Quarter-Centennial Celebration of the founding of the Swedish Colony in the

Woods of Maine, June 25th, 1895 [ed. by S. J. Estes], Portland, Maine, 1895.

The Story of New Sweden, by Wm. Widgery Thomas, jun., in *Collections and Proceedings of the Maine Historical Society,* 2nd ser., Vol. vii., pp. 53 foll. and 113 foll., Portland, 1896. [This is written by the founder, who was an U.S.A. consul in Sweden, and in 1870 collected a small party of fifty-one persons to settle in his own State, where they have largely prospered on the banks of the Aroostook. The prevailing religion appears to have been Baptist. The colony has largely helped the development of the State of Maine.]

3.—SETTLEMENTS IN THE NORTH WEST.

The two most important books on the larger Swedish settlements are :—

History of the Swedes in Illinois, edited by Ernest W. Olson, in collaboration with Anders Schön and Martin J. Engberg, The Engberg-Holmberg Publishing Co., Chicago, two volumes, 1908.

A History of the Swedish Americans of Minnesota, compiled and edited by A. E. Strand, The Lewis Publishing Company, Chicago, three volumes, 1910.

More popular is the one volume by Alfred Söderström : *Minneapolis Minnen Kulturhistorisk axplockning från quarnstaden vid Mississippi,* Minneapolis, 1899.

4.—GENERAL DESCRIPTIONS AND POPULAR SKETCHES.

G. F. Peterson : *Sverige i Amerika : Kulturhistoriska och biografiska teckningar,* The Royal Star Co., Chicago, 1898.

O. N. Nelson : *History of the Scandinavians and successful Scandinavians in the U.S.,* two volumes, Minneapolis, 1893.

Lars P. Nelson : *What has Sweden done for the United States?* Chicago, 1903. [A popular essay on occasion of a national commemoration, but full of information in a convenient form.]

Carl Sundbeck : *Svensk-Amerikanerna,* Stockholm and Rock Island, 1904. [Records of a journey undertaken with the support of the Swedish Government, and likely to be useful to immigrants.]

P. Waldenström : *Genom Norra Amerikas förenta Stater : Reseskildningar,* Stockholm and Chicago, 1890.

5.—RELIGIOUS HISTORY OF THE SWEDES IN U.S.A.

G. Unonius : *Minnen från en sjuttonårig vistelse i Nordvestra Amerika* (1841-1858), published in 1862, with a *Bihang* [in answer to some remarks on Dr. Norelius' book, particularly as to his relation to Esbjörn], published at Stockholm in 1896.

E. Norelius: *De Svenska Luterska församlingarnas och Svenskarnes Historia i Amerika*, Rock Island, Illinois, 1890.

Henry Eyster Jacobs: *A History of the Evangelical-Lutheran Church in the U.S.*, fifth ed., Scribner and Sons, N.Y., 1907 (being volume four of the general *American Church History*).

The Augustana Synod, 1860-1910, Rock Island, 1910 [a jubilee volume containing papers of much interest].

Missions Förbundets Minnesskrift, 1885-1910 [a twenty-five years' jubilee volume], Chicago, 1910.

B.—DETACHED NOTES ON THE EARLY SWEDISH SETTLEMENTS IN THE UNITED STATES, 1841-1860.

(By Dr. Toffteen).

Before 1860 the Swedes that emigrated to America came generally by sailing ships. The emigrants were then not very numerous, and, as they generally came in parties, with the view of settling together, it is possible to trace them to the settlements which they founded.

Since 1860 the emigration has been very much larger, and has gone by the Atlantic emigration steamers. No larger parties, settling at one place, are known. The following is a concise sketch of the Swedish settlements in the United States between 1841 and 1860.

1.—Pine Lake, Wisconsin.—1841.

With the exception of a few adventurers, that may have come here in earlier times, the first considerable settlement of Swedes was the one that was led by the Rev. G. Unonius. This party was made up of some well-to-do Swedes, who expected to settle here, but were also animated by the old Viking spirit, desirous of adventures. They came to America in 1841, and founded a colony at Pine Lake, Wis. About 1850 most of the old settlers had, however, moved away, and several of them returned to Sweden.

2.—Brocton, Massachusetts.—1844.

In 1844 came a little company, led by Daniel Larson, from Haurida, Småland, and settled in Brocton, Mass. Their motive for emigration was the expectation to better their economic conditions here. They had been moved by reading the letters of Unonius to the Swedish papers.

3.—New Sweden, Pennsylvania.—1845.

Peter Kassel and four other families from Kisa, Östergötland, migrated here in 1845, and settled, or rather founded, the New Sweden settlement in Jefferson Co., Pa. A desire for adventures seems to have been the primary motive for this migration.

4.—Bishop's Hill, Illinois.—1845-1854.

Erik Jansson, and members of a sect founded by him, and generally known as the Jansonists, began to migrate in 1845. Their chief centre in Sweden was Biskopskulla. They settled in Henry Co., Ills., and called their colony Bishop Hill. The largest number of this colony came in 1846, but new additions of the colony continued to come until 1854. Religious persecution by the ecclesiastical and civil authorities in Sweden was the motive for this emigration.

5.—Chicago, Illinois.—1846-1852.

Some members of the Pine Lake colony moved early to Chicago. In 1846 emigration parties were organized in Sweden for the purpose of settling in Chicago. These parties came from different localities. In 1846 came fifteen families; in 1847 forty families; in 1848 about 100 families; in 1849 some 400 Swedes, and in 1850 about 500; in 1851 and 1852 some 1,000 each year. Economic reasons were the motives for these emigrations, and from this time onward the chief motive for emigration from Sweden has been a desire to better the economic conditions of the people concerned.

6.—Andover, Illinois.—1846-1849.

In 1846 about seventy-five persons left Kisa, Östergötland. They came that year no further than Buffalo, N.Y. In the next years others joined them, and a part of them started on canal-boats to go west. They reached Henry Co., Ills., in 1848, and founded there the Andover colony. This colony was increased in the following year, 1849, with some 300 Swedes from Kisa and Grenna. Rev. L. P. Esbjörn was among the emigrants that year. The Andover colony extended early into Swedona and Ophicus, and became the largest Swedish colony at that time.

7.—Sugar Grove, Pennsylvania, and Jamestown, New York. —1848.

The other part of the Swedes that came to Buffalo, N.Y., in 1846, went southward in 1848, and settled in Sugar Grove.

This party was also increased in 1847, and new emigrants joined them in the following years. A number of them finally settled down and founded the Swedish colony at Jamestown, N.Y.

8.—Houston, Texas.—1849.

About fifty Swedes came here in 1849, in company with Mr. M. S. Swenson, and settled in Houston, Texas, where Mr. C. Swenson already owned property.

9.—Chisago Lake, Minnesota.—1850-1851.

Some 100 Swedes from Helsingland and Medelpad came to New York in 1850. Most of them settled in Knox and Henry Counties, Ills. A few of them, however, went north the next year, and founded the colony of Chisago Lake, Minn. In 1853 a large number from Kronoberg joined this colony. Among the emigrants, 1851, was also Dr. Norelius.

10.—Manitowoc and Waupaca, Wisconsin.—1850.

One hundred and eleven emigrants left Gefle in 1850. Some of them settled in Galva, Watago and Henderson, Ills., but a large part of them went north, and founded the Swedish settlements in Manitowoc and Waupaca, Wis.

11.—Galesburg, Illinois.—1851.

About 100 Swedes from Northern Skåne settled, in 1851, in Galesburg and Knoxville, Ills. The following year a still larger company of emigrants, these also from Northern Skåne, joined the Galesburg settlers. Rev. T. U. Hasselquist, founder of the Augustana Synod and Augustana College, was in this company.

12.—La Fayette, Indiana.—1852.

A considerable number of Swedes migrated in 1852 from Grenna, and settled in La Fayette, Ind. In the two years following large numbers were added, and the settlement was extended by small colonies in West Point, Attica, Millford and Yorktown, Ind.

13.—St. Charles, Illinois.—1852.

The same year a number of emigrants from Westergötland settled in St. Charles, Ills.

14.—Vasa, Minnesota.—1853.

A large number of emigrants from Northern Skåne came to America in 1853, under the leadership of Colonel Hans

Mattson. They went up north, and founded a colony at Vasa, Goodhue Co., Minn. New emigrants, chiefly from North-Eastern Skåne, poured into this colony the following years, and in 1860 this had become one of the largest Swedish settlements in America.

15.—STOCKHOLM, WISCONSIN.—1854.

The following year, 1854, a very large number of Swedes left Vermland. It had now become known in Sweden that Minnesota and Wisconsin, with their beautiful lakes and colder climate, reminded much of Sweden. Consequently the larger number of these sons of Vermland went north and settled on the shores of Lake Pepin, near the Vasa settlement in Minnesota. The new settlement at Lake Pepin was called Stockholm.

16.—ROCKFORD, ILLINOIS.—1852-1854.

While thus many new comers went into Wisconsin and Minnesota, letters from the earlier emigrants to their friends at home led many emigrants, in the years 1852-1854, to settle in Illinois. Many of these, chiefly from Småland and Westergöt-land, came to Rockford, Ills., where very soon a large Swedish colony flourished.

17.—CARVER COUNTY, MINNESOTA.—1853-1854.

In 1853 a number of people from Westergötland went up into Minnesota and founded a settlement in Carver Co. Next year their number was increased, and several Swedish colonies sprang up in that county.

18.—SCANDIAN GROVE, MINNESOTA.—1856.

Soon the Swedes began to push further and further into Minnesota, and in 1856 a large number of people from Northern Skåne founded a colony in Scandian Grove, Minn.

By this time railroads were extended into the West, and Atlantic travel was done by steamships. Since 1860 large numbers have come over; many of these have stopped in the old Swedish colonies of Illinois and Minnesota; many also have settled in Pennsylvania and the eastern cities. But a considerable number have gone West, into Iowa, Kansas, Nebraska, Colorado and even California, with stray settlements in other States like the Dakotas. In Kansas and Nebraska, however, are the largest settlements of later years, and the smoky steel district in Kansas is now well known as largely a Swedish settlement with a prosperous population. Others, like New Gotland and Gothenburg, Nebraska, testify to the number and the prosperity of the Swedes in those parts of America. Bethany College, Kansas, founded by Dr. Swenson, is an important institution belonging to the Augustana Synod.

In the meantime many Swedes have remained in the larger, and for that matter also in the smaller, western cities. While there are considerably more than 100,000 Swedes in Chicago, Minneapolis counts them by 50,000 to 75,000, and St. Paul, Minnesota; Denver, Colorado; Omaha, Nebraska; Kansas City, Saline, Lindsborg and McPherson, Kansas; San Francisco and Oakland, California, have large numbers of Swedes.

The following is a summary of the figures given by the Rev. P. Peterson, emigrant missionary in New York. He has printed them in the fullest and most complete form in a paper contained in the *Missions Förbundets Minnesskrift*, 1885-1910, pp. 48 fol., which includes those for 1908.

1821-1860	....	23,558 forty years.
1861-1870	....	63,851 ten years.
1871-1880	....	115,922 ,,
1881-1890	....	291,776 ,,
1891-1900	....	226,266 ,,
1901-1908	....	211,319 eight years.

1,032,692

The figures for the years 1899-1908 have been :—

1899	12,797
1900	18,650
1901	23,331
1902	30,894
1903	46,028
1904	27,763
1905	26,595
1906	23,310
1907	20,589
1908	12,809

242,766

Average, 24,276.

Therefore, though there is a falling off in recent years, and a great drop in the year of industrial depression (1908)—as there was in the immigration generally from other countries—the figures for the last decade, 1901-1910, will almost certainly largely exceed those for 1891-1900, when they are forthcoming.

29

INDEX.

For the purposes of this Index ä and ö have been treated as == œ, œ ; but å has been put last under a.

30

Made in the USA
Middletown, DE
23 April 2018